FLIGHT-FREE
EUROPE

GREAT BREAKS BY RAIL, ROAD & SEA

Published by Time Out Guides Ltd, a wholly owned subsidiary of Time Out Group Ltd.
Time Out and the Time Out logo are trademarks of Time Out Group Ltd.

© **Time Out Group Ltd 2008**

10 9 8 7 6 5 4 3 2 1

This edition first published in Great Britain in 2008 by Ebury Publishing
A Random House Group Company
20 Vauxhall Bridge Road, London SW1V 2SA

Random House Australia Pty Limited 20 Alfred Street, Milsons Point, Sydney, New South Wales 2061, Australia
Random House New Zealand Limited 18 Poland Road, Glenfield, Auckland 10, New Zealand
Random House South Africa (Pty) Limited Isle of Houghton, Corner Boundary
Road & Carse O'Gowrie, Houghton 2198, South Africa

Random House UK Limited Reg. No. 954009

Distributed in US by Publishers Group West
Distributed in Canada by Publishers Group Canada

For further distribution details, see www.timeout.com

ISBN 978-1-84670-087-3

A CIP catalogue record for this book is available from the British Library

Printed and bound by Firmengruppe APPL, aprinta druck, Wemding, Germany

The Random House Group Limited supports The Forest Stewardship Council (FSC), the leading international forest
certification organisation. All our titles that are printed on Greenpeace approved FSC certified paper carry the FSC logo.
Our paper procurement policy can be found at www.rbooks.co.uk/environment

Time Out carbon-offsets all its flights with Trees for Cities (www.treesforcities.org).

Time Out Guides Limited
Universal House
251 Tottenham Court Road
London W1T 7AB
Tel + 44 (0)20 7813 3000
Fax + 44 (0)20 7813 6001
Email guides@timeout.com
www.timeout.com

Maps Pinelope Kourmouzoglou, Kei Ishimaru

Back cover photography by (left to right) Shannon Mendes; Jonathan Cox; DB AG.

Photography by page: 3 Heloise Bergman; 5, 272 Rob Greig; 6, 249 Tanya Sassoon; 7 (top left), 273 Danube Express; 7 (top middle), 13 (middle), 16 (bottom), 20, 21, 24, 27, 29, 162, 163, 165, 167, 168, 247, 251, 233 Karl Blackwell; 7 (bottom middle), 265 (bottom middle) Elan Fleisher; 7 (bottom right) Stuart Abraham; 13, 244 Polferries; 15 (top), 213, 214, 217, 218 swiss-image.ch; 15 (bottom) Richard Lumborg-The Idea Works Ltd; 19, 34, 35, 37, 39, 40, 42 Oliver Knight; 25 Jean-Christophe Godet; 44, 45 Don Muschter Steden; 47 Heloise Bergman; page 50 GNTB/ Andrew Cowin; pages 51, 54 Alamy; 57, 184, 185 (left), 190 Rajko Radovanic; 60, 61, 66 Alex Lloyd; 68, 69, 70, 72 (bottom), 74 Isle of Man Department of Tourism and Leisure; 72 (top) Stephen Davison; 76, 77 (left) Tamsin Shelton; 77 (right) Jamie Large; 83, 84, 86 Stuart Abraham/www.jersey.com; 84 (top left) Jersey Tourism; 90, 91, 95, 96 Tourism Flanders; 98 Brian Daughton; 99 (left) Falite Ireland South West; 102 David Doyle; 105 Nick Slocum/Whale Watch West Cork; 106 Jacques Hampe/Strasbourg Office of Tourism; 107 (left) Yves Noto-Campanella/ Strasbourg Office of Tourism; 107 (right), 110 Airdiasol Rothan/ Strasbourg Office of Tourism; 109 Arblaster & Clarke; 112, 113, 116 JP Campomar, Ville de Avignon; 120 Doug Houghton/Scottish Viewpoint; 121 (left) Alistair Peebles; 121 (right), 122 Getty Images; 134, 135 (left) SIBA/ Brigitte Ruiz; 141 Tim Brenner; 144 Claire Boobyer; 145 (right) Michelle Grant; 150, 246, 253, 255, 256 (left) Olivia Rutherford; 154, 155 (left), 160 Stéphane Lerendu; 155 (right), 157, 158 Pierre Witt/Les Gets; 170, 171, 174 Gianluca Moggi; 176, 178 Fjord norde as Terje Rakke /Nordic Life AS/Fjord Norway; 185 (right), 188, 189, 203 (left), 205, 208 Fumie Suzuki; 186, 187 Rafael Estepania; 192, 193 (right), 196 (top) Turespaña; 193 (left), 195, 196 (bottom), 262 Chris Moss; 199 VisitFlam/E.A. Vikesland; 202, 207 Cathy Phillips; 203 (top right) Matt Field; 203 (bottom right), 206 Britta Jaschinski; 212 Christian Perret; 220 Bergen Tourist Board; 225 Tove K. Breitstein; 226 VisitFlam/ Per Eide; 229 Abi Tallis; 237 (top left), 241 Artur Zyrkowski; 237 (bottom left), 240, 242 Polska Organizacja Turystyczna; 237 (right) Maciej Rawluk; 243 Trevor Jones, Wolsztyn Experience; 256 (bottom right), 270 Jon Santa Cruz; 264, 265 (bottom right), 269 DB AG; 265 (top middle), 268 www.tourspain.com; 265 (right top), 266 Lydia Evans.

Featured establishments/artists: pages 7 (bottom left), 10, 11, 13 (bottom), 31, 78, 81, 99 (right), 101, 103, 115, 127, 128, 131, 135 (right), 139 (left), 145, 147, 150 (left), 159, 173, 177, 197, 209, 210, 256 (top right), 221, 222, 228, 229 (left), 230, 232, 234, 265 (left).

The editor and writers would like to thank Harriet, Theo and Matthew Albert, Ilaria Bardessono, Damir Biuklic, Nigel Burch, Charlotte Cooke-Priest, Heather Gilbert, Colin Keldie, Jake Lingwood, Lene Lunde, Amanda Monroe, Dorli Muhr, Paola Musolino, Peter Newcombe, Rianne Ojeh-Steenbergen, Michael Peck, Tom Rendall, Carly Simpson, Peer Sips, Martyna Szmytkowska, Ruby Vrolijk and John and Vivienne Whiffen. Special thanks to all the Time Out writers whose work forms the basis for some of these chapters.

Contents

Introduction

With the opening of the High Speed 1 railway line between St Pancras International and the Channel Tunnel, flight-free travel to Europe has become a practical option. It's also the most enjoyable and environmentally intelligent way of taking a holiday. So put your airport anxieties and no-frills nightmares behind you and take the train, and the boat, and the bus...

Written by **Chris Moss**, Editor

Flight-free travel is better, smarter and faster than it's ever been. For a moment, it seemed the sudden and exponential rise of the budget airline might hasten the demise of surface travel, but, also rather suddenly, a number of factors have come into play to make flying look less than wonderful.

The most obvious one is global warming. A passenger on a Eurostar train travelling from St Pancras International to Paris Gare du Nord produces about 5.5kg of carbon dioxide; the same person on a flight from London Heathrow airport to Charles de Gaulle would produce 60kg of carbon dioxide. Throw in transfers between air terminals and city centres, and flying just doesn't fit with the environmentalist consensus.

But concern for the planet isn't the only reason to eschew the aeroplane. If it were, we'd walk everywhere, shun cars and taxis, or perhaps just stay at home reading books written by George Monbiot.

Flight-free travel's main strength is pleasure – it is just lovely and somehow very human to slow down, stick to the ground, see the world as you move through it, and meet fellow travellers – and at the same time not to have to suffer the stresses and frustrations of airports.

Of course, overland travel is nothing new. Until the 1950s, when the de Havilland Comet and Boeing 707 revolutionised civil aviation, most long-distance passenger travel was by rail or by sea, with buses and cars for shorter hops. Fewer people went abroad in those days, and they tended to think of travel in terms of Grand Tours, transatlantic crossings, adventures on the Nile and intrepid explorations.

InterRail

PLAN YOUR JOURNEY THROUGH EUROPE

European trains take you swiftly and efficiently from city centre to city centre.

Take a high speed train from Paris to Lyon in only two hours or make the train your hotel, boarding a night train in Berlin and waking up in Zurich, Krakow, Malmö, Paris, Warsaw or Vienna. With an InterRail Pass, the choice is yours. See the map below for an indication of journey times between major European cities.

FREE TO EXPLORE EUROPE

TRAVEL TIMES

This is why many of the people who want to sell you flight-free transport like to package their services in the trappings of nostalgia and glamour. The Venice Simplon-Orient-Express and new Danube Express are the most obvious examples, but even the cross-Biscay ferries have cinemas and casinos, and most of us are wont to buying a mini-bottle of bubbly when the Eurostar revs up as it leaves London.

THE OPTIONS

Flight-free means lots of things, but what it most often means is catching a train. While driving, cycling, walking, catching ferries and riding on buses are all practical and fun options – and all feature prominently in this book – they have fewer advantages than the railways. The train is fast, comfortable and predictable (on the Continent) and you can walk around and socialise. It is safe and the network is extensive – there is a global grid of iron rails connecting northern Portugal to Saigon, and Europe is where most of the busiest hubs and spokes are concentrated.

THE RAILWAYS

Buy a good map like the Thomas Cook Rail Map Europe and trace the black lines with your finger. The thicker lines are main lines – some of them high-speed ones – and the thinner ones are branch lines running through smaller towns and villages. Europe, you will see, is well covered.

To tap into this vast network, you have to get across the Channel, and taking the train through the UK is at best a bore and at worst a logistical nightmare. British trains are often slow, dirty and ugly, and they are invariably expensive. That said, the relocation of the Eurostar terminus to St Pancras has made for much-improved connections from the Midlands, the north of England and Scotland. Holiday-weekend track maintenance aside, the services on the west and east coast main lines are speedy these days – Virgin's Pendolinos between Manchester and London take 2 hours 15 minutes, while National Express East Coast, which took over from GNER in December 2007, connects York to London in just 1 hour 51 minutes.

One UK service worth singling out is the Scotrail Caledonian Sleeper service connecting London Euston with Glasgow, Edinburgh, Aberdeen, Inverness and Fort William. It's charming and restful, and you can get haggis and malts as you travel through the night. If you are thinking of doing the Aberdeen-Orkneys trip described in this guide, this is a service to consider. See the Directory at the back of this book for details.

FAST TRACKS

The Eurostar has failed to live up to expectations. When the Channel Tunnel project was under discussion in the 1980s, Britons were promised lines from Manchester to Milan, from Glasgow to Ghent. But by the time the first Eurostar service started rolling in 1994, all the so-called Regional Eurostar plans had been shelved. Indeed, it took another 13 years for the London-to-tunnel service to get a dedicated line.

Rail fans love to argue that fast trains are a viable alternative to planes and the opening of said line – High Speed 1 – would seem to support their cause. In reality, only a handful of services can really compete for time with jets. These would include London to Paris (2hrs 15mins), London to Brussels (1hr 51mins), London-Cologne (4hrs 41 mins) and also the service to Paris Disneyland. Seven European countries have united to create Railteam, a Europe-wide network of fast lines that will bring other hubs – including Basle, Barcelona and Zurich – a lot closer by 2010. It also promises to make booking much easier, with a central website, www.railteam.eu, that goes live in 2009.

Meanwhile, there are other pleasures to be had. For a start, a rail journey begins at the gloriously refurbished St Pancras station in London, one of the few places where Victorian and 21st-century architectural ideas collide and come up with something truly beautiful. If you get there a bit early, there may even be time for a drink in 'Europe's longest champagne bar'.

Then, once you get onto the Continent, you tap into the shimmering, hi-tech world of the ICE, the Thalys, the AVE. These enigmatic names denote the missile-like trains that provide our European brothers and sisters with fast, efficient services between major cities. Every few months, news reports from Spain, Germany, Italy and France tell us a new line has been opened, and a new record set; many regular inter-city services now commute at speeds of 260mph, while the current world record was set in April 2007 by the 25,000-horsepower French V150 TGV, which peaked at 357.2mph.

THE MAN ON THE TRAIN

Mark Smith was station manager for Charing Cross, London Bridge and Cannon Street railway stations in London in the early to mid '90s, and also worked as a European rail agent issuing tickets and advising other travel agents on train travel across Europe. When he retired from British Rail in September 2007, he created the website www.seat61.com to provide rail enthusiasts with advice on the best train times, routes and fares from the UK to Europe. His tips for pleasurable, cost-cutting rail travel are:

● Use German Railways' impressive online timetable, http://bahn.hafas.de (English button upper right) to go from Seville to St Petersburg or from Nice to Helsinki; use the same site for buying tickets to or through Germany, Austria, Scandinavia, central and eastern Europe, or call German Railways' UK office on 08718 808066.

● When comparing train fares with flights, remember that trains are centre to centre with no extra to pay to reach remote airports, there are no baggage fees or weight limits, no airport taxes or fuel surcharges, and infants go free. A sleeper train may save you a hotel bill, too.

● Always book a couchette or sleeper for an overnight train ride, for both comfort and security. Booking just an ordinary seat is a false economy.

● For journeys from Britain to France, Switzerland, Spain and Italy, the best way to buy tickets is online at www.raileurope.co.uk (French Railways' UK subsidiary) or French Railways' own site, www.voyages-sncf.com (English-language button bottom left). Or you can buy tickets by phone from Rail Europe on 0844 848 5 848, but there's a £6 fee for phone bookings.

● You can book City Night Line sleeper trains from Brussels to either Berlin or Hamburg, Paris to Munich, Cologne to Prague, Vienna or Copenhagen online at www.bahn.de/citynightline, buying a connecting Eurostar ticket to Paris or Brussels at www.eurostar.com or a Eurostar+Thalys ticket to Cologne at www.raileurope.co.uk.

● Feel free to take your own food and drink (and even wine or beer), it's allowed.

● Never travel without a good book and a corkscrew.

SMILE!
YOU ARE IN FORMENTERA

ESPAÑA

The sea will surprise
you like never before

Formentera
Illes Balears

www.illesbalears.es
www.spain.info

FERRIES, COACHES AND CARS

This is not a great era for ships, not if you consider people's perceptions of them. Cruises are, for all the marketing and attempts at reinvention, still largely viewed as either floating luxury troughs or be-funnelled rest-homes, and the arrival of a 15-deck behemoth is viewed by responsible tourism types as only slightly less damaging than an armed Hemingway or a bikini-ed mosque visitor.

Ferries, meanwhile, are regarded along the same lines as piers, kiss-me-quick hats and Jim Davidson – just not very pleasant. Yet, around 20 firms operate dozens of services out of the main British ports and on the continent there are hundreds of operators, large and small. Forced to comete with planes and trains, many have bought new vessels that are more spacious, more comfortable and faster. For trips arounds Scandinavia, the Baltic, Greece, Croatia and the Scottish Isles, the ferry has all the virtues of the cruise – peace, weather, space to stroll – and hardly any of its vices.

If ferries are old-fashioned and a bit middle class, travelling by coach is strictly proletarian. The word is dated, grubby, slow-sounding; a 'coach' may serve a purpose for a rugby match piss-up or for a hard-up student's initiatory bolt from home, but it just won't do for a holiday. The rest of the world uses a variation of the word 'bus' for its long-distance services and, funnily enough, the buses on offer in France, Germany and Spain are sleeker, faster and newer than, say, those used on the National Express service between Birmingham and

THE BOY ON THE BUS

Benji Lanyado, 24, is a travel writer and edits YounginEurope.com, He discovered the wonders of bus travel during trips around Europe over his university summer breaks. Here are his reasons for being cheerful on the back seat:

● Buses have never been glamorous. No steaming hulk of a bus ever pulled into a station and picked up Marilyn Monroe. No... because buses are the people's transport. Think of it like a football stadium. Where is the best banter? Where are the local characters? In the cheap seats, of course.

● Buses stop at quirky little dives in the middle of nowhere for delicious local broth and sweet coffee. Buses hug coastlines and mountainsides that no train could conquer. Limit yourself to trains and you could miss vast chunks of the continent. If you want to travel the beautifully rugged Albanian Riviera, or swing through the forests of northern Estonia, or travel the southern Turkish coast, a bus is your only option.

● Planning a multi-stop trip is easy. Bus users have the wonderful Eurolines (eurolines.com), which covers the majority of Europe on one site. There's even an 'InterRail' equivalent, courtesy of the rough-and-ready chaps at Busabout (busabout.com).

● The prices are a joy. In Eastern Europe you can span fair-sized countries for under a tenner.

● People think that buses are one up from the donkey and cart in the convenience stakes. Not so. Most Eurolines affiliates are surprisingly perky; with deep seats, wide berths, cup holders, decent loos and communal TVs hovering overhead.

● Travel during the day and you can get the entire back seat to yourself. But, yes, you will get the occasional stinker. In this eventuality, the best thing to do is get drunk, strike up a conversation, and you'll be amazed at how the hours fly by.

noflights●.com

Call 0844 357 0288 or visit www.noflights.com

Travelling without Flying...
A World of Possibilities

European and Worldwide holidays by Rail, Road or Sea

Blackpool Pleasure Beach. On the upside, firms such as market leader Eurolines – which transports between 500-600,000 passengers to Europe every year on about 500 routes – are upgrading their vehicles and offering on-board 'luxuries' such as picture windows, reclining seats and seat belts. Like trains, most coach services go from centre to centre and, for shorter journeys, their times compare favourably with flights.

A coach is – in green terms – far better than a car. But the latter has obvious advantages when it comes to providing freedom and flexibility. Keen cyclists apart, the car is the only practical mode of transport for exploring the trails of Spain's Picos de Europa national park, the villages of southern Eire or the vineyards of the Rhône valley. It is also the only way you can achieve the James Bond high of Europe's ultra-fast motorways, remote lanes and coastal hairpins. A few years ago, car hire was daylight robbery anywhere except in the US, but now there are great deals across Europe.

HOW GREEN IS ALL THIS?

Train travel produces a tenth of the greenhouse gases per passenger per mile of aeroplanes. In 2007, Eurostar unveiled plans to reduce its carbon dioxide emissions by 25 per cent by 2012. The plan is to install energy meters on trains to encourage drivers to drive more economically, fit controls to reduce energy consumption from lighting, heating and air conditioning, and source more electricity from 'green' energy companies. There are also schemes that intend to get more people into the carriages by using space better.

Friends of the Earth claim that if all passengers who normally fly between London, Paris and Brussels switched to the train, it would reduce carbon emissions by 200,000 tonnes per year – the annual carbon footprint of Oxford.

The latest coaches coming off the production lines meet Euro Emissions Standard IV – currently the most stringent level for nitrogen oxide, hydrocarbons, carbon monoxide and other emissons. Most of us probably won't check whether we are boarding a Volvo B12B with a Jonkheer body or a MAN Van Hool T9 Altano, but as the EU moves towards punitive measures for smelly, smoky transport companies, those that make money out of our overland trips will be forced to invest in flash new buses.

AND HOW CHEAP?

Eurostar tickets, whether you buy them directly from the firm or from an authorised agent – details in the Directory at the back of this book – never quite compare with the 2p to Venice half-lies touted by the budget airlines. At press time, the lead-in return fare for London-Paris was £59, London Brussels was £59 and London-Lille was £55. Eurostar sold 800,000 of these bargain tickets in 2007, so no one can claim they are hidden from view or embedded in some remote website link.

Eurostar also sells tickets to destinations in France, Belgium and Netherlands, as well as to the German hubs of Cologne, Aachen and Frankfurt. For longer trips, through fares can be purchased from RailEurope (the UK agent for French firm SNCF) and Deutsche Bahn, as well as non-affiliated ticket agents such as European Rail, Ffestiniog Travel and International Rail; these can be competitive if you book well in advance (though the

booking websites are usually a frustrating click fest) and InterRail, at £242 for 22 days continuous travel, is still a budget blowout. See the Directory for websites and telephone numbers.

Look out for offers and deals, and check what your ticket includes. For instance, when you buy a ticket to Brussels you can travel on to any Belgian station free within the next 24 hours. You can also travel on to any other station in the Netherlands free – within 24 hours – when you buy a Eurostar ticket to a Dutch station.

Coaches can be dirt cheap. A London–Warsaw one-way ticket typically costs £48 with Eurolines, and prices remain the big draw for coach travel. As major firms begin to launch passes and offers, they present a genuine alternative to the InterRail.

Cars – bought or hired – are dirty, slow and accident-prone. They are flight-free and at rental rates from £20 a day they are affordable, but unless you can have or can rent a hybrid it's a choice that could be expensive for the environment.

All this is so much logistics, so much being green and good. But flight-free travel is mainly about an attitude to leisure. Having chosen your mode of transport to get from A to B, you'll still have days, perhaps weeks, in which to enjoy yourself and explore a city, a region, perhaps a whole continent. The itineraries in this book, while allowing plenty of time for resting, eating and drinking, are intended to be a celebration of all the different ways people can move around. Once you alight from the coach or disembark at the port, you still have it all to do: cycling, canoeing, climbing; swimming and sailing; trams and steam trains; Segways and shoe leather. You may even, having avoided the sky – and the airport – for your main trip, decide to take off and do a balloon flight or hang-glide off a cliff; that's not the kind of flight we are trying to break free from.

WHY AND HOW THE FLIGHT-FREE GUIDE?

Over several years, Time Out produced a number of publications with titles such as *Fly Europe* and *Europe by Air*. The rise of the low-cost airline was a catalyst for these and reflected the public need for short, sharp city guides.

A new demand for inspirational, environmentally aware travel ideas prompted the present book. The journeys are all tried and tested, and, we believe, affordable and practical. The only press trips that were accepted were for the ski chapter and the boxes on champagne, Aegean cruising and the Orient Express train. RailEurope assisted with several tickets and passes, Eurostar provided a return ticket to Lille and Brittany Ferries and SeaFrance each provided a return sea-crossing. All other chapters were funded independently.

In keeping with the spirit of the book, we asked our writers to travel flight-free at all times. On the few occasions when flights were used to get us home – due to time pressures – the flights were offset.

ADVERTISERS

We would like to stress that no establishment has been included in this guide because it has advertised in any of our publications and no payment of any kind has influenced any review. The opinions given in this book are those of Time Out writers and are entirely independent.

HOW TO USE THIS BOOK

ABOUT TIME OUT CITY GUIDES
This is the first edition of *Time Out Flight Free Europe*, one of an expanding series of more than 75 travel guides produced by the people behind the successful listings magazines in London, New York, Chicago, Sydney and many more cities around the world.

THE LOWDOWN ON THE LISTINGS
Addresses, telephone numbers and websites have been included, as have details of other selected services and facilities. However, owners and managers can change their arrangements at any time. Before you go out of your way, we strongly advise you to call and check opening times and other particulars. While every effort has been made to ensure the accuracy of the information contained in this guide, the publishers cannot accept responsibility for any errors it may contain.

HUBS, TRIPS AND JOURNEYS
The four 'Hubs' chapters focus on cities easily reached by train from St Pancras International. These constitute holidays or short breaks in themselves and also serve as excellent gateways to the European rail network.

The 'Trips' chapters contain practical overland routes from cities or ports in the UK to European cities or regions; travelling time ranges from 90 minutes to more than a day.

The 'Journeys' chapters celebrate travelling for its own sake; the text guides you from the moment you sit down on the bus, train or ferry right to the end of your 'grand tour' of a region, country or several countries.

TELEPHONE NUMBERS
Local phone numbers are listed in this guide. To dial them from abroad, use your country's exit code (00 in the UK, 011 in the US) or the + symbol (on many mobile phones), followed by the country code, followed by the number as listed (you may have to drop the initial zero). For country codes, *see p280*.

LET US KNOW WHAT YOU THINK
We hope you enjoy Time Out Flight Free Europe, and we'd like to know what you think of it. We welcome tips for places that you consider we should include in future editions, and take notice of your criticism of our choices. You can email us at guides@timeout.com.

JOURNEY TIMES
In 'Hubs' and 'Destinations' chapters, we give the time taken by the writer for his or her main journey – where possible this is the fastest route available. Other information and alternative routes are provided in the Travel Information section towards the end of each chapter.

ATTRACTIONS
Next to this symbol are the main reasons for taking a trip, such as 'budget', 'family-friendly', 'food & drink' and 'romance'.

TRANSPORT ICONS

	Train		Steam train
	Tram		Car
	Bus		Motorcycle
	Bicycle		Segway
	Camel		Horseriding
	Ship		Ferry
	Canoe		Sailing boat
	Kayak		Rowing boat

TREES ARE GREENISH
Each trip in this book is marked with tree symbols that indicate how green we think it is. Our consultant Graham Simmonds, Chief Executive of Trees for Cities, asked us to remind readers that 'this is an instinctive, non-scientific appraisal of each trip. It's not an exact measurement of how much CO2 a person uses on a holiday, but an evaluation of how green a trip appears to be in general terms':

Carbon heavy and no special redeeming features

Beginning to think about green travel

Carbon thoughtful, but no prizes

Eco-intelligent travel experience

Deep green, planet-saving holiday

Hubs

Hubs

UNITED KINGDOM

North

LONDON

LILLE

PARIS

FRANCE

Bay of Biscay

SPAIN

Sea

NETHERLANDS

GERMANY

COLOGNE

BRUSSELS

BELGIUM

CZE
REPU

LUXEMBOURG

AUSTR

SWITZERLAND

SLO

ITALY

Arc de Triomphe p24

Paris

ROUTE London ▶ Paris

Paris has it all: romance and reading matter on the *rive gauche*, medieval alleyways, café society, and delicious cuisine without a celeb chef in sight. Add galleries packed with art and sculpture from all the great European schools and some of the world's most striking modern and postmodern architecture, and you have the ultimate city for the cultured flâneur. The city is renascent, and perfect for the weekend.

Written by **Chris Moss**; 'Fizzing with excitement' by **Ruth Jarvis**

Centre Pompidou p25

Les Deux Magots p27

THE TRIP

This is a trip worthy of a toast at St Pancras's new champagne bar. Getting to Europe couldn't really be easier than it is today, short of taking a private helicopter from your house to the Deux Magots. As you pull out of the artfully reinvented station, wave to passengers on the inter-city East Midlands trains. You'll be in Paris before they get to Sheffield. The train is into tunnels seconds after the platform is left behind and from then on it's full-tilt to France. In the olden days – the 1990s – the engine had to chug along till it made it to the new tracks in France but now the 68 miles (109 kilometres) of track between London and the tunnel – nicknamed High Speed 1 – have been upgraded. A Eurostar record of 208mph (334.7kmph) was set on the line in July 2003. The ordinary speed is somewhat lower – an average of 186mph (300kmph), hence the call centre number of 08705 186 186 – but even at this pace the only views you get are blurry: greenish, rolling Kent, flattish dun-coloured Pas-de-Calais and then Paris's rather nondescript suburbs as you approach the Gare du Nord. You've arrived.

 St Pancras International ▶
Paris Gare du Nord
2 hours 15 minutes

 Art; culture; food & drink; romance

Dinner & Show at 7pm from €145 • Show at 9pm : €99, at 11pm : €89

Montmartre - 82, boulevard de Clichy - 75018 Paris
Reservations : 01 53 09 82 82 - www.moulin-rouge.com

THE DESTINATION

Paris, for all its differences, has this in common with London: it is always being reborn. King Philippe-Auguste filled it with trade guilds in the 13th century to create an urban bourgeoisie to counter the power of the Church and the feudal lords; in the 17th century, Jean-Baptiste Colbert commissioned lavish building work to create a city fit for 'Sun King' Louis XIV; and in the 19th, Baron Haussmann made it the maquette for all the world's aspiring cities.

The latest sign of a renaissance is 104, an enormous arts and media centre that opened in summer 2008 in a building that used to be home to the city's undertakers. It is part of an elaborate scheme to revive the run-down north-east of Paris – and a key element in Socialist mayor Bertrand Delanoë's plan to create a Paris fit for the 21st century.

Modelled on the successful regeneration of the 13th arrondissement on the Left Bank of the Seine, the plan is to turn this previously desolate neighbourhood into a cultural hub, with a multiplex arthouse cinema not far from 104, as well as shops and affordable social housing.

In 2006, the first tramway to be opened in Paris in nearly a century enhanced the connections between the city and its southern satellites. The plan for the north-east also includes the tram, plus a series of walkways crossing the périphérique, the eight-lane motorway that marks the limits of Paris 'proper'.

Most significant of all has been Delanoë's attempt to tame the traffic in Paris. In summer 2007, he launched **Vélib**, a free bicycle scheme that was an immediate success.

Next to come is the Automobiles-en-Libre-Service, which will make 2,000 electrically powered vehicles available to subscribers, who can drive the cars away without booking at dozens of sites 24 hours a day - and then park them anywhere in the city.

With all this ambition and thrusting modernity, it's a relief to stroll around a Paris where none of it matters. There are many ways to do this multi-faceted city – there are icons of modernist architecture, museums and galleries, existentialist cafés and royal gardens galore – but for a perfect weekend, explore the river, a handful of world-class galleries and see the first real version of Paris – the city of the Capetians.

DAY 1: **ART AND ARCHITECTURE**

Lovers of Paris – and even more so those who fell in love in Paris – claim the city is worth a lifetime of weekend trips. Sights like the Eiffel Tower, the Arc de Triomphe, the Centre Pompidou and Notre-Dame are among the most celebrated and photographed places on the planet. You certainly wouldn't want to rush them just to tick boxes, so bear in mind that Paris's pleasures are quite spread out. At the same time, this is the city of the flâneur and the boulevardier – Paris was, literally, made for walking. A lot of iconic vistas and buildings can be taken in by just strolling off the Avenue des Champs-Elysées, loitering in the Jardin des Tuilleries and getting lost around the Latin Quarter. At some stage it's also almost obligatory to hike to the top of the hill at Montmartre and take in the whole of the city from the sugary-white dome of the Sacré Coeur.

PARIS

Vélib
www.en.velib.paris.fr

Jardin des Tuileries

To get started on a flâneuring tour, take a metro from your hotel to the Bir-Hakeim station. You will debouche at the base of the **Eiffel Tower**. Perhaps no building better symbolises Paris than the tower. Maupassant claimed he left Paris because of it, William Morris visited daily to avoid having to see it from afar – and it was originally meant to be a temporary structure. The radical cast-iron tower was built for the 1889 World Fair and the centenary of the 1789 Revolution by engineer Gustave Eiffel (whose construction company still exists today). Construction took more than two years and used some 18,000 pieces of metal and 2,500,000 rivets. Vintage double-decker lifts ply their way up and down; you can walk as far as the second level. There are souvenir shops, an exhibition space, café and even a post office on the first and second levels.

Views can reach over 65 kilometres on a good day, although the most fascinating perspectives are of the ironwork itself, whether gazing up from underneath or enjoying the changing vision as the lift rises.

Walk along quai Branly, and follow the curve of the Seine until you reach the Pont des Invalides. Cross the river and continue down avenue Roosevelt till you hit the Champs-Elysées. For all its fame, the boulevard is essentially a traffic route – or jam, as is often the case – and it's a long, noisy hike all the way up to the Arc de Triomphe. Far better to head south-east past the Grand Palais and Petit Palais – both built for the 1900 Exposition Universelle – and into the **Jardin des Tuileries**.

The gravelled alleyways of these gardens have been a chic promenade since they opened to the public in the 16th century; and the popular mood persists with the funfair that sets up along the rue de Rivoli side in summer. André Le Nôtre created the prototypical French garden with terraces and a central vista running down the Grand Axe through circular and hexagonal ponds. As part of Mitterrand's Grand Louvre project, fragile sculptures such as Coysevox's winged horses were transferred to the Louvre and replaced by copies, and the Maillol sculptures were returned to the Jardins du Carrousel; a handful of modern sculptures has been added, including bronzes by Laurens, Moore, Ernst, Giacometti, and Dubuffet's *Le Bel Costumé*.

IM Pei's glass pyramid will draw you inexorably towards the **Louvre,** the huge palace that evolved between the reigns of King François I (1515-47) and President François Mitterrand (1981-95) to become arguably the most important art gallery in the world. Much like the building itself, the Louvre's collections were built up over the centuries. They encompass a rich visual history of the western world, from Ancient Egypt and Mesopotamia to the 19th century. One of the most impressive things about the Louvre is the way it juxtaposes architecture and content. Look up from a case of Greek or Roman antiquities and you might see an 18th-century painted ceiling, or two doves by Braque.

Some 35,000 works of art and artefacts are on show, divided into eight departments and housed in three wings: Denon, Sully and Richelieu. Under the light-flooded atrium of the glass pyramid, each wing has its own entrance, though you can pass from one to another. The main draw is, of course, the paintings and sculpture. Two glass-roofed sculpture courts contain the famous Marly horses on the ground floor of Richelieu, with French sculpture below and Italian Renaissance pieces in the

Eiffel Tower
Champ de Mars
01 44 11 23 45
www.tour-eiffel.fr

Jardin des Tuileries
rue de Rivoli

Louvre
rue de Rivoli
01 40 20 50 50
www.louvre.fr

Denon wing. The Grand Galerie and Salle de la Joconde (home to the *Mona Lisa*), like a mini Uffizi, run the length of Denon's first floor with French Romantic painting alongside. Dutch and French paintings occupy the second floor of Richelieu and Sully.

Continue east along rue de Rivoli – the neighbourhood to your left, Les Halles, is a rather ugly nexus of entertainment, commerce and kebabs – and, turning left at rue du Renard, you will wind up at the **Centre Pompidou**.

Modern architecture in Paris really took off with the Centre Pompidou, designed by Richard Rogers and Renzo Piano. This benchmark of inside-out high-tech is as much of an attraction as the Musée National d'Art Moderne within – as is the piazza outside, which attracts street performers and pavement artists. Opened in 1977, the 'Beaubourg' holds the largest collection of modern art in Europe. Sample the contents of its vaults (50,000 works of art by 5,000 artists) on the website, as only a fraction – about 600 works – can be seen for real at any one time. There is a partial rehang each year.

COFFEE, CAKES, SARTRE

Nowhere on earth are there so many literary associations in so small an area as in St-Germain-des-Prés. Hop on the metro to St Michel, exit muttering 'when I was in Paris, boul' Mich', I used to...' (*Ulysses*), and take the rue de l'Hirondelle passageway to the right of the fountain.

Centre Pompidou
(Musée National d'Art Moderne)
rue St-Martin
01 44 78 12 33
www.centrepompidou.fr

THE LUNCH BOX

Some people use the morning Eurostar just for a swift business meeting and then zoom back in the afternoon. Boring. But if you want to show you are a bon viveur and spontaneous enough to qualify for an existentialist's polo neck, then how about going in and out for lunch?

There are plenty of eateries around Gare du Nord, but only a handful are top-notch. **Chez Michel** is just behind St-Vincent-de-Paul church, a few minutes' walk from Gare du Nord – and while the area isn't particularly classy, the food is. Thierry Breton is from Brittany and sports the Breton flag on his chef's whites. His menu is stacked with hearty offerings from said region. Marinated salmon with purple potatoes served in a preserving jar, pickled herring-style, is succulently tender; so, too, is the abalone.

Just west of the station, **Pétrelle** is popular with fashion designers and film stars, not least because Jean-Luc André is as inspired a decorator as he is a cook. A faded series of early 20th-century tableaux is one recent flea market find, but behind the style is some serious substance. The €29 no-choice menu is huge value for money (on our last visit, marinated sardines with tomato relish, rosemary-scented rabbit with roasted vegetables, deep purple poached figs); or you can splash out with luxurious à la carte dishes such as tournedos Rossini. If you're looking for a quick and delicious lunch near Montmartre, visit André's annexe, Les Vivres, next door.

Spring is where Michelin inspectors go on their day off. Young American chef Daniel Rose has wowed the critics since opening this sleek 16-seat bistro in 2006, serving a no-choice four-course menu that changes every day according to what he finds at the place des Fêtes market. On a late spring day this might result in a velvety cauliflower soup (made without cream), chunky octopus salad with potatoes, radishes and herbs, poached guinea hen with root vegetables, and baked apple with French toast. A meal feels like a big dinner party, with Rose the affable host. Reservations obligatory.

Chez Michel *10 rue de Belzunce, 01 44 53 06 20*
Pétrelle *34 rue Pétrelle, 01 42 82 11 02*
Spring *28 rue de la Tour d'Auvergne, 01 45 96 05 72*

This will bring you out on rue Gît-le-Coeur. At no.9, on your right, is the Relais Hôtel Vieux Paris, the Beat Hotel. It's been smartened up since a drug-addled William Burroughs wrote *Naked Lunch* here, but pictures of the Beats adorn the wall and Mme Odillard will show fans photos of those wild times in a signed copy of Brian Chapman's book *The Beat Hotel*.

Walk on to join quai des Grands-Augustins, opposite Les Bouquinistes, where, at no.51, you'll find **Lapérouse**, one of the most romantic restaurants in Paris. The eaterie was formerly a clandestine rendezvous for French politicians and their mistresses; the tiny private dining rooms upstairs used to lock from the inside. Chef Alain Hacquard does a modern take on classic French cooking: his beef fillet is smoked for a more complex flavour; a tender saddle of rabbit is cooked in a clay crust, flavoured with lavender and rosemary and served with ravioli of onions. It's not cheap – a half-bottle of Pouilly-Fuissé will set you back nearly €35 – but it is gorgeous. Lapérouse was a literary hotspot from 1870: its small salons – designed for dangerous liaisons – hosted the likes of Sand, Maupassant, Zola, Dumas and Hugo.

After lunch, turn left down rue Dauphine, where Alain Fournier, author of *Le Grand Meaulnes*, lived at no.24, and drop down rue Mazet. The restaurant Magny, where George Sand smoked cigars with Flaubert, Gautier and Turgenev at Sainte-Beuve's literary dinners, was at no.3; it's now called Azabu.

Crossing rue St-André-des-Arts, go through the archway at no.59 to find a charming covered passage and the back entrance of Procope. Dating from 1686, it's the city's oldest café and boasts Voltaire, Rousseau, the Marquis de Sade, Beaumarchais, Balzac, Verlaine, Hugo, La Fontaine and Anatole France among its former customers. The food, unfortunately, is mediocre, but upstairs you can see Voltaire's marble desk and a letter from the imprisoned Marie-Antoinette.

From here, turn right into boulevard St-Germain and walk west past the metro station. Just after the corner with rue Bonaparte is **Les Deux Magots**, a favourite hangout of Jean-Paul Sartre and Simone de Beauvoir in the closing years of the war. Covert messages were exchanged between members of the Resistance in the café's toilets, over which a charming dame pipi still presides. The Deux Magots' literary associations are many – the walls are covered with photos of Hemingway and the Surrealists. While the terrace is filled with St Tropez types, the interior is still dignified and quiet enough to attract writers – even if they're just penning postcards.

The hot chocolate at Les Deux Magots is good (and the only item served in generous portions) – but, like everything else, it's pricey. Visit on a weekday afternoon when editors come by, manuscripts in hand, to the inside tables, leaving enough elbow room to engage in some serious discussion.

To the right, further along boulevard St-Germain, is Les Deux Magots' existentialist sister, **Café de Flore**, where Sartre and de Beauvoir virtually lived at the beginning of the war.

Bourgeois locals crowd the terrace tables at lunch, eating club sandwiches with knives and forks, as anxious waiters frown at couples with pushchairs or single diners occupying tables for four. Black American writers James Baldwin and Richard Wright enjoyed the liberated spirit here; Baldwin completed *Go Tell It on*

PARIS

Lapérouse
51 quai des Grands-Augustins
01 43 26 68 04

Les Deux Magots
6 pl St-Germain-des-Prés
01 45 48 55 25
www.lesdeuxmagots.com

Café de Flore
172 blvd St-Germain
01 45 48 55 26
www.cafede-flore.com

the Mountain in the Flore. These days the café awards its own writer's prize, and if you stay long enough you may see a famous face – Paul Auster or Paulo Coelho perhaps, both of whom have been known to drop in when they're in town.

If you decide to sleep over in St-Germain-des-Prés, choose between the modern, stylish **La Villa**, with its faux crocodile skin on the bedheads and crinkly taffeta over the taupe-coloured walls; and the more moderately priced, but stylish **Le Clos Médicis**. Designed more like a private townhouse than a hotel, it's located by the Luxembourg gardens: perfect if you fancy starting the morning with a stroll among the trees.

DAY 2: MEDIEVAL PARIS

The Ile de la Cité is where Paris was born around 250 BC, when the Parisii, a tribe of Celtic Gauls, decided to found a settlement on this convenient bridging point of the Seine. Romans, Merovingians and Capetians followed, in what became a centre of political and religious power right into the Middle Ages: royal authority at one end, around the Capetian palace; the Church at the other, by Notre-Dame.

When Victor Hugo wrote his *Notre-Dame de Paris* in 1831, the Ile de la Cité was still a bustling quarter of narrow medieval streets and tall houses: 'the head, heart and very marrow of Paris'. Taking the metaphor literally, Baron Haussmann performed a marrow extraction when he supervised the expulsion of 25,000 people from the island, razing tenements and some 20 churches, and leaving behind large, official buildings – the law courts, the **Conciergerie**, Hôtel-Dieu hospital, the police headquarters and the cathedral. The lines of the old streets are traced into the parvis in front of **Notre-Dame**.

Perhaps the most charming spot on the island is the western tip, where Pont Neuf spans the Seine. Despite its name, it is in fact the oldest remaining bridge in Paris, begun under the reign of Henri III and Catherine de Médicis in 1578 and taking 30 years to complete. Its arches are lined with grimacing faces, said to be modelled on some of the courtiers of Henri III. In 1991, the bridge (or rather a full-size facsimile of it) starred in Leos Carax's budget-busting film *Les Amants du Pont Neuf*.

Down the steps is a leafy triangular garden, square du Vert-Galant. You can take to the water here on the **Vedettes du Pont Neuf**. On the bridge's eastern side, place Dauphine, home to restaurants, wine bars and the ramshackle Hôtel Henri IV, was built in 1607, on what was then a sandy bar that flooded every winter. It was commissioned by Henri IV, who named it in honour of his son, the future King Louis XIII.

The brick and stone houses, similar to those in place des Vosges, look out over the quays and square. The third, eastern side was demolished in the 1860s, when the new Préfecture de Police was built. Known by its address, quai des Orfèvres, it was immortalised on screen by Clouzot's eponymous film and Simenon's Maigret novels. It's a tranquil, secluded spot.

The towers of the Conciergerie dominate the island's north bank. Along with the Palais de Justice, it was once part of the Palais de la Cité, the residential and administrative complex of the Capetian kings. It occupies the site of an earlier Merovingian fortress and, before that, the Roman governor's house. Etienne Marcel's uprising prompted Charles V to move the royal retinue

La Villa
29 rue Jacob
01 43 26 60 00
www.villa-saintgermain.com

Le Clos Médicis
56 rue Monsieur-le-Prince
01 43 29 10 80
www.closmedicis.com

Conciergerie
2 blvd du Palais
01 53 40 60 97

Notre-Dame
pl du Parvis-Notre-Dame
01 42 34 56 10
www.cathedraledeparis.com

Vedettes du Pont Neuf
sq du Vert-Galant
01 46 33 98 38
www.vedettesdupontneuf.com

to the Louvre in 1358, and the Conciergerie was assigned a more sinister role as a prison for those awaiting execution. The interior is worth a visit for its prison cells and the vaulted Gothic halls. On the corner of boulevard du Palais, the Tour de l'Horloge, built in 1370, was the first public clock in Paris.

Sainte-Chapelle, Pierre de Montreuil's masterpiece of stained glass and slender Gothic columns, nestles amid the nearby law courts. Enveloping the chapel, the Palais de Justice was built alongside the Conciergerie. Behind elaborate wrought-iron railings, most of the present buildings around the fine neo-classical entrance courtyard date from the 1780s reconstruction.

Sainte-Chapelle
6 blvd du Palais
01 53 40 60 97

FIZZING WITH EXCITEMENT

The new TGV route from Paris to Strasbourg means that you can now travel by train from Paris to the Champagne region in only 45 minutes (Gare de l'Est to Reims). However, a boon though fast train times may be for most European travel, there are certain very important advantages to be gained by taking a coach tour to, and of, Champagne. First, since you need transport to flit from one château to the next, it means you don't have to worry about getting around when drunk. Second, and of key importance, how many crates of champagne do you think you might be able to carry on to the TGV and through a Paris station change? Probably not as many as the three you can bring back with a wine tour specialist. And, if you think three crates might break the budget, bear in mind that buying direct from champagne houses knocks a significant amount off the prices: non-vintages start at around €15.

A tour with wine travel specialist Arblaster & Clarke is, typically, a three-day, two-night weekend that includes visits to four houses, two tutored tastings and tutorials, and on-demand advice from a wine expert. The journey over there is long, though the tedium is usually ameliorated by the inevitable wine purchases. All group tours are by their nature sociable, but group tours that actively require you to drink are more sociable than most.

Reims itself is less splendid than might be expected of somewhere at the centre of one of the world's most profitable beverage industries. It has a grey, northern cast to it and a 1970s feel to its arcades and neon-lit high street. That said, it has a landmark cathedral, some decent restaurants, good markets and malls, and a historic branch of Galeries Lafayette. There are also several museums, including a UNESCO World Heritage Site abbey, now a history museum, and the Musée de la Reddition, housed in the map room of General Eisenhower's headquarters, where the German army formally surrendered to the Allies in 1945. But if you're here for the bubbly, you won't have a lot of free time (and you may need a lie down in the little you have).

With a standard Arblaster & Clarke tour, the Friday night is taken up with an extensive comparative tasting at the tour-base, the Hôtel de la Paix, a smart Best Western, followed by (non-inclusive) meals at a choice of restaurants. Two favourites are Brasserie le Boulingrin (48 rue de Mars) and La Vigneraie (14 rue de Thillois). Over the weekend, you will be shown round several chateaux of varying styles and, depending on the package, you may be invited to a chateau for a formal meal with a different champagne accompanying every course.

Visiting wine producers is always a pleasure, but this tour is particularly enjoyable, perhaps because the winemakers' passion and pride at working in one of the world's greatest and most exacting closed shops is evident as they guide you round their *caves*, explain their production methods and answer your questions, particularly in the smaller places such as the husband-and-wife operation at Gausson, in Ay. In contrast, big-name Taittinger seems corporate and production-line.

Arblaster & Clarke (*www.winetours.co.uk*, 01730 263111) runs a variety of tours to the Champagne region, starting at £299 per person. You can travel by coach and ferry from London, Folkestone or Dover or join the group in Reims if you prefer the Eurostar experience – and don't plan to buy more champagne than you can carry.

PARIS

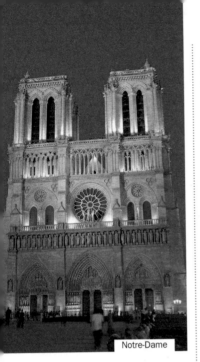
Notre-Dame

After passing through security, you can visit the Salle des Pas Perdus, busy with plaintiffs and barristers, and sit in on cases in the civil and criminal courts. Across boulevard du Palais, behind the Tribunal du Commerce, place Louis-Lépine is occupied by the Marché aux Fleurs, where horticultural suppliers sell flowers, cacti and exotic trees. On Sundays, they are joined by caged birds and small animals in the Marché aux Oiseaux.

The Hôtel-Dieu, east of the marketplace, was founded in the seventh century. During the Middle Ages your chances of survival here were, at best, slim; today the odds are much improved. The hospital originally stood on the other side of the island facing the Latin Quarter, but after a series of fires in the 18th century it was rebuilt here in the 1860s.

Notre-Dame cathedral dominates the eastern half of the island. On the parvis in front of the cathedral, the bronze 'Kilomètre Zéro' marker is the point from which distances between Paris and the rest of France are measured. The **Crypte Archéologique**, hidden under the parvis, gives a sense of the island's multilayered past, when it was a tangle of alleys, houses, churches and cabarets. Despite all the tourists, Notre-Dame is still a place of worship, and holds its Assumption Day procession, Christmas Mass and Nativity scene on the parvis. Walk through the garden by the cathedral to appreciate its flying buttresses. To the north-east, a medieval feel persists in the few streets untouched by Haussmann, such as rue Chanoinesse, rue de la Colombe and rue des Ursins, though the crenellated medieval remnant on the corner of rue des Ursins and rue des Chantres was redone in the 1950s for the Aga Khan.

The capital's oldest love story unfolded in the 12th century at 9 quai aux Fleurs, where Héloïse lived with her uncle, Canon Fulbert, who had her tutor and lover, the scholar Pierre Abélard, castrated. Héloïse was sent to a nunnery.

BED, BOARD, BAUDELAIRE

For a bite to eat and a spot of shopping take the footbridge to the Ile St-Louis, a tranquil, unspoiled corner of Paris and one of its most exclusive residential addresses. There are pretty views from the tree-lined quays, and the island still retains the air of a tranquil backwater, curiously removed from city life.

There's a splendid view of the flying buttresses of Notre-Dame, and a decent meal of tripe or a well-dressed frisée aux lardons to be had at **Brasserie de l'Ile St-Louis**. Ask for a table at the western end from the terraces.

Rue St-Louis-en-l'Ile – lined with fine historic buildings that now house quirky gift shops and gourmet food stores (many of them open on Sunday), quaint tearooms, stone-walled bars, hotels and restaurants – runs the length of the island. The grandiose Hôtel Lambert at no.2 was built by Le Vau in 1641 for Louis XIII's secretary, and has sumptuous interiors by Le Sueur, Perrier and Le Brun. At no.51 – Hôtel Chenizot – look out for the bearded faun adorning the rocaille doorway, which is flanked by stern dragons supporting the balcony. There's more sculpture on the courtyard façade, while a second courtyard hides craft workshops and an art gallery.

Across the street, at no.54, is the **Hôtel du Jeu de Paume**. With a discreet courtyard entrance, 17th-century beams, private garden and a unique timbered breakfast room that

Crypte Archéologique
pl Jean-Paul II
01 55 42 50 10

Brasserie de l'Ile St-Louis
55 quai de Bourbon
01 43 54 02 59

Hôtel du Jeu de Paume
54 rue St-Louis-en-l'Ile
01 43 26 14 18
www.jeudepaumehotel.com

was once a real tennis court built under Louis XIII, this is a charming and romantic hotel. These days it is filled with an attractive array of modern and classical art. A dramatic glass lift and catwalks lead to the simple and tasteful rooms.

At no.31, famous ice-cream maker Berthillon still draws a crowd. and no.69 houses **Mon Vieil Ami**, where Antoine Westermann has created a true foodie destination. He may be one of Alsace's greatest chefs, but his bistro cooking draws on all the regions of France and gives it a modern slant. Even the classic Ile St-Louis dining room has been successfully refreshed with black beams, white perspex panels between wall timbers, and a long, black table d'hôte down one side.

Baudelaire wrote part of *Les Fleurs du Mal* while living at the Hôtel de Lauzun at 17 quai d'Anjou; he and fellow poet Théophile Gautier also organised meetings of their dope-smokers' club on the premises. A couple of centuries earlier, Racine, Molière and La Fontaine resided as guests of La Grande Mademoiselle, cousin of Louis XIV and mistress of the Comte de Lauzan. The hôtel, built in 1657, stands out for its scaly sea-serpent drainpipes and trompe-l'oeil interiors.

If you like to rock and roll – gently – in bed, then check in to **Paris Yacht**. Bobbing peacefully on the Left Bank opposite the Ile St-Louis, this two-cabin houseboat can accommodate up to four guests. The terrace on the upper deck provides the ideal setting for a romantic dinner. The peaceful 17th-century townhouse **Hôtel des Deux-Iles** offers 17 soundproofed, air-conditioned rooms done out in vaguely colonial style. Attractive features include a tiny courtyard off the lobby and a vaulted stone breakfast area. The equally pleasant **Hôtel le Lutèce**, just up the road, is run by the same management.

TRAVEL INFORMATION

At least one **Eurostar** train departs St Pancras for Paris every hour between 5am and 9pm. Most are direct services.

WHEN TO GO
Year-round; spring and autumn are special.

USING THE HUB

Paris is the principal hub for France's SNCF railway network, as well as the high-speed TGV network that connects the capital to all the major cities. There are frequent, fast services from Gare du Nord to Amiens, Boulogne and Haute-Picardie, as well as to Belgium, the Netherlands, Cologne and the UK; from Gare de l'Est to north-east France, Luxembourg, Germany and Switzerland; from Gare St-Lazare to Normandy; from Gare Montparnasse to Brittany, Chartres and south-west France; from Gare d'Austerlitz for the Loire Valley, south and south-west France, and Spain; from Gare de Lyon to south-eastern France, the Auvergne, Provence, the Alps and Italy; there are night trains from Gare d'Austerlitz to the south and from Gare de Bercy to Italy. There is a frequent RER (high-speed metro) service between Gare St-Lazare and Versailles-Rive Gauche. See the Directory at the back of the book for more information about international connections.

Further reading

Adam Gopnik *Paris to the Moon*
Charles Dickens *A Tale of Two Cities* It was the best of times, it was the worst of times...
Marcel Proust *The Remembrance of Things Past* Belle époque Paris through the fictionalised life of the author.
Émile Zola *Nana* The great chronicler of Parisian life.
Victor Hugo *Les Misérables* The book that became the musical.

Websites

www.edible-paris.com
Personalised itineraries for eating your way around Paris.
www.paris-art.com
All about art in Paris, although you'll need to read French.
www.pidf.com
The official tourist website.

Mon Vieil Ami
69 rue St-Louis-en-l'Ile
01 40 46 01 35

Paris Yacht
quai de la Tournelle
06 88 70 26 36
www.paris-yacht.com

Hôtel des Deux-Iles
59 rue St-Louis-en-l'Ile
01 43 26 13 35
www.deuxiles-paris-hotel.com

Hôtel le Lutèce
65 rue St-Louis-en-l'Ile
01 43 26 23 52

Eurostar
www.eurostar.com

Grand'Place p35

Brussels

ROUTE London ▶ Brussels

The Belgian capital is an enigma. A French-speaking enclave in a Flemish region of a bilingual country where the safest option is to speak English, it is cosmopolitan, cultured, and a little bit confusing. But locals will tell you that you can eat, drink and party better here than in Paris – and now that there's a super-fast train into the heart of Brussels you don't have to get a job with the EU to discover it.

Written by **Edoardo Albert**

Grand'Place p35

Manneken-Pis p34

THE TRIP

Get on at St Pancras. Get off at Bruxelles-Midi two hours later. Couldn't be much easier. The journey through the Kentish countryside is unremarkable as are the initial stages in France. But when the line turns east, looking out of the window reveals 'le plat pays' (the flat land), which was Jacques Brel's and is now yours. It's a country where church steeples emerge from morning mists and trees march in lines beside ditches. This has been contested ground many times, which is something to reflect upon as you arrive in Brussels and the heart of Europe. Compare the magnificent glass arch of St Pancras to the uninspiring collection of struts and concrete at Bruxelles-Midi. Then again, survey the platforms and you'll see not only the Eurostar, but the burgundy-red Thalys, the ice-white ICE trains and the silver TGV Atlantique. This is a major hub with lines carrying bureaucrats, bankers and powerbrokers into the unloved, largely unelected powerbase of the modern European superstate. But if the bureaucracy gets too much, the inter-city trains are pretty good, too, and Antwerp and Ghent are both less than an hour away.

 St Pancras International ▸ Bruxelles-Midi **1 hour 51 minutes**

 Art; food & drink

THE DESTINATION

'Every day is a song for a holiday.' Not long ago a pink neon sign bearing that slogan appeared on the portico of the old stock exchange in Brussels during the Christmas market festivities. But this gnomic little sign said something important about the city. For a start, there was the fact that the sign was in English, an accepted lingua franca on the streets of the EU capital. What with Brussels being officially bilingual, the language choice also negates the need for producing it in both French and Flemish (one without the other is unthinkable; English is uncontroversial). Then there's the question of what it actually means. Like a Magritte painting, at first glance it seems clear enough, and then you dig deeper (how can a day be a song?) and before long it's all about as clear as the EU constitution. Maybe double meanings are unavoidable in a fractured country. After all, the Flemings and the Walloons watch different TV stations, sing different versions of the national anthem and have different school systems. In recent polls of the 100 greatest Belgians in history (carried out, of course, by different French- and Flemish-speaking TV stations) there was virtually no agreement in the results (with only Father Damien the leper-priest, Eddy Merckx the cyclist, and Jacques Brel the singer-songwriter making the top ten in both lists). No one agrees about anything. Whatever the reason for the anomaly that is Belgium, this is its quirky capital and the locals have a flair for having fun and enjoying their free time – perhaps that's what the 'song' idea is all about: having a party every day. Enjoy.

EXPLORE

Rather than planning everything, visitors to Brussels are well advised to leave enough space in their schedule for a surprise or two. While the grandiose architecture will stop you in your tracks, the rest is there for you to sort through and put together in any order that takes your fancy. In Brussels, the spaces in between are just as important as the sights. The city centre is compact and appealingly walkable – though don't neglect the trams – and it is on these meanderings between square and palace, museum and statue, that you start to get a feel for what Brussels is really about.

Now, if proof positive is required of the fundamental insanity that's about the only thing left locking the Belgians together, what image comes to mind when you think of Brussels? Is it the Grand'Place, the UNESCO-listed World Heritage Site that Victor Hugo described as 'the most beautiful square in the world'? Is it the beer, the food or the expense-account consumers at the EU? Could be, but chances are that you've thought of a little naked boy urinating into a basin. Yes, where Paris has its lofty tower, New York its meaningful statue and London its sober clock, Brussels has the **Manneken-Pis**. If you really have to see it – and the idea is better than the reality – then leave Grand'Place from the south side and follow the crowds past the lace and tapestry shops into rue de l'Etuve. Here stands the Manneken-Pis, one of the world's most disappointing tourist draws. Like the *Mona Lisa* it's so much smaller than you expect, but the boy is fortunately elevated on

Manneken-Pis
rue de l'Etuve, Brussels
www.manneken-pis.com

a baroque pedestal to give him some grandeur. Around him are gated railings, only opened by the person whose sole job it is to dress him in his various costumes: Euro-jogger, Santa Claus, a condom on World AIDS Day, and so on. A framed sign gives a calendar of upcoming costume days. The current statue was made in the 17th century by Jérôme Duquesnoy. Stolen by the British in 1745, then again by the French in 1777, it was smashed by a French ex-con in 1817, who was given life for doing so. Its origins are unknown, though it is naturally endowed with local myth as well as a never-ending pee. Since 1985, the lad has had a similarly incontinent sister, the **Jeanneke-Pis**, squatting in impasse de la Fidelité, off rue des Bouchers, and now the weeing company has expanded to include **Zinneke**, a dog doing what you'd expect.

Having relieved yourself of this must-see, wander into the Grand'Place. It has always been a focus for the social and cultural life of the city, whether as a medieval market, a parade ground, a place of execution, a concert venue or, until the 1980s, a short cut for traffic and a car park for coaches. Now a pedestrian zone, it changes colour and character according to the season: flower-strewn in summer, fairy-lit for Christmas. It is the starting point for any tour of the Lower Town, with the tower of the **Hôtel de Ville** (Town Hall) as its distinctive landmark. Legend has it that the Hôtel de Ville's architect, in despair at the way the tower seems to unbalance the rest of the building, climbed it and then descended rather faster. This may be the reason for not allowing visitors to climb up there these days, though a series of elegant official rooms can be visited on the guided tour. The most flamboyant of them is the 18th-century Council Chamber, awash with gilt, tapestries,

Jeanneke-Pis
impasse de la Fidelité, off rue des Bouchers, Brussels

Zinneke
rue des Chartreux, Brussels

Hôtel de Ville
Grand'Place, Brussels
02 279 43 65
tourist information 02 513 89 40

THE LUNCHBOX

Another thing to factor in to the strangeness quotient: it now makes sense to go to Brussels for lunch. Take a mid-morning train, arrive at lunchtime, eat, digest and head back home for tea. Of course, for the plan to work the eateries need to be close to the station, so to facilitate Belgian lunchbreaks here are three restaurants within easy walking distance.

Coming out of the station, head towards the centre of town up the broad boulevard de l'Europe, which rather appropriately morphs into avenue de Stalingrad before opening into place Rouppe. Here you'll find **Comme chez Soi**, complete with two Michelin stars. But awayday meals don't have to be haute cuisine and highly priced; a few hundred metres southwest, on rue Notre-Seigneur, there are two excellent options. **La Grande Porte**, which does indeed have a big door, has both a cosy bar and modern restaurant serving the Belgian classics like mussels and steak. It's also open late if you're staying overnight. A few steps further down the street, look out for the vine-covered house that looks like it should be in a Bruegel painting. **Les Petits Oignons** is an unfussy French/Belgian restaurant where food is cooked with finesse and arrives in invigorating portions.

Comme chez Soi *23 place Rouppe, 02 512 29 21, www.commechezsoi.be*
La Grande Porte *9 rue Notre-Seigneur, 02 512 89 98*
Les Petits Oignons *13 rue Notre-Seigneur, 02 512 47 38, www.petits-oignons.be*

mirrors and ornate ceiling paintings. Brussels' only secular Gothic building, the town hall remains in practical, everyday use as the seat of the Mayor of Brussels.

The houses on the square were once made of wood until the French bombardment of 1695, which destroyed over 4,000 buildings and flattened everything except the tower of the Hôtel de Ville, which was used by the gunners to take aim. Under the command of the mercantile guilds, the square was rebuilt in under five years, in stone, with fine bronze and gold detail. As each guild jostled for power and influence, it branded each house with individual markings and a name (although some pre-date the guilds).

North west of the Grand'Place, **Ste-Catherine** was designed in 1854 in neo-Gothic style by Joseph Poelaert, and almost became the stock exchange before opening as a church in 1867. Tucked between the buttresses is an ancient pissoir, giving a novel twist to the phrase holy water.

Directly north of Grand'Place is a museum featuring perhaps the only figure to rival the Manneken-Pis as a national symbol, and he's a boy, too – Tintin. The **Centre Belge de la Bande Dessinée** is located in a beautifully restored Victor Horta department store (whose ground-floor café can be partaken of without a ticket). It features a revamped Tintin section to coincide with his 75th birthday celebrations in 2004, as well as lesser-known Belgian comic characters, plus the all-too-well-known Smurfs. Apparently, when the genius behind the sky-blue woodland creatures, Pierre Culliford (or Peyo as he became known), attended art school his teachers said he had no future as an artist. If you've children in tow, beware of the erotic works on the third floor. If you've not, just around the corner from the museum, rue St-Laurent was, until World War II, the location of the city's legal brothels. It was all explained in Jacques van Melkebeke's book, *Imageries Bruxelloises*: 'My son, never come here... these are bad women...and what's more, I believe it's outrageously expensive!'

Given the place that comics hold in Belgian life, it should come as little surprise that puppetry also has a venerable history in the city. All that remains today is **Théâtre du Toone**. This company of marionettes has been performing shows for generations, sometimes with more gusto than audiences might have expected: in 1932, in front of the burgomaster and other notables, the puppet Woltje and his wife gave an unexpected spin to 'wooden' performances. Following protests, the offending parts were chopped. Today, productions are still done in the Bruxellois dialect. The atmosphere balances out incomprehension, though you may be lucky enough to catch *Hamlet* in Brussels English.

Charlotte Brontë taught in Brussels, boarding in a house that was later demolished to make way for the **Palais des Beaux Arts**, the recently reinvigorated arts institute. Brussels is the uncredited model for the backdrop of her novel, *Villette*, but Charlotte did not think much of the Belgians:

'If the national character of the Belgians is to be measured by the character of most of the girls in the school, it is a character singularly cold, selfish, animal and inferior. They are besides very mutinous and difficult for the teachers to manage – and their principles are rotten to the core.'

Ste-Catherine
pl Ste-Catherine, Brussels
02 513 34 81

Centre Belge de la Bande Dessinée
20 rue des Sables, Brussels
02 219 19 80
www.stripmuseum.be

Théâtre du Toone
21 petite rue des Bouchers, Brussels
02 511 71 37
www.toone.be

Palais des Beaux Arts
23 rue Ravenstein, Brussels
02 507 84 44
www.bozar.be

Still, she was positively polite in comparison to the poet Charles Baudelaire, who grew to hate the Belgians during his monetarily induced exile in the country, although the fact that syphilis was eating away at his brain might have had something to do with it.

The Belgians, my word, push
Imitation to excess,
And if they get smallpox,
It's just to be like the French.

Of course, the epitome of Belgium's brand of suburban strangeness is René Magritte. He lived in the large and anonymous commune of Jette, in a house ideal for the most respectable and bourgeois of Surrealists by reason of its very anonymity. The house opened as the **Musée Magritte** in 1999. This huge house had been divided into three separate apartments; René and his wife Georgette rented the ground and attic floors. Visitors can see many elements of the building in his paintings: the blue walls and fireplace from *La Durée Poignardé* – although there's no steam locomotive puffing forth – the sash windows, glass doors, staircase and other bourgeois elements that Magritte manipulated so effortlessly.

The Magrittes came to a compromise over the colour scheme: Georgette preferred brown for the doors, stairs and panelling, while René insisted on the clashing salmon pink dining room, electric blue lounge and lime green bedroom. René and Georgette led quiet lives; the artist painted some of his masterpieces from his Renoir and Vache periods in a suit and bow tie. Visitors can see original works, documents, letters and photos on the first and second floors – 17 of the 19 rooms are open to the public. The Magrittes moved out in 1954, and the building was bought by two Belgians and restored between 1993 and 1999 as a permanent homage to a surreally typical Belge. As Magritte said of *Man in the Bowler Hat*, in which a face is obscured by a bird: 'Everything we see hides another

Musée Magritte
135 rue Esseghem, Brussels
02 428 26 26
www.magrittemuseum.be

thing, we always want to see what is hidden by what we see, but it is impossible. Humans hide their secrets too well.'

The tiny border commune of Koekelberg is home to Brussels' most bizarre and overblown church: the **Basilique du Sacré Coeur**. Commissioned by Léopold II in 1905, this vast structure, an extraordinary mix of Gothic and art deco with a lit-up cherry-coloured crucifix on top, took seven decades to finish.

Of course, there might be a simpler explanation for Belgium: beer. Drinking is a part of Belgian culture. The range of bars and beers speak not only of the national history, but also of a drinking culture that is easily as significant as wine with Burgundy or tea with England.

At the centre of this is beer. Not just any old beer, but some 600 varieties in almost as many colours and flavours, and brewed by everyone from reclusive Trappist monks to major multinational concerns. Most bars serve around 20 types; some stock 200. They'll be served, with a 's'il vous plaît' from the waiter or barman, in a specially shaped and logoed glass, plonked on to a logoed beermat. If you want to tempt sudden death by beer, there's **La Mort Subite**. Named after a card game and a variety of fruit beer whose hangovers often produce longings for mortality, the popularity of this classically dissolute café soon saw the name pass into legend. Be warned, though: this is one of few venues to serve the local Gueuze, to be handled with care. Alternatively, to drink in some strange vibes, you could do worse than **La Fleur en Papier Doré**. As the haunt of the Surrealists, this quirky venue would make a mint from the tourist trail were it not stuck on an obscure, steep, grey street whose only function is to connect the Lower and Upper Towns, which just makes it more perfect. It attracts the more unusual tourist, happy to gawp at the doodles and sketches and stagger around in Magritte's wonky footsteps. Just north of Grand'Place, **A La Bécasse** comes as a surprise. From the street, all that marks its presence is a red neon light, hinting there's something tacky involved. Not at all. Look down at your feet and see the stone and brass welcome mat fixed to the pavement. Follow the alley through the houses and you see the Dickensian-style bottle windows. Behind is an ancient tavern where customers sit at long tables and have their beer, including draught Lambic, poured from jugs by aproned waiters. It's of the same genre and ownership as **L'Imaige de Nostre-Dame** nearby.

Naturally, with drink must come food, and Belgian food is sublime. The country boasts 105 Michelin stars and you'll be hard pushed to eat a bad meal in Brussels. For a thoroughly Belgian blowout, we recommend **Belga Queen**, where everything is unashamedly Belgian. The restaurant sits in a vast bank building with original pillars and a massive stained-glass skylight, giving an air of loftiness and space. Yet once at the table, it can feel surprisingly intimate (though couples alone are rare – this seems to be a place to go with a crowd). The BQ is renowned for its oyster bar, where heaving seafood platters are composed. The unisex toilet doors are transparent, and it's up to you to work them out.

A cheaper option is **Bij den Boer**. The Farmer's looks a bit like a transport caff and can seem a little intimidating from the outside as it's always packed with local customers. The restaurant is famous for its mussels and bouillabaisse, and prices are rather good for the area, in particular the four-course menu. On the other hand, the service can be quite infuriatingly slow. The staff are friendly enough, and dash around at a rate, but never, it seems, towards your table. But persevere and you will leave feeling mightily satisfied. This is Belgium at its shoulder-shrugging best.

As for places to stay, Brussels is stuffed with expense-account driven hotels. The positive side of that, for visitors, is that prices often plunge at weekends and during the summer, so it pays to check for deals. Try the newish (opened 2006) **Hotel Orts**, in a perfect location for sightseeing and nightlife; kitsch, nautically themed **Noga**; the aptly named **Welcome**; or, for something more designed, **Monty Small Design Hotel**.

IN THE AREA

ANTWERP

There are plenty of reasons to visit Antwerp, diamonds, Rubens, architecture and food all being among them. But what it's really good for is wave-your-hands-in-the-air-like-you-just-don't-care clubbing fun. Yes, cut another notch on to Belgium's bedpost, this supposedly sleepy country is home to the best nightlife in northern Europe. This reputation derives from the city's status as a fashion capital, a gay centre and a place at ease with itself. Locals sashay from one spot to another in a bid to decide what's hot and what's not. Us mere mortals can check www.noctis.com or drop into urban shops like **Fish & Chips** to pick up flyers. Also check out www.myspace.com/mysubscape for info on no-nonsense monthly parties in the city park.

A quick word about clothing: only the more underground clubs will welcome skate shoes and baggy jeans; in the mainstream, it's always best to dress up and impress the doormen. One exception is **Petrol**, a laid-back place where funky house alternates with electronica, drum 'n' bass and reggae, and where people can be whatever they want.

A good starting point is the legendary **Café d'Anvers**, which was a church and cinema before its transformation to a kicking club in 1991. Expect progressive house from Thursday to Saturday, with resident DJs including local luminaries like Isabel, Prinz, Tweety and Filliz.

Popular gay club **Red & Blue** has taken over from the Fill Collins Club on Saturdays. It's a men-only affair, but there are also mixed one-nighters, including Café de Love, Studio 54 and Colorbar, on other nights.

Industria, meanwhile, is one of Antwerp's more sparkling sin bins. Saturday night is the Bonthuys party at this beautiful old factory space with progressive house and funky soul spun by residents Bill, Mystique and Pollux. For something a little fresher, how about mixing sounds with sushi? **Stereo Sushi** is just what it says on the tin – a funky evening meal followed by partying until 5am at weekends.

The more alternative crowd prefers the rolling drum 'n' bass and scratchy electronica of the quite weird and somewhat wonderful **Kaaiman**, set in an atmospheric cellar in the dock area. For one-off parties, it's also a good idea to click on to www.5voor12.com, a production company that stages major club events throughout the country as well as irregular nights

Grand'Place p35

at **De Cinema**. This particular venue accommodates Couleur d'Anvers, a night of African and black music held on the first Saturday of the month.

International hotspot Antwerp is also now included on the tour circuit of various travelling superclubs including Sensation (www.sensation-white.com), which calls into town every spring.

As for somewhere to stay, the **New International Youth Hostel** is a ten-minute walk south of the train station and has rooms as well as dorms. Right in the centre of the old town, **Hotel Villa Mozart** has 25 luxury rooms.

The tourist office, **Toerisme Antwerpen**, is helpful.

GHENT

On a scale of Belgium's cities, with party-central Antwerp at one extreme and preserved-in-aspic Bruges at the other, Ghent lies comfortably in between. It has more listed buildings than the rest of Belgium put together, an ancient castle and a cathedral containing some of the world's most important works of art. But it doesn't allow its past to muzzle its present: Ghent is a thriving port, university city and the nerve centre of Belgium's digital industries. Given its many attractions it's surprisingly free of visitors and the locals seem content to keep it that way. So let the tourist hordes stay on the train to Bruges; your stop comes first.

Ghent is just half an hour from the centre of Brussels. Four fast trains an hour travel between the two cities. From Gent St Pieters station take any one of five trams into town (nos.1, 10, 21, 22 or 40; pay on board).

Although all of Ghent bears wandering, its architectural highlights lie, conveniently for the time-strapped tourist, along the same curving street in the town centre, although the road suffers a number of confusing identity changes along the way. From St Michielsbrug (St Michael's Bridge) over the River Leie you'll see the beautiful buildings overlooking the Graslei (Herb Quay) and Korenlei (Corn Quay), most built during the Flemish

De Cinema
12 Lang Brilstraat, Antwerp
03 226 49 63
www.decinema.be

New International Youth Hostel
256 Provinciestraat, Antwerp
03 230 05 22
www.niyh.be

Hotel Villa Mozart
3 Handschoenmarkt, Antwerp
03 231 30 31
www.bestwestern.com

Toerisme Antwerpen
13 Grote Markt, Antwerp
03 232 01 03
www.visitantwerpen.be

Renaissance but some dating from 1000 AD. Crossing west over the bridge you'll come to **St Niklaaskerk**, an outstanding piece of Scheldt Gothic architecture built in the 1200s. Its interior is dominated by an over-the-top Baroque altarpiece.

A short way further down the street stands the **Belfort** (Belfry), first built in the 14th century and later heavily restored. Its interior – containing both a carillon and a bell museum – is worth the entrance fee for the view over the city and the neighbouring cathedral.

Ghent's first cathedral was founded (as St Peter's) by the Brabant-born St Bavo in the seventh century. Built over six centuries, the current **St Baafskathedraal** is remarkable as much for its high and late Gothic style as for the noted works of art it contains. Laurent Delvaux's elaborate rococo pulpit, in oak and marble, is the first thing you see on entering, and Peter Paul Rubens' *Entry of St Bavo into the Monastery* is displayed in the north transept. Its undisputed masterpiece is *The Adoration of the Mystic Lamb* by Hubert and Jan van Eyck. The painting is on display in the De Villa chapel, crowded in high season but worth the wait. Entry costs €2.50 and also includes the loan of a recorded commentary. Because the painting is so rich in detail, this is recommended, taking you as it does through the complexity of the painting panel by panel. The picture depicts a scene from the Apocalypse according to St John, the colours so bright and glistening that the painting lights up the whole chapel. South and west of the cathedral are Ghent's shopping streets, such as crowded Veldstraat, south from St Niklaaskerk, and the more attractive Magaleinstraat and Koestraat, which lies to the south of the Belfort.

The **Guild of Guesthouses in Ghent** has 66 families who offer B&B accommodation, from a room in a cosy private home to a self-contained suite in a 17th-century cloister. The **City of Ghent Tourist Office** can also help with accommodation.

TRAVEL INFORMATION

Eurostar runs several services a day to Brussels, with fares one way starting from £29.50. Onward railway travel in Belgium on the same day is free.

WHEN TO GO
Anytime, but spring, summer and autumn are obviously warmer.

USING THE HUB

There are frequent services between Brussels Midi and Antwerp, Brugge, Gent, Oostende and Liége. There are ICE and Thalys services to Aachen, Cologne and Frankfurt in Germany and to Rotterdam and Amsterdam in the Netherlands. There are direct, high-speed trains between Brussels and Basel, Montpelier, Paris, Strasbourg and Zurich, a regular if rather slow (around 15 stops) train to Luxembourg Gare and a night service to Hamburg and Berlin. During the summer there are special direct trains to Marseilles. Visit the Belgian trains website (www.b-rail.be/main/E/) to check timetables and download brochures and also see the Directory at the back of the book for more information about international connections.

Further reading
André de Vries *Cities of the Imagination: Brussels*
Hergé *Tintin in Tibet* Hergé's own favourite among the many Tintin books he wrote.
Charlotte Brontë *Villette* Set in a thinly-disguised version of Brussels, Villette is often unjustly overlooked next to *Jane Eyre*. It shouldn't be.
Christopher Booker *The Great Deception* A history of the European Union.

Websites
www.brusselsinternational.be
The official tourist website.
www.europa.eu
The polyglot (23 languages!) website of the European Union.
www.eureferendum.blogspot.com
For the other view on the nascent superstate.

St Niklaaskerk
Cataloniestraat, Ghent
09 266 56 60
www.stniklaas.com

Belfort
17A Botermarkt, Ghent
09 233 07 72
Closed Nov-Mar

St Baafskathedraal
St-Baafsplein, Ghent
09 225 49 85
www.sintbaafskathedraal-gent.be

Guild of Guesthouses in Ghent
www.bedandbreakfast-gent.be

City of Ghent Tourist Office
Belfort, 17A Botermarkt, Ghent
09 226 52 32

Eurostar
www.eurostar.com

Palais de Beaux Arts p48

Lille

ROUTE London ▶ Lille

With the new, shorter travel times following the opening of the high-speed line through Kent, Lille moves from being an excellent weekend break destination to a realistic choice for a day out, at least for those who live in southern England. Although part of France for 350 years, the city's lovely medieval centre is still redolent of the classic wool towns of Flanders. The grand architecture and cobbled streets of Vieux Lille stretch between the Canal de la Deule, the northern border of the inner city, and an enjoyably confusing complex of main squares comprising the town centre.

Written by **Edoardo Albert**

Vieille Bourse p46

Grand' Place p46

THE TRIP

You emerge from the long, ear-popping tunnels under London near Dagenham and carry on through a landscape of mingled marsh and industry before crossing the Thames just past Dartford. Then it's 15 minutes of Kent, sheep, and perhaps a misty view of the green fields before disappearing under the sea. The Channel Tunnel may be a marvel of engineering, and it is the longest undersea tunnel in the world at 23.5 miles (37.9 kilometres), but it's the most boring part of the journey. Still, it only takes 21 minutes before you emerge in France. You can immediately see the change, although there are few geological or ecological differences between Nord-Pas-de-Calais and the county of Kent. Here the land is defined by planting and ploughing, by forest and field, rather than wood and hedge. Through it, the train moves, smooth as a Gallic smile, past villages clustered around their steepled church, and modern farm buildings that are as ugly in France as they are everywhere else. Some Lille trains go on to Disneyland, so you might well find yourself sharing a carriage with short princesses, excited ducks and voluble ogres.

 St Pancras International ▶
Lille-Europe **1 hour 20 minutes**

 Art; budget; shopping

THE DESTINATION

Lille-Europe station is the usual concrete, steel and glass construction that passes for railway architecture today. Off the train, out of the station (there's a tram stop directly beneath your feet as you cross the plaza) and there in front of you, looming like a great, marooned glass ship, is the first of Lille's many shopping opportunities: **Euralille**. Some 140 shops, cafés, restaurants and a huge Carrefour supermarket mean that if you want to make a swift shopping trip to France and return the same day – more than feasible for southerners with the short travel time to Lille – then this is an obvious port of call.

A WALK ON THE OLD SIDE

Even if shopping is your thing, best to leave Euralille until later. You don't really want to be carrying bags around all day, and besides, there are other, more interesting shopping opportunities a short walk away. Head past Euralille and then the town's second station, Lille-Flandres, with its row of fountains out front and grand 19th-century arch inside.

Going straight down the road opposite the station will bring you to the first of Lille's grand squares, the place du Théâtre. The theatre in question is **L'Opéra de Lille**, an Italian-style opera house designed by Louis-Marie Cordonnier and completed in 1914, just in time to be commandeered by the occupying Germans who staged over 100 performances there during the four years of the Great War. Tickets need to be booked well in advance, as shows sell out fast.

Opposite the opera house is the Vieille Bourse, the old stock exchange, consisting of 24 houses around a central courtyard. Walking through it, you'll find second-hand book stalls, a flower market and, often, chess players deep in concentration. Continue through into Lille's Grand' Place (officially known as place du Général de Gaulle, after Lille's home-boy hero). The cobbled streets around here are largely traffic free, and the grand houses built in the Flemish style, although embellished in a manner unseen in the Protestant Netherlands, make a theatrical backdrop to the great square.

Exit the square via rue Rihour. Ahead lies the remaining wing of the Palais Rihour, the old residence of the Dukes of Burgundy that burned down in 1916. Only the wing containing the palace chapels survived. This is now the location for the city's helpful **tourist office**. Stop by to pick up free maps and guides, and consider investing in the City Pass (€18 for one day, €30 for two) that provides entry to Lille's tourist attractions, and unlimited travel on the city's bus, tram and metro systems. You could also go on the hourly mini-bus tour that runs from outside the tourist office; the trip takes 50 minutes and costs €9.50 (free with the City Pass).

It's now 90 years since the end of the Great War and the carnage that brought an end to 19th-century progressivism. The tourist office runs battlefield tours to Ieper (Ypres) in Belgium, running every Saturday from 16 February to 20 December. The tour costs €45 per person (€40 with City Pass) and is in English; call in at the office or phone +33 359 579 400 to book.

Duly armed with pamphlets and future plans, leave the tourist office and set off on some serious local sightseeing. Head back

Euralille
www.euralille.com

L'Opéra de Lille
2 rue des Bons Enfants
03 28 38 40 50
www.opera-lille.fr

Tourist Office
42-44 pl Rihour
08 91 56 20 04
www.lilletourism.com

towards Grand' Place and then go north from there into the narrow streets of Vieux Lille. It's hard to believe, as you walk the cobbled streets past sleek design shops and fashionable boutiques snuggling comfortably within their 17th-century suits, that 20 years ago this was a broken-down quarter of the city, with property so cheap even poor people could afford to live there. It's still properly inhabited, with real, day-to-day-requirement shops nestled in among those selling lifestyles.

Lille's pâtisseries are irresistible. Try one or two to find out, possibly at **Confiserie Brier**. But if you'd like to taste just why General de Gaulle would send his personal driver from the Elysée Palace all the way back to Lille to pick up a parcel of waffles, visit **Meert** and settle back, in its tearoom, into the 19th century. Little seems to have changed since then, with the wrought-iron lacework and copper fronted display cabinets much the same as when the young de Gaulle sat next to his *maman*, wolfing waffles. The shop first opened in 1761, on its current site, and settled on its final look 78 years later, in 1839. In the years since it's stubbornly resisted fashion, serene in the knowledge that waffles sell.

Should you need something a little more substantial, nearby there's a fine restaurant devoted to fish, L'Huitrière, tucked in behind a truly beautiful fishmonger, **A l'Huitrière**. Even if you have no intention of eating there, take a look at the shop. The exterior and interior are decorated with exquisite art deco mosaics by Breton artist Mathurin Mehaut, and the produce is arranged with similar care for appearance and texture. The restaurant has been Michelin-starred since the 1930s, although it's not nearly as striking to look at as the fish shop.

Also within the easily walkable confines of Vieux Lille is the fromagerie **Philippe Olivier**. The eponymous owner is an expert in local cheeses and has, in proper investigative mode, revived many a moribund regional cheese. Consider fellow passengers on the train home when deciding on the whiff-level of your purchases. For those intent on returning with bags stuffed with goods, a good plan is to browse along rue Basse, rue des Chats Bossus and rue de la Monnaie, although all the roads around here are worth a look.

Before leaving Vieux Lille we must point you towards a godless example of ecclesiastical architecture. Turn into rue du Cirque and there, on your right, is the façade of the cathedral of **Notre-Dame-de-la-Treille**. The church itself was begun in the 19th century in a neo-Gothic style. Money ran out and the building was only completed in the 1990s. Brutally blank slabs of concrete bring a juddering halt to the weathered stone of the cathedral's nave, while above the door something resembling a climbing frame has been installed – perhaps intended as a route by which an outraged pious aesthete could ascend either to heaven or to lob a brick through the rose window.

Some solace from this desecration can be found in the nearby **Musée de l'Hospice Comtesse**, a former hospital, founded in the 12th century, rebuilt in the 18th and now a museum of Flemish art, furniture and ceramics.

Confiserie Brier
118 bis rue Esquermoise
03 20 55 35 55

Meert
27 rue Esquermoise
03 20 57 07 44
www.meert.fr

A l'Huitrière
3 rue des Chats Bossus
03 20 55 43 41
www.huitriere.fr

Philippe Olivier
3 rue du Curé St-Etienne
03 20 74 96 99

Notre-Dame-de-la-Treille
pl Gilleson
03 20 55 28 72
www.catholique-lille.cef.fr

Musée de l'Hospice Comtesse
32 rue de la Monnaie
03 28 36 84 00
www.musenor.com
Closed Tue

WORLD CLASS ART AND SHOPPING

Lille might not be one of France's biggest or most beautiful cities but it is home to the country's second most important art collection, the **Palais des Beaux Arts**. For much of the 19th century, Lille, a centre of industry and commerce at the time, was bursting at its seams. To provide some much needed room the neighbouring communes were incorporated into the city, and much of its monumental architecture dates from this time of prosperity and expansion. The place de la République was the first square to be imprinted with this new civic pride, and standing on it is the museum. It has important works by Flemish, Dutch, Spanish and Italian masters, including Rubens, Donatello and Tintoretto, but its real strength is in, logically enough, 19th-century French art, including some works important in art history by Jacques-Louis David, Eugène Delacroix, Gustave Courbet and Pierre Puvis de Chavannes.

Big department stores line rue Nationale, running west from Grand' Place, while the main shopping centre is the pedestrian zone between rue de Paris and rue de Bethune, from the main squares to the Palais des Beaux Arts, with pretty well all the national and international chains represented. But the best shopping in town is to be found at the Sunday morning flea market in the working-class Wazemmes district, south-west of the Palais des Beaux Arts. You can buy chicory from farmers, Mont des Cats cheese and fresh couscous from food stalls, and rummage for bric-a-brac and clothes. In the lead up to Christmas there is a daily market in place Rihours, near the tourist office, which many Britons visit to do their seasonal shopping. The local love of markets is taken to its conclusion on the first weekend in September when the whole town turns into a gigantic street market for La Braderie. Traders come from all over Europe, setting up some 10,000 stalls selling to between one and two million visitors. The market dates from the Middle Ages and, if you come on its weekend, come for the market: everything else is closed.

Out of town, but easily accessible by metro or tram, Roubaix is factory outlet heaven, with discounts of 30 to 70 per cent on usual retail prices. Trams and buses stop at McArthur Glen mall with its designer-label stores, and a bus will take hardcore bargain hunters to L'Usine for some warehouse-style rummaging after Nike, Dior and YSL.

After all that shopping, you'll need somewhere to park the bags. One option is just to get back on the train, but if you can do a night in Lille, and have the money, then a hotel that doubles as a national monument is the **Hermitage Gantois**. Built in the 15th century as a hospice, it was recently converted, chapel and all, into a luxury hotel. Non-guests will need a certain amount of nerve to push open the glass doors and advance down the corridor towards reception if they're not carrying a gold-plated AmEx card, but don't be browbeaten, as the hotel is obliged to allow sightseeing. Go in, tell the staff at the desk you want to look around, and admire how the expense-account half live.

Just as beautiful, and almost as expensive, is the **Couvent des Minimes**, next to what remains of the old port of Lille (don't get too excited, it's a quay leading off from the River Deûle; almost all Lille's waterways were covered over in

Palais des Beaux Arts
pl de la République
03 30 06 78 00
www.pba-lille.fr
Closed Tue

Hermitage Gantois
224 rue de Paris
03 20 85 30 30
www.hotelhermitagegantois.com

Couvent des Minimes
17 quai du Wult
03 20 30 62 62
www.alliance-hospitality.com

the 19th century). The hotel itself is a converted convent, with a beautiful cloister. Cheaper options, both conveniently located near to the railway station, include **Hotel Flandre Angleterre** and **Hotel du Moulin d'Or**.

IN THE AREA

Roubaix, ten kilometres to the north-east of Lille, has, like its larger neighbour, a flair for combining art and shopping – and here the art is shown in the unlikely location of the municipal swimming pool. It's no ordinary **Piscine**, having been designed in an art deco style by JP Philippon of Musée d'Orsay fame, and today sculptures by the likes of Camille Claudel stand around the pool, illuminated by the light pouring through the two rising-sun stained-glass windows, while paintings are displayed in the shower rooms and changing cubicles.

TRAVEL INFORMATION

Lille has two metro and two tram lines connecting the city to the surrounding communes, as well as numerous bus routes. Fares are low, with a day pass on metro, tram and bus costing €3.50. Buying a City Pass from the tourist office also provides you with free travel on public transport.

While the centre of Lille is not ideal for cycling – cobbled streets are liable to play havoc with your fillings – there is a comprehensive system of bike paths leading right out into the countryside. Bikes can be hired from **Ch'ti Vélo**, **Holiday Bikes** or **Etablissement Léger Cycles**.

For those who want to reduce their carbon footprint but are unsure if they've got the legs to manage it, **Transpole**, the Lille-area transport authority, rents out e-bikes. These are like ordinary bikes except for the fact that some of the energy released when going downhill or peddling along on the flat is stored, to help you when a climb looms. Transpole also hires out Segways, those rather peculiar-looking grown-up trolleys. E-bikes and Segways are available from the Oxygène station at place des Buisses, next to Lille Flandres station, and near the Pont de la Citadelle on Champ de Mars by the citadel.

WHEN TO GO

You're not going to Lille for the weather. Serious shopping is probably better done in milder weather, so spring and autumn are ideal, but anytime is possible.

USING THE HUB

Lille is an important railway junction for northern France and is a useful hub for southern and western France if you want to avoid passing through Paris. From Lille-Flandres station there are regular services to Arras, Boulogne-sur-Mer, Calais, Lens, Saint-Pol-sur-Ternoise and Charleville-Mézières. From Lille-Europe, there are direct TGV services to Avignon, Boulogne-sur-Mer, Bordeaux, Lyon, Marseille, Montpelier, Nantes, Nice, Rennes, Toulouse and Tours. There are also frequent Eurostar services from Lille-Europe to Brussels. See the Directory at the back of this book for more information about international connections.

Further reading

Émile Zola *Germinal* Life down t'pit.
Charles Williams *The Last Great Frenchman: A Life of General de Gaulle* Good popular biography of Lille's most famous son.

Websites

www.lilletourism.com

Hotel Flandre Angleterre
13 pl de la Gare
03 20 06 04 12
www.hotel-flandre-angleterre.fr

Hotel du Moulin d'Or
15 rue du Molinel
03 20 06 12 67
www.hotelmoulindor.com

Piscine
23 rue de l'Espérance
03 20 69 23 60
www.roubaix-lapiscine.com

Ch'ti Vélo
10 av Willy Brandt, between Lille-Flandres station and Euralille shopping centre
03 28 53 07 49

Holiday Bikes
2 rue Gustave Delory
03 20 57 02 25

Etablissement Léger Cycles
64 rue Léon Gambetta
03 20 54 83 39

Transpole
08 20 42 40 40 (0.12 €/min)
www.transpole.fr

Ludwig Museum; Dom p53

Cologne

ROUTE London ▶ Brussels ▶ Cologne

One of Germany's liveliest cities is less than five hours from London. Home to the nation's busiest carnival and loveliest urban waterway, Cologne can easily fill a weekend. In summer, a Mediterranean atmosphere reigns in the Old Town, along the landscaped banks of the Rhine and on the many tourist craft offering day trips and cruises to Düsseldorf, Bonn and beyond. A magical time to visit the cathedral city is during Cologne Nights in July, when music and a firework display boom over an illuminated convoy of boats.

Written by **Peterjon Cresswell**

Köln Hauptbahnhof

THE TRIP

Take the morning Eurostar from London St Pancras to Bruxelles-Midi, where a change of platforms allows you to hook up with Thalys or ICE services linking the Belgian capital with Cologne. As the train pulls out you see the best and worst of Europe's most fractured capital: no-man's-land neighbourhoods decimated to make way for the cross-city rail; the dinky corner bars; the spike of the Hôtel de Ville that withstood the French bombardment of 1695; and the vast billboard of Tintin and Snowy that dominates Gare du Midi. Passing the sleek Guillemins station in otherwise seedy Liège, you creep into Germany with only a bleep to remind you of a border crossing – although German soon becomes the first language of the four announced over the tannoy. Sooner than you know it, the train is pulling into Köln Hauptbahnhof, Germany's busiest rail hub. Above the long row of platforms gleams the sign '4711 Echt Kölnisch Wasser' for the famous Eau de Cologne. Across from the panelled frontage towers another local icon, so close you can hear the station announcements on its steps: Cologne Cathedral, the Dom. You have arrived.

 St Pancras International ▸ Köln Hbf **4 hours 41 minutes**

 Drink; nightlife; history

THE DESTINATION

A regional capital in Roman times, the fourth most prominent ecclesiastical centre after Jerusalem, Byzantium and Rome for medieval Christians, and a pioneer of Germany's industrial age, Cologne displays history in abundance despite the substantial Allied bombing of World War II. A media hub, gay mecca, carnival centre and riverside resort, Cologne is also Germany's party city, with four areas of nightlife activity dotted along the ring road that winds around the compact, walkable centre. In summer, the Rhine and the green spaces around it come into their own, and a relaxed, timeless mood graces the city. The crocodiles of tourists, pointy umbrellas directing gaggles of foreigners and scores of schoolchildren diligently completing questionnaires congregate for one reason and at one place: the Dom.

EXPLORING THE CITY

Walk into the two-floor tourist office opposite the **Dom** and the vintage black-and-white postcards on sale show an immediate post-war scene of mountains of rubble – 90 per cent of Cologne's Old Town was destroyed – and the cathedral, almost intact, rising above it. The Allies knew not to bomb it. Although started in 1248, Germany's biggest tourist attraction was only completed 650 years later thanks to a campaign inspired by the 19th-century Romantic movement. A Gothic style gradually replaced the Romanesque one and for a while, until the erection of the Eiffel Tower, the spires were the tallest construction on earth. 'Towering' doesn't do it justice. Think: hulking, looming, monumental. Within, highlights include the Shrine of the Three Kings behind the high altar, the Gero Crucifix and some of the world's oldest stained-glass windows, dating from 1260. Climbing the 157-metre, 509-step south tower to the 100-metre-high observation platform, the view is overwhelming, but walk behind the building at street level, and you find gargoyles depicting local politicians and personalities, even one of Hennes the billy goat, mascot of local football club IFC Köln. Some 90 craftsmen work here every day – the Dom is still a creation in motion. Its façade is being painstakingly cleaned by lasers – sandblasting would be too abrasive.

The raised pedestrianised area on which it stands was repaved in the 1970s and '80s to incorporate the major museums nearby and unify the city and river into one landscaped public space. Tel Aviv artist Dani Karavan was responsible for the sculptures and the line in the concrete pointing towards the Rhine representing the route of war time deportations; Eduardo Paolozzi created the riverside garden, fountains and bronze paving stones to suggest ships bobbing in the Rhine when there were docks here. Cagoule-wearing stewards are there to advise you to walk round the terrace outside the Kölner Philharmonie beside the Dom so that your footsteps do not disturb rehearsals or concerts below.

Two other cultural landmarks stand nearby: the **Römisch-Germanisches Museum** has the same dimensions as the Roman villa that once stood here, its mosaic of Dionysus perfectly preserved on what was the dining room floor; and the **Ludwig Museum** has a renowned collection of Russian avant-garde and American pop art, as well as 180 original Picassos.

COLOGNE

Dom
179 4055
www.koelnerdom.de

Römisch-Germanisches Museum
4 Roncalliplatz
221 24438
www.museenkoeln.de/rgm

Ludwig Museum
1 Bischofsgartenstrasse
221 26165
www.museenkoeln.de/ludwig

Year-round, especially in summer, tourist ships of all descriptions glide down the Rhine past Cologne Cathedral, right in the heart of the city. You only need to wander five minutes from the Dom or the main station to the river to find the jetties lined up by Hohenzollern Bridge, times, prices, panoramic routes and destinations clearly signposted by each one. A little further along, by Deutz Bridge, stands a bike-hire place – some river services do special deals for cyclists on certain days. Cologne's role as a relaxing, eco-friendly destination was never better illustrated.

Three main companies ply their trade here: K-D Linie, Kölntourist and Dampfschiffahrt Colonia. Of the three, long-established K-D has by far the biggest schedule, having instigated river tourism here with the sailing of the wooden steamship *Concordia* between Mainz and Cologne in 1827. These days K-D ('Cologne-Düsseldorf') runs services to Bonn, sightseeing cruises down the Rhine and themed boat tours, such as the one playing classical music heading for August's annual Beethoven Festival (www.beethovenfest.de) in Bonn. A popular trip for families is to the Sea Life Centre in Königswinter (www.sealifeeurope.com), with 3,000 creatures, a touch pool with starfish and a deep-sea basin with a 360-degree glass tunnel. An extra €1.50 with a combined return ferry ticket from Cologne allows admission. Many boats are equipped with a children's play area, including a paddling pool, a slide and swings. There are family meal deals too. On Tuesdays two cyclists can travel for the price of one, while on Wednesdays there are reduced combined rates for adults and children.

Most of K-D's summer traffic is down to the Rhine Gorge, the narrowest point of the river between the North Sea and Switzerland. This beautiful stretch, lined with medieval castles in various states of disrepair, is steeped in legend, something akin to a German Avalon. Most famously of all, near St

Goarshausen stands the rocky outcrop of Lorelei, much celebrated in song and poetry. Here a Rhine maiden would comb her long, blonde hair enticing sailors to crash in the then treacherous waters with her mysterious song. Near Königswinter, the Dragon's Cliff is where Siegfried, hero of the *Nibelungenlied*, slaughtered the dragon but lost his strength by bathing in its blood afterwards. An electric railway runs from the summit to Königswinter 1.5 kilometres away.

Wine is a big industry here. Koblenz, at the confluence of the Rhine and Mosel rivers, is a major centre, although there is little else to see there apart from the early 13th-century mainly Romanesque church of St Castor. To combine an afternoon's city stroll with a cruise from Cologne, your best choices are Bonn and Düsseldorf. Bonn, the all-but forgotten capital of former West Germany, is best known as the birthplace of Beethoven. His house (www.beethoven-haus-bonn.de) is now a museum containing a handful of his original instruments and ear trumpets. The third richest city in Germany, Düsseldorf typifies the post-war boom, the fashionable shops along focal Königsallee as glamorous as you'll find anywhere in the country. The biggest cultural attraction here is a 90-strong collection of works by Paul Klee, the basis for the permanent exhibition at the Kunstsammlung Nordrhein-Westfalen (www.kunstsammlung.de), which is to be found on Grabbeplatz.

All three ferry companies offer standard, round-trip tours of the Cologne area lasting about an hour for a rather reasonable €6, and all lay on themed tours in winter (in particular in the run-up to Christmas) and evening ones in summer.

Kölntourist *Konrad-Adenauer-Ufer, 121 600, www.koelntourist.com*

Dampfschiffahrt Colonia *Lintgasse 18-20, 257 4225, http://dampfschiffahrt-colonia.de*

K-D *Frankenwerft 15, 208 8318, www.k-d.com*

COLOGNE BY DAY

The tall, thin gabled buildings of the surrounding Old Town were almost entirely reconstructed after 1945 except for a couple with tell-tale struts sticking out of the top floor, used to lift furniture outside the narrow edifice. A hive of tourist-friendly taverns provide traditional local black pudding, mashed potato and apple sauce ('Himmel un Ääd'), marinated beef and potato pancakes; Hans and Ulrike Frömmer offer a warmer welcome than most at the **Stapelhäuschen**, which also has 34 reasonably priced rooms.

These eateries are complemented by equally traditional brewery outlets, Brauhäuser, or Weetschaften as they are known in the sing-song local dialect. The beer they brew, Kölsch, top-fermented and served in thin Stange glasses, is fundamental to the city's identity. Although frowned upon by Stein-guzzling Germans everywhere else, it is thoroughly enjoyed by both visitors and residents as the perfect light summer drink. A blue-aproned Köbes, or waiter, completes the picture.

Cologne makes much fuss of its 12 Romanesque churches. **Gross St Martin**, with its clover-leaf choir, was the tallest structure in the city until the Romantics got to work on the Dom. Perhaps of more interest are the ones dotted around the medieval city, each with its own story. A couple are found around the **Wallraf-Richartz Museum/Fondation Corboud**, where an impressive display of Old Masters is hidden behind a controversial exterior that the city embellished with artists' names against the wishes of the architect. Here, by Judengasse, was the centre of Jewish culture, scoured by medieval pogroms and later eradicated by the Nazis. The remains of a ninth-century synagogue, beside a Roman palace complex, are still being dug up, but plain to see is a 12th-century mikvah, or ritual bath, the staircase and water level of which are visible through the glass. Here also is the **Farina-Haus**, the home of the world's oldest fragrance company, which is named 4711 after the number given by Napoleon's reorganisation of the city's addresses into one long list.

Pavement plaques show the remains of the city walls and the dock area of Roman times. You can see these also on a mural map on the walls of the **Alte Römerschänke**, another classic Altstadt pub. Hohe Strasse is still Cologne's main shopping arcade, just as it was for the Romans.

Away from the mainly pedestrianised ancient centre, cyclists rule the streets – to avoid becoming another notch on the handlebars, listen out for loud bell rings. If you want to join them, there is a bike hire stall (723 627) by Deutz Bridge that rents by the hour or day and runs organised tours.

Parks and green spaces characterise the west of the city, where the 2006 World Cup venue RheinEnergie-Stadion and the famous national football coaching school are based. Cologne is Germany's sports hub – the **Sport & Olympia Museum** is located on the riverbank, with its rooftop court. Exhibitions trace the history of sport and games since ancient times, highlighting along the way Germany's sporting achievements and the 'English passion for betting'.

While Hohenzollern Bridge makes an iconic tableau with the Dom and Central Station, the less picturesque Deutz Bridge leads to the upcoming district of the same name across the river. Mocked for generations as *schälzig*, (cross-eyed), locals on the opposite bank have forever been in the shadow of the Dom and

Further reading

Mandy Aftel *Essence and Alchemy: A Book of Perfume* Its history and recipes for brewing your own pongs.
Kate Sedley *The Three Kings of Cologne* The queen of medieval mystery stories.
Max Hastings *Bomber Command* How so much of Cologne came to be flattened during World War II.

Websites

www.koelntourismus.de
Comprehensive city website.

Stapelhäuschen
1-3 Fischmarkt
0221 257 7863

Gross St Martin
An Gross St Martin
0221 257 7924

Wallraf-Richartz Museum/Fondation Corboud
39 Martinstrasse
0221 211 19
www.museenkoeln.de/wallraf-richartz-museum

Farina-Haus
21 Obenmarspforten
0221 399 8994
www.farina.eu

Alte Römerschänke
23 Am Bollwerk
0221 258 0650

Sport & Olympia Museum
1 Rheinauhafen
0221 336 090
www.sportmuseum-koeln.de

COLOGNE

Old Town. This is slowly changing with the building of the Triangle Tower, a new high-speed (ICE) train station, a new concert arena and the headquarters of national air carrier Lufthansa. 'Schälzig ist Chic' is the PR motto.

COLOGNE BY NIGHT

Whatever the good intentions, the west bank remains Cologne's entertainment centre, with nightlife hubs at the main junctions of the inner ring-road. The Belgian Quarter, Belgisches Viertel, is the most grown-up, directly west of the Dom. Walk here along Friesenstrasse, which provides as good a start to the night as any, with classy cocktail bar **Vic** and lively **Dos Equis** the pick of the bunch. The DJ-oriented **6 Pack**, with its six tall fridges full of bottled beers, may be the best bar in town. Moving south, the student-oriented Quartier Lateng, or Latin Quarter, is set around Zülpicher Strasse, where **Stiefel** is the most characterful option. The Latin Quarter mingles with the less studenty Südstadt, or St Severin quarter, near Ubierring. The **Ubier Schänke** is bohemian and the **Fiffi Bar** attracts a good mix of people.

For cocktails, **Sir Peter Ustinov's Bar**, named after a regular guest of the **Dom Hotel**, can't be beat and the hotel itself is possibly the best in town. For top-notch gastronomy, head to the panoramic 11th floor of the Hotel im Wasserturm for Hendrik Otto's Michelin-starred masterpiece, **La Vision**. In Nippes, just north of the Ring, **Paul's Restaurant** is another food destination.

Stylish accommodation options include the riverside **Hyatt Regency** and, near the station, the comfortable four-star **Four Points**. Less exclusive options are the **Hopper Et Cetera** and the pleasant **Lint Hotel** in the Altstadt. The budget **Good Sleep** is great for the price and location near the Dom.

TRAVEL INFORMATION

Tickets from the UK to Cologne can be booked through **DB UK**. Return fares from London to Cologne, on Eurostar to Bruxelles-Midi and then the ICE or Thalys train to Cologne, start from £79 per person.

WHEN TO GO

Spring, summer and autumn are best.

USING THE HUB

Germany has several important rail hubs, including Berlin, Dresden, Frankfurt, Hamburg, Nürnberg, Munich and Stuttgart. From Köln Hbf station there are frequent, fast ICE services to Berlin, Dusseldorf, Dortmund, Essen, Bonn, Bremen, Frankfurt, Hamburg, Hannover, Koblenz, Leipzig and Munich.

International, high-speed trains connect Cologne with Amsterdam (using ICE trains) and Brussels (using high-speed Thalys trains), and there are night through trains to Copenhagen, Luxembourg, Milan, Minsk, Moscow, Prague, Vienna and Warsaw. Some ICE services call at the city's Köln-Deutz station instead of Köln Hbf. See the Directory at the back of this book for more information about international connections.

Vic
16 Friesenstrasse
0221 135 116

Dos Equis
62 Friesenstrasse
0221 133 898

6 Pack
33 Aachener Strasse
0221 254 587

Stiefel
18 Zülpicher Strasse
0221 211 636

Ubier Schänke
19 Ubierring
0221 321 382
www.ubierschaenke-koeln.de

Fiffi Bar
99 Rolandstrasse
0221 340 6211
www.fiffibar.de

Sir Peter Ustinov's Bar
Dom Hotel, 2A Domkloster
0221 202 4375

Dom Hotel
2A Domkloster
0221 20240
www.lemeridien-domhotel.com

La Vision
Hotel im Wasserturm, 2 Kaygasse
20080
www.hotel-im-wasserturm.de

Paul's Restaurant
2 Bülowstrasse
766 839
www.pauls-restaurant.de

Hyatt Regency
2A Kennedy Ufer
828 1234
www.cologne.regency.hyatt.com

Four Points
2 Breslauer Platz
16510

Hopper Et Cetera
26 Brüsseler Strasse
924 400
www.hopper.de

Lint Hotel
7 Lintgasse
920 550
www.lint-hotel.de

Good Sleep
19-21 Komödienstrasse
257 2257
www.goodsleep.de

DB UK
08718 80 80 66
www.bahn.co.uk

Destinations

Destinations

Bergen

NORWAY

OSLO

ORKNEY

STAVANGER

DENMARK

Aberdeen

Edinburgh

North Sea

Newcastle

Heysham

ISLE OF MAN

DUBLIN

REPUBLIC OF
IRELAND

Liverpool

HOLLAND

NETHERLANDS

AMSTERDAM

Rosslare

UNITED KINGDOM

Harwich

The Hague

CORK

Fishguard

LONDON

BELGIAN
BEACHES

Cologne

GERMAN

Penzance

Weymouth

Poole

Portsmouth

BRUSSELS

BELGIUM

Plymouth

CALAIS

LUXEMBOURG

Frankfurt

ISLES OF SCILLY

JERSEY

Reims

LUXEMBOURG

Atlantic Ocean

BRITTANY

PARIS

STRASBOURG

Mur

Nantes

FRANCE

BERNE
SWITZERLAND

Bay of Biscay

Lyon

PORTES
DU SOLEIL

Milan

AVIGNON & AROUND

TURIN

BORDEAUX

Avignon
Nîmes
Arles

Santander

Marseille

Nice

Bilbao

NICE &
THE RIVIERA

ESPAÑA VERDE

Zaragoza

Corsica

Oporto

Barcelona

MADRID

Sardinia

PORTUGAL

SPAIN

Valencia

Mallorca

LISBON

Ibiza

Mediterranean Sea

Seville

ALGIERS

TUNIS

0   400 km

0   200 miles

MOROCCO

ALGERIA

TUNISIA

Marrakech

Côte d'Opale p63

Calais

ROUTE	Dover ▶ Calais ▶ Wissant ▶ Audresselles ▶ Wimereux ▶ Boulogne ▶
	Audenfort ▶ Ardes ▶ Oye-Plage ▶ Calais

Cycle off the ferry at Calais and turn right for a leisurely three-day circular bike ride, taking the scenic route around the Nord-Pas-de-Calais region, covering no more than 45 kilometres a day, visiting beaches, fishing villages, local markets and some historic sites.

Written by **Gavin McOwan**

Coastal cycle path p67

Road to Audenfort p65

THE TRIP

The ferry crossing is only an hour and a half, and quite gentle unless there is a storm brewing. Not bad, considering that this is one of the busiest passenger and vehicle maritime routes in the world, and the boat is steaming across one of the most congested shipping lanes to be found anywhere. As the white cliffs of Dover fade behind you, those on the other side of the Channel, south-west of Calais, come in to view. You'll be cycling towards the gentle rolling hills that you can see above the cliffs once you've disembarked and navigated the Calais one-way system.

Seeing that the journey time is so short, there's hardly time to explore the boat or try the restaurant. SeaFrance is a French firm so the food is decent – but the real thing awaits. It costs from just £10 (Saturday price) each way to catch the Dover-to-Calais ferry, your bike goes for free and there are no hidden taxes – making it better value than any budget airline flight to the Continent. All in all this is the easiest, cheapest, closest and greenest non-flying holiday it is possible to have from these shores.

 Folkestone ▸ Calais
1 hour 30 minutes

 Food & drink; active break

THE DESTINATION

With its reputation for militant dockers, English booze cruisers descending on its supermarkets and asylum seekers invading the Channel Tunnel from the other direction, Calais is the bit of France most Brits can't wait to get out of, too busy to give it a second glance as they adjust to driving on the right and negotiate the autoroute that heads toward Brittany, Burgundy or Provence – somewhere, anywhere, more interesting, more French. Even cyclists tend to head straight to the railway station and throw their bikes on to a southbound train; Calais isn't even indexed in most cycling guides to France, although it is the nearest foreign port to British soil. But cycle off the ferry, turn right past Sangatte – and no, there won't be an asylum seeker in sight – and within 15 minutes you find yourself on one of the most scenic stretches of coastline anywhere in France.

The dramatic white cliffs of the Côte d'Opale mirror Dover's, discernible across the Channel, but unlike their Kentish rivals these are backed by sweeping dunes and fringed with long golden sandy beaches that make for ideal sunbathing, lazy picnics and easy beach riding.

Inland the rolling countryside of the Parc Naturel des Caps offers near-empty roads and idyllic pastoral scenery, the ideal ingredients for a moderately challenging weekend's cycling – all just 20 kilometres from Calais. In fact this is perfect cycling country: the volume of traffic is but a fraction of that found on English country roads, and in a land where cycling is so revered, the respect motorists show towards cyclists is almost humbling. What's more, the whole trip can be completed over a weekend.

DAY ONE: CALAIS TO WIMEREUX & BOULOGNE

Given Calais's proximity to England it is no surprise that its history is bound to the island across La Manche. For over two centuries, from 1347 to 1558, Calais was an English town. Following his victory at the Battle of Crécy in 1346 King Edward III captured the town after a vicious 11-month siege that starved the courageous citizens of Calais into surrender. Before cycling off down the coast take note of Rodin's masterful statue, *Les Bourgeois de Calais* (*The Burghers of Calais*), erected in 1888 in front of Calais's oversized town hall. It's a vivid depiction of the group of defeated, ravaged men who volunteered their lives in exchange for the King's promise that he would spare their fellow citizens. The Burghers, too, were later pardoned when Edward's queen, Philippa of Hainault, begged him to spare their lives.

There is little else of historical interest in Calais as virtually the entire town, including the only concentration of English Tudor architecture in France, was flattened in World War II. In May 1940, Calais stood firm to the bloody end against German forces as the town and British and French troops were sacrificed while Dunkirk was being evacuated. Four years later Calais was again a major battleground when the Allies ejected the Germans.

Still today, some 60 years later, the British invade these shores on a massive scale and on a daily basis – Dover and Calais are the world's busiest passenger ports – only now the invaders come in white vans, coaches and 4x4s to plunder the supermarkets and discount booze warehouses.

From the town centre follow the signs to Sangatte, south-west out of Calais, and within minutes you're out on the open road, the D940, a minor road that stays close to the coastline all the way to Wimereux. This is the Côte d'Opale, so-called because the impressive chalk cliffs give the sea an opaque milky-green hue. For a panoramic view of this sweeping stretch of coarse-grass dunes and broad, empty beaches – like so much in this part of France it is underrated, but must be one of the most beautiful stretches of coastline in the country – cycle up to the lookout point at Cap Blanc-Nez, just south of Sangatte, where you can see the ferries scuttling across the Channel all the way back to Dover.

The English connection continues a little further south at the small village of Wissant (meaning 'White Sand' in old Flemish) where it is believed Julius Caesar set off for his second invasion of Britain in 54 BC. Wissant was an important port until it silted up around the 16th century; today the small fishing village appears almost engulfed by the huge sand dunes around it and fishermen have to drag their flobarts – small boats – across the sand to the ocean by tractor. If the tide is going out and the sand firm and wet, it is a joy to cycle for several kilometres along the broad beach – the finest in a string of fine beaches on this coast – and watch the kitesurfers and sand-yachters at play.

Rejoin the D940 south of Wissant for around six kilometres before turning right up to another spectacular lookout point, the Cap Gris-Nez headland where there is a lighthouse and views up and down the coast.

Of course, all this sea air and pedalling will build up a healthy appetite and the best place for lunch is Audresselles, another small fishing village with an abundance of seafood cafés housed in squat whitewashed fishermen's cottages. **Au P'tit Bonheur** is a cosy restaurant serving no-frills crabs, moules and lobster or, if the sun is shining you can eat on the beach on one of the huge, black flat-topped rocks dotted in the sand – they make perfect picnic tables. If you just want to quench your thirst the very local **Chez Eric's** is a good place for a beer and a croque-monsieur. You can end the first day in either the beach resort of Wimereux or the port town of Boulogne-Sur-Mer, four kilometres further south: each has its own charm. If rosbifs complain that Calais lacks Gallic atmosphere, Boulogne, with its 13th-century ramparted citadel and bustling street market is one of the liveliest and most historically interesting towns in the region, while belle époque but slightly raffish Wimereux is as French as an old bicycle with a string of onions slung over the handlebars. Stroll along the promenade in summer and it's easy to picture Jacques Tati's Monsieur Hulot enjoying his vacances here.

There's a good selection of brasseries and hotels in Wimereux, but it's hard to beat **L'Atlantic**, which has simple modern rooms with balconies and one of the best seafood restaurants in the region; both come with sea views. Also right on the seafront is **La Goëlette**, a homely but stylish chambres d'hôtes (B&B) with four bedrooms with polished wooden floors and a bright, airy feel. (Book in advance and ask for one of the front rooms.)

There is such a surprising dearth of interesting accommodation in Boulogne that **L'Enclos de l'Evêché**, an elegant mansion in the old town, with high-ceilinged spacious rooms, wooden floors and antique furniture, is a stand-out choice. The guesthouse's restaurant is good enough to attract non-guests but, if you have

Au P'tit Bonheur
2 rue Jeanne d'Arc
03 21 83 12 54

Chez Eric's
68 rue Edmont Marin
03 21 32 98 79

L'Atlantic
Digue de Mer, Wimereux
03 21 32 41 01
www.atlantic-delpierre.com

La Goëlette
13 Digue de Mer, Wimereux
03 21 32 62 44
www.lagoelette.com

L'Enclos de l'Evêché
6 rue de Pressy, Boulogne
03 91 90 05 90
www.enclosdeleveche.com

Chez Jules
pl Dalton, Boulogne
03 21 31 54 12

the energy, head downtown to **Chez Jules**, a local institution serving everything from pizzas out of the huge wood-fired oven to fancy brasserie fare and – not surprisingly, as Boulogne is France's most important fishing port – excellent local seafood.

DAY TWO: **BOULOGNE INLAND TO AUDENFORT**

If you are in Boulogne on a Saturday, the morning market is an unmissable gathering of local characters and superb regional produce spilling out on to the cobblestones of place Dalton, in front of the majestic church of St Nicolas. Delicious local cheeses, wild mushrooms and farmyard-fresh veg all look so appetising that you may regret coming by bicycle: you'll want to take so much of it home with you. Cheese-lovers should visit the outstanding **Phillippe Olivier**, one of the best fromagiers in northern France, with around 300 varieties in stock. Place Dalton is the thriving heart of Boulogne and the only part of the lower city to retain its pre-war character. From here it's a ten-minute schlep, or five-minute huff and puff on the bike, up the Grand Rue to the walled Haute Ville. Built on Gallo-Roman foundations, the impressive ramparts, decorated by 17 turrets, make for a pleasant stroll with outstanding views of the town and port. But despite such solid defences, Boulogne, like Calais, was also bagged by an invading English monarch when Henry VIII ordered its capture in 1544. Inside the walls, many of the old buildings have been impressively restored and there are new restaurants and shops lining the main street, rue de Lille. For this next leg, you'll need a very good map to find the right road to Audenfort – and study it carefully before setting off. It is perhaps no surprise that in this part of the world Michelin's online maps (www.viamichelin.com) are far more effectual than Google's. They are invaluable if you want to explore the countryside while avoiding main roads. To take the scenic route from Wimereux to Audenfort head for the D233 (just after the train station), get on to the D251 at Belle-et-Houllefort, and then the D191, which takes you almost all the way there. You'll probably get lost a few times, but that is part of the fun in this idyllic corner of rural France. Many visitors are surprised to find such pleasant pastoral scenery so close to the pancake-flat industrial sprawl that surrounds Calais – breathing in the country air and smells of the farmyard, it feels a world away. There are no major sights in the area, just meander your way eastwards through the Parc Naturel des Caps, passing sleepy farmhouses and châteaux; the undulating green hills are easy on the eye but plenty steep enough (when carrying panniers) to provide a challenging ride.

In most French villages there is little to do in the evening aside from eat and then sleep, and if you've been cycling all day you'll want to do both well, so choose your accommodation carefully. The **Auberge du Moulin d'Audenfort**, a converted 17th-century mill where the River Hem still runs through the building, scores highly on both counts. The menu of hearty regional food is just the job to restore some energy after a day spent in the saddle, and excellent value. Terrine of rabbit in white beer and hazelnuts followed by knuckle-end of lamb in thyme and garlic, with a 'trilogy' of crèmes brûlées to finish costs just €19. One of the local cheeses, the Vieux Lille, is so pungently earthy you can taste the farmyard it came from. And if a bellyful of food and good wine doesn't send you to sleep, the babbling river will.

Phillippe Olivier
43 rue Thiers, Boulogne
03 21 31 94 74
www.fromage-online.de
The website is in German

Auberge du Moulin d'Audenfort
impasse du Gué, Audenfort
03 21 00 13 16
www.lemoulindaudenfort.com

Auberge du Moulin d'Audenfort p65

DAY THREE: **BACK TO CALAIS**

For many Frenchmen and women, Sunday is no longer a day of rest; it is a day for squeezing into lycra, meeting up with friends and going on a long bike ride. Cycling in rural France on a Sunday morning is a joy for the simple fact that cars on the road are outnumbered by cyclists, all of whom greet you with a cheery bonjour. If you do most of your cycling on crowded British roads or commuting to work, this feels wonderfully liberating.

From Audenfort it is a fairly steep haul northwards up the D224, once again through picturesque countryside. From the brow of the hill there are fine views of the English Channel, Dunkirk and Calais to the north and Flanders to the east. Continue to the town of Ardes and keep your eyes open for the D228. The ride back to Calais from here is the least interesting leg of the journey, though still fairly quiet and pleasant enough as the road (the D228, then D229 and D219) follows a canal toward the coast and the Platier d'Oye Nature Reserve, a stopover for migratory birds on their way back north in spring. From here swing eastwards on to the D119 at Oye-Plage, parallel to the flat sand dunes and marshy beaches. You can stop for a picnic here before getting back on the ferry, but Calais's unsung beach, on the other side of town west of the port, is a much nicer option. Better still, head into town for a final culinary and shopping splurge.

Given that booze, rather than food, is the priority for most day-trippers to Calais, picking out a decent restaurant from the scores of mediocre ones is a challenge. There are plenty of cheap moule-frites joints if that's all you have time for, but it's worth seeking out one of Calais's excellent mid-range seafood eateries. These places are quite formal – so you'll have to change out of your cycling gear – but after the weekend's endeavours a slap-up fishy feast is in order. Book ahead at weekends.

A five-minute ride out of town heading west, **Aquar Aile** is located on the fifth floor of an ugly modern apartment block but has fabulous views of the seafront. This is one of the finest fish restaurants in town, with friendly service and terrific oysters. **Le Channel** is Calais' most famous restaurant but remains excellent value for the full French with all the trimmings. The owners have recently opened a fine cheese and wine shop

Aquar Aile
255 rue Jean Moulin, Calais
03 21 34 00 00
www.aquaraile.com

Le Channel
blvd de la Résistance, Calais
03 21 34 42 30
www.restaurant-lechannel.com

around the corner (1 rue André Gerschell, 03 21 34 44 72). To the east of the port, the nautically themed **Le Grand Bleu** serves superb local seafood fresh from the fish market across the road.

One of the few drawbacks of cycling rather than driving in France is that you can't load up with wine to bring home – so at least remember to stuff an empty backpack into your panniers: a case of half a dozen bottles should fit snugly. When buying such a small quantity, quality is paramount, so heed the locals' advice and go to a small wine shop rather than a supermarket or cash 'n' carry – they may be cheaper but the quality varies widely. **Le Bar à Vins** is a little shop/wine bar in the centre of town where Luc Gille, the friendly and knowledgeable owner, has been buying 'only the wines I like and would drink myself' from small producers all over France for 20 years. Belly, panniers and backpacks full, from his shop it is a five-minute wobble back on to the ferry.

IN THE AREA

This journey can be completed in three days by anyone with a reasonable degree of fitness – or even two days by the super-fit. It can also be easily extended south-west to Normandy, or even all the way to Brittany.

Cycling to the historic port town of Dieppe, taking in the misty marshes of the Somme, will take another two days from Boulogne. Return from Dieppe to Newhaven with **Transmanche Ferries** or to Newhaven or Portsmouth with **LD Lines**. A further two days will take you to magical Honfleur, one of the most beautiful harbours in Europe, and glitzy Deauville. Return from Le Havre to Newhaven or Portsmouth with LD Lines.

The Normandy beaches and Bayeux lie between the ports of Caen, at the heart of cider and calvados country, and Cherbourg. The Norman coastline becomes rugged to the west, the cycling more challenging, the weather more severe – so bring along the waterproofs. Return from Caen to Portsmouth or from Cherbourg to Poole or Portsmouth with **Brittany Ferries**.

For aspirant Tour de Francers, the seven-to-ten-day ride from Calais to Brittany provides an unforgettable journey, taking in the wild Atlantic coast and Mont St Michel before sailing home from the walled city of St Malo. Return from St Malo to Poole or Plymouth with **Condor Ferries** or to Portsmouth with Brittany Ferries.

Looking north, those with no home to go to can take on the LF1 cycle path all the way to Den Helder in the Netherlands.

TRAVEL INFORMATION

SeaFrance operates 30 daily crossings on the Dover–Calais route. Foot passenger services: Dover to Calais from 08.15 to 19.30, Calais to Dover 08.30 to 19.30. Foot passenger fares, with bicycle, are from £12 each way. A car and up to five passengers starts from £26 each way if booked online. The crossing time is 1.5 hours.

If you have a fold-up bike, it is possible to catch the Eurostar to Calais' Frethun railway station and take your bike on board.

WHEN TO GO

Spring to late summer; book accommodation and ferries well in advance if planning to go during the school summer holidays.

Further reading

Patricia Fenn *Calais, Boulogne and the North of France* Extremely informative on local food and wine, as well as hotels, beaches and local markets.

Websites

www.viamichelin.com
www.uk.pas-de-calais.com
Half-day cycle routes in Nord-Pas-de-Calais.

CALAIS

Le Grand Bleu
8 rue Jean-Pierre Avron, Calais
03 21 97 97 98
www.legrandbleu-calais.com

Le Bar à Vins
52 pl d'Armes, Calais
03 21 96 96 31

Transmanche Ferries
www.transmancheferries.co.uk

LD Lines
www.ldline.co.uk

Brittany Ferries
www.brittany-ferries.com

Condor Ferries
www.condorferries.co.uk

SeaFrance
0871 22 22 500
www.seafrance.com

Castle Rushen p71

Isle of Man

ROUTE Heysham ▶ Douglas

Take the ferry from Liverpool or Lancashire to the land of three-legged
men, kippers and ancient castles. After a Full Manx breakfast there are
fells to climb and panoramic views across the Irish Sea, then it's down
to an ancient port for a pint of the local hoppy beer and scallops in butter,
followed by tales of Viking daring and Celtic myth.

Written by **Michael Hodges**; 'Motorcycle Mecca' by **Ben Wilkins**

National Folk Museum p73

THE TRIP

Set in the middle of the Irish Sea, the Isle of Man for centuries played a crucial role in the seafaring and trade links between Britain, Ireland and, more unexpectedly, Scandinavia. Today, it is only a 2.5-hour ferry ride away from the port of Liverpool, or about 3.5 hours from Heysham in Lancashire. In past times, the god Manannan was said to veil the island in fog to save it from marauders and these days the crossing can still be misty, but landfall is more assured than for Viking freebooters. The highlight of the journey is the rising hump of 2,034-foot Snae Fell, Norse for 'Snow Mountain', the highest point on the island, although the concrete modernist eccentricity of the Douglas ferry terminal is almost equally awe-inspiring, albeit in a very different way. If you haven't seen it already on the ferry, then look out at the terminal for the triskelion, the three-legged man symbol – said to originate from the battle technique of Manannan, who, when the fog failed to conceal the island on one occasion, changed himself into three legs, rolled downhill and hurled the invaders back into the sea.

 Liverpool ▶ Douglas **2 hours 30 minutes**

 Active break; history; landscape; wildlife

National Folk Museum p73

THE DESTINATION

As Ken Dodd once pointed out, 'No man is an island, apart from the Isle of Man.' His remark in many ways encapsulated a society set aside from the mainland mainstream and determined to maintain its own identity, whether it be the continued running of a motorcycle race that anywhere else would have been banned for being too dangerous to running its own affairs through the world's oldest continuous parliament. But now the island is looking to reinvent itself as a place to go on weekend breaks, on the basis of its fantastic scenery, access to great seafood and a unique history. The main force behind this reinvention is the **Manx National Heritage** an organisation that combines the role of Ministry of Culture, National Trust and National Parks Authority. The organisation is in the happy position of having much to promote, not least the **Tynwald**, the world's oldest continuous parliament (5 June is Tynwald Day when the members of parliament gather on Tynwald Hill in the centre of the island to open parliament in a ceremony that goes back 1,000 years).

Man is only 33 miles long and 13 miles wide, with the bulk of the northern half being fell and mountain, so it's no surprise that the towns are dotted around the coast where, since 3,500 BC, men have gained their livelihood from the sea. To see their Neolithic tombs go to the remarkably intact burial chambers at **Cashtal yn Ard** (the Castle of the Heights). You shouldn't find it difficult to find somewhere to stay; there are B&Bs galore and some 20 campsites. At the other end of the scale, large hotels include the **Mount Murray Hotel**, between Douglas and Castletown, with an 18-hole golf course and leisure centre, or, if you prefer an indoor swimming pool and casino, both sensible options in winter, there's the **Douglas Hilton**.

Manx National Heritage
01624 648000
www.gov.im/MNH/

Tynwald
Douglas
01624 685500
www.tynwald.org.im

Cashtal yn Ard
Nr Cornaa, on the way from Glen Mona

Mount Murray Hotel
Santon
01624 661111
www.mountmurray.com

Douglas Hilton
Central Promenade, Douglas
01624 662662
www.hilton.co.uk/isleofman

CASTLETOWN

Castletown, ten miles south of the capital Douglas, is named for **Castle Rushen**, a low set, medieval stone fortification that looks across a pleasantly eccentric square featuring a memorial to the islanders who fell in the world wars (for opening times of the castle and other attractions run by Manx Heritage, contact the **tourist office**). In the centre of the square is a pillar dedicated to the wonderfully named Colonel Cornelius Smelt, Lieutenant Governor of Man, who died in 1832 'aged 82 in the 28th year of his government'.

Castle Rushen was once 'the fortress of the Kings and Lords of Mann'. The clock on the castle wall gives some idea of the castle's provenance, bearing the legend 'Eliz Reg 1597'. Cut through to the shoreline from the square and you'll find a wide bay with the airport on the northern side. The small, whitewashed building in front of you is a preserved 18th-century grammar school that started life in the 13th century as St Mary's Chapel.

The harbour beyond is home to yachts and pleasure cruisers in summer and, if you're nautically inclined, the shipping forecast is put in the window of Castletown Harbour office.

DOUGLAS

For ferry passengers Douglas is their first landfall. If you do land here make sure to visit the **Manx Museum**, minutes walk away from the docks, where you will find a fibreglass relief model of the island in the first room.

The museum is generally impressive, especially the new Viking exhibition that puts the island's Norse history in context. Vikings were not only pirates but farmers too, masters of the Irish Sea and, from Man, rulers for nearly 500 years of a kingdom that included the Western Isles – the last Viking king died in 1265. However, if you've only five minutes to spare then stick to the map room, which is an excellent way to familiarise yourself with the island's topography.

As well as the expected high-street shops, the island's two breweries are in Douglas. The biggest, **Okell's**, brews a variety of northern English-style creamy ales, but the smaller **Bushy's** produces lively and hoppy bitters.

PEEL

Like castles? Like kippers? Like tall concrete chimneys? Then you'll love Peel. The capital of the west coast is only half an hour's drive across the middle of the island from Douglas, yet it has a perceptibly different atmosphere, produced in part by the grotesque modern garbage incinerator behind the town but more by the fact that it faces the wilder, western seas. Incinerator aside, Peel is very much a seafaring town and is, appropriately, home to an interactive museum dedicated to the island's sea history. The **House of Manannan** was reopened in July 2007 after a half-million pound revamp and is well worth a visit, in particular for the multi-media tour and the almost unbelievably camp video presentation by the Irish actor JP McKenna. He stars as Manannan, the Celtic deity and shape shifter who lives on a nearby mysterious island and who protects Man from invaders by shrouding it in an impenetrable fog.

NOTES

Castle Rushen
Castletown
01624 648000

Tourist Office
Douglas Ferry Terminal
01624 686799
www.visitisleofman.com

Manx Museum
Kingswood Grove, Douglas
01624 648000

Okell's
Kewaigue, Douglas
01624 699400
www.okells.co.uk

Bushy's
11 Church Street, Douglas
01624 611101
www.bushys.com

House of Manannan
Mill Rd, Peel
01624 648000

MOTORBIKE MECCA

Motorcycle racing dominates the biggest event in the Isle of Man's calendar: the TT. The year 2007 was the centenary of the first Tourist Trophy races, when gentlemen raced ill-equipped, underpowered and downright unreliable motorcycles on the island's roads. Today, the very best riders, and fastest bikes, can lap the 37.75-mile mountain circuit at an average speed of 130mph. Only 11 riders finished the gruelling inaugural event, their clothes holed from the acid used to try to damp the dust on the un-metalled roads.

During these 100 years, the Isle of Man has become the spiritual home of motorcycle racing. People come from the world over to enjoy the racing and to ride the same roads that the competitors race on. Try doing that at a Grand Prix.

Of course, the other reason people come, in these days of over-sanitised sport, is to get close to the action. Try sitting on the hedge alongside the Cronk-y-Voddy straight, only a couple of yards from bikes flying past at over 180mph. You can't get much closer to the action than that. The bikes rush up the hill and over the rise, the noise of the exhaust muted and distant, until they're on you and you're hit by a wall of air and the wailing exhaust note. Don't blink or you'll miss the buzz, as they appear to rip apart the fabric of space around you. In short, if you only go to one bike race in your life, make it this one.

Even if you don't have a bike, the island during TT week is unlike anywhere else. To get the full flavour, park yourself at the Creg-ny-Baa pub with a pint and marvel at the bikes on the run down from Kate's Cottage, front wheels in the air, as they drop down towards you.

The racing might be what brings in the crowds but it's almost a backdrop to the crowds themselves. Thin, fat, short and tall; the legion of bike fans is an entertainment in itself. You don't need to be a petrolhead to appreciate the TT, but we'd be kidding if we tried to claim it doesn't help. But don't forget to book early because the ferry and accommodation fill up months before the event.

Visit the island during TT week for the racing, the crowds and the party atmosphere, but come at other times to ride the circuit at your own pace. Only then can you truly experience riding the mountain section of the course with no other traffic. After finishing the beautifully broad and sweeping tarmac of the mountain section, reflect on your ride with a beer at the Creg-ny-Baa pub. Did we mention that there are no speed limits on the mountain section?

TT dates: 30 May to 12 June 2009; 29 May to 11 June 2010; 28 May to 10 June 2011.
Creg-ny-Baa pub, *Mountain Road, Creg-ny-Baa, 01624 676948.*

One group of invaders that Manannan failed to halt were the Vikings and the museum's main exhibit is the replica longship that was sailed here by a joint crew of Manxmen and Norwegians in 1979.

Like many places in the British Isles, Man has great seafood that is not always cooked that well, but what it does get right is the kippered herring. The Manx style of kipper is less strongly flavoured than the Whitby or Craster varieties and **Moore's Traditional Curers** claims to be the last traditional curer on the island. As well as kippers Moore's produces bacon, crab claws, and, in the autumn season, the island's noted queen scallops (all of which can be posted home if you are not inclined to put kippers in your luggage).

RICH GROUND, LONG WALKS

The Kings and, later, the Lords of Man didn't go in for modernisation – horses were preferred to tractors over most of the island until after World War II – and as a result an immensely rich landscape has survived, varying from the bleak beauty of the high fells to unspoilt beaches and a patchwork of fields that retain the same hedge and wall boundaries they did centuries ago. This patrimony is best displayed at the **National Folk Museum**, in the far south of the island, where ancient farming techniques are preserved amid whitewashed thatched cottages. The lack of intensive farming also meant the survival of much of the archaeology of the Viking periods and there is an extensive network of public rights of way.

There are walks all over the island of varying degrees of difficulty, but the big one is Raad ny Foillan, or Road of the Gull, which follows the majority of the island's 100-mile coastline. There are seven sections to the hike, which you can do in stages over a visit or, alternatively, the entire trail can be walked in about six days. In the high country, Snae Fell is worthy of comparison with the Pennines or the mountains of Skye with which it once shared a kingdom. There is a café at the summit operated by the **Snaefell Mountain Railway** and from there you can, weather permitting, see Ireland, England, Scotland and Wales; a vantage point offered nowhere else in these islands. The walking here is exhilarating and tough but remember fog can come down very quickly on the mountain, even in summer.

If you're looking for less exposed rambling, the island's 17 national glens offer covering woodland and tumbling streams. Dhoon Glen, near Ramsey, and Glen Mooar, near Kirk Michael, both feature delightful waterfalls, but if you've children with you opt for Silverdale Glen. A little inland from Castletown along the Silverburn river outside Ballasalla you'll find Rushen Abbey at the glen's mouth. Bleak and squat, built in the soft slate of the island, the abbey contrives to be a simultaneously cosy and desolate collection of stunted towers. The Silverburn is browner than silver, heavy with earth washed down from the fells if there has been rain. The burn runs down from Silverdale Glen, offering the choice of three walks of different levels of difficulty, although none is too hard, with the longest being eight miles. Look out for brown trout as you go along and eventually you'll come to a stone bridge. Built around 1250 it is one of the last packhorse bridges in the British Isles – built by the monks of Rushen Abbey to bring produce in from their farms in the north of the island.

ISLE OF MAN

Moore's Traditional Curers
Mill Rd, Peel
01624 843622
www.manxkippers.com

National Folk Museum
Cregneash Village
www.gov.im/mnh/

Snaefell Mountain Railway
01624 675222
Closed in winter

The Sound

Further downstream you'll find a boating lake, a Victorian carousel (powered by water) and **Craftworks Studio**, where the children can paint ceramics and you can drink tea.

For real aficionados the best time to visit is during the island's two walking festivals, over six days in late June (22-27 June 2008) and four days in October (9-12 October 2008).

THE CALF OF MAN

Man's little offspring is just south of Cregneash and lies across the Sound, a third of a mile of racing currents and jagged rock outcrops that have taken their share of ships. Local legend ascribes the Sound to the feet of the Irish giant Finn MacCooil (one wonders what Manannan thought of that). There are seasonal boat trips to the island running from Port St Mary and Port Erin. Back on the mainland, the bumps and mounds you'll find on the Meayll peninsula are the Parade, an ancient defensive settlement that now features a grass-roofed restaurant, a car park and a visitor centre with a glass wall opening on to what might be the best view from a café in the British Isles (try the fish soup, made from freshly caught local produce each day for £5.25). The visitor centre is excellent, explaining the wildlife, social history and legends associated with the Sound in a quick video presentation. It is especially pleasant to walk here in spring and summer, when flowers on the Calf of Man and the Meayll peninsula include the wonderfully named purple milk-vetch, bird's-foot trefoil, spring squill and sea campion. Elecampane, which was once cultivated as a salve for wounds, also grows wild here.

As you come out of the restaurant look to the right of the car park to a white cross. This is the Thousla Cross, erected in tribute to the bravery of the Manxmen who rescued the crew of a French schooner run aground in the treacherous currents between Man and the Calf in 1858.

You are now at the southernmost point of the island and, if you are walking the Road of the Gull, you are 95 miles from the start whether you turn left or right. If you want to walk a dog here you can't head west as the farmer allows access to walkers but not their dogs.

SHARK ATTACK

On the western coast you may be lucky enough to see grey seals dragged up on to the rocks or, out in the Sound, the dorsal fins of basking sharks – if you do then report them to Manx Heritage, which keeps a running tab on the appearances of these majestic plankton eaters. You may also see whales – both Minke and Orca are found off the Man coast. But if the fauna won't come to you, then go to them: the **Foillan Beg** sails out of Peel harbour and offers basking shark tours. It claims to be a 'wise operator, trained to minimise disturbance to marine animals', although presumably not all of them, as fishing trips are run as well.

MOTORBIKES

Famously, the Isle of Man, outside of the towns and villages, doesn't have a speed limit. This may help explain its attraction to bikers. The other draws are, of course, the **TT** race that dominates the island in May and the **Grand Prix** in late August.

Craftworks Studio
Silverdale Glen
01624 823244
www.craftworks-studio.co.uk

Foillan Beg
Peel harbour
07624 434457
mal.kelly@manx.net

Isle of Man TT
www.iomtt.com

Isle of Man Grand Prix
www.iommgp.com

Reminders of the TT dot the northern side of the island; there are wall plaques and memorials to riders who have died in the notoriously dangerous races or, more simply, the orange signs that alert the riders to coming bends. Because the race is entirely on open roads, with all the dangers that implies, there is no other competition quite like it in the world. And since it is on open roads, many young bikers come here to emulate their heroes, sometimes, sadly, fatally.

INDUSTRIAL HERITAGE AND RAILWAYS

Although the island is selling itself on its Celtic and Viking heritage, it is also one of the most important historical sites of the Industrial Revolution, when lead, silver and zinc mining attracted engineers from across the British Isles to Man. The most impressive surviving example of this heritage is the Manx Heritage-run **Laxey Wheel**. Set in a typical east coast glen, the wheel is a great feat of Victorian engineering, using the power generated by the torrent that dashes down the glen to lift water from the mines below. Now an emblem of the island and invariably busy in spring and summer, it is worth waiting for the coach trips to pull away and spending a little time in front of a machine that combines usefulness with an almost Heath Robinsonesque whitewashed beauty.

Beneath the wheel you'll find, after a 15-minute walk, the village of Laxey itself and the aptly named **Mines Tavern**. The food here is home-made and rather good by pub standards, especially the shepherd's pie, although quite why the chef looked so distressed when we asked for salad remains a mystery. Don't be put off, however, for as the name of the pub implies, you are amid industrial heritage: the walls carry pictures of the old workings and the men who laboured at them, and the bar is an ingenious re-creation of an electric train.

If you went to the pub first and, after a pint or two, are of the opinion that a 15-minute walk up hill is probably 14 too far, then simply go into the back garden and look down at the less celebrated second Victorian waterwheel. This will also give you a chance to wander around the small but appealing parish church, and to take in an attractive viaduct just outside the toy town Laxey station. There are 40 miles of railway on the island operated by four different lines: the **Isle of Man Steam Railway** runs from Douglas to Port Erin; the **Manx Electric Railway** between Douglas, Laxey and Ramsey; the electric **Snaefell Mountain Railway** from Laxey to the summit of the mountain; and the small **Groudle Glen Railway**, from the glen to the coast.

TRAVEL INFORMATION

The **Isle of Man Steam Packet Company** runs ferries from Liverpool (2hrs 30mins to 2hrs 40mins) and Heysham in Lancashire (3hrs 15mins to 3hrs 45mins depending on tides) to Douglas. Fares start from £35 return for an adult foot passenger, and for a car and two passengers the cost can be as low as £98 return, although at times when you're actually likely to want to visit fares start from £168.

WHEN TO GO

When it's sunny. The island is full of bikers in May and August.

Further reading

George MacDonald Fraser *Flashman* Fraser was a longtime resident of the Isle of Man. The Flashman books tell what happened to the school bully after the end of *Tom Brown's Schooldays*. Hall Caine *The Manxman* Now almost forgotten, Hall Caine was one of most popular authors of Victorian times and set many novels on the Isle of Man.

Websites

www.iomtt.com
The TT website.
www.iommgp.com
And the Grand Prix one.
www.isleofman.com
Comprehensive island website.

Laxey Wheel
Laxey
www.iomguide.com/laxeywheel.php

Mines Tavern
Captains Hill, Laxey
01624 861484

Isle of Man Steam Railway
www.iomguide.com/steamrailway.php

Manx Electric Railway
www.mers.org.im

Snaefell Mountain Railway
01624 675222
www.iomguide.com/mountainrailway.php
Closed in winter

Groudle Glen Railway
www.groudleglenrailway.com

Isle of Man Steam Packet Company
08705 523523
www.steam-packet.com

Porth Conger St Agnes p79

Isles of Scilly

ROUTE Penzance ▶ St Mary's ▶ St Agnes ▶ St Martin's ▶ Tresco ▶ Bryher

Leave your car behind with a sea voyage to the far-flung Isles of Scilly and a taste of Britain at its most exotic. Family adventures, outdoor pursuits and romantic hideaways can all be found in this beautiful, unspoiled archipelago, where life is ruled by the sea and the seasons. As walking, cycling and sailing are visitors' only options for exploring, this is one of the greenest destinations around. Cut your carbon footprint even more and pitch a tent at one of four idyllic campsites, then wake up to sensational views, the purest air imaginable and breakfast on the beach.

Written by **Tamsin Shelton**

En route from St Martin's p80

St Martin's p80

THE TRIP

Since the seasonal crossing from Penzance to St Mary's on the *Scillonian III* leaves in the morning, passengers usually arrive in Cornwall the night before. But beware of filling up on a full English breakfast – converging currents off Land's End mean the voyage can be choppy, hence the ample supply of sick bags, buckets and mops. Don't be put off, however. The trip is where the adventure begins and, as the Cornish coast slips away, look out for dolphins swimming alongside. Strike up conversation with fellow passengers and you will soon hear accounts of generations of family holidays spent in the Scillies. When, three hours later, these tiny outposts of rural England come into view you'll see why.

The *Scillonian III* docks at Hugh Town, St Mary's 'capital'. If you're staying on St Agnes, St Martin's, Tresco or Bryher your luggage is transferred to one of the launches that ply between the islands. They jostle alongside the mothership while the crew form a chain and pass bags along to the appropriate boat. The system is well honed, thanks to coloured luggage labels, and you will soon be on your way for the last leg of your journey.

 Penzance ▸ St Mary's
2 hours 40 minutes

 Active break; beaches; family holiday; wildlife

Hell Bay Hotel p82

THE DESTINATION

The Isles of Scilly are scattered 28 miles off Land's End and benefit from their position in the Gulf Stream with mild winters and warm summers, though they are sometimes battered by Atlantic storms. The frost-free climate allows subtropical vegetation to flourish and flower farms to grow narcissi in October; indeed, wildflowers seem to bloom in every crevice. While carefully managed tourism is the economic mainstay of the community, fishing and farming are important occupations for the 2,000 inhabitants, who are proud of the islands' status as an Area of Outstanding Natural Beauty. Their resilience and resourcefulness have kept the Scillies a very special place to visit and the welcome offered to visitors is genuinely warm. Deciding on which island to use as a base is difficult as each has its distinct character and fervent supporters. Staying on more than one offers a chance to really savour Scillonian life and form what could be a lifelong allegiance.

ST MARY'S

The largest of the Isles, at just over four square miles, St Mary's has the greatest variety of activities, shopping, eating and accommodation options. Get your bearings by climbing Garrison Hill, which rises up at the end of the promontory west of Hugh Town, for sweeping views of the archipelago. The hill is named after the 18th-century fortifications built here, but the dominant structure is the 16th-century, eight-pointed Star Castle, built as a defence against the Armada. A visit to the **Isles of Scilly Museum** reveals a treasure trove of loot recovered from shipwrecks, artefacts illustrating Scillonian life from prehistoric to modern times, and an 1877 pilot gig – a traditional wooden rowing boat. Gig racing is the main sport here and island teams compete on Wednesdays and Fridays in summer. You can cheer the crews on from the passenger boats that follow each race on a course from Samson to the Hugh Town quay.

Heading east, Telegraph Road leads towards the interior, passing **Carreg Dhu** (pronounced 'Crake Dew'). This small volunteer-run subtropical garden may not be as famous as Tresco's, but it's a peaceful place to rest and admire plants that would not survive on the mainland. Nearby is the **Longstone Heritage Centre**, which has a Made in Scilly gift shop and a local history display, as well as a café with marvellous views. From Porthcressa Beach, a pretty sheltered bay on the south side of Hugh Town, a path loops round Peninnis Head, passing intriguing rock formations such as the Kettle and Pans close to the lighthouse. Beyond lies Old Town Bay, the island's main port until the 17th century.

East of here, Porth Hellick bay is overlooked by a monument to Rear-Admiral Sir Cloudesley Shovell, who steered his fleet on to the rocks during a storm in 1707, losing 2,000 men. This disaster led to the 1714 Longitude Act, which offered a large prize to whoever could find a method of accurately determining longitude at sea. A mile north is Pelistry Bay, one of St Mary's most gorgeous beaches; a sandbar to Toll's Island forms at low tide – it's dangerous to swim here at high tide, however.

There are several ways to explore St Mary's. Hire a bike from **Buccabu Hire** by Porthcressa Beach, take to horseback

Isles of Scilly Museum
Church Street, St Mary's
01720 422337

Carreg Dhu
Telegraph Road, St Mary's
01720 422404

Longstone Heritage Centre
St Mary's
01720 423770

Buccabu Hire
by Porthcressa Beach, St Mary's
01720 422289

(**St Mary's Riding Centre**) or take a vintage bus tour with **Island Rover**. The community bus, a relic retired from mainland service, circles the quiet leafy lanes during the summer. There are between 30 and 40 miles of coastal paths and nature trails, and it's possible to walk right round the island keeping the sea in view at all times. This is the best way to discover St Mary's rich prehistoric heritage, from the impressive Bronze Age village at Halangy Down in the north to the chambered cairns on the east.

Most accommodation is found in Hugh Town, and ranges from the **Garrison campsite** and **Garrison House B&B**, with Aga-cooked breakfasts, to hotels in memorable buildings such as the **Star Castle Hotel**, converted from the military stronghold overlooking town. If you've built up an appetite exploring the island, stop off at the **Carn Vean** licensed café and tea gardens at Pelistry. For fresh fish and seafood with a beach vibe, the **Boat Shed** at Porthmellon opens from 11am to midnight.

ST AGNES

Admirers of St Agnes say the lack of a hotel has helped the island to preserve its unique qualities. Visitors either camp or rent a cottage, which gives a sense of belonging, albeit temporarily, to Britain's most south-westerly community. The peace is palpable once you step on to Porth Conger quay after the bustle of St Mary's harbour, unless you're heading for **Troy Town Farm Campsite**, in which case the quiet will be broken by the throb of farmer Tim Hicks's tractor come to fetch the luggage. Take the sandy path that hugs the coast, then clamber over the rocks for a first glimpse of Troy Town. The campsite is set in small grass fields just above the shoreline, with mesmerising views of Bishop Rock Lighthouse, the bird-sanctuary island of Annet and the jagged Western Rocks. Seals often swim in close for some humanwatching. The beach just below and its rock pools are a constant draw for children, when they're not choosing delicious home-made ice-cream from the farm shop. Troy Town is the only dairy farm in the Scillies and the shop also sells its milk, yoghurt, clotted cream, beef, pork and vegetables. Food miles don't get much lower than this.

One of the greatest draws for families visiting the Scillies is their safety, and children can happily explore and be sent on errands unaccompanied, tasting a freedom usually denied to them elsewhere. St Agnes's Post Office is the perfect place to send a child with a shopping list and some pocket money. This Aladdin's Cave stocks an astounding array of food, alcohol, books, toys and holiday paraphernalia. The pasties are essential for a day at the beach, of which the finest is Covean. When the tide is out cross the sandbar to the island of Gugh (rhymes with 'dew') to find wildflowers, a Bronze Age standing stone and a burial chamber. From Covean, head uphill to the **Covean tea rooms** for man-size portions of cake, or downhill to the **Turk's Head**. The most south-westerly pub in Britain also has one of the most spellbinding views; its sun-trap terrace is a glorious spot to enjoy a seafood platter and a pint of Doom Bar.

A short walk from the campsite leads to a miniature stone maze, said to have been laid out by the lighthouse keeper's son in 1729. The beach below is covered in small cairns of perched pebbles, as if Andy Goldsworthy has passed this way – add your own to this anonymous artwork. Paths criss-cross the wild

ISLES OF SCILLY

St Mary's Riding Centre
Maypole, St Mary's
01720 423855

Island Rover
01702 422131
www.islandrover.com

Garrison campsite
Hugh Town, St Mary's
01720 422670

Garrison House B&B
Hugh Town, St Mary's
01720 422972

Star Castle Hotel
01720 422317
www.star-castle.co.uk

Carn Vean café
Pelistry, St Mary's
01720 422701

Boat Shed
Porthmellon, Hugh Town, St Mary's
01720 423881
www.the-boatshed.co.uk

Troy Town Farm Campsite
01720 422360
www.troytown.co.uk

Covean tea rooms
St Agnes
01720 422620

Turk's Head
St Agnes
01720 422434

heathland of Wingletang Down, taking ramblers all round the island via such spots as Beady Pool, so-called because it's still possible to find beads washed up from a wrecked 17th-century trading ship. Above the cove, two huge boulders indented with a yard-deep basin form the Giant's Punchbowl, the most bizarre rock formation on the Scillies.

ST MARTIN'S

This most northerly of the Isles lays claim to the loveliest beaches and the clearest waters, something that few who disembark at Lower Town's low-water quay would dispute. The white sand and crystalline water resemble the Caribbean, an effect enhanced by the upmarket appearance of the **St Martin's on the Isle Hotel**, which enjoys magnificent sunsets and views across to uninhabited Teän and St Helen's. The hotel's restaurant, Teän, was awarded a Michelin star in January 2008 – the menu includes stand-out starters of Cornish mackerel and Scillonian sea bass as a main course.

Rival beach Middle Town is backed by dunes, sheltering the smoothly run **St Martin's Campsite** just behind. Like the St Agnes site, families have been returning for years, sometimes even to the same favourite pitch. Children quickly form friendships and wander off on shell-gathering forays at low tide, crab-hunts at the quay or trips to the barn to borrow books or buy eggs and vegetables. The lack of traffic makes the island one big adventure playground, and children won't miss TV or computers here.

The spinal road linking Lower, Middle and Higher Towns provides head-clearing views of the archipelago and connects the island's services, from the food-serving **Sevenstones Inn** at the west end to **St Martin's Bakery** at the east. Both are run by self-taught baker Toby Tobin-Dougan, whose lovingly crafted loaves, croissants and pastries cause daily queues to form outside the bakery. Nearby is a cluster of other enterprises, including the Post Office Stores, North Farm Gallery, Glenmoor Gift Shop and **Polreath Tea Rooms & Guesthouse**. The road heads downhill to the high-water quay at Par Beach, a perfect crescent of crunchy white sand. From here it's a short walk past the gig sheds, tennis court and cricket pitch to **St Martin's Vineyard**, which produces white, red and sparkling wines in old flower fields. Tasting tours are available and the shop sells the wines and other local products. Next door is the **Little Arthur Café**, serving the freshest meals made from delicious home-grown and local organic ingredients – booking is essential.

Footpaths allow easy wandering over purple heather and golden gorse and down to the deserted northern beaches at Great and Little Bays. From the latter, White Island (pronounced 'wit') can be reached at low water to explore Underland Girt, a huge underground cave, but watch out for the incoming tide. The island's natural wildness contrasts with the neat rows of carnations and narcissi cultivated at **Churchtown Farm**. Visitors can call in to find out more about this historic Scillonian industry and send flowers to the mainland.

TRESCO

Lying between St Martin's and Bryher, Tresco has a somewhat manicured appearance and is certainly the most commercial of the off-islands. Its unusual status as the mini empire of the

St Martin's on the Isle Hotel
St Martin's
01720 422090
www.stmartinshotel.co.uk

St Martin's Campsite
St Martin's
01720 422888
www.stmartinscampsite.co.uk

Sevenstones Inn
St Martin's
01720 423560

St Martin's Bakery
St Martin's
01720 423444

Polreath Tea Rooms & Guesthouse
St Martin's
01720 422046

St Martin's Vineyard
St Martin's
01720 423418
www.stmartinsveineyard.co.uk

Little Arthur Café
St Martin's
01720 422457

Churchtown Farm
Higher Town, St Martin's
01720 422169

Dorrien-Smith family, which leases it from the Duchy of Cornwall, contributes to this feeling of just-so orderliness. Nevertheless, Tresco is a charming island with its fair share of gorgeous, empty beaches like Pentle and Appletree Bays, and its world-renowned **Abbey Gardens**, a must-see for any visitor.

The subtropical gardens dominate Tresco's southern half and also offer a shop, a café and the Valhalla exhibition of ship figureheads. Founded by Augustus Smith in 1834 around the ruins of a 12th-century Benedictine priory, these 17 acres cram in over 20,000 exotic plants from 80 countries, including proteas, date palms and cacti – rather like Kew without the glass. Wandering among such floral fecundity is a heady experience and a reminder of the favoured position of the Scillies. Yet at Tresco's northern end the cliffs bear the brunt of storms and the island becomes more rugged. Here, the ruins of King Charles's Castle and Cromwell's Castle can be explored and bloodthirsty children will be thrilled by views of the replica gibbet atop Hangman's Island, a large rock where 500 Royalists are said to have been executed on one day during the Civil War.

Straddling the island's centre are the genteel settlements of Old and New Grimsby. The expensive Island Hotel and the sailing school are located at Old Grimsby, while the Estate Office, pub/restaurant/B&B New Inn, impressively stocked Tresco Stores, bike hire and Gallery Tresco are on the west side at New Grimsby. For all accommodation options, including dozens of self-catering and timeshare cottages, see www.tresco.co.uk.

BRYHER

A short boat ride from Tresco but a world away in mood is Bryher, population 78, the smallest community of the Isles. There is a strong sense of self-sufficiency here, illustrated by the fine 'hedge veg' stalls set out by smallholders. These help-yourself, honesty-box booths selling seasonal fruit, vegetables, preserves and even bulbs and flowers can be found all over the islands, and are a particular boon to campers and self-caterers.

Northern Bryher offers spectacular views from Watch Hill, Shipman Head Down and Badplace Hill above Hell Bay. Nothing stands between these rocks and Newfoundland, so watching the

Star Castle Hotel p79

Abbey Gardens
Tresco
01720 424105

Further reading

RL Bowley *The Fortunate Isles: The Story of the Isles of Scilly*
Andrew Cooper *Secret Nature of the Isles of Scilly* Comprehensive illustrated guide to the flora and fauna.
Paddy Dillon *Walking in the Isles of Scilly: A Guide to Exploring the Islands*
Michael Morpurgo *Why the Whales Came*; *The Wreck of the Zanzibar*; *Arthur, High King of Britain* Historical novels for children set in the Scillies.

Websites

www.scillyonline.co.uk
Locally run resource for visitors and residents on all aspects of life on Scilly.
www.simplyscilly.co.uk
Official Tourist Board website.
www.scilly.gov.uk
Council of the Isles of Scilly website.
www.scillywebcam.com

Fraggle Rock
01720 422222

Bryher Campsite
01270 422886

Hell Bay Hotel
01720 422947
www.tresco.co.uk/stay/hell-bay

Rat Island Sailboat Company
Porthmellon, St Mary's/Tresco
01720 422060

Bennetts Boatyard
Green Bay, Bryher
07979 3933206
St Martin's
07881 802964
www.bennettboatyard.com

Isles of Scilly Diving School
Higher Town, St Martin's
01720 422848
www.scillydiving.com

ScillyDiving
Higher Town, St Martin's
01720 423420
www.scillydiving.com

St Mary's Riding Centre
Maypole, St Mary's
01720 423855
www.horsesonscilly.co.uk

Island Wildlife Tours
42 Sally Port, St Mary's
01720 422212
www.islandwildlifetours.co.uk

Scilly Walks
01720 423855
www.scillywalks.co.uk

Isles of Scilly Steamship Company
0845 710 5555
www.islesofscilly-travel.co.uk

Tourist Office
Hugh Street, St Mary's
01720 422536

surf crash in is an exhilarating sight. By contrast the east and south coast have safe, clear waters ideal for divers, and Rushy Bay, overlooking uninhabited Samson, is one of the best beaches in the Scillies. Former children's laureate and Bryher devotee Michael Morpurgo has set several of his books here, and young fans will enjoy discovering the landscapes that inspired him. They'll also enjoy the huge home-made pizzas at the **Fraggle Rock** pub or fresh pasties from Bryher Stores. Both are handy for the discreet **Bryher Campsite**, sheltered between two hills with views to Tresco. Wilder views from the **Hell Bay Hotel** on the exposed west side come with a much steeper price tag.

ACTIVITIES

You can't escape the outdoors in the Scillies, and why would you want to when it's so beguilingly beautiful?

Get out on the water with the **Rat Island Sailboat Company**, which offers sailing and windsurf instruction plus kayak, boat and equipment hire, or, if you're on Bryher or St Martin's, with **Bennetts Boatyard**. For a different perspective get under the water on a diving course or snorkelling safari run by the **Isles of Scilly Diving School**. Keen divers can charter a boat from **ScillyDiving** to explore some of the Scillies' 150-odd dive sites. If you just want to sit back and enjoy the view, take a special trip on one of the island launches to see puffins, seabirds, seals and Bishop Rock Lighthouse. Ask at the quays for details.

Landlubbers can saddle up at **St Mary's Riding Centre** for hacks through the countryside, suitable for all abilities. To discover the islands' remarkably diverse flora and fauna, join a guided walk with **Island Wildlife Tours**. An archaeological ramble with **Scilly Walks** will help you make sense of Britain's densest concentration of Bronze Age monuments.

TRAVEL INFORMATION

The **Isles of Scilly Steamship Company**'s *Scillonian III* sails regularly from March to the end of October from Penzance to St Mary's. Crossing time is 2hrs 40mins. Fares start at £76 adult or £38 child (2-15 years) for a saver return.

The helpful **Tourist Office** offers comprehensive accommodation listings and a vacancy service.

Inter-island launches run daily throughout the season according to the tides. Check times at the islands' quays.

WHEN TO GO

With the *Scillonian III* timetable running from March to the end of October, it is possible to visit by boat through three seasons. Spring flowers come early and migrating birds stop off on their journey making this a good time for nature-lovers, though autumn brings even more migrating birds, some of them very rare. Tresco opens all year round, and there are always many exotic plants in flower. Even in the height of summer the beaches are never remotely crowded and sunshine hours are above the national average. Enterprises that lie dormant during the quieter months while locals get on with the day job swing into action and accommodation can be very hard to find at short notice. The campsites book up months in advance, so plan your trip to the Scillies well ahead.

St Aubin's Harbour p87

Jersey

ROUTE   Poole ▶ Jersey

With fun to be had in, on and around Jersey's pristine coast, the littoral minded can sail, surf, swim or dive into the crystal depths. And after exploring the ancient country lanes, the woods and valleys, you'll have an appetite worthy of the island's gourmet restaurants, cosy cafés and seafood shacks.

Written by **Sam Le Quesne**

Portelet p88

Durrell Wildlife Conservation Trust p86

Poole ▸ Jersey
3 hours

Active break; beaches; family
holiday; food; watersports

THE TRIP

The fastest route to Jersey is to take the high-speed ferry with Condor Ferries from Poole, which operates every two-to-three days in spring and autumn and has daily sailings in summer and holidays (between November and mid-March there is only a slow service from Portsmouth). Having made the train journey to Poole (around 2hrs from London Waterloo), you will need to allow 20 minutes to walk to the ferry terminal and allow an hour for check-in. Two vessels work this fast route, both accommodating 750 passengers and 185 cars. Straightforward bar, restaurant and shopping facilities help the time pass quicker, as does the opportunity to plant the sprogs in front of a DVD in the children's area. Be on deck as you near Jersey so you can see the sea-sculpted architecture of the coastline surge into view. Jersey's beaches, cliffs and coves have changed little over the centuries, even if the port of St Helier now presents a thoroughly modern skyline. There is a great sense of occasion as the boat slows in its approach past the majestic outline of Elizabeth Castle, with the busy traffic of small craft zipping around you.

THE DESTINATION

It may not be big, but Jersey is certainly clever. With just 45 square miles of land and fewer than 90,000 residents, this beautiful island has managed to keep its identity when all around are losing theirs. True, it is a British territory (you'll find M&S and Boots on the high street, you can buy a sausage roll from a bakery or a pint of bitter in a pub), but this is no ordinary chip off the mainland block. For one thing, the States of Jersey has its own political system, with its own tax laws, healthcare and judiciary, all of which mean the flavour (and, some would argue, the quality) of life here is palpably different to anywhere else in Britain. And this same idiosyncratic spirit extends to the appearance of the island, which owes just as much to its nearest neighbour, France, as to the sovereign influence of Her Maj. Street names are almost all in French (or what you might take to be French: many of them are, in fact, in Jèrriais, the island's native language); the architecture of the granite farm buildings, the ancient network of narrow lanes and the lush, sloping fields are strongly reminiscent of the topography of rural Normandy, just across the water. Even the local residents mostly have French names.

But, to dispel some common misconceptions, let's be clear that English is indeed the language of Jersey (although some – albeit a dwindling number – still speak Jèrriais) and sterling is the currency (of which there is also a Jersey version – featuring highly satisfying pound notes in the place of coins, and quaint watermarks of long-lashed Jersey cows).

Of the island's 12 parishes, the capital, St Helier, is the financial, commercial and residential hub. Known locally simply as 'town', it encompasses the main pedestrianised shopping area (with its Victorian covered markets selling locally grown fruit and veg, and trawler-fresh fish and seafood), as well as the commercial port, the ferry terminal and the highest concentration of restaurants, bars and nightlife. Also in town is the award-winning **Jersey Museum**, which provides a cogent and entertaining overview of island life, past and present. And just around the corner, the newly housed **Jersey Tourism** has a wealth of information on what to see and how to see it – its map of the island's cycle routes is well worth picking up, and you can hire a bike to go with it from nearby **Zebra**. Alternatively, car hire outlets abound in this area of town, where you'll also find the brand-new bus station serving all corners of the island (for timetables, see www.thisisjersey.com).

THE MAGNETIC NORTH

At the top of the compass is Jersey's most elevated shoreline, where rose-tinted granite cliffs tumble down to the sea. You'll find miles of great walking and hiking, with the largest network of footpaths accessed via Les Platons car park (where an occasional bacon roll van makes for a satisfying ersatz picnic) and the area known as Égypte (be sure to bring a container in late summer or early autumn, as the brambles here are heavy with juicy blackberries). But perhaps the most satisfying cliff path around these parts is the four-mile single-file track that connects two of Jersey's prettiest ports, Bonne Nuit and Bouley Bay. The former, a picturesque little fishing harbour, has a small but perfectly formed patch of golden sand, especially popular with young children due

JERSEY

Jersey Museum
The Weighbridge, St Helier
01534 633300
www.jerseyheritagetrust.org

Jersey Tourism
Liberation Place, St Helier
01534 448800
www.jersey.com

Zebra
9 Esplanade, St Helier
01534 736556

Corbière Lighthouse p88

Bouley Bay Dive Centre
Les Charrieres de Boulay, Trinity
01534 866990

Water's Edge Hotel
Bouley Bay, Trinity
01534 862777
www.watersedgehotel.co.je

Pure Adventure
01534 769165
www.purejersey.com

Hungry Man
Rozel Harbour, Trinity
01534 863227

Navigator
Granite Corner, Havre de Rozel, Trinity
01534 861444

Durrell Wildlife Conservation Trust
Les Augres Manor, La Profonde Rue,
Trinity
01534 860000
www.durrellwildlife.org

Gorey Watersports
Longbeach, Grouville
07797 816528

to its colony of tame ducks who spend their days waddling up and down the slipway. There's also a simple, friendly café with a charming terrace, and a good line in cappuccinos, freshly filled sarnies and local dairy ice-cream.

Bouley Bay, on the other hand, is a little more action-packed. A tortuous two-lane road (the venue for an annual motor race) winds down to the harbour itself, where you'll find access to a pretty pebble beach (you can park on the roadside by the Black Dog pub, if there are no allocated spaces left). The steeply shelving beach and superb underwater visibility make Bouley Bay a great spot for swimming (to which end, a well-maintained landing stage is permanently moored a few hundred yards offshore) and, especially, for snorkelling and diving. **Bouley Bay Dive Centre** is right next to the beach (as is a lively little trailer caff, offering fry-ups and seafood), should you want to make a day of it. And for those lodging at the beautifully located **Water's Edge Hotel** home is just a few steps away.

Also up north is the lovely beach of Plémont, which is well worth the climb down the several flights of concrete steps that save you having to tackle the precipitous cliffs that encircle this funnel of golden sand (at high tide it disappears entirely). There's often a small wave here, which is ideal for belly-boarding and body surfing but works up enough power on a rough day to knock junior swimmers off their feet. More good swimming is to be found just around the corner at Grève de Lecq, another sandy, popular beach with plenty of shelter from the surrounding headlands. But if this all sounds a little tame, you can take a more adrenalin-fuelled approach to these cliffy coves by getting in on the coasteering action courtesy of **Pure Adventure**, which organises everything from rock-scrambling and sea kayaking to dinghy sailing and power boating. And finally, bookending the northern fringe of the island are the rugged clifftop ruins of Grosnez Castle, at the eastern tip, and the colourful pier and decent eateries of Rozel Harbour to the west – try the **Hungry Man** on a budget or the **Navigator** for a seafood odyssey.

Heading inland from here leads to the enclave of agricultural fields, picturesque farmhouses and sleepy 'green lanes' (where 15mph speed limits give precedent to leg and pedal power) that is the parish of Trinity. This is also where you'll find the world-renowned **Durrell Wildlife Conservation Trust**. Devoted entirely to the preservation and propagation of endangered species, this beautiful, rambling facility belongs to an enlightened age of zoo-keeping. The late naturalist and author Gerald Durrell may no longer be headquartered in the Trust's 16th-century manor house, but his pragmatic, upbeat approach to conservation is still at the heart of everything that goes on here.

EASTERN DELIGHTS

With the houses and beaches of France in plain sight (in fact, don't be surprised if your mobile picks up a text message welcoming you to the French networks), the east coast has an appropriately foreign flavour. The beaches here are more like those you'd associate with holiday snaps – craggy and pine-fringed, the brightly coloured sails of dinghies and windsurfers crisscrossing in the bay. You'll find great swimming, as well as waterskiing and windsurfing – courtesy of **Gorey Watersports** – on the sand and sea-grass sweep of Grouville Bay, while at the top of the beach the picture-postcard Gorey Harbour is watched over by **Mont Orgueil Castle**. The austere façade of this 13th-century castle conceals a vast range of rough and tumble children's activities (from dressing up and fighting with wooden swords, to monkeying around in the panoramic play area), along with some expertly curated historical exhibits charting the castle's construction and the varied fortunes of its tenants. Contemplate this new information over a drink (and, perhaps, some excellent food) at the **Castle Green** gastropub or on the terrace of harbourside **Suma's**, where polished service and views of the floodlit castle make great additions to some low-key fine dining.

Beyond the castle is St Catherine's Bay, where a huge breakwater provides welcome shelter (and, by the way, excellent mackerel fishing – feathers, bait and cheap rods are all available from the hole-in-the-wall shops on the breakwater itself). But if you'd rather have a less bloody encounter with the local marine life, why not join up with one of the **National Trust for Jersey**'s regular rock-pooling tours? Or, better still, just meet your fish on the plate, along with mountains of fresh side dishes and a wonderful view to ponder, on the terrace of the **Driftwood Café**.

Out of sight of the sea, meanwhile, is the splendid **Longueville Manor Hotel**, where country house surroundings and a world-class restaurant are a temptation to never stray beyond the property's 14th-century gates.

SOUTHERN COMFORTS

The best time to visit the south-eastern tip of the island is at low tide, when you will be treated to the sight of some extraordinary rock formations, almost lunar in their otherworldliness. If you have the time (and stamina) to explore this area properly, Jersey Tourism organises a superb programme of low-tide walks – notably the 'Moon Walk' among the rocks and pools, and the 'Twin Towers' romp, which connects the dots between the area's historic Martello towers. And seafood fans' take note: in the evening, the beachside café just down the road from here transforms into **Green Island Restaurant**, a cosy and convivial joint serving excellent fish and fruits de mer.

Dead centre on Jersey's south coast is St Aubin's Bay, a wide reach of sand extending from the edge of town to cute St Aubin's harbour. It is on the quays surrounding this old-fashioned harbour, with its busy community of local sailors and fishermen, and its romantic fort just a couple of hundred yards off the pier heads, that you'll find an enclave of excellent drinking and dining options. Choose between the historic **Old Court House** pub or the spanking new **Boat House**, a waterside bar, brasserie and restaurant rolled into one. But serious foodies will want to try the fusion menu and laid-back, beachy vibe at the **Salty Dog**. All of which make St Aubin's a great place to base yourself, either in the sweet **Beechwood House** guesthouse or the swankier **La Haule Manor**.

At the town end of the bay, amid the thriving area surrounding St Helier harbour (known to everyone as 'the waterfront'), the marina is ground zero for yacht charters, rubber dinghy trips and fishing jaunts – again, **Pure Adventure** are the people to talk to. The majority of the best dining options are within walking distance of here, too – notably the Michelin-starred **Bohemia** or the small but perfectly groomed **Rojo** – as well as the most central hotels. Of

Mont Orgueil Castle
Gorey, St Martin
01534 8532920
www.jerseyheritagetrust.org

Castle Green
La Route de la Côte, St Martin
01534 840218

Suma's
Le Mont de Gouray, St Martin
01534 853291

National Trust for Jersey
01534 483193
www.nationaltrustjersey.org

Driftwood Café
Archirondel, La Route de la Côte, St Martin
01534 852157

Longueville Manor Hotel
Longueville Road, St Saviour
01534 725501
www.longuevillemanor.com

Green Island Restaurant
Green Island, St Clement
01534 857787

Old Court House
Le Boulevard, St Aubin's Harbour, St Brelade
01534 746433

Boat House
1 North Quay, St Aubin, St Brelade
01534 744226

Salty Dog
Le Boulevard, St Aubin's Harbour, St Brelade
01534 742760

Beechwood House
High Street, St Aubin, St Brelade
01534 767547

La Haule Manor
La Neuve Route, St Brelade
01534 746778
www.lahaulemanor.com

Pure Adventure
01534 769165
www.purejersey.com

Bohemia
Green Street, St Helier
01534 880588

Rojo
10 Bond Street, St Helier
01534 729904

JERSEY

these, the boutique **Club Hotel & Spa**, the upmarket **Pomme d'Or** and the old-school **Grand** are the best. And, even if the rack rate at the Grand might send you scurrying for the tourist office's B&B list, do try to make time for a cocktail or three in its chicer-than-thou Champagne Lounge, before heading round the corner to the island's best pasta joint, the intimate and affordable **La Cantina**.

But if it's beach life you're after, make a beeline for the next bay along, St Brelade's, where a wide stretch of immaculately maintained golden sand is surrounded by what is arguably some of the most striking scenery in Jersey: at one end, a fisherman's chapel with sloping cemetery and ancient jetty; at the other, the cliffs and striped tower of Ouaisne. The beach is wide and long enough to feel uncrowded even on an August bank holiday, and an elegant promenade with various kiosks and restaurants – notably an award-winning, glass-fronted **Pizza Express** – mean that it's possible to stay on and around your deckchair from morning till dusk. But if you get itchy feet, the idyllic cove of Portelet is just beyond the headland, waiting to be explored. This tiny bay curls around a grass-topped outcrop, complete with ancient burial site, whose secluded vantage points can be accessed via a small sand causeway or, as the tide rises, a short swim from the beach. Alternatively, if you prefer your views with a pint in your hand, you'll get them in spades overlooking the bay at the **Old Portelet Inn**.

WESTERLY WAVES

If you love to surf, the west coast is where you'll be spending most of your time. And you'll be in good company, whatever the season, for even on a rain-lashed, steel-clouded December afternoon, you will still find a crowd of local surfers paddling out into the vast Atlantic-battered expanse that is St Ouen's Bay. Stretching over several miles of pristine sand, fringed by rugged dunes and storm-blasted pines, and uninterrupted by any development, this bay is one long, wild and wonderful beach. People come here to surf (if you need a board or lessons, ask the lads at **Jersey Surf School**), to skim across the sand on blokarts (talk to **Pure Adventure**), to beach-cast for bass (for that, you're on your own) or simply to light a barbie and watch the sun set between the reef-mounted La Rocco Tower far out in the bay and the lonely, majestic sentinel of Corbière Lighthouse at its southernmost point. And if you haven't brought a picnic, don't worry, you can join the surf bums, the families and the flip-flopped drifters either at the **Watersplash Beach Bar & Diner** or at **Big Vern's** for a beer, a burger or a bit of both.

Turning back inland from here brings you to the quintessential country parishes of St Mary and St Lawrence. Many of the island's 46 miles of 'green lanes' are to be found in these rural parishes, and you can walk for hours among the potato fields, cattle pastures and farms, where you'll find honesty boxes offering crates of delicious apples or bags of ruby-red tomatoes to passers-by. But to travel an even greater distance (a couple of centuries, say), immerse yourself in the island's past at **Hamptonne Country Life Museum** in St Lawrence, where a perfectly restored 17th-century farm continues untouched by the passing of time. Also in St Lawrence is a snapshot of the island's more recent history in the form of the **Jersey War Tunnels**, which relates fascinating, often moving perspectives of the German Occupation of the island during World War II.

Club Hotel & Spa
Green Street, St Helier
01534 876500
www.theclubjersey.com

Pomme d'Or
Liberation Square, St Helier
01534 880110
www.seymourhotels.com

Grand
Esplanade, St Helier
01534 722301
www.grandjersey.com

La Cantina
7 Pierson Road, St Helier
01534 724988

Pizza Express
La Route de la Baie, St Brelade
01534 499049

Old Portelet Inn
La Route de Noirmont, St Brelade
01534 741899

Jersey Surf School
The Surf Shak, Watersplash, St Peter
01534 484005
www.jerseysurfschool.co.uk

Watersplash Beach Bar & Diner
La Grande Route des Mielles, St Peter
01534 482885

Big Vern's
La Grande Route des Mielles, St Peter
01534 481705

Hamptonne Country Life Museum
La Rue de la Patente
01534 863955
www.jerseyheritagetrust.org

Jersey War Tunnels
Les Charrieres Malorey
01534 860808
www.jerseywartunnels.com

JERSEY

IN THE AREA

It is only a short hop from Jersey across the water to St Malo, and the many attractions of Guernsey are just under an hour's boat ride away, but if you're thinking of making a day trip, there is really only one place to go: the island of Sark. Measuring just three miles by half a mile, this shard-like protuberance of granite cliffs and gorse-covered headlands is home to one of the most unusual communities in the British Isles. Here you'll find no cars, just a handful of shops and a smattering of restaurants, and an intricate network of sandy tracks and tree-shaded lanes that wind between sloping fields and meadows on their journey down to the sea. In the place of beaches are craggy inlets and smugglers' coves with romantic names and clear, cold water in which to plunge on a hot summer's day. The charm of this place is, in many ways, its sheer inaccessibility, and the resulting sense of peace and isolation. And the calm atmosphere among the shops of the tiny main street and the terraces of the various hostelries feels entirely unaffected, as does the welcome at the island's various hotels.

Sark is a naturalist's paradise, with a myriad unspoiled habitats for local marine life and sea birds, as well as all manner of wild plantlife to admire (for information on walks, see www.sark.info). Also well worth a look is La Seigneurie, the 18th-century seat of the island's feudal seigneurs. Formal gardens and the grand architecture of the main house make it ideal for a leisurely stroll on a sunny afternoon. But for something a little more feral, point your bike in the direction of the north end of the island, where the bluebell-strewn Eperquerie Common is a paradise in springtime, while the elaborate nooks, crannies and rock corridors of the Boutique Caves beneath are there to be explored at low tide throughout the year. Legends abound about smugglers storing their wares in these subterranean chambers, and this same Peter Pan allure is very much present in the Gouliot Caves, over to the west, whose secret Jewel Cave is so well hidden that it can only be accessed in the company of a qualified guide.

With appetite duly whetted, stop for a snack at **Squires Restaurant** or a pub lunch at the **Bel Air Inn**. And if you can't tear yourself away, the picturesque **Dixcart Bay Hotel** or the foodie **La Sablonnerie** offer good, affordable accommodation.

Get there and away on the high-speed **Marin Marie** ferry (50mins from St Helier). And to get around faster than your legs will carry you, hire bikes from **A to B**, **Avenue** or **Sark Cycle Hire**.

TRAVEL INFORMATION

Condor Ferries also operates out of Weymouth (journey time, 3hrs 25mins; daily sailings in summer and peak holidays, twice weekly out of season). Having made the train journey to Weymouth (around 2hrs 30mins from London Waterloo), you will need to allow ten minutes to walk from the train station to Weymouth ferry terminal. If you enjoy a slow boat, Condor also operates a conventional ferry service every day except Sunday from Portsmouth year-round, complete with cabins, a panoramic bar – and a 10.5-hour crossing.

WHEN TO GO

Summer. Surfers come in spring and autumn.

Further reading

John Nettles *Bergerac's Jersey* Out of print but you know you want it.
Rosanne Guille *Sark Sketch Book*
Douglas Botting *Gerald Durrell: The Authorized Biography* The life of Jersey's most famous adopted son.

Websites

www.jersey.com is an excellent, exhaustive resource.

JERSEY

Squires Restaurant
01481 832422

Bel Air Inn
01481 832052

Dixcart Bay Hotel
01481 832015

La Sablonnerie
01481 832061

Marin Marie
www.manche-iles-express.com

A to B
01481 832844

Avenue
01481 832102

Sark Cycle Hire
01481 832276

Condor Ferries
www.condorferries.co.uk

Zeebrugge p96

Belgian Beaches

ROUTE London ▸ Brussels ▸ Ostend

You want a quick trip to sun-dappled European beaches basking in the heat? Don't just think Med. There can be few beaches easier to reach than the 69 kilometres of unbroken sand where Belgium squeezes in between France and the Netherlands to dip its toe in the North Sea. Once there, the pace is perfect for settling down to some serious eating, low-gradient cycling and, should the weather turn inclement, a huge range of indoor sights and activities.

Written by **Edoardo Albert**

Mercator p94

THE TRIP

Well, it couldn't really be any easier. Catch the Eurostar from the new St Pancras terminal and two hours later you're at Bruxelles-Midi station. The Eurostar fare also covers onward railway journeys within Belgium, so it's not even necessary to queue up for an onward ticket; simply hop on to the next train for Ostend – Oostende in the local language – and a little over an hour later you're there. (Blankenberge, Zeebrugge and Knokke-Heist also have direct rail connections to Brussels.) Depending on how long you have to wait for your onward train, it shouldn't take more than four hours between leaving St Pancras and arriving at your hotel.

There's one thing parents should bear in mind during the journey: you have to pay €0.50 to use the toilets at Bruxelles-Midi, so make sure you have some change with you. There is a machine at the entrance to the toilets that will change down €1 and €2 coins, but having nothing but notes to hand means buying something, anything, in a desperate rush while a three-year-old is doing the cross-legged hopping dance under your feet. Anyone want to buy a Tintin keyring?

 St Pancras International ▸
Ostend **3 hours 42 minutes**

★ Beaches; family holiday; food & drink; shopping

Where can you snap up the latest fashions and the finest seafood?

If you like haute cuisine as much as you like haute couture you'll find the Flemish coast, in northern Belgium, a treat to visit. Here you'll discover the very best food the sea has to offer in its many gourmet restaurants. Why not sample a glass of wine at one of the area's Michelin-starred restaurants? And what better way to build up an appetite than by exploring the plethora of chic boutiques that stock all you could want in designer clothing, shoes and jewellery? After all, when you're eating five-star food, you'll want to look the part. **Find out in Flanders**

flanders
belgium

The Flemish Coast   www.visitflanders.co.uk

THE DESTINATION

The Belgian coast may not seem to have immediate appeal, given its cool latitude, the mud-brown surf of the North Sea, and the memories of war that linger in the abandoned gun emplacements pointing out to sea but, as always with Belgium, it pays to look beneath the surface. Up until the 19th century the unstable sands meant there wasn't much there apart from shifting dunes and itinerant shellfish scavengers – whence the fondness for mussels. Kings Leopold I and II changed everything by determining that the country should have its own, somewhat colder, version of the French Riviera. But in some ways their most important legacy wasn't the patina of regal approval, but Leopold II's coast tram (de Kusttram). The tram runs the entire length of Belgium's beaches, making this area one of the easiest to get around in Europe, and one of the best for families intent on doing more than just lie on a beach.

RIDING ON DE KUSTTRAM

Many a family lives in thrall to the transport obsession of its younger members, so for those with a young Thomas fanatic the **Kusttram** provides both a uniquely useful method of getting up and down the coast and an attraction in its own right. It's a train! In the road! If you can, grab the rear window seat for a panoramic view as the vehicle clangs its way from De Knokke in the east to De Panne in the west, some 70 halts in all. It stops at all the resorts on the coast and means that should the crowds and the beach-front apartments grow too stifling in one place, then a short trip can see you alighting among grass-covered dunes and relatively empty beaches. The trip from one end of the line to the other takes about two and a quarter hours, making all the coast accessible wherever you are staying. The service is used by tourists and locals alike with a tram every 20 minutes in winter, while in summer it functions almost like a metro, with the next service following after only five to ten minutes. Major stops have ticket offices, with the most useful fare for tourists being the €5 day pass (€1.50 for 6-11s; under-6s free) that allows unlimited travel for the day. Validate the ticket by inserting it into one of the machines in the tram; there's one by each of the three doors (note: if the machine says 'gesloten' it's not working). The central doors offer access without steps for those pushing push- or wheelchairs. Major stops have useful maps of the local area.

OSTEND

Ostend, with some 69,000 inhabitants, is the largest city on Belgium's coast. Indeed, Ostenders will tell you that it's the only city on the coast. And historically speaking, that's not far from the truth: along with Niuewpoort it was the only seaside settlement for centuries. Leopold II – intent on rivalling the French Riviera – made it one of Europe's most fashionable destinations but World War II wreaked much devastation, with post-war planners and developers leaving their own inimitable mark in the shape of some undistinguished apartment blocks, all jostling for that elusive sea view. The Channel Tunnel broke many of the ferry links between Ostend and Britain, but now the city has woken up both to its past and its potential future. Owing to its central position on the coast Ostend makes an

BELGIAN BEACHES

Kusttram
www.dekusttram.be

ideal holiday base, with nowhere much more than an hour away, and it also offers the greatest range of activities should the wind turn northerly and the temperature plummet. Indeed, there's a good case for saying that the city is a four-season destination, with winter offering brisk walks along the promenade overlooking a wide and deserted beach, followed by a cosy snuggle in to a neighbourhood bar or tea room, while summer means a packed beach and buzzing promenade.

As Ostend cannot depend on its weather, there are many activities and sights on offer – far more than you'd find in an equivalent Mediterranean resort. Try walking along the quay, from the Seamen's Memorial towards the railway station. First you'll pass the Fish Market (Visserskai), selling the morning's catch, then the **Nordzeeaquarium** (North Sea Aquarium). Younger children will enjoy the tanks showing some of the fish, crustaceans and cephalopods in the nearby sea, although teenagers might not be impressed by the low-key exhibits. A little further on more evidence of Ostend's maritime connections are provided, first by the *Amandine*, the last local trawler to fish in Icelandic waters, and now a restored museum ship, and in the yacht haven, the *Mercator*, a three-masted sailing ship that was the training vessel for officers in Belgium's merchant navy from 1932 to 1960.

Alternatively, catch the Kusttram from the railway station (towards Knokke) and hop off two stops later ('Duin en Zee') at the excellent **Earth Explorer**, a scientific theme park. Here are interactive exhibits explaining the workings of earth, air, wind and fire (note that if you get into the flume ride that runs through the volcano you end up, rather unexpectedly, getting wet at the end of the journey if you're sitting in the front). It's too good to leave for a bad day (in which case it can get unpleasantly crowded). Just behind the Earth Explorer, towards the dunes, there is an excellent playground and a short walk beyond squats **Fort Napoleon**, Europe's only intact Napoleonic fort, with a bistro inside and a fine, if expensive, restaurant stuck on the side. From the fort a minute's walk takes you over the dunes to a broad stretch of beach mercifully free of apartment blocks (and spot the later, World War II era, gun emplacements as you go).

But Ostend isn't only sand and science: art is represented in the eerie pictures of James Ensor (1860-1949). The **Ensorhuis** is where he lived and worked from 1875 to 1916. For something more up to date it's worth walking about a mile from Wapenplein, the central square (which turns into an ice rink from late November to 6 January), through the Leopold Park, to **PMMK, Museum voor Moderne Kunst-Aan-Zee** (Museum for Modern Art by the Sea). The surrounding area also contains the highest concentration of the tile-faced belle époque buildings that once filled Ostend, before bombs and builders did their worst. They can give one the curious impression of being in an old-fashioned municipal swimming pool, but are certainly better than the undistinguished apartment blocks erected in replacement.

Mammon-related amusements are to be found in the pedestrianised shopping streets around Wapenplein – fashion and shoes are well represented – and at the beachfront casino **Kursaal**, which also serves as a concert venue.

There may be a bad restaurant in Belgium but you'll struggle to find it. The Belgians seem to have succeeded in marrying the

Nordzeeaquarium
Visserskaai, Oostende
059 50 08 76
http://users.skynet.be/
noordzee.aquarium/

Amandine
35-Z Vindictivelaan, Oostende
059 23 43 01
www.amandine-museum.be

Mercator
Jachthaven Mercator, Oostende
059 70 56 54
www.zeilschip-mercator.be

Earth Explorer
128B Fortstraat, Oostende
059 70 59 59
www.earthexplorer.be

Fort Napoleon
Vuurtorenweg, Oostende
059 32 00 48
www.fortnapoleon.be

Ensorhuis
27 Vlaanderenstraat, Oostende
059 80 53 35

PMMK, Museum voor Moderne Kunst-Aan-Zee
11 Romestraat, Oostende
059 50 81 18
www.pmmk.be

Kursaal
Monacoplein, Oostende
059 70 51 11
www.kursaaloostende.be

Thermae Palace Hotel

finesse of French cookery with the hearty good appetite of northern Europeans, so no piddling around with perfectly formed gastronomic statements that wouldn't sate an anorexic: here the food fills the stomach as well as pleasing the palate. As for recommendations, are you sick of those over-designed eateries that strive for individualism but end up looking and feeling exactly the same? Then try the **Wiener Kaffeehaus** opposite the railway station where chintz remains defiantly king. There's a small terrace with lovely views over the yacht haven, but for the full effect venture inside for fake flowers, figurines, friendly service and exceptional crêpes.

The best place to stay, as far as views and history are concerned, remains the **Thermae Palace Hotel**, Leopold's old villa. In the centre of the old part of town, the **Golden Tulip Bero** is a modern and family-friendly hotel (the playroom and swimming pool come in handy if the weather turns). Or put the surfeit of apartments to your advantage: rent one. Try www.lacotebelge.be or www.panimmo.be. The local **tourist office** is exceptionally helpful; call in for maps, advice and help with planning your stay. If you're aiming on seeing a number of Ostend's sights, get an Ostend City Pass from the tourist office: for €19.90 (€9 children) it gives entrance to pretty well all Ostend's attractions, including those we've mentioned above, as well as the Atlantic Wall Museum (*see page 97*).

CYCLING

The coast is flat and full of bicycle lanes and tracks. So get on your bikes! There is no better way to get around when the weather's good. Cycle lanes are usually separated from road traffic and you can cycle the length of the coast, as well as heading inland for quieter rambles along waterways and lanes. All the resorts have places where you can hire bicycles, from ordinary mountain bikes to those four- and six-seater contraptions designed to exhaust parents and exhilarate children ('faster, Dad, faster'). In a fine example of joined-up transport thinking, the Belgian railway company, SNCB (look out for a capital B in an oval), hires out bikes from major stations (although note that they do not provide children's cycles). The local tourist offices

Wiener Kaffeehaus
28 Vindictivelaan, Oostende
059 23 89 10
www.wienerkaffeehaus.be

Thermae Palace Hotel
7 Koningin Astridlaan, Oostende
059 80 52 74
www.thermaepalace.be

Golden Tulip Bero
1A Hoftstraat, Oostende
059 70 23 35
www.hotelbero.be

Tourist Office
2 Monacoplein, Oostende
059 70 11 99
www.inenuitoostende.be

Nico Karts
44A Albert I Promenade, Oostende
059 233 481
www.nicokarts.be

Sandra-Strandfietsen
16 Albert I Promenade, Oostende
0478 407 921

Bredene
www.bredene.be

De Haan
www.dehaan.be

Old Corner
25 Koninklijke Baan, De Haan
059 23 30 50
www.oldcorner.be

Blankenberge
www.blankenberge.be

Sea Life
116 Koning Albert I Laan, Blankenberge
050 42 42 00
www.sealife.be

Serpentarium
146 Zeedijk, Blankenberge
050 42 31 63
www.serpentarium.be

Mini Train Expo
Leopold III-plein, Blankenberge
0477 31 53 79
www.minitrainexpo.be

Hotel Beaufort
11 De Smet de Naeyerlaan,
Blankenberge
050 42 92 61
www.hotelbeaufort.be

Zeebrugge
www.zeebrugge.be

Knokke-Heist
www.knokke-heist.be

are good sources of information, or to do some pre-planning see www.visitbelgium.com/bike.htm. In Ostend bikes can be hired from **Nico Karts** or **Sandra-Strandfietsen**.

EAST FROM OSTEND

Heading east from Ostend, the first resort you come to is **Bredene,** with its extensive camp grounds. Not the most handsome of places, but it has the advantage of not having a promenade, thus the beach is not defaced by the ugly line of apartment blocks that seals shore from sea too often along the coast. But a little further along the coast that problem is solved completely. **De Haan** is head and shoulders the prettiest resort on the Belgian coast and it does this by ensuring its head and shoulders don't protrude too high into the sky. Stringent planning regulations mean that no building can have more than a couple of storeys, and careful restoration has ensured that most of its original belle époque buildings remain in pristine condition. The quiet streets, large expanses of open, green spaces, playgrounds and, of course, the beach mean that this is probably the best resort on the coast for a family with younger children. Within frisbee flight of the beach **Old Corner** provides child-pleasing food and wallet-friendly beds.

Continuing east, **Blankenberge** is the opposite of De Haan: brash beachfront apartments (although many beautiful buildings survive in the town centre), a pier, endless retail opportunities and, in summer, heaving crowds. If you like a buzz, this is the place to be. Add in the marine attractions of the coast's largest and best aquarium, **Sea Life**; the reptilian charms of the **Serpentarium**, right on the promenade; and the transport attractions of the model railway exhibition in the train station (**Mini Train Expo**); and you have a lively resort. As a place to stay, and eat, **Hotel Beaufort** escapes the apartment block blight by dint of being in a listed building.

Zeebrugge is a working container port, one of Europe's biggest. The coast tram gives you a good chance to see the huge ships unloading. The final resort, and the eastern terminus of de Kusttram, is **Knokke-Heist**, Belgium's capital of bling. It's the sort of place people stay to be seen, so to take a look at them have a stroll along the promenade and admire the designer togs and designer bods. To stay in appropriate style book in to **Manoir du Dragon**. Something considerably less expensive can quickly be reached, however. Either walk briskly, or hire a bike (note that bikes can't be taken in), and head east along Kustlaan and then Bronlaan to **Het Zwin** nature reserve. It's the largest sanctuary on the coast, with 150 hectares of dunes and beach as they used to be before the rest of Belgium decided it needed its own slice of sea view. Breathe deep. Next stop: Holland.

WEST FROM OSTEND

If you only have time to head one way from Ostend, go east. But the trusty coast tram runs west, too, and the most notable attraction is only a short distance from Ostend. Get off at Domein Raversijde for 50 hectares of dunes and the **Atlantic Wall Museum**, an intact section of the coastal defences that the Germans built to prevent an Allied landing during World War II. The tram passes below the mute guns, but it still gives one pause for thought when you look out to the bare beaches and think how exposed the men coming ashore many miles west in Normandy must have been to murderous gunfire.

From **Middelkerke** to the end of the line (and the end of Belgium) at **De Panne**, resorts and apartment blocks are interspersed with areas of undeveloped dunes. It's generally quieter, which does make it well suited to a restful off-season break. Even at rush hour the cars are few and the people relaxed. A good base is the modern **Hotel Apostroff** in Koksijde, which is a fine place to de-stress. And at the penultimate stop there are the singular pleasures of **Plopsaland** (yes, you are reading that right), a Belgian theme park much loved by local children. Where better to end a trip to this gently surreal country?

IN THE AREA

Ostend, Blankenberge, Zeebrugge and Knokke all have rail links to Bruges, with trains every hour. The journey time is short (not more than a quarter of an hour) and the effort well worth it. From here, onward connections put pretty much the whole of Belgium, and neighbouring Luxembourg, within easy reach.

TRAVEL INFORMATION

Eurostar runs several services a day to Brussels, with fares one way starting from £29.50. Onward railway travel in Belgium is free, so you can both arrive at, and leave, your destination by waving your Eurostar ticket at the ticket inspector.

Bicycles can be taken on to the coast tram.

Transeuropa Ferries runs from Ramsgate to Ostend (motor vehicles only, no foot passengers) with a sailing time of five hours, while **P&O** runs from Hull to Zeebrugge (14 hours sailing). As well as cars, P&O takes foot passengers and there's a courtesy bus on to Zeebrugge or Bruges. Transeuropa Ferries fares range from £70 to £112 return for a car and up to nine passengers. The fares on the P&O ferry from Hull to Zeebrugge start from £196 return (car and two passengers).

WHEN TO GO

Year-round, but don't expect much beach time during the winter.

Further reading

Hugo Claus *The Sorrow of Belgium* Life under occupation during World War II.
Harry Pearson *A Tall Man in a Low Land: Some Time Among the Belgians*
Rudy Rucker *As Above, So Below: A Novel of Peter Bruegel*

Websites

www.toerisme-oostende.be
www.visitflanders.co.uk
Useful tourist website.

Manoir du Dragon
73 Albertlaan, Knokke Heist
050 63 05 80
www.manoirdudragon.be

Het Zwin
Knokke Heist
050 60 70 86
www.zwin.be

Atlantic Wall Museum
636 Nieuwpoortsesteenweg, Raversijde
059 70 22 85
www.west-vlaanderen.be/raversijde

Middelkerke
www.middelkerke.be

De Panne
www.depanne.be

Hotel Apostroff
38 Lejeunelaan, Koksijde
058 52 06 09
www.apostroff.be

Plopsaland
De Panne
www.plopsaland.be

Eurostar
www.eurostar.com

Transeuropa Ferries
www.transeuropa.co.uk

P&O
www.POferries.com

North Main Street

Cork

ROUTE Fishguard ▶ Rosslare ▶ Cork City ▶ County Cork

A short car-ferry ride and an easy drive to Ireland's second city is an opportunity to shift down a few gears and soak up the atmosphere of a place that moves at its own pace. Sample some of the best cuisine in Ireland, brave the traditional dishes, quaff the local brew – and then head for the coast to visit an array of resorts and sandy coves. For the more adventurous, there is also the chance to explore the rugged landscape of West Cork and experience some of the best whale watching in Europe.

Written by **Brian Daughton**

River Lee p100

Farmgate Café & Restaurant p103

THE TRIP

From Fishguard it's a fairly short jaunt – between two and three-and-a-half hours depending on the type of ferry and the prevailing weather conditions – across the Irish Sea to Rosslare. Perhaps for such a short journey time it's not worth renting a cabin but Stena Line offers upgrades for a reasonable £15 extra to the comfortable armchairs of the first-class lounge, where it's easy to pass the entire trip in a relaxing doze, perusing the selection of newspapers or sipping the complimentary tea or coffee. Should you require it, an evening meal or tipple can also be provided at a reasonable cost by efficient and friendly staff. If you are not a night owl there are also crossings that depart just before noon, in the mid afternoon and in the early evening.

Upon landing in Ireland it's an easy onwards journey. There's a daily train service that runs to Cork from Rosslare via Limerick Junction, and there are also frequent buses. However, if you want to explore beyond Cork, you'll need to take, or hire, a car. From Rosslare it's a two-and-a-half hour drive through rolling, rich farmland. For the most part the road follows the line of the coast, giving views of the sea on your left.

 Fishguard ▶ Cork
4 hours 30 minutes

 Food & drink; wildlife

THE DESTINATION

'Irish by birth but Cork by the grace of God,' is the phrase locals proclaim in homage to their birthplace. Outside the gravitational pull of Dublin, Ireland's second city has a keen sense of its own worth and character. Despite a relatively small population (170,000), the city punches above its weight and is, to date, the smallest city ever to be the European Capital of Culture (in 2005). Well served by the second largest natural harbour in the world, it was once a thriving merchant city and in the days of ocean travel the final stop before crossing the Atlantic.

CORKING

One of Cork's favourite sons, the writer Frank O'Connor, once described his native city as having a 'tattered grace'. Though no longer entirely accurate, there is a frayed edge to the beauty of Cork and this is part of its allure. The city derives its name from the word Corcaigh, Gaelic for 'marshland', and that's just where it's built. The city was founded by St Finbarr in the sixth century as a monastic settlement. Legend has it that Cork's patriarch flung a giant serpent across the wastelands below the monastery. Its body is said to have forged the two branches of the River Lee when it fell back to earth.

The neo-Gothic cathedral of **St Finbarr** is built on the site of the old monastery and its two spires are a prominent sight in the city. The river does fork on entering Cork and meets again where it spills out into the harbour. The centre is, in fact, a tear-shaped island and this helps give the town its calm, village atmosphere. Some of the main thoroughfares were waterways, until they were covered over in 1704, and you can still see the moorings and steps leading up to some of the old merchants' houses. Of course, put a town and canals anywhere near each other and you end up with comparisons to Venice but Cork's real charms are made of earthier stuff. Much of it is in the topography. From the flat plain of the island centre the city spreads out quite steeply into the surrounding hills. Perhaps nowhere is the phrase 'downtown' more appropriate.

The city will appeal to the flâneur (a word that some claim is derived from the Irish word for 'libertine') in you, but to induce a bit of poetic reverie in your meanderings, you may need to first sup a pint of the black stuff. Murphys and Beamish are the two stouts brewed locally, which explains the faint whiff of malted barley you sometimes get along the southern quays. The city is blessed with some real Irish pubs that have so far held firm against the commercial temptations of 'Oirishness'. You could try **Roundy House** or, if you fancy a coffee next to an open fire with a view of the river, then the **Quay Co-Op** is your best bet. One of Cork's favourite places for a morning 'jar' is the **Long Valley** and it's possibly the best introduction to the city. The tradition of the 'slow pint' lives on here. As your stout slowly settles, unfold your newspaper, sit back, breathe in the 'tick tock' pulse of the place and observe what floats in on the morning tide. Peckish? Not to worry – the sandwiches here are legendary, at least for their size. Try the roast beef – perfect fuel for a stroll around the city. The Long Valley may have been the first place to see the potential for the gourmet sandwich.

Just around the corner from the Valley is Cork's oldest hotel,

St Finbarr
Bishop Street, Cork
021 496 8744

Roundy House
1 Castle Street, Cork
021 422 2202
www.theroundy.com

Quay Co-Op
24 Sullivan's Quay, Cork
021 317026
www.quaycoop.com

Long Valley
10 Winthrop Street, Cork
021 427 2144

CORK

the **Imperial**. Thackeray and Dickens once stayed and the hotel retains something of its 19th-century opulence. If something a little less grand is required, the guesthouses along the Western Road are centrally located, good value for money and popular with visitors. Try **Crawford House** or **Killarney House**. **Isaacs Hotel**, just north of the river, is a good base from which to explore the city.

TOP OF THE HILL TO YOU

Patrick Street – known locally as 'down Panna' – is Cork's main thoroughfare. In 2005, when the city was the European Capital of Culture, the road was spruced up by Catalan architect Beth Galí but despite the 'Ramblas' treatment, it is not as interesting as other streets in the city, being mainly home to the usual chains. Try continuing north across Patrick's Bridge and up the steepest hill in Ireland – St Patrick's Hill. It's worth the climb for the fantastic view of the city and the Georgian terraces running off to the right. But before you make your assault on the hill, look up to your left to the clock-bearing steeple with a gilded salmon perched on top. It is affectionately known as the 'four-faced liar' due to the fact that the four clocks on each of its faces tell a different time.

Another area worth a saunter is the grid of pedestrian streets and lanes tucked away between Patrick Street and Paul Street. This is Cork's Huguenot Quarter, where refugees fleeing religious persecution sought sanctuary. Today, it's home to craft shops and cafés. The **Ginger Bread House** does a brisk trade in coffee, pastries and sandwiches, as does **Insomnia**, which has a craft shop attached to the café. Also in the area is the **Vangard Gallery**, with interesting exhibits of Irish artists.

Of course, any river city worth its banks must have a water-side walk, and in this Cork does not disappoint. The Lee Walkway starts by the old distillery on the North Mall. From the centre, cross over any of the bridges to the north bank, turn left and follow the quay down to the distillery. With the river on your left, follow the tarmac path until you come to a recently constructed pedestrian bridge. Cross over and the path will eventually lead you on to the Mardyke. Straight ahead is the southern entrance to University College Cork. Follow the path up to the main quad to the **Lewis Glucksman Gallery** on your right. This splendid building of wood and steel was shortlisted for the Stirling Prize in 2005 and has been a welcome addition to the cultural life of the city. It provides a much more uplifting experience than Cork's other major gallery, the **Crawford**, which can be a fairly dispiriting affair. However, the restaurant at the latter is run by the celebrated Ballymaloe House, which ensures the food is more inspiring.

FITZGERALD'S PARK

To reach the park, retrace your steps from the university to the Mardyke. Turn left, and just past the Cork Cricket Club you'll find the entrance on your right. Cut through the park diagonally in a north-westerly direction, which will bring you to Cork's only cast-iron suspension bridge, known locally as the 'Shaky Bridge'. Before leaving, if some rest and recreation is needed, the park has a well-equipped children's playground, plus a child-friendly café and restaurant overlooking what is possibly the most

Isaacs Hotel

Imperial
79 South Mall, Cork
021 427 4040
www.flynnhotels.ie

Crawford House
Western Road, Cork
021 427 9000
www.crawfordguesthouse.com

Killarney House
Western Road, Cork
021 427 0290
www.killarneyguesthouse.com

Isaacs Hotel
48 MacCurtain Street, Cork
021 450 0011
www.isaacs.ie

Ginger Bread House
Paul Street, Cork
021 427 6411

Insomnia
19 French Church Street, Cork
021 427 9701

Vangard Gallery
Carey's Lane, Cork
021 427 8718
www.vangardgallery.com
Closed Aug

Lewis Glucksman Gallery
University College, Cork
021 490 1844
www.glucksman.org

Crawford
Emmet Place, Cork
021 490 7855/restaurant 021 427 4415
www.crawfordartgallery.com

CORK

Ballymaloe House

beautiful stretch of the River Lee. The **Cork Public Museum**, dedicated to Irish history, is also in the park and worth a visit. To continue the walk, cross the bridge and follow the steps up to Sunday's Well Road. Here you turn right and follow the road back into the city. However, you could detour and visit **Cork City Gaol**, which is now a museum. Look for the gaol sign on your left by the church.

ANOTHER PINT – AND SOME PIG'S TROTTERS

In Cork 'you're no one until you've been thrown out of the **Hi-B**'. The pub itself is a tiny room up a creaking staircase. On entering, you may think you've trespassed into someone's living room. Usually, there is a huddle of regulars arranged around the semicircular bar with Brian O'Donnell, the owner, holding court behind the counter – listen in on the wit, repartee and general banter at the bar. Take a pew at the counter if you dare, or retreat to the open fire in the corner, where you can warm your feet. For a winter walker the place is pure joy. Be warned though, that despite the air of cosy frivolity, Brian O'Donnell runs a tight ship and he can be notoriously prickly. Some of the cardinal sins are throwing coal on 'his' fire and ordering a non-alcoholic drink. Mobile phones can also incur wrath. Oh, and serving pints to women. You may want to challenge him on this one.

The English Market, entered via the vast, wrought iron gates on Princes Street or from the Grand Parade, is slap bang in the middle of the island centre. It's Europe's largest covered market – especially popular on rainy days – and is without doubt the heartbeat of Cork. It's a communal space where the great, the good and the poor gather to mingle, chat and, as they say locally, 'get their messages' (shop for food). While the origins of the market can be traced back to James I in 1610, the present building dates from 1786. In the Napoleonic Wars it even supplied corned beef to Wellington's troops. In 1980, however, it was badly damaged by fire but fortunately was refurbished by the Cork Corporation to an award-winning design.

There is no exclusivity around food here. You can buy everything from tripe to organic lamb. The market's commitment

Cork Public Museum
Fitzgerald's Park, Cork
021 427 0679

Cork City Gaol
Sunday's Well Road, Cork
021 430 5022
www.corkcitygaol.com

HI-B'
108 Oliver Plunkett Street, Cork

Spaniard p104

to traditional Cork favourites such as crubeens (pig's trotters), drisheen (blood sausage), corned mutton, spiced beef tripe and locally sourced beef and fish has seen its reputation soar. This is where the Cork cook stocks up and the market has been integral to the blossoming food culture in the region. With over 50 stalls arranged around three central aisles and different sections for meat, fish and vegetables it has the feel of a North African souk, given a Victorian makeover.

Having ogled some food you may well want to eat. Without doubt, your best bet is the **Farmgate Café & Restaurant**, which is located above the fountain at the Princes Street end of the English Market. The posters on the wall leading up the steps from the market to the restaurant are a comprehensive guide to everything that is going on. At the top of the stairs on your right is the balcony café section of the Farmgate, which is a great spot to soak up the beguiling hustle and watch the bustle of the market below. If in need of something more substantial, head across to the restaurant section, behind the glass front. It serves up possibly the best lunch in town, with a firm commitment to sourcing locally and in season. To emphasise this ethos Kay Harte, the owner, points up to the menu board, saying, 'What's on that board is what you get in the market below. Next month, you won't get a tomato out of me.'

Cork also has a healthy music and theatre scene. The four-day **Cork Jazz Festival**, usually held in late October, is a big draw for hundreds of musicians and thousands of music fans each year. The **Cork Opera House** has an all-year programme of drama, musicals and dance as well as opera. For traditional Irish music and a well-pulled pint try **An Spailpin Fanach**.

EAST COUNTY CORK

Heading east from the city on the N25, then turning off at Midleton in the direction of Ballycotton you'll come to **Ballymaloe House**, the restaurant, hotel and café run by the family of Irish TV chef Darina Allen. The sumptuous set lunch and five-course evening meal are worth starving for. If you feel inspired to hone your culinary skills, the **Ballymaloe Cookery School** is in the nearby village of Shanagarry.

Also in Shanagarry is the **Stephen Pearce Pottery & Gallery**, which sells the work of local artisans as well as pots, plates and bowls by Stephen Pearce himself.

Now fed and shopped, it's time for some air. Hop back into the car and drive for ten minutes to Ballycotton and the coast. To start the clifftop walk, go to the end of the village where the road splits. Follow it to the right upwards past an abandoned dance hall called the Cliff Palace. From there, with the sea on your left, follow signs for the East Cork Way. Take the coastal path, and you'll arrive in Ballyandreer after an hour's stroll. There is a lovely sandy cove here, perfect for cooling off on a summer's day. This walk is particularly popular with twitchers on account of the variety of birdlife to be seen.

Of course, there's nothing that works up a thirst more than a good walk. On returning to Ballycotton, slake that thirst at the **Inn by the Harbour**. Mary Rose and Gerry Lynch, the owners, also organise deep-sea angling from the inn's two fishing boats as well as providing accommodation and food. Other options in town include **McGraths**, a family-run pub in the middle of town,

Farmgate Café & Restaurant
English Market, Cork
021 427 8134

Cork Jazz Festival
www.corkjazzfestival.com

Cork Opera House
Emmet Place, Cork
021 427 0022
www.corkoperahouse.ie

**An Spailpin Fanach
(The Wandering Labourer)**
27 South Main Street, Cork

Ballymaloe House
021 465 2531
www.ballymaloe.ie

Ballymaloe Cookery School
Shanagarry
021 464 6785
www.cookingisfun.ie

Stephen Pearce Pottery & Gallery
Shanagarry
021 464 6807
www.stephenpearce.com

Inn by the Harbour
Ballycotton
021 464 6768
www.innbytheharbour.com

McGraths
Main Street, Ballycotton
021 646 085

Further reading

Frank O'Connor *An Only Child Memoir* by Cork's best-known writer.
Seán Ó Faoláin *Collected Stories*. Born in 1900, Ó Faoláin portrayed the lives of Cork's working and middle classes, against the backdrop of a failing church and the decline of Irish nationalism.
Gerry Murphy *End of Part One*. Selections from Murphy's previous work, together with 30 new poems portraying *'The Psychopathology of Everyday Life'*.

Websites

www.corkslang.com
Do you know your 'gauzer' from your 'gash'? Learn to speak like a local.
www.peoplesrepublicofcork.com
Listings and lively forums by Corkonians.
http://homepage.eircom.net/~cork county/index.html
The role of Cork City and County in the Anglo-Irish War of liberation.

An Lon Dubh (The Blackbird)
Ballycotton
021 464 6274

Fishy Fishy Café
Market Place, Kinsale
021 470 0415
www.fishyfishy.ie

Man Friday
Lower Road, Scilly
021 477 2260
www.manfridaykinsale.ie

Blue Haven
3 Pearse Street, Kinsale
021 477 2209
www.bluehavenkinsale.com

Spaniard
Kinsale
021 477 2436
www.spaniard.ie

Bulman Pub
Summercove, Kinsale
021 772 131
www.thebulman.com

Stena Line
08705 707070
www.stenaline.co.uk

and **An Lon Dubh** pulls a good pint and has a cosy ambience. Further east on the N25 you'll come to Youghal, the only walled town in Ireland, the old home to Walter Raleigh and where John Huston filmed *Moby Dick*.

SOUTH CORK: KINSALE

Kinsale, 18 miles south from Cork, was the site of the Battle of Kinsale, which occupies a place in the Irish psyche analogous to Hastings for the English. As well as being home to the world's oldest yacht club, it has an unusually high concentration of fine restaurants. The pubs, however, counterbalance any hint of snootiness and the 'craic' here is popular with weekenders.

One restaurant receiving plaudits is the stylish **Fishy Fishy Café**. The owner, Martin Shanahan, opened the restaurant with a mission to make the Irish 'lose their fear of fish'. He has the phone numbers of all the fishermen who work out of Kinsale and is often seen planning the day's menu standing on the harbour wall with the phone glued to his ear. His firm belief is that 'fish is a gift and we use what the sea offers up'. The restaurant only serves lunch (noon-4pm) and it doesn't take reservations. Martin's advice: 'Turn up and make sure you have some money in your back pocket' (credit cards are not accepted).

Other good restaurants include the long-established **Man Friday**, which is a pleasant ten-minute walk from the town centre. The **Blue Haven**, in the heart of Kinsale, is renowned for its food and charm.

There is a regular bus service from Cork to Kinsale.

SCILLY WALK

The walk to Scilly and the harbour begins from the **Spaniard** pub, which is just off the Cork road. From the clapboard house follow the signs for the walk. The path takes you back down to the harbour as you head out to the point and Charles Fort. Originally built in 1681 to rebuff the threat of a Dutch invasion it functioned as a British garrison until 1922. Just before the fort is the **Bulman Pub**, which is popular for drinks inside and, weather permitting, outside by the sea wall opposite. From Charles Fort follow the path past the entrance down to a small pebbled beach which is good for a quick dip when the tide is in. You can either turn back, or continue on down the gravel path to the point, known locally as 'Preachain' (Irish for crow). There, there's not much else to do apart from throwing yourself on the grass and breathing in the salt air.

TRAVEL INFORMATION

The crossing with **Stena Line** takes between two and three-and-a-half hours. If travelling to Fishguard from elsewhere by public transport, look out for offers.

In the summer season there is usually a direct ferry from Swansea to Cork. This service was suspended in 2007 and negotiations are currently ongoing with a new operator.

WHEN TO GO

Ireland is green for a reason. It rains, often. Summertime, though, offers the best chance of good weather, although the pubs and restaurants are welcoming whatever the weather.

WHALE WATCHING

West Cork is one of Europe's premier whale-watching sites. This is due to the surrounding continental shelf being relatively short, extending a mere 100 miles before plunging into deeper ocean waters. This makes the sea off West Cork an ideal breeding ground for the herring and sprat that the whales feed on. It also means that whales in Ireland can be seen quite close to the shore.

Nic Slocum, who runs **Whale Watch West Cork** with his wife Wendy, is a trained zoologist and has been watching whales for 20 years. He is committed to a sustainable approach to whale and dolphin watching and is keen to impart knowledge of marine conservation to his passengers – you'll soon be talking about 'blows', 'backs' and 'baitballs' like an expert. His twin-engine catamaran – *RV Voyager* – operates out of Castlehaven harbour, less than a mile from the fishing village of Union Hall in West

Cork – 90 minutes by road from Cork city. Huge, 30-ton Minke whales and, even bigger, the mighty Fin whale – the second largest mammal in the world – are routinely sighted, as well as Humpbacks and the occasional Killer whale.

For food afterwards, try **Dinty's Bar** in Union Hall or **Hayes' Bar** in nearby Glandore. Both are family-run pubs with good reputations. If you feel inspired to make an occasion of it, there's **Annie's Bar** in the beautiful village of Castletownsend. Many have eaten there and beaten a path back to its door.

Whale Watch West Cork *Union Hall, County Cork, 028 33357, www.whalewatchwestcork.com*
Dinty's Bar *Union Hall, 028 33373*
Hayes' Bar *Glandore, 028 33214*
Annie's Bar *Castletownsend, 028 36146*

Petite France p108

Strasbourg

ROUTE London ▶ Paris ▶ Strasbourg

The capital of Alsace is an undiscovered gem that hasn't had the numbers of British visitors it deserves. It's not just the home of the European Parliament: it's a historic city with great venues for food, drink, culture and nightlife, and only a little over five hours on the train from London.

Written by **Sue George**

Cathédrale Notre-Dame-de-Strasbourg p108

Petite France p108

THE TRIP

Who said crossing Paris had to be a nightmare? Just five minutes' walk from the Gare du Nord in Paris is the Gare de l'Est – a smaller and sweeter station selling all the essentials (beer, sandwiches, glamorous lingerie) for a trip east. Once you're on the TGV service – which, since its inception in summer 2007, has cut the travelling time from Paris to Strasbourg by half – settle down as the suburbs whizz past. That's the last you'll see of the metropolitan world for more than 250 miles. Then it's pancake-flat fields, interspersed with rolling woods, Champagne vineyards, a few villages and the occasional lake, until about half an hour outside Strasbourg. As the train winds its way into the Alsace region, pine forests hug steep slate cliffs and picturesque hamlets nestle in the valleys. Chunks of wood piled up outside every cute little half-timbered cottage let you know that you're travelling through roaring-log-fire country – it's almost enough to make you get out and go for a long country walk. Strasbourg station, a 19th-century building surrounded by what looks like a glass doughnut, is a five-minute walk from the historic city centre.

 St Pancras International ▶
Strasbourg **5 hours 11 minutes**

 Food & drink; history; luxury; romance; winetasting

THE DESTINATION

With the whole of the city centre a UNESCO World Heritage Site, and a restaurant and shopping culture infused with the expansive expense accounts of the members of the European Parliament, the capital of the Alsace region offers a great holiday for anyone interested in a food and drink break set among beautiful buildings. The miracle is that the architecture has survived, given Strasbourg's tumultuous past: an independent city state for many centuries, and an important river port, it has been fought over many times. But, despite the wars, centuries of architecture are still in amazingly good nick.

The Strasbourg of the Middle Ages remains obvious in its street layout and religious buildings. The **Cathédrale Notre-Dame-de-Strasbourg** is an extraordinary Gothic construction, with just one, rather spindly, spire but a remarkable abundance of external statuary – from virtues stabbing vices with their lances to a full complement of wise and foolish virgins, one of whom looks as if the thought of seduction by the devil has left her drooling.

The city has an exceptional concentration of buildings from medieval times up to the late 16th century, both elaborately decorated ones for rich merchants (like the Maison Kammerzell restaurant, *see below*) and plainer ones for more ordinary folk. Built in stone on the bottom storey so that they wouldn't rot on the area's swampy ground, the overhanging upper floors of the half-timbered houses make for some narrow streets. All the buildings are topped with steep roofs and have three storeys of dormer windows – there for storing grain and drying hides, because cellars would flood. Most of these houses are in the oldest part of the city – Petite France – which was the millers' and tanners' district. The roads, which appear to be named in both French and German, are deceptive: what seems to be German is, in fact, Alsatian dialect.

In 1681, Strasbourg was annexed by the French, and became the regional capital, which led to another golden age for the city. The most notable of many buildings built at that time is the **Palais Rohan**, now home to the **Musée des Arts Décoratifs**, with interior decor from the original palais apartments; the **Musée des Beaux-Arts** – housing works by Raphael, Goya and El Greco among others; and the **Musée Archéologique**, with its collection of finds from the Iron Age onwards. For an all-round look at the history of the area, there's also the sweet and atmospheric **Musée Alsacien**.

Strasbourg was annexed by the German empire from 1871 to 1918, and the city expanded and improved greatly during this time, although it took many years for its inhabitants to admit as much. The wide boulevards north of the place de la République, such as avenue des Vosges, are worthy of a wander: the grand architecture is surprisingly impressive.

After the horrors of Nazi occupation during World War II, Strasbourg – being so close to the German border and knowing at first hand the advantages of a united Europe – became the home of many major European institutions. The impressive buildings of the European Quarter, built in the 1990s, can be easily seen from the boat trip that travels around the city (**Batorama**). Other bang-up-to-date buildings include the

Cathédrale Notre-Dame-de-Strasbourg
pl de la Cathédrale
03 3 88 21 43 34
www.cathedrale-strasbourg.asso.fr

Palais Rohan
2 pl du Château
03 88 52 50 00
www.musees-strasbourg.org

Musée des Arts Décoratifs
2 pl du Château
03 88 52 50 08
www.musees-strasbourg.org

Musée des Beaux-Arts
2 pl du Château
03 88 88 50 68
www.musees-strasbourg.org

Musée Archéologique
2 pl du Château
03 88 52 50 00
www.musees-strasbourg.org

Musée Alsacien
23-25 quai St-Nicolas
03 88 52 50 01
www.musees-strasbourg.org

Batorama
15 rue de Nantes
03 88 84 13 13
www.strasbourg.port.fr/visites-en-bateaux.htm

Académie de la Bière p111

Musée d'Art Moderne et Contemporain. Opened in 1998, it has significant work from Rodin to the present day, via Picasso, Arp and several Fluxus notables.

All of these sights can be visited more cheaply with a Strasbourg Pass, which offers various freebies including a boat trip, while other attractions allow entry at half price. It is available from the **tourist office**.

HOTELS

For out and out luxury, the place to stay has to be **Château de l'Ile** – a (natch) château in the countryside about 13 kilometres away in St-Oswald. There, your wellbeing can be tended in hammam and jacuzzi, you can exercise in the pool or wander in the elegant grounds. Most people, though, will want a city-centre residence, but it's worth settling your dates well in advance as hotels can book out on the three and a half days every month the MEPs are in town.

One of the best-known hotels is the **Regent Petit France**, slap in the middle of the medieval centre. In fact, many of the city's hotels date back centuries. **L'Hôtel du Dragon** can put up a pretty good fight as the oldest, being first recorded in 1345, and right on the river to boot. Also suitably historic is **L'Hôtel Beaucour**, a 17th-century mansion that used to be an umbrella factory. The **Hôtel Cathédrale**, so close to the cathedral you are practically in it, has fantastic views but don't expect to sleep in – the bells ring from first thing in the morning to last thing at night. The **Hôtel Suisse**, also near the cathedral, looks as picture-postcard perfect as any Swiss scene.

ALL ABOARD THE GRAVY TRAIN

With literally hundreds of restaurants to choose from, it's clear that the Strasbourgeois love their food – although how they manage to stay so slender on a diet of Alsatian specialities, cheese, ham and foie gras, lightened only slightly by a mountain of *choucroute,* is a bit of a mystery.

Musée d'Art Moderne et Contemporain
1 pl Jean-Hans Arp
03 88 23 31 31
www.musees-strasbourg.org

Tourist Office
17 pl de la Cathédrale
03 88 52 28 28
www.ot-strasbourg.fr

Chateau de l'Ile
4 quai Heydt, Strasbourg-Oswald
03 88 66 85 00
www.chateau-ile.com

Regent Petit France
5 rue des Moulins
03 88 76 43 43
www.regent-hotels.com

L'Hôtel du Dragon
12 rue du Dragon
03 88 35 79 80
www.dragon.fr

L'Hôtel Beaucour
5 rue des Bouchers
03 88 76 72 00
www.hotel-beaucour.com

Hôtel Cathédrale
12-13 pl de la Cathédrale
03 88 22 12 12
www.hotel-cathedrale.fr

Hôtel Suisse
2-4 rue de la Râpe
03 88 35 22 11
www.hotel-suisse.com

Petite France p108

Maison Kammerzell
11 pl de la Cathédrale
03 88 32 42 14
www.maison-kammerzell.com

Chez Yvonne
10 rue du Sanglier
03 88 32 84 15
www.chez-yvonne.net

La Cloche à Fromage
27 rue des Tonneliers
03 88 52 04 03
www.cheese-gourmet.com

Le Buerehiesel
4 parc de l'Orangerie
03 88 45 56 65
www.buerehiesel.com

Poêles de Carottes
2 pl des Meuniers
03 88 323 323
www.poelesdecarottes.com

Sophie Peirani
61 rue du Fosse des Tanneurs
03 88 52 00 66

Colette Ravier
11 rue de l'Epine
03 88 75 94 80

Frick-Lutz
16 rue des Orfèvres
03 88 32 60 60
www.frick-lutz.fr

Arts et Collections d'Alsace
4 pl du Marché aux Poissons
03 88 14 03 77
http://artsetco.perso.cegetel.net/

One of the most famous eateries is **Maison Kammerzell**, overlooking the cathedral. Its Alsatian specialities, such as *choucroute* with three different sorts of fish, are perfectly set off by the 1427 building with its bottle-bottom windows and mural decor. Strasbourg is also known for its traditional, cosy, wood-walled restaurants, called *winstuben*. **Chez Yvonne** is a great example but there are many others. **La Cloche à Fromage** is probably he world's only all-cheese restaurant, where every dish – except the chocolate fondue – has cheese in it.

Haute cuisine anyone? There's a three-star Michelin restaurant in town, in the shape of **Le Buerehiesel**. With lunch from Tuesday to Friday costing €35 (without wine), you could almost convince yourself that it's a bargain.

After all that rich food, vegetables are probably sounding quite unusually attractive. **Poêles de Carottes** offers organic vegetarian food at reasonable prices.

For a more down-home snack, a local speciality is the *tarte flambée* or *flammekueche* – a bit like a pizza without the tomato but with onions and bacon. It makes a perfect accompaniment to a beer down the pub.

CONSPICUOUS CONSUMPTION

As befits a city floating in euros, there's no shortage of places anxious to part you from them. There's the usual array of French department stores and chains – Printemps, Galeries Lafayette, Fnac and Monoprix – around the place Kléber. But the interesting shops are the small ones, such as that of **Sophie Peirani**, who makes imaginative women's hats, bags, scarves and jewellery. Or **Colette Ravier**, who makes well-cut women's clothes. To take home Alsatian delicacies, **Frick-Lutz** offers foie gras, a wide range of delicious sausages and other meaty stuff. For linen, glassware and pottery in Alsatian style, there's the **Arts et Collections d'Alsace**.

But the most famous shopping option of all, going since 1570, is the Christmas market, which opens at the end of November each year and runs to New Year's Eve.

SANTÉ ET ENCORE

Around every corner, there's usually some kind of drinking establishment: with venues of all types, from hip bars to raucous pubs, there's no reason to stay entirely sober. Alsace is both a beer and wine centre, and both are in plentiful supply. The **Académie de la Bière** has over 70 beers on offer and, with food too, is a friendly place to down a few. The **Frères Berthom** styles itself as a village of beers, some brewed by Trappist monks.

For wine, head to **Au Verre à Soi**, a sophisticated and charming place with 30 wines by the glass, snacks and occasional live jazz to add to the utterly civilised recorded variety. Other hip venues include **Jeannette et les Cycleux**, which gets full marks for quirkiness – the eponymous bicycles are coming out of the walls. **L'Epicerie** is laid-back and atmospheric but fills up quickly.

For some live bands or themed clubbing – like salsa or traditional *bal musettes* – check out **La Salamandre**. Not quite cool enough for you? Maybe the beautiful people gracing the sofas at **Le Seven** are more your style.

Strasbourg is packed with arts and culture, and a great one-stop shop for tickets and information is **La Boutique Culture**. It is housed in a 13th-century apothecary's shop, which is probably the oldest in Europe. Whether your interest is in opera, theatre, music (ancient or modern), art or dance, staff know about it here – from world-class mainstream to the fringiest of the fringe. There are also a few decent cinemas: for English-speakers, the two **Star cinemas** are independents that show arty, indie and quality Hollywood films in the original language with French subtitles.

THE GREAT OUTDOORS

Perhaps one of the reasons the Strasbourgeois stay slim is the exercise they get. Step, without due care and attention, out of any building, and a bike hurtling past might knock you off your feet, even with the 400 kilometres of specially built cycle paths. Hire a bike at **Vélocation** and you can do as they do – or perhaps even cycle into the nearby countryside. But there are more unusual options. One requiring no effort at all is the **Éco'Pouss** – an electric tricycle that seats three and looks like a plastic kiddie car with a roof. Then there's the **Segway**, a mode of transport that almost defies description: standing in a shopping trolley being pushed by your mum comes the closest. Travel by Segway simply requires you to stay upright as it moves along the pavement.

TRAVEL INFORMATION

Return fares from London to Strasbourg start at £89 in standard class. For bookings visit the **Europe Travel Centre**.

WHEN TO GO

Spring, autumn and winter – lots of snow and a huge market.

Further reading

In-depth tourist information in English on Strasbourg is thin on the ground. *Strolling in Strasbourg*, only available in Strasbourg, is an excellent book with six themed, guided walks and plenty of information. €4 from the Tourist Office.

Websites

www.ot-strasbourg.com
The official tourist office site.
www.europarl.europa.eu
The European Parliament...

Académie de la Bière
17 rue Adolph Seyboth
03 88 22 38 88
www.academiedelabiere.com

Frères Berthom
18 rue des Tonneliers
03 88 32 81 18
www.lesfreresberthom.com

Au Verre à Soi
23 rue de l'Arc-en-Ciel
03 88 22 18 88

Jeannette et les Cycleux
30 rue des Tonneliers
03 88 23 02 71
www.lenetdejeannette.com

L'Epicerie
6 rue du Vieux Seigle
03 88 32 52 41

La Salamandre
3 rue Paul Janet
03 88 25 79 42
www.lasalamandre-strasbourg.fr

Le Seven
25 rue des Tonneliers
03 88 32 77 77

La Boutique Culture
10 pl de la Cathédrale
03 88 23 84 65

Star cinemas
18 rue du 22 Novembre
27 rue du Jeu-des-Enfants
03 88 32 44 97
www.cinema-star.com

Vélocation
La Grande Verrière, pl de la Gare
10 rue des Bouchers
03 88 24 05 61/03 88 23 56 75
www.velocation.net

Éco'Pouss
10 ave Molière
www.ecopouss.com

Segway
7 pl du Marché au Cochons de Lait
www.segwaytour.fr

Europe Travel Centre
1 Regent Street, London SW1
0844 848 4070
www.raileurope.co.uk

St Bénezet Bridge p114

Avignon & Around

ROUTE London ▸ Avignon ▸ Nîmes ▸ Arles

A relaxing trip to a relaxing city, where history, shopping and good food
and wine are the order of the day. And – when the heat gets too much, or
you want to explore a little more – there's no shortage of routes out of the
city, whether that means exploring the Roman monuments in nearby cities
or indulging in the Provençal idyll of the countryside nearby.

Written by **Sue George**

Place de l'Horloge p117

THE TRIP

Leave around noon. Stop by St Pancras' champagne bar and then grab a pasty for lunch, in the full knowledge that you'll be enjoying a Provençal dinner that very evening. In summer, the direct service means you can just sit back and think of France, perhaps flicking through Peter Mayle or Lawrence Durrell on the way.

The rest of the year, going to Avignon from the UK involves changing in France, at either Lille or Paris, though only masochists would choose the latter. The TGV trains on the Lille–Avignon route are duplex – the best views are from the upper deck, so try to reserve your seat there. The time speeds by as you watch the flat plains of northern France change to the more varied, drier south with the mountains visible in the distance. The TGV skirts towns and plunges through verdant scenery, though it all whizzes by teasingly fast.

On arrival the heady smells of Provence hit you as soon as you get off the train at Avignon TGV station, to the south of the city – not to be confused with the central SNCF station. A *navette* (or shuttle bus) meets the train and will get you to Avignon city centre in 10 minutes.

 St Pancras International ▸
Avignon TGV **5 hours 49 minutes**

 Architecture; food & drink; history

THE DESTINATION

Since the TGV- Mediterranée line – opened in 2001 – made Avignon a feasible weekend escape for well-heeled Parisians, the city of the popes has become an elegant holiday destination and a gateway to Provence.

Avignon has held a strategic place on the River Rhône since ancient times. But it was during its period as the capital of Christianity – the 14th century, when the popes found the Vatican a touch unruly and moved to Avignon – that the city began to flourish, with artists, merchants and politicians coming in their wake. A few popes and some 70 years later, the papacy had returned to Rome to stay. But Avignon wasn't about to give up its prestige and briefly had its own pope. Its grand and well-kept buildings show it was still a significant city until well into the 18th century.

This history is visible everywhere you look. Avignon is a walled city with its ramparts intact. Stand at one of the gates to the city, say in front of the station, or out on the bridge looking inland, and they encircle it completely. Another good view is from the park at the Rocher des Doms, where the gardens look over the Rhône and the city.

Most roads lead to the city's main square, place de l'Horloge, around which are ranked several cafés, the town hall – with its huge clock – and the opera house. Just off the square is Avignon's most significant site: **Le Palais des Papes** – or Palace of the Popes. Built in the mid 1300s, and perhaps the most important Gothic palace in Europe, it was built as a fortress as well as a palace and towers ominously over its neighbours. It housed the 14th-century popes and their large entourages; later, it was a barracks and a prison. Vast rooms (now empty, having been wrecked during the French Revolution) were built to scare the living daylights out of the pope's friends, enemies and minions. Its 25 rooms encompass the austere and the gaudily decorated, and a helpful audioguide gives you a handle on what used to happen where.

A few minutes' walk away, the **St Bénezet Bridge** – otherwise known as le pont d'Avignon – is the city's best-known landmark. Once you've realised that this is the pont d'Avignon whose song you probably learnt at school, the annoying little ditty will be running around your head all day. But, in fact, no one has ever danced on the bridge – except perhaps the odd tourist – and it's not a nursery rhyme invented some time in the Middle Ages but a tune from a 19th-century comic opera. The bridge was built from the 12th century, damaged several times by floods on the Rhône, and was rebuilt at various times up to the 17th century when the Avignonians gave up on it – as a result, the bridge ends suddenly in the middle of the river.

With the city's religious background in mind, you'd expect churches aplenty, and here they are – from the 12th-century **Cathédrale Notre-Dame-des-Doms**, the building topped with its bright golden Madonna, to the **Eglise St-Didier** with its 14th-century frescoes. Avignon is also bountifully supplied with museums. The **Musée du Petit Palais** was built as a palace for the archbishops and now houses more than 300 paintings from the period between the Middle Ages and the Renaissance, including works by Botticelli, Carpaccio and Giovanni di Paolo.

Le Palais des Papes
6 rue Pente Rapide
04 90 27 50 73
www.palais-des-papes.com

St Benezet Bridge
rue Ferruce
04 90 27 51 16
www.palais-des-papes.com

Cathédrale Notre-Dame-des-Doms
pl du Palais
04 90 82 12 24

Eglise St-Didier
pl St-Didier
04 90 86 20 17

Musée du Petit Palais
pl du Palais
04 90 86 44 58

Musée Calvet
65 rue Joseph Vernet
04 90 86 33 84
www.fondation-calvet.org

Hôtel d'Europe

ie **Musée Calvet** has an excellent collection of fine art from
edieval tapestries and sculptures, to paintings by Édouard
anet, Pierre Bonnard and Raoul Dufy.

For something right up to date, the **Collection Lambert** hosts
me top-notch 20th- and 21st-century art. Art dealer Yvon
mbert has given Avignon his collection on a 20-year loan and
w a series of temporary exhibitions present works by artists
ch as Cy Twombly, Nan Goldin and Jean-Michel Basquiat.

An Avignon Passion pass – free at your first full price attraction
offers discounts on all Avignon attractions, including guided
urs and trips outside of town. At every attraction the passes
e practically thrust upon you and you'd be hard pressed to
iss being offered one if you are doing any sightseeing at all.

BED TO LAY YOUR HEAD

itering for all pockets from the loftiest of expense accounts to
e tightest of budgets, Avignon is chock-full of accommodation
tions, so staying here is easy – except during the Festival in
ly where booking far in advance is best. Probably the most
imorous hotel is the **Hôtel de la Mirande** in the shadow of the
lais des Papes. Given that the hotel used to be a cardinal's
lace – and is decorated like one to boot – it's not surprising
at it's one of the Leading Small Hotels of the World. Elegance
a slightly lower tariff is on offer at **Hôtel d'Europe**. This hotel
n the Michelin guide since 1900 and host to guests ranging
im Napoleon to Tennessee Williams – sits in a beautiful
e-filled square. **Hôtel Cloître St-Louis** was once part of a
onastery, and it sits peacefully and a little fastidiously just
f the hubbub of rue de la République.

3ut it's not just high-end accommodation, there's a plethora
middle-range hotels too, such as **Hôtel Bristol** conveniently
uated right at the bottom of rue de la République main drag.
there's the **Mercure Pont d'Avignon** in a quiet area right
ar the bridge, with on-site car parking for those who need it.
it the cheaper end of the spectrum, **Hôtel Colbert** is
mething of a quiet haven, with Provençal-styled rooms and

Collection Lambert
Hotel de Caumont
5 rue Violette
04 90 16 56 20

Hôtel de la Mirande
4 pl de la Mirande
04 90 85 93 93
www.la-mirande.fr

Hôtel d'Europe
12 pl Crillon
04 90 14 76 76
www.hotel-d-europe.fr

Hôtel Cloître St-Louis
20 rue Portail Boquier
04 90 27 55 55
www.cloitre-saint-louis.com

Hôtel Bristol
44 cours Jean Jaurés
04 90 16 48 48
www.bristol-hotel-avignon.com

Mercure Pont d'Avignon
rue Ferruce
04 90 80 93 93
www.accorhotels.com

Hôtel Colbert
7 rue Agricol Perdiguier
04 90 86 20 20
www.lecolbert-hotel.com

Hôtel Mignon
12 rue Joseph Vernet
04 90 82 17 30
www.hotel-mignon.com

Le Palais des Papes p114

Campsite
04 90 80 63 50
www.camping-avignon.com

Restaurant Christian Etienne
10 rue de Mons
04 90 86 16 50
www.christian-etienne.fr

La Fourchette
17 rue Racine
04 90 85 20 93

La Compagnie des Comptoirs
83 rue Joseph Vernet
04 90 85 99 04
www.lacompagniedescomptoirs.com

L'Opera Café
24 pl de l'Horloge
04 90 86 27 17 43

Le Brigadier du Théâtre
17 rue Racine
04 90 82 21 19
www.lebrigadier.com

Au Tout Petit
4 rue d'Amphoux
04 90 82 38 86
www.autoutpetit.fr

Caves Breysse
41 rue des Teinturiers
04 32 74 25 86

Le Café de la Comedie
15 pl Crillon
04 90 85 74 85

Bouteillerie at the Palais des Papes
04 90 27 50 85

air-conditioning that is very welcome on a stifling summer night.
Hôtel Mignon has small rooms but is well designed and good value for the price you'll pay.

From April to October, there's a large **campsite** on Ile de la Barthelasse, which sits in the river between central Avignon and the new town. A free shuttle boat takes you to and fro.

MUNCH

You're not likely to go hungry in Avignon, which seems to have a restaurant for every day of the year, and encompasses the good, bad and indifferent; the traditional and the innovative; the quiet and formal, and comparatively raucous.

The aforementioned Hôtel de la Mirande has one of Avignon's top-flight restaurants, serving the hautest of haute cuisine. On Tuesday and Wednesday nights it offers the more informal table d'hôte – where a small number of people eat in the kitchen with the chef. **Restaurant Christian Etienne** is another excellent choice, with set menus from reasonable to very expensive. It even has a *menu du cochon* – all types of piggy delights for you to eat – a menu for pigs as well as of them.

Inexplicably, there's an orange decor in many of Avignon's restaurants, but it doesn't detract from the great food. At **La Fourchette**, one of the best mid-price restaurants, the food is classic Provençal, with a modern twist and local wines. **La Compagnie des Comptoirs**, located in an 18th-century house with vaulted ceilings, does Provençal-eastern fusion. There's a bar and DJ, and in the summer an elegant courtyard garden to chill out and drink in.

Still on the orange-coloured theme, **L'Opera Café** is by far the most salubrious eatery on the square, even if the service is stress-laden – for some reason the staff run around like headless coqs sportifs and seem to be in a constant state of panic. Still, it's a good place to sit outside and people-watch.

Le Brigadier du Théâtre serves straight-down-the-line Provençal food. Its high-camp decor – think cherubs and chandeliers – adds to the atmosphere.

One of Avignon's rising stars is **Au Tout Petit**. It doesn't look much from the outside, but the French-Thai food is terrific, and the staff warm and English-speaking.

Apart from the July festival, most restaurants are shut on Sunday and many take Monday off too. So on Sunday morning go to the covered market at Les Halles and pick up some picnic grub. Les Halles might not be much to look at inside, although its 'green wall' – basically a hedge covering a wall – is rather fun, but there's a host of stalls selling olives, quiches, pâtisserie and other goodies.

Wine from the local Rhône region is what you want to go for here, although much of it is drunk in restaurants rather than bars. The **Caves Breysse** offers regional wine by the glass and **Le Café de la Comedie** is a nice little establishment on a pretty square. If taking wine home with you, the **Bouteillerie at the Palais des Papes** – reached either at the end of the Palais des Papes tour or directly through its entrance at place de l'Amirande – offers guided tastings of Côtes du Rhône wines, and sells 55 regional wines at cellar prices.

The village of Châteauneuf du Pape – home of the world-famous wine – is only 18 kilometres away from Avignon, but as there is no public transport service there you'll have to take a cab or an organised tour. All-day wine tours for two to six people, including cellar visits, wine museums and tastings, are available via www.avignon-wine-tour.com.

CREDIT CRUNCHING

With money flowing like the local wine, suitable places to spend it are thick on the ground. While boulevard de la République is the place for your H&Ms and Zaras, the swankiest shopping is to be had in rue Joseph Vernet. **Cacharel**, for instance, is at no.8. Among many other clothes shops on that road, **Façonnable** at no.30 and **Ventilo** will both prove sadly tempting.

Au Jardin de Provence has beautiful things for the home. Back towards place de l'Horloge, **Pylones** at 21 rue St Agricole sells funny little toys for adults.

If your budget is modest, try rue des Marchands. The street's most famous and picturesque shop is **Mouret** – a hat shop dating from 1860, with many cute chapeaux for sale. **La Cure Gourmande**, a biscuit-come-sweet shop with all kinds of crystallised fruit on sale, will send you straight to the dentist.

Wandering towards place Pie, **Liquid** has drinks and drink-related gadgetry that you'd never have imagined, let alone considered, before. As well as the great wines of the region – Châteauneuf du Pape, Gigondas, St Joseph and Crozes Hermitage – it also sells unlikely sounding drinks like wild plum Kushi tea and rose lemonade.

ALL EYES AND EARS

The **Avignon festival**, founded in 1947 and held every July, marks three weeks celebrating European theatre and sees the city teeming with people. There's all sorts of performances on offer, in around 20 different venues from small chapels to the Honour Courtyard in the Palace of the Popes.

Year-round, the city boasts three theatres, including the **Théâtre Municipal**, which has performances of opera, ballet, theatre and orchestral music.

The **Utopia** cinemas have repertory screenings of US indie, classic old Hollywood and European films, all in the original language with French subtitles. There's jazz at the Utopia cinema through the auspices of **AJMI** – a jazz and improvised music promoter and record label.

This isn't really a clubbing city but there are still a few must-go places. The **Red Zone** caters for the city's resident and visiting youth, who dance to all types of music depending on the night. Avignon's best-known gay bar is **Le Cid Café**.

MEET THE ROMANS: NÎMES AND ARLES

When the Roman Empire conquered France 2,000 years ago they had to show those Gauls – *pace* Asterix – just who was boss. The result: the area around has some of Europe's most notable Roman monuments, all of which are readily accessible on a short train trip. At Nîmes, **Les Arènes** is the best-preserved amphitheatre in the world. Dating from the first century AD, it's constructed out of huge blocks of stone two storeys high, with 60 stone arcades facing the street, and seating for 20,000 spectators. When it was built, it hosted day-long spectacles: its complete state means it's all too easy to imagine petty criminals

Cacharel
8 rue Joseph Vernet
04 90 86 19 19

Façonnable
30 rue Joseph Vernet
04 90 82 35 88

Ventilo
28 rue Joseph Vernet
04 90 85 26 51

Au Jardin de Provence
2 rue Petite Fusterie
04 90 86 29 38

Pylones
21 rue St-Agricole
04 90 82 30 45
www.pylones.com

Mouret
20 rue des Marchands
04 90 13 42
www.chapelier.com

La Cure Gourmande
24 ue des Marchands
04 90 82 65 35

Liquid
37 rue Bonneterie
04 90 85 19 89
www.liquidboutique.fr.st

Avignon festival
04 90 27 66 50
www.festival-avignon.com

Théâtre Municipal
20 pl de l'Horloge
04 90 82 81 40

Utopia
Manutention: 4 rue des Escaliers Ste Anne
Republique: 5 rue Figuiere
04 90 82 65 36
www.cinemas-utopia.org

AJMI
04 90 86 08 61
www.jazzalajmi.com

Red Zone
25 rue Carnot
04 90 27 02 44

Le Cid Café
11 pl de l'Horloge
04 90 82 30 38
www.lecidcafe.com

Les Arènes
blvd des Arènes, Nîmes
04 66 21 82 56
www.culturespaces.com

being torn apart by lions and gladiators stabbing each other in the jugular. If your imagination needs any extra stimulation, bullfights are held here every September. In the meantime, climb up to the highest tier of original stone seats – in classical times, reserved for slaves and women – and look at the imposing arena spread out below.

Roman Nîmes also has the **Maison Carrée** – a rectangular Roman temple of beautifully undamaged Corinthian columns set atop a stone plinth. For a view of the whole city, climb up the Tour Magne, which is one of the original lookout points and stands to the north of the city centre.

While Nîmes is a fully functioning commercial centre with other museums, restaurants, bars and hotels, the much smaller town of Orange is its equal in terms of heritage.

Offering a more pacific view of the Roman period, the enormous **Théâtre Antique** is the best-preserved Roman theatre in the world. Comedies, plays and debates were held here, grandstanding the then-importance of Orange to the Empire. A world-famous music festival is held here in July and August; clearly, the Romans knew a thing or two about acoustics.

A ruined temple lies next to the theatre, and the city's museum is just across the street. To the north of the town, the Arc de Triomphe stretches over both sides of what is now a heavily trafficked road – formerly the Via Agrippa, which ran between Lyon and Arles.

Arles has both a Roman amphitheatre, **Les Arènes** and a Roman theatre, **Théâtre Antique**. The amphitheatre is one of the oldest in the world and still hosts bullfights. The theatre, however, was ransacked after the Romans left and is now in rather a sorry state that, to some, adds atmosphere.

Instead of travelling by train to Arles, you could opt for a more aquatic route and take one of **Mireio**'s river cruises there from Avignon, which includes lunch on the way.

IN THE AREA

To get right out into the countryside, you'll have to give the train a miss and opt for roads. The **bus station** is right next to the SNCF station, and a lot less salubrious. But it's a great transport hub for places near and far.

The chichi village of **St-Remy-de-Provence** is only 40 minutes away by bus, but it's in another world, one where you can walk into your own lotus-eating dream. Set in the foothills of the Alpilles mountains, St-Remy has some lovely hotels such as **Le Mas des Carassins**. You can always spend the day sleeping by the pool; more energetic types can hike along the nearby GR trail – riding and cycling are available too.

There's also some more gentle sightseeing on offer: Van Gogh spent a lot of time in St Remy and painted *De sterrennacht* (*The Starry Night*) here, although you won't find much in the way of correspondence between the local geography and Van Gogh's rendering of it. There's a **permanent collection** of his paintings and drawings on show at 8 rue Estrine.

The village also boasts a famous native son: the 16th-century seer Nostradamus was born in St-Remy, in a modest house that is still standing. We wonder if he foretold that his home town would now be a second residence to so many arty Parisians?

Maison Carrée
pl de la Maison Carrée, Nîmes
04 66 36 26 76

Théâtre Antique
rue Madeleine Roch, Orange
04 90 51 17 60
www.culturespaces.com

Les Arènes
rond-point d'Arènes, Arles
04 90 49 36 86
www.arenes-arles.com

Théâtre Antique
rue de la Calade, Arles
04 90 49 36 25

Mireio
Allées de l'Oulle, Avignon
04 90 85 62 25
www.mireio.net

bus station (gare routière)
5 ave Monclar, Avignon
04 90 82 07 35

St-Remy-de-Provence
www.saintremy-de-provence.com

Le Mas des Carassins
1 chemin Gaulois, St-Remy-de-Provence
04 90 92 15 48
www.masdescarassins.com

Van Gogh collection
8 rue Estrine, St-Remy-de-Provence
04 90 92 34 72

Carpentras, also just 40 minutes away, is rather an industrialised town but with an interesting centre. It has the oldest synagogue in France, dating from the 14th century, and a few other low-key museums and a cathedral. But it is a pleasant, not-too-touristy place to soak up the atmosphere or enjoy the Friday market. One of the Marquis de Sade's châteaux – Château de Mazan – is only 15 kilometres away. It's now been transformed into a luxury hotel.

Far be it from us to suggest it, but if you should decide to hire a car, then the whole of this region opens up for you. The Luberon area, brought to the world's attention by Peter Mayle's A Year in Provence, retains much of the charm that brought him there in the first place, and has a procession of pretty villages. Try Roussillon – an ochre-red village set in pine forests. Next to the village is a Sentier des Ocres (Giants' Causeway) – a natural park of jagged red ochre cliffs. Or Gordes, set on a steep hill, and dominated by its château.

There's also Fontaine-de-Vaucluse, a medieval village tucked into a valley in the Vaucluse mountains. Its main claim to fame is that its river gushes straight out of a cliff-face; no one has yet managed to find its source. Provence is full of such places: just get in the car and drive.

TRAVEL INFORMATION

Return fares from London to Avignon start at £99 return in standard class. The time that is quoted at the beginning of this chapter is for the summer-only direct service, which operates on Saturdays. During the rest of the year, the best option is to change at Lille-Europe and you'll arrive at Avignon TGV in anything from six hours nine minutes, to six hours 25 minutes. It may be possible to do the journey in slightly less time, but when this book was going to print the only faster time (five hours 51 minutes) involved travelling across Paris.

Keep your stress levels low by changing in Lille, where you just have to get the lift to another platform, rather than braving the route via the capital. Changing trains in Paris means crossing town to another station, with all the lugging of cases through the crowds and up the metro stairs that that implies.

The services to Nîmes and Arles usually depart from the SNCF station, Avignon Centre: it's 27-31 minutes to Nîmes and 15-20 minutes to Arles. Sometimes TGV trains bound for Toulouse stop at Nîmes – a journey of just 17 minutes – while on occasions a bus plies the 'rail' route to Arles (proving that the 'rail replacement service' is not uniquely British).

Book through **Rail Europe**. The Nice-bound Motorail service stops at Avignon en route, should you want to take your car down there. Passage can also be booked through Rail Europe. Further information on travel and accommodation is available from the **tourist office** in Avignon.

WHEN TO GO

The summers are long, hot and dry, with only the occasional thunder storm to disturb the buzz of the cicadas in the olive trees. Winter time can bring cold blasts of wind with the Mistral, spring produces new growth and pleasant temperatures, and autumn sees the sometimes torrid summer heat relent.

Further reading

Peter Mayle *A Year in Provence*. The classic book about a couple who decided to live their French dream by buying a run-down Provençal farmhouse. He followed it up with *Toujours Provence* and *Encore Provence*.
Lawrence Durrell *The Avignon Quintet*. A set of novels about rich Europeans in France, Switzerland and Egypt before, during and after World War II. These experimental novels – *Monsieur, Livia, Constance, Sebastian* and *Quinx* – have loose plots encompassing themes of war, the Knights Templar, mortality, sexual identity, and Nazism.
Iain Pears *The Dream of Scipio*. A novel comprised of three stories set in Avignon – in 475, 1340, and 1943. All look at what happens when one man tries to preserve the noble values of his civilisation against what he sees as cruel and barbaric, yet powerful, outsiders.
Edwin Mullins *Avignon of the Popes: City of Exiles*. An in-depth history of 14th-century Avignon when it was, briefly, the most important city in Christendom.

Websites

www.ot-avignon.fr
The useful website of the local tourist authority.
www.avignon-et-provence.com
And for further afield in the province.

Château de Mazan
pl Napoléon, Mazan
04 90 69 62 61
www.chateaudemazan.fr

Rail Europe
0844 848 4070
www.raileurope.co.uk

Avignon office de tourisme
41 cours Jean Jaures, Avignon
04 32 74 32 74
www.avignon-tourisme.com

Kitchener Memorial p123

Orkney

ROUTE   Aberdeen ▶ Kirkwall

Need a reason to brave the North Sea crossing to Orkney? How about the Northern Lights in winter, almost perpetual daylight in high summer, World Heritage Site status for its Neolithic heartland, a Viking tradition, astonishing seascapes and more history than most people can handle without a stiff drink. Just as well there are two whisky distilleries. Even aquaphobes should board the ferry to Kirkwall.

Written by **Keith Davidson**

Pier Arts Centre p122

Ring of Brodgar p125

THE TRIP

f you're travelling to Orkney in midwinter it is a mistake to look out of your cabin window. What you glimpse will be motile, white-trimmed, chaotic, and quite capable of killing you in seconds – and that's only with winds of force 6 and 7. The strange thing is that, while first-timers are laying on their beds, thinking, 'I'm going to die!' all the Orcadians will be sipping at pints of beer in one of the ship's bars, sitting in the cinema, shopping, or even enjoying a meal in the restaurant. They have endured this many times before and have faith in NorthLink's safety record. For newbies, it's a trauma worth enduring, however, because there is a truly world-class reason to visit Orkney exactly in midwinter, more of which below.

By contrast, summer might not guarantee a smooth sailing – the North Sea never does – but it will bring far more daylight. As you head north in the evening – departures are always 5pm, weather permitting – there is an opportunity to see the east coast of Scotland slide by while you stand out on deck: up from Aberdeen, past the tip of Buchan, across the Moray Firth, then up and into Kirkwall. Welcome to Orkneyjar.

 Aberdeen ▸ Kirkwall
6 hours

  Beaches; history; landscape; walking; wildlife

Stenness stones p125

Albert Hotel
Mounthoolie Lane, Kirkwall
01856 876000
www.alberthotel.co.uk

Sands Hotel
Burray
01856 731298
www.thesandshotel.co.uk

Creel
Front Road, St Margaret's Hope, South Ronaldsay
01856 831311
www.thecreel.co.uk

Pier Arts Centre
Victoria Street, Stromness
01856 850209
www.pierartscentre.com

Julia's Café-Bistro
Ferry Road, Stromness
01856 850904

THE DESTINATION

Orkney is the single name applied to the group of islands lying immediately off the north coast of Scotland. There are around 70 overall and just 17 are inhabited. The largest and most populous is known simply as the Mainland, home to the principal towns of Kirkwall and Stromness, as well as most of the major attractions. The Mainland and the islands immediately to its south-east are joined by causeways and tend to be the focus for most visits.

Even taken together the largest linked islands (Mainland, Burray, South Ronaldsay) are fairly modest in size, so travelling around by car hardly constitutes a journey of any heft; this is not Route 66. The real Orkney tour takes place in another dimension altogether: time. A scant 2,000 years takes in its role as a Royal Navy base during the world wars, its years under the charge of the Scottish kings, centuries of Viking control and the extraordinary late Iron Age remains from the time of Christ. Push back further to its amazing Neolithic sites at Skara Brae, Maes Howe and elsewhere, and you hit 3100 BC. Meanwhile, a 2007 archaeological dig provided solid evidence that Mesolithic people were here nearly 9,000 years ago. Even visitors who meander round the Mainland with no set agenda can still bump into things older than the Egyptian pyramids. Although that's not to say that the 21st century hasn't left its mark…

RIGHT HERE, RIGHT NOW

The ferry from Aberdeen, with its many entertainments, should tip off travellers that they may have left mainland Britain behind but not its comforts. This hits home even harder if you stay at the lately refurbished **Albert Hotel** in Kirkwall. The exterior gives no indication of the boutique, cosmopolitan sensibility of the rooms. You could say much the same about the **Sands Hotel** down on Burray, a former 19th-century herring station. Unremarkable outside, inside the accommodation is simple and contemporary, chiming in well with the waterside location.

On South Ronaldsay the **Creel** has long been acknowledged as the best restaurant in the islands and it also has three bedrooms upstairs for anyone who fancies a stopover.

In terms of 21st-century attractions, the **Pier Arts Centre** at Stromness not only leads the way locally, but stands as one of the best regional arts centres anywhere in the UK. Relaunched in 2007 after a £4.5 million redevelopment, this is not a polite, provincial space for pleasant landscapes and inoffensive still lives. Owing much to the vision of its founder, the late Margaret Gardiner, who counted key figures from the St Ives scene as friends, the Pier has work by Barbara Hepworth, Ben Nicholson and Roger Hilton as well as the likes of Eduardo Paolozzi and local artists. If all the creativity gives you an appetite, **Julia's Café-Bistro** is nearby.

IN TIME OF WAR

Scapa Flow is simply a big stretch of water sheltered on all sides by islands. It is one of the world's best anchorages and has been used as such since Viking times. It came to prominence in the 20th century as the Royal Navy's main wartime base, acting as a focus for moments of high drama and startling loss.

Just a few weeks after the declaration of war in 1939, a German U-boat sneaked in to Scapa Flow from the east and sank the HMS *Royal Oak*, killing more than 800 men. This prompted Churchill to order the building of causeways, blocking off the eastern approach. There are four of these 'Churchill Barriers' linking the Mainland to the tiny islands of Lamb Holm and Glimps Holm, then to Burray and South Ronaldsay. Italian prisoners of war worked on their construction and also left behind one of the most curious reminders of that period – a beautiful little chapel on Lamb Holm. With its simple façade and detailed interior – largely the work of prisoner Domenico Chiocchetti, who died in 1999 – the Italian Chapel is entirely anomalous in the low, windswept landscape but profoundly moving at the same time.

Immediately after World War I, Scapa Flow was used to house 74 vessels from the defeated German Imperial Navy as precise peace terms were thrashed out. Talks dragged on into the summer of 1919, at which point the local German commander, lacking up-to-date information, decided to scuttle the lot. On 21 June that year something like 400,000 tons of warship went to the bottom. Despite extensive salvage work, three battleships and four light cruisers are still there, making Scapa Flow one of the UK's premier diving sites.

In a footnote to the Great War, and three years before the German fleet sabotaged itself, the waters off Orkney had become the final resting place for a hero of the British Empire, Field Marshal Lord Kitchener. This was the man whose distinctive pointing finger and walrus moustache featured on a famous recruitment poster at the outset of the conflict. In June 1916, he boarded the HMS *Hampshire* at Scapa Flow, set for a diplomatic mission to Russia. Just off the west coast of the Orkney Mainland, the vessel hit a mine and sank. Only a dozen men survived from a complement of 655. In 1926, the people of Orkney built a simple memorial tower for Kitchener at Marwick Head, the nearest point to the wreck. In season, breeding seabirds cry and wheel around the soaring cliffs. All year round, Marwick Head is somewhere to stand and look south to Hoy and beyond, and to watch the North Atlantic swell and crash against the land. Just a few miles south at Yesnaby, also on the Mainland's west coast, the cliffs and sea stacks are perhaps even more spectacular. From both locations, you can see Scotland in the distance.

SCOTS AND SCOTCH

When the Vikings arrived in these islands in the eighth and ninth centuries, Scotland was only just forming as a unified kingdom. That meant Orkney came under an effective Norse control that lasted all the way through to the 15th century. Scottish authority in the islands, then, is a Johnny-come-lately phenomenon of fewer than 600 years. The best place to get a flavour of this timespan is at the 16th-century Tankerness House in Kirkwall, home to the **Orkney Museum**. Displays go through the islands' entire story, from Stone Age to present day, and set visitors up nicely for outdoor explorations of the famous sites. If all these retrospectives put you in the mood for more traditional accommodation in Kirkwall, try the **Lynnfield**, with its almost Edwardian atmosphere. Its bar is also a great place to

ORKNEY

Orkney Museum
Broad Street, Kirkwall
01856 873191

Lynnfield
Holm Road, Kirkwall
01856 872505
www.lynnfieldhotel.co.uk

sample various types of **Highland Park** single malt Scotch. The distillery, which dates from the 18th century, is just along the road. Orkney's other distillery, Scapa, is not open to the public but its output can be found in the islands' pubs.

ORKNEYJAR

One of Kirkwall's stand-out features is the sandstone bulk of the 12th-century **St Magnus Cathedral**. Romano-Gothic in style, it was built when the islands formed a Norse fiefdom and was dedicated to the memory of Magnus Erlendsson, Earl of Orkney, who was murdered on the orders of his cousin in 1115. A rounded plaque inside the entrance reads, 'This is none other but the House of God, and this is the Gate of Heaven,' a description some Orcadians would apply to the islands.

The Viking period left behind a lot more than the cathedral, however. Place names have obvious Scandinavian roots, while the word Orkney itself derives from Orkneyjar, Old Norse for 'island of the seals', although this is pre-dated by the Gaelic name of Insi Orc, 'island of the wild boar'. The boars are long gone, the seals remain.

The most obvious big-ticket Viking remains are to be found in the north-west corner of the Mainland at the Brough of Birsay. Getting to this tiny tidal island, which can be reached on foot for only a few hours a day, is an adventure in itself. Originally a Pictish settlement, then the centre of Norse power from around the ninth century until Kirkwall became the focus in the 12th, it has the remains of a Viking church and its surrounding village, although the buildings are now really little more than floor plans. It may lack the grandeur of St Magnus Cathedral, but standing out here on the western edge of the islands, you get a real sense of a medieval Viking colony where the King of Norway held sway and local spats between Anglo-Saxons and Normans 500 miles south were purely incidental.

SOUND OF IRON

The Vikings were an impressive lot but the islands' late Iron Age inhabitants left behind something that may eclipse Norse endeavours: the Broch of Gurness to the north of the Mainland. There are brochs, fortified stone towers, all over the Scottish Highlands and Islands, but the example at Gurness is an archaeological wonderland. Dating to around 200 BC, it has the remains of the central defensive structure surrounded by the extensive ruins of an attached settlement. Visitors can simply wander among these, musing on place names that would see Tolkien weep with joy. Gurness is on Eynhallow Sound, a stretch of water between the Mainland and Rousay. Go there at dusk and you might have the entire site to yourself. The sound of geese carries over from the neighbouring island, the light is an extraordinary sinking blue, and don't worry about any abrupt snorting noises. That will be a seal breaching the water nearby and clearing its nose.

HEART OF THE MATTER

In the late 1990s, UNESCO took a look at the various Neolithic stone circles, burial chambers and other sites on the west of the Orkney Mainland, had a think, then declared them a World Heritage Site just before the turn of the Millennium. One of only

Highland Park
Holm Road, Kirkwall
01856 874619
www.highlandpark.co.uk

St Magnus Cathedral
Broad Street, Kirkwall
01856 874894

2 such cultural sites across the UK, it was dubbed the Heart of Neolithic Orkney. At many locations, like the Standing Stones of Stenness or the Ring of Brodgar – by the Lochs of Stenness and Harray – you can simply walk among ancient monuments, up close and personal. The **Stenness stones** originally numbered a dozen although only four survive, but they are huge – the biggest nearly 18 feet – and date back at least 5,100 years. With a low sun behind them casting long shadows, they look like the monolith from *2001: A Space Odyssey*. But these are real, and far more evocative for it. The nearby **Ring of Brodgar** may only be 4,500 years old, but it is more complete, with 36 of the original standing stones still in place.

The most celebrated Neolithic site on the Mainland is probably **Skara Brae**, on the west coast by Sandwick. It was uncovered in 1850 after a severe winter storm blew away sand and soil. Excavation revealed something quite incredible: a working village occupied between 4,500 and 5,100 years ago. The astonishing thing about the dwellings is the detail of domesticity from a period that has been typically characterised as savage. The houses have fireplaces, dressers, rudimentary toilets, sleeping spaces and more. The replica house on site and the visitor centre explain all.

You can touch the stones at the Ring of Brodgar, you can walk by the houses at Skara Brae, but nothing can compare to the experience on offer at **Maes Howe** by Stenness. A large chambered burial tomb bang in the Neolithic Heartland and dating back around 5,000 years, it was built so the entrance passage lined up with the setting sun at the moment of the winter solstice in December. This sounds fairly clever although possibly humdrum – sunlight hitting a wall – but witnessing the event is a revelation and worth a trip to Orkney all on its own. The chamber itself is a marvel of the prehistoric mason's craft, while it was later sacked by Vikings who left runic graffiti along the lines of 'I rule', 'So do I', 'See how high I can reach', 'Ingigerth is well fit' and 'I'm totally ace at runes, me'.

At the winter solstice, those privileged few with an entry ticket – places are limited – stand in a darkened space with a hardwired connection to people just like themselves from thousands of years ago. The sun lines up gradually with an incandescent burst of light at the chamber's rear wall building to a peak at the very moment when our local star appears to reach its annual southernmost point in the Orcadian sky. If you're religious, it will be spiritual. If you're a dyed-in-the-wool atheist, you still might need a long walk and large dram afterwards.

Finally, no description of Neolithic Orkney can omit the **Tomb of the Eagles** by Cleat at the bottom of South Ronaldsay. A private, family-run site, this is another 5,000-year-old chambered cairn discovered by farmer Ronnie Simison on his land in 1958. The Simisons subsequently developed the attraction, building a user-friendly visitor centre to house the artefacts and human skeletal remains found inside the cairn, the latter having been buried with white-tailed sea eagle talons and, sometimes, entire birds, hence the name.

The tomb itself is around 20 minutes' walk from the visitor centre, through farmland, and perched on a clifftop looking out to the heaving North Sea and riotous Pentland Firth. It's a low crawl in through the entrance passage and the Simisons have

Stenness stones
Stenness, Mainland
www.orkneyjar.com/history/standingstones

Ring of Brodgar
Sultigeo, Mainland
www.orkneyjar.com/history/brodgar

Skara Brae
Sandwick, Stromness
www.orkneyjar.com/history/skarabrae

Maes Howe
Stenness
www.orkneyjar.com/history/maeshowe

Tomb of the Eagles
Cleat, South Ronaldsay
01856 831339
www.tomboftheeagles.co.uk

Further reading

George Mackay Brown *Beside the Ocean of Time* One of the great 20th-century poets.
George Mackay Brown *Greenvoe*
Hermann Palsson & Paul Edwards *The Orkneyinga Saga: A History of the Earls of Orkney*
James Miller *Scapa*
Caroline Wickham-Jones *Orkney: A Historical Guide*

Websites

www.orkneyjar.com - for the heritage of the islands.
www.orkney.gov.uk - local council services.
www.orcadian.co.uk - local newspaper.
www.buyorkney.com - Orcadian products
Most of the major Neolithic sites on the Orkney Mainland are under the care of Historic Scotland (www.historic-scotland.gov.uk) while other places of interest are listed by the official tourist organisation, Visit Orkney (www.visitorkney.com). These websites will give details of locations and opening times. Visit Orkney also has some useful links for other organisations and facilities across the islands and runs the tourist office in Kirkwall (6 Broad Street, 01856 872856).

Scapa Flow Visitor Centre
Lyness
01856 791300
www.scapaflow.co.uk

Orkney Ferries
Shore Street, Kirkwall
01856 872044
www.orkneyferries.co.uk

NorthLink Ferries
08456 000449
www.northlinkferries.co.uk

Pentland Ferries
01856 831226
www.pentlandferries.co.uk

John O'Groats Ferries
01955 611353
www.jogferry.co.uk

Tourist Office
6 Broad Street, Kirkwall
01856 872856

left some skulls in one of the chambers. Walking back along the cliff tops, at the right time of year, you might see a seal colony with pups on the shingle beach in Ham Geo.

AND IN THE BEGINNING...

Even on Orkney you eventually run out of history. But then and now the summer sun sets late, and on cold, clear nights in winter the sky can put on a show unknown in more southerly latitudes. The Northern Lights, or Aurora Borealis, a veritable kaleidoscope of fast flickering reds, greens and purple-blues, is a result of particles in the solar wind crashing into the high atmosphere above the North Pole. Board the ferry and sail nort and you might see the same things as the first settlers, making this the most extravagant time jump of all.

IN THE AREA

Having done the Mainland and its linked islands, you might want to get on a small ferry and head for some of the others. Hoy is famed for its western cliffs and the 450-foot sea stack called the Old Man of Hoy, while it's also home to the **Scapa Flow Visitor Centre** at Lyness, which tells the story of the anchorage, particularly during the world wars. The waters off Flotta, east of Hoy, are particularly good for porpoises, dolphins and whales. Rousay, north of the Mainland, has another late Iron Age broch that is arguably better than the example at Gurness just over Eynhallow Sound. Like many of the islands, Westray is good for seabirds (peak season is May to July) while Papa Westray still has rare corncrakes. Sanday literally means 'the sandy island' and has great beaches, as does Stronsay. One of the other natural attractions on the latter, however, is the Vat of Kirbuster, a collapsed coastal cave with impressive rock arch. Seals are seen everywhere, all year round. **Orkney Ferries** sails between the Mainland and 13 of the other islands.

TRAVEL INFORMATION

NorthLink Ferries runs two services: the main sailing from Aberdeen to Kirkwall on the Orkney Mainland (6 hours) and a shorter hop from Scrabster in Caithness to Stromness, also on the Orkney Mainland (1 hour 30 minutes). The other year-round service comes from **Pentland Ferries**, which operates from Gills Bay in Caithness to St Margaret's Hope on South Ronaldsay (1 hour). All take cars. From May through to September, **John O'Groats Ferries** runs a foot passenger service from John O'Groats in Caithness to Burwick on South Ronaldsay (40 minutes). The **Tourist Office** is in Kirkwall.

WHEN TO GO

May, June and July have least wind, least rain and loads of daylight. In midsummer the sun rises around 4am and doesn't set until roughly 10.30pm. By contrast, December is dark, and often wet and very very windy, but it also affords the opportunity to see the winter solstice at Maes Howe. 'Cyclonic becoming north or north-east; 6 to gale 8, occasionally severe gale 9 for a time. Rough, occasionally very rough later. Rain. Moderate or good,' is a typical weather forecast for a December sailing.

Brittany

| **ROUTE** | Plymouth ▶ Roscoff ▶ Morlaix ▶ Dinan ▶ St-Malo ▶ Vitré ▶ Forêt de |
| | Paimpont ▶ Carnac ▶ Quimper ▶ Brest |

Embark on an overnight ferry to the Breton port of Roscoff for a break of two halves: a luxury bender of health treatments, spa hotels and Michelin-starred cuisine, interspersed with rambling, windsurfing, sailing and horse-riding. After that, take a quick zip around Brittany's more intriguing corners before heading back across the Channel, with the brave crewing their own yacht home.

Written by **Jonathan Lee**

Le Temps de Vivre p131

Le Jardin Exotique p129

Plymouth ▶ Roscoff
6 hours

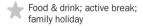
Food & drink; active break;
family holiday

THE TRIP

Short straw or long? Pick the *Pont-Aven*, Brittany Ferries' new luxury cross-Channel ship, and you might well think you were back in the glory days of maritime travel. With room for 2,400 passengers and 650 cars, she's a gleaming behemoth with designer cabins – complete with porthole windows and mosaic-tiled bathrooms – plus an art deco piano bar, haute cuisine restaurant, cinemas, decent shops, a swimming pool and even a kennel (the introduction of pet passports means that it's now possible to take Rover or Tiddles on holiday too). Le Grand Pavois, tucked away at the stern, is the only nod to the bad old days: a thumping nightclub-cum-bar hosting live acts and bingo.

The short straw is the *Pont L'Abbé*, which plies the same run but is let down by lacklustre bars and tired cabins: best avoid this old warhorse if you can.

The trip across the Channel takes between six and eight hours, leaving plenty of time to wave Plymouth's chain-riddled, concrete centre goodbye and prepare yourself for something altogether more sophisticated over the water.

THE DESTINATION

Perched on Finistère's Bay of Morlaix, Roscoff is a back to nature resort par excellence. Think restorative seaside retreat – spotless streets, bracing sea air, upmarket hotels and miles of spectacular white-sand beaches – with a good dash of 21st-century sophistication courtesy of health centres and modern sports facilities. A warming Gulf Stream and abundant terroir and sea provide plenty of raw material for gastronomes to get their teeth into as well.

With just 4,000 residents, the town manages to remain compact and unspoilt, despite the visitors quadrupling the population in high season. Bretons may have descended from the Celts of Britain but present-day attitudes couldn't be more different: expect quality eateries and bracing outdoor pursuits rather than the plastic tat emporia and lager-fuelled yobbery of so many British seaside towns.

The port's origins as a 16th-century corsair town – settled by privateers who plundered galleons to fund the king's coffers – are very much in evidence: head for the old town to find a good clutch of 16th-century merchants' houses, many sporting ornate gargoyles and chimeras.

You'll dock at the modern deep-water Port du Bloscon, which is situated just east of the Vieux Port (old port) and a 20-minute walk from the historic centre. First, stock up on supplies: **Algoplus** sells a good selection of maritime foodstuffs such as langoustine bisque and salmon and seaweed rillette, while you can pick up some quality vintages direct from the grower at **Peter Newcombe's Roscoff's Wine Seller**. While you're there, the **Criée de Roscoff** is a working fish market with exhibits and simulated trawler trip, offering a fast-track immersion into Roscoff's fishing industry.

BONNIE PRINCE AND JOHNNY ONION

Flat as a crêpe, Roscoff is very pedestrian-friendly and can be crossed in well under an hour on foot.

Start at the helpful **Office Municipal de Tourisme** and bone up on the town's famous visitors, which include Mary Queen of Scots – who set ashore at just five years of age in 1548 upon her engagement to François, the future King of France – and Bonnie Prince Charlie, who fled here after his bid to return English and Scottish thrones to the Stuarts ended in bloody defeat at Culloden in 1746.

You should also pick up a map for the self-guided heritage trail, a circular tour that takes in 24 of the town's most interesting landmarks. Highlights include the Chappelle Ste-Anne – a windblown chapel clinging defiantly to the headland and a touchstone for sailors – and the 16th-century Notre-Dame-de-Croas-Batz, a spirited Gothic affair in the old town sprouting an impressive sundial, wooden cherubs, flying buttresses and stone-carved caravel boats and figures, crowned by a preposterously ornate Renaissance tower.

Those keen on saving shoe leather should jump on the **Petit Train**, while A Fer et à Flots tours offer good one-day excursions by boat and train around the bay and countryside (June-Sept, details from the tourist office).

An unmissable attraction is **Le Jardin Exotique**, a small,

BRITTANY

Algoplus
02 98 61 14 14
www.algoplus-roscoff.fr

Peter Newcombe's Roscoff's Wine Seller
02 98 61 24 10
www.roscoffswineseller.com

Criée de Roscoff
02 98 62 39 26

Office Municipal de Tourisme
46 rue Gambetta
02 98 61 12 13
www.roscoff-tourisme.com

Petit Train
www.petit-train-bretagne.com
June-Sept, 35-min tours depart old port

Le Jardin Exotique
BP 54
02 98 61 29 19
www.jardinexotiqueroscoff.com

well-tended botanical garden on the east side of town and home to some 3,000 subtropical species including spiky Mexican agaves and perfumed Californian lilies. A granite outcrop affords excellent views across the Bay of Morlaix, while ponds, waterfalls and a Japanese bridge make it a great place to while away a couple of tranquil hours.

Meanwhile, the fastest way to get to grips with the classic Breton look – string of onions, beret, rickety bicycle, stripy jumper – is at the **Maison des Johnnies et de L'Oignon Rosé**. This excellent museum uses rare footage and photos to bring the history of Brittany's onion sellers to life: during the inter-war boom years, some 1,500 'Johnnies' touted 10,000 tonnes of plaited pink onions around the UK every year. Although the peddlers now number just two dozen, Appellation d'Origine Contrôlée status could see throngs of Johnnies taking to the saddle once more.

SUN, SAND AND SEAWEED

Offering numerous ways to tussle with wind and wave, Roscoff will tire the most hardened adrenaline junkie. More sedate pursuits include health spas, walking, horse-riding and golf.

You'll find Roscoff's sailing centre, **Centre Nautique de Roscoff**, in the old port. Throw yourself into the drink on dinghies, catamarans, kayaks and cruises while the kids get to play in the seaside kindergarten (July-Aug).

The **Centre de Glisse**, seven kilometres west up the coast near Santec, offers kayaking, sand-yachting, wave-skiing and speed-sailing. Or you can play tennis at the **Lagadenou tennis courts** on the west side of town, scuba dive at the **Aquacamp** two kilometres west, play golf 13 kilometres away at **Carantec** or ride at the **Centre Equestre du Mouster** eight kilometres away in St-Pol-de-Léon.

Roscoff's Centre de Thalassothérapie is a must-stop for anyone keen to wrap themselves in puréed seaweed or enjoy an anti-stress massage. It ranks as one of the best thalassotherapy centres in France, but be warned: this is a temple of health rather than beauty and its clinical, white-tiled treatment rooms and matronly efficiency are a million miles from fluffy robes and candles. Bathing capped visitors follow a strict timetable of treatments, which range from algae wraps (you'll feel like a giant heated spring roll), high-pressure douches (essentially a carwash, with you as the car) and *polper rouler* massage (a half-hour pinch-athon). Themed packages offer the best value for money, while there's also a swimming pool, jacuzzi and sauna.

A simple walk along the beach is the best antidote for such a pummelling: head for the insider's choice, plage de Traon Erc'h near Le Jardin Exotique, a tucked-away crescent of white sand just 25 minutes' stroll from the town centre.

SCOFF AWAY IN ROSCOFF

For such a compact town, Roscoff's culinary scene punches way above its weight. Seafood is the mainstay – mackerel, pollock, seabass, crab and lobster are landed by the buckletload – while eateries range from affordable rustic backrooms and crêperies to pricey Michelin-starred numbers.

For a buzzy experience, try **Le Surcouf**. Probably the best mid-priced eaterie in town, it's always packed with families and smart

Maison des Johnnies et de L'Oignon Rosé
48 rue Brizeux
02 98 61 25 48

Centre Nautique de Roscoff
quai Charles de Gaulle
02 98 69 72 79
www.roscoff-nautique.com

Centre de Glisse
plage du Dossen
02 98 29 40 78

Lagadenou tennis courts
02 98 61 23 73

Aquacamp
La Ruguel
www.aquacamp.fr

Carantec
02 98 67 09 14

Centre Equestre du Mouster
02 98 69 51 48

Roscoff's Centre de Thalassothérapie
rue Victor Hugo
02 98 29 20 00
www.thalasso.com

Le Surcouf
14 rue Amiral Réveillère
02 98 69 71 89
www.jalima.fr

business types, all tucking in to steaming bowls of fish soup and icy towers of oysters, mussels, prawns and langoustines.

If your idea of a perfect meal is to be served an endless round of ornate splodges – each described in excruciating detail – then try the Michelin-starred **Le Temps de Vivre**. Jean-Yves Crenn gives local produce such as artichokes, black pudding, crab and onions the haute cuisine treatment, but it's all a tad earnest.

You're on far safer ground with fellow Michelin star-bagger **Le Yachtman at Le Brittany hotel**. The setting is hard to beat, with a cavernous fireplace, wooden beams, deep leather seats and good views across the harbour, while chef Loïc Le Bail majors on seabass, scallops and local veg, and his lobster *kig ha farz* is the stuff of legend.

Simplicity reigns at **La Moule au Pot**, a small seafood restaurant in the old town. Dishes are unfussy with staples including red onion compote, moules frites and seafood lasagne. Exposed stone walls and a flower-scented terrace provide pleasant backdrops.

Those seeking affordable fine dining should try the **L'Ecume des Jours**, situated in a 16th-century house right on the quay. Nicole and Michel Quéré serve updated seafood classics such

Le Temps de Vivre
pl Lacaze Duthiers
02 98 61 27 28
www.letempsdevivre.net

Le Yachtman at Le Brittany hotel
blvd Ste-Barbe
02 98 69 70 78
www.hotel-brittany.com

La Moule au Pot
13 rue Edouard Corbière
02 98 19 33 60

L'Ecume des Jours
quai d'Auxerre
02 98 61 22 83

GETTING THERE UNDER YOUR OWN SAIL

If the luxury cabins of the *Pont-Aven* don't quite shiver your timbers, crewing a yacht offers a more exhilarating way of crossing the Channel. Solo travellers who know their spinnakers from their poop decks can offer their services to 'hitch' their way to France, while groups can charter an entire boat. The 116-mile trip from Plymouth to Roscoff takes 18-24 hours depending on the weather, while the Channel Islands are 14-16 hours away. Other destinations in France include Morlaix, Treguier and St-Malo. The season runs from April to October.

CREWING

This is an ad hoc system so don't bank on a specific departure day. Your strategy: pin up details of your requested trip – together with a brief summary of your nautical skills – on a yacht club noticeboard in Plymouth and wait for the call.

There are some 20 local clubs, and the Royal Western Yacht Club of England, on Plymouth's Queen Anne's Battery, is a good place to start. During the summer, the confident turn up at the clubs on Sunday morning to tout their skills in person.

Those looking to brush up on their nautical skills before setting sail should contact one of the UK's sailing clubs: try the London Corinthian Sailing Club (www.lcsc.org.uk), the Bromsgrove Boaters (www.bromsgroveboaters.co.uk) or the Bristol Sailing Association (www.bristolsailing.org.uk) – all are good sailing clubs running regular cross-channel trips and lively social events.

CHARTERING

Chartering your own yacht across the Channel offers a full-on Captain Bligh experience. Liberty Yachts on Plymouth's Queen Anne's Battery is a good bet, offering a choice of ten boats sleeping up to eight people with a supplied skipper and skipper's mate, depending on your group's experience.

The boats come with full mod cons including showers, central heating, cookers and oil skins but don't expect to be sinking barrels of rum and singing sea shanties: you'll work hard during the voyage and cook for any supplied crew. Hire charges start at around £500 for the weekend (low season) with skipper, fuel, mooring and food adding around £200 per day. Unsurprisingly, stag weekends are barred.

Liberty Yachts
01752 227911, www.libertyyachts.co.uk
Royal Western Yacht Club of England
01752 660077, www.rwyc.org

as foie gras with pink onion marmalade and lobster and scallops with saffron. Set menus start at a reasonable €20 per head. The nearby **Les Alizés** is a more spartan gastro affair: there are great sea views from the open-plan dining room while oysters, lamb, fresh fish, grilled lobster and smoked salmon are on offer.

A good budget, late-night option is **Marie Stuart**, a friendly check tablecloth-type eaterie serving good pizza and pasta.

And as for drinking, many restaurants have bars, but for longer Breton cider-powered sessions try the old port's **Le Winch Bar** on quai Charles de Gaulle or the nearby **Bar Ty Pierre**.

WHERE TO STAY

Roscoff offers an excellent selection of hotels in every price bracket and a good campsite just outside town. Be aware that many hotels shut up shop between mid November and February.

The breezy 16-bedroom **Hôtel du Centre**, situated on Roscoff's old port, is arguably the town's best-priced and well-located hotel, offering minimalism with a seaside twist. Beyond deckchair stripes and funky bathrooms are excellent sea views, a good in-house restaurant and decent terrace.

Traditionalists with deeper pockets should check out **Le Brittany**. Situated on an outcrop a few hundred yards from the town centre, this rebuilt merchant's mansion resembles an ancestral home with tapestries, blazing fires, dark-wood Breton furniture and a snug bar, while a pool and spa up the pampering ante. The restaurant is the highlight but the bedrooms, a little boxy and characterless, can't quite match the opulence and the whole experience borders on the formal.

The **Hôtel Aux Tamaris** is one of the most characterful places in town. A nautical theme can so often conjure up images of stuffed albatrosses and piped sea shanties, but this immaculate hotel pulls it off in grand style. Sails stretch across ceilings, bright rooms bear the monikers of boats, islands and lighthouses and teak furniture and portholes abound. You're on a quiet street right on the sea overlooking the Ile de Batz, while the bar resembles the interior of a luxury yacht.

Hôtel Le Temps de Vivre is a designer retreat in the old town. The owners have converted a corsair's residence into a boutique 15-bedroom establishment with cutting-edge furniture, good sea views, open-plan bathrooms and Wi-Fi access.

If you're stuck during high season, try the **Armen Le Triton**. It may resemble a land-locked cruise liner, but its 45 rooms are keenly priced. If nothing else, you can offer owner Olivier Vidie a few words of encouragement – he's painstakingly transforming a 1970s frill-fest into a modern establishment with simple rooms and decent balconies. Large gardens and tennis court make up for its slightly inland position.

Of course, there's always the canvas option at **Camping de Perharidy 'Aux Quatre Saisons'**. The campsite is situated two kilometres west of the town centre and offers 200 pitches for tents, caravans and campervans, plus rentable bungalows and mobile homes. Facilities include washrooms, a small selection of shops, laundry and tourist information centre. It's hardly the Ritz, but kids are well catered for thanks to on-site minigolf, table tennis and pétanque, and sea kayaking, diving, fishing and golden sands are all nearby.

Les Alizés
quai d'Auxerre
02 98 69 75 90

Marie Stuart
28 rue Amiral Réveillère
02 98 61 28 06

Le Winch Bar
02 98 61 15 80

Bar Ty Pierre
1 rue Gambetta
02 98 69 72 75

Hôtel du Centre
Le Port
02 98 61 24 25
www.chezjanie.com

Le Brittany
blvd Sainte-Barbe
02 98 69 70 78
www.hotel-brittany.com

Hôtel Aux Tamaris
49 rue Edouard Corbière
02 98 61 22 99
www.hotel-aux-tamaris.com

Hôtel Le Temps de Vivre
pl Lacaze Duthiers
02 98 19 33 19
www.letempsdevivre.net

Armen Le Triton
rue du Docteur Bagot
02 98 61 24 44
www.hotel-letriton.com

Camping de Perharidy 'Aux Quatre Saisons'
April-Oct, Le Ruguel
02 98 69 70 86
www.camping-aux4saisons.com

BATZ AND BOULES

Back to the 1950s anyone? The **Île de Batz**, a ten-minute ferry chug from Roscoff's old port, is pure Famous Five territory. Just two by four kilometres, it's a wind-swept hideaway of stone cottages and heather, the odd grazing pony and long empty stretches of beach – perfect for shy sun-seekers and inept boules players alike. Biking, horse-riding and birdwatching are options, while **Le Jardin Exotique Georges Delaselle** on the south-eastern tip is a marvel. Founded in 1897, this recently replanted garden hosts more than 2,000 species, including an outstanding collection of palms.

Island accommodation is basic, but try the **Grand Hôtel Morvan** or chambres d'hôtes at **Ti Va Zadou**. A good self-catering option is a two-person gîte at **Ti Ma Bro**.

Of the smattering of eating and drinking possibilities, **Le Bigorneau Langoureux** on the approach road to the dock, is one of the best: a tapas-style bar offering wine by the glass and excellent snacks. Good local produce such as confit d'oignon and organic blonde beer can be found at the boulangerie and pâtisserie **La Marée Gourmand** just up into Bourg village.

IN THE AREA

Roscoff offers good rail connections to some of Brittany's most inspiring corners and onward connections to neighbouring Normandy, the Loire and the Atlantic coast.

Half an hour down the line is Morlaix, an old port town on the doorstep of several parish closes – impressive churchyards featuring ossuaries and churches dating from the 15th to the 17th centuries. Further east, the citadel town of St-Malo makes a good buzzy coastal base, with regular ferries back to the UK.

Those intrigued by the area's Celtic heritage should head for Carnac on Brittany's southern coast, home to around 2,000 prehistoric megaliths. If you're warming to the mystical theme, seek out the Forêt de Paimpont, 30 kilometres west of Rennes and accessed by bus from the capital. The forest is good walking territory but, more importantly, is Merlin's old stomping ground and home to Fontaine de Barentone, the wizard's spring.

Architectural highlights include Dinan, situated just north of Rennes, and the smaller Vitré, found close to the Normandy border. Both are well-preserved medieval cities with all the embellishments of castles, ramparts and cobbled lanes. To the south-west, Quimper boasts an impressive Gothic cathedral.

TRAVEL INFORMATION

Brittany Ferries runs up to three outward and two return journeys a day between Plymouth and Roscoff (dropping to six days a week, Jan to mid Mar). Crossings take around six hours during the day and eight hours overnight. Fares for a car plus two passengers start at £230 return. Two-berth cabins on the *Pont-Aven* start at £35 each way for overnight crossings, while the far less plush *Pont L'Abbé* offers two-berth couchettes (without en suite bathrooms or toilets) from a bargain £15 each way.

WHEN TO GO

June-September.

Further reading

Gwyn Griffith *Goodbye Johnny Onions* A history and elegy for stripy jumpers, strings of onions and, in fact, a whole lost world.

Sébastien Minguy *Roscoff: Images du Passé* History through a lens: fascinating and, in places, moving.

Guy de Maupassant *Selected Short Stories* The master of the short story.

Websites

www.roscoff.fr
The official town site.

www.roscoff-tourisme.com
And the tourist office site.

www.kervarker.org
Learn the Breton language online.

www.iledebatz.com
In French only.

Île de Batz
www.iledebatz.com

Le Jardin Exotique Georges Delaselle
April-Nov
02 98 61 75 65
www.jardin-georgesdelaselle.fr

Grand Hôtel Morvan
Pors Kernoc
02 98 61 78 06

Ti Va Zadou
Bourg
02 98 61 76 91
www.guidesdecharme.com

Ti Ma Bro
Le Bar Hir
02 98 61 79 18
www.ti-ma-bro.fr

Le Bigorneau Langoureux
Débarcadère
02 98 61 74 50
www.lebigorneaulangoureux.com

La Marée Gourmand
Venoc
02 98 61 74 33

Brittany Ferries
www.brittany-ferries.com

Arcachon p140

Bordeaux

ROUTE London ▶ Paris ▶ Bordeaux

As you'd expect, Bordeaux is overflowing with top-quality wine and
fantastic regional and gourmet food to match, but it offers much more.
The city is packed with beautiful neo-classical and Beaux Arts architecture,
parks, galleries and museums, as well as a thriving nightlife scene, while
the surrounding areas have sandy beaches, medieval villages, pretty rivers
and breathtaking châteaux.

Written by **Jill Starley-Grainger**

Port d'Arcachon

Cap Ferret p140

Caudalie Vinothérapie Spa p140

THE TRIP

With just one change necessary, the train journey from London to Bordeaux is fairly straightforward, taking around seven hours door to door. Eurostar arrives at Gare du Nord in the north of Paris, while the trains for Bordeaux depart from Montparnasse in the south, so here you're faced with the only difficulty of the trip: you have to get across the city on line 4 of the metro – a bit of a hassle when you're laden with luggage. If you book straight through with Eurostar, more than an hour is always allowed for your cross-city transit, although it usually takes between 30 and 40 minutes. From Montparnasse, a three-hour journey on a TGV takes you to Bordeaux St-Jean station, whence it's a 20-minute walk or a fast bus, tram or taxi to the city centre. The train ride south passes through grassy rolling hills and cities, including Poitiers and Angoulême, and you'll see plenty of cows and a large wind farm out of your window. Food and drink, including some decent French wine, are usually available in a restaurant car on board, but it's mostly uninspiring pre-packaged sandwiches, so you're better off taking a picnic.

St Pancras International ▸
Bordeaux St-Jean
6 hours 40 minutes

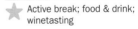 Active break; food & drink; winetasting

THE DESTINATION

With its prime location in sunny south-west France and a young, affluent population, Bordeaux is a fantastic city for a weekend break. Recently named a UNESCO World Heritage Site for its lovely belle époque centre, it's packed with plenty of diversions for day and night. Head an hour in any direction for everything from beaches and boats to châteaux and spas.

In the UK, the entire region is often referred to as Bordeaux, but properly named it's the Aquitaine region. To the west of Bordeaux city are the calm, warm waters of the Bay of Arcachon, with great swimming and wildlife spotting, and the more tempestuous Atlantic coast, providing some of Europe's best surfing. North will take you to the geographically dull, but oenologically outstanding, Médoc, where you can enjoy wine-tasting at the châteaux of the world's most famous vineyards. South is the Lot, filled with miles and miles of flat roads and pine forests, perfect for family cycling and camping holidays. But the richest rewards start an hour to the east, with UNESCO World Heritage Sites, fortified villages, gorgeous vineyards, crumbling castles and magnificent châteaux. Keep going just a little further, around two-and-a-half hours east of Bordeaux, and you're bang in the Périgord region (known simply as 'the Dordogne' in the UK), with the incredibly pretty Dordogne river, beautiful villages and, yes, more châteaux.

If your visit is short, it's best to stay in the city of Bordeaux and take day trips to the lovely town of St-Emilion and its surrounding vineyards, the Bay of Arcachon for bird-spotting and sun-bathing, and the intimate, luxurious wine spa Caudalie for pampering among the vines. But there's so much to do in the region that it easily fills a one- or two-week holiday, in which case it's better to take a gîte and visit Bordeaux city on day trips.

Booking ahead is a necessity for certain elements of a trip to Bordeaux, especially for visits to fine restaurants and vineyards. You can't just rock up and expect to get in. Depending on the star status and size of the restaurant or vineyard, you should book anywhere from a few days to a few weeks in advance, especially for the most famous vineyards, such as Château Margaux and Château Latour, where it's best to book at least a month ahead, although the best introduction for complete beginners is probably at **Château Mouton Rothschild** (for reservations, email visites@bphr.com; €25), one of the few first-growth châteaux easily accessible to outsiders.

CULTURE

In the past few years, Bordeaux has really turned itself around from a crumbling 18th-century relic to a thriving, buzzy city. This is largely thanks to huge amounts of money being invested in renovating the old town, riverfront and docklands, attracting a young population and securing it UNESCO World Heritage status and the Rugby World Cup in 2007. It has a dozen museums and innumerable galleries covering art, history, shipping, wine and more, but where this forward-looking city really excels is in the modern and futuristic. Your first stop should be the contemporary art museum **CAPC**. Housed in a magnificent 19th-century warehouse on the Garonne river, CAPC is home to hundreds of works from the mid-20th century to today, including pieces by the

BORDEAUX

likes of Gilbert and George and Anish Kapoor. The permanent collection is on rotating display, and a series of temporary exhibitions takes over part of the space.

Fans of the architect Le Corbusier should make their way to the suburb of Pessac. In this otherwise ordinary area is Cité Frugès, a neighbourhood of houses designed by Le Corbusier in 1926 for the workers of a sugar foundation. The simple square, white boxes were a long way from being dream homes for the 1920s working class families for whom they were intended, but in recent years, they've been snapped up and renovated by fans of Modernism. At the **Maison Municipale Le Corbusier** you can take a short tour through one of the houses, then follow a self-guided walk through the neighbourhood.

Towards Bacalan docks, down a long, slightly dodgy-looking back road, is the unmissable, quirky **Le Garage Moderne**. It's a multi-functional space of garage, modern art gallery, café and sometimes nightclub, all housed in a former warehouse. The café is friendly and the art gallery entertaining, but the main draw is, in actuality, the garage, and this is true even for non-car fans. In fact, it does a big sideline in bicycles. Visitors are welcome to wander around the garage, where some of the disused cars have been turned into installation artworks. And should your automobile or bicycle be in need of a repair, you don't simply bring it here and drop it off. This is a co-operative where the members join in. Come here to use the tools to fix your vehicle or bicycle yourself, get advice, lessons and assistance from the knowledgeable male and female mechanics, or, for complicated work, pay them a fee to do the work for you.

SHOPPING

You can find everything from haute couture to trendy boutiques in Bordeaux, and the pedestrianised old town makes for a pleasant shopping experience. All the big names are here, but where Bordeaux shines is in wine and food, including local specialities, such as canelés. Shops are usually open Mondays to Saturdays from around 10am to 7pm and closed on Sundays.

For clothes shopping, those with cash to splash will want to get lost in the Golden Triangle, the area between allées de Tourny, cours Georges Clemenceau and cours de l'Intendance. Here you'll find Christian Dior, Hermès, Cartier, Louis Vuitton et al. A little further south on the long, pedestrianised rue St-Catherine, you'll find classy department store Galeries Lafayette, adorable baby shop Natalys and a host of high-street favourites, including Etam, H&M and Zara. Poke around rue du Pas St George and rue des Remparts for smaller, independent shops and boutiques.

A Bordeaux speciality everyone should try is the scrumptious canelé, a small eggy sponge flavoured with rum and vanilla. The most famous speciality shop is **Baillardran**, which sells the sticky sweets singly or in boxes.

Even if you're planning vineyard visits, you might want to stock up on wine in the city. Some vineyards have no wine available to sell to the public, while others keep only a limited supply. One of the most beautiful wine shops in the city is **L'Intendant**, with four floors of bottles to choose from, but since it specialises in the grands crus, don't expect bargains. This is instead a place to visit to find wines you're unlikely to get anywhere else in the world, and for the ones you'd get in the UK, the prices are marginally better.

Château Mouton Rothschild
05 56 73 21 29
www.bphr.com

CAPC Le Musée d'Art Contemporain
Entrepôt Laîné, 7 rue Ferrère, Chartrons
05 56 00 81 50
Closed Mon

Maison Municipale Le Corbusier
4 rue Le Corbusier, Pessac
05 56 36 56 46
www.officiecultureldepessac.net

Le Garage Moderne
1 rue des Etrangers, Bacalan
05 56 50 91 33
www.legaragemoderne.org

Baillardran
Galerie des Grands Hommes
05 56 79 05 89
www.baillardran.com
Branches throughout the city centre

L'Intendant
2 aallées de Tourny
05 56 81 18 87

Seeko'o p140

EATING

Where fine wine flows, excellent food follows, and that's certainly true of Bordeaux. You won't have to look far to find a decent meal, from simple snack bars to Michelin stars. The regional specialities are seafood, especially oysters and eel, beef, asparagus, prunes and mushrooms. Cooking varies from refined or fussy (depending on your perspective) to hearty or lardy (again…), with plenty of rich sauces in the rustic restaurants, and froths, foams and jus at the other end. Luckily, the area has such as a strong wine and food heritage that it's difficult to have a bad meal.

Leading the gourmet brigade is **La Tupina**, where Jean Pierre Xiradakis dishes up regional cuisine in a relaxed atmosphere. The restaurant has a country house theme, and while the food is rustic, it has a sophisticated edge. The seasonal menu might include roast black pig loin with mashed potatoes and gravy or a hearty cassoulet, but it's worth trying the special ingredient-led menus, with every course, including dessert, based on a single, seasonal ingredient, such as tomato or mushroom.

For Michelin-starred magnificence, visit **Le Chapon Fin**, located in an unusual art nouveau building. The restaurant creates exquisite dishes, such as lightly roasted John Dory with chilled lentil cake and warm truffle cream, at one of Bordeaux's swankiest addresses in the old town.

Fans of fromage should pay homage at **Baud et Millet**, a restaurant with a large menu of cheese-based dishes. Don't miss a visit to the chilly, dark cheese cellar, where you'll see a range of unusual French cheeses, perhaps including the local Tome d'Aquitaine, a goat's cheese bathed in Sauternes sweet wine.

Other restaurants worth seeking out include **Chez Greg Le Grand Théâtre**, the trendiest eatery in town, and **Le Bouchon Bordelais**, which offers a modern take on regional cuisine.

For light meals and snacks, visit **L'Orangerie** for great views of the park, **L'Autre Salon de Thé** for its teas and pastries, and **Le Grand Café** for city-centre people-watching.

SLEEPING

Brits have been flocking to Bordeaux since Eleanor of Aquitaine married King Henry II in the 12th century, and we were the primary catalyst for spreading the word around the world about

La Tupina
6 rue Porte de la Monnaie
05 56 91 56 37
www.latupina.com

Le Chapon Fin
5 rue Montesquieu
05 56 79 10 10
www.chapon-fin.com

Baud et Millet
19 rue Huguerie
05 56 79 05 77
www.baudetmillet.fr

Chez Greg Le Grand Théâtre
29 rue Esprit des Lois
05 56 31 30 30
www.chezgreg.fr

Le Bouchon Bordelais
2 rue Courbin
05 56 44 33 00
www.bouchon-bordelais.com

L'Orangerie
Jardin Public, entrance cours de Verdun
05 56 48 24 41

L'Autre Salon de Thé
11 rue des Remparts
05 56 48 55 43

Le Grand Café
65 cours de l'Intendance
05 56 52 61 10

the quality of Bordeaux wines, so British visitors are sure to get a warm welcome. Most hotels are of the refined olde worlde variety, but more and more, such as Seeko'o, which opened in 2007, are targeting a younger market.

For luxury, the **Regent Bordeaux** has just reopened after an extensive renovation. The decor is very Marie Antoinette and the location unbeatable – just across from the Grand Opera right in the heart of the city. Another option is the four-star **Le Burdigala**, which has nice, spacious rooms and friendly service.

One of the chicest sleeps in the city is **Seeko'o**, a new design hotel in a modern building overlooking the river north of the centre near the trendy dockside area. For charming country hotel ambience in a fantastic old-town location, try **La Tour Intendance**.

Bargain beds with a difference can be found at **Une Chambre en Ville**, a small hotel in a former art gallery in the city centre, and **Hôtel Acanthe**, which has low prices in a good area.

BEYOND THE CITY LIMITS

For a spa day with local flavour take the short 15-minute cab ride to **Caudalie Vinothérapie Spa** outside Bordeaux. Located in an excellent Grand Cru Classe vineyard, the intimate spa feels very French and sophisticated. All the treatments use Caudalie's patented products, which feature the powerful antioxidants of wine-grapeseed oils. While waiting for treatments, take a dip in the small thermal pool, get steamy in the hammam or recline in the indoor and outdoor relaxation areas.

Hop on a train in Bordeaux, and you can be hitting the beach in less than an hour at the beautiful Bay of Arcachon. By rail, the main access point is Arcachon, a friendly seaside resort at the bottom near the Atlantic, but you can also start at the tip of the bay, La Teich, which is about ten minutes closer to Bordeaux.

Arcachon itself is full of attractive restaurants, shops and cafés, and its sandy beaches are pretty and calm enough for families. It does get very busy, though, so if you're seeking peace and quiet, you'll be better off heading elsewhere. Take the ferry across the bay to swanky Cap Ferret, a headland with the bay on one side and the Atlantic on the other. Watch millionaires pose on their yachts on the bay side while you recline on the quiet sandy beach, or take surfing lessons on the Atlantic side. You can hire bicycles from most towns around the bay, and the 70 kilometres of flat, easy cycle paths take you through quaint oyster farming villages and along pretty coastal routes. Just outside Arcachon is the dramatic Dune du Pyla, Europe's tallest sand dune, with the Atlantic on one side, the bay on the other and pine forests behind.

Wildlife-lovers shouldn't miss the magnificent, 120-hectare **Parc Ornithologique du Teich**. A protected nature reserve, it's host to more than 260 species of birds, 80 species of which are permanent residents. You'll need at least an hour, but preferably two or three, to stroll around the wetlands, spotting white storks, black kites, kingfishers and hoopoes.

IN THE AREA

Less than an hour east of Bordeaux is some of the region's most beautiful scenery. The rolling hills of the **Entre-deux-Mers** are host to pretty vineyards, small and large châteaux, historic villages and the UNESCO World Heritage town of St-Emilion. If you just want to

Regent Bordeaux
2-5 pl de la Comédie
05 57 30 44 44
www.regenthotels.com

Le Burdigala
115 rue Georges Bonnac
05 56 90 16 16
www.burdigala.com

Seeko'o
54 quai de Bacalan
05 56 39 07 07
www.seekoo-hotel.com

La Tour Intendance
16 rue de la Vieille Tour
05 56 44 56 56
www.hotel-tour-intendance.com

Une Chambre en Ville
35 rue Bouffard
05 56 81 34 53
www.bandb-bx.com

Hôtel Acanthe
12-14 rue St-Rémi
05 56 81 66 58
www.acanthe-hotel-bordeaux.com

Caudalie Vinothérapie Spa
chemin de Smith Haut-Lafitte, Bordeaux-Martillac
05 57 83 82 82
www.caudalie.com

Parc Ornithologique du Teich
Maison de la Nature du Bassin d'Arcachon, Le Teich
05 56 22 80 93
www.parc-ornithologique-du-teich.com

Entre-deux-Mers
Office du Tourisme, 4 rue Issartier, Monsegur
05 56 61 82 73
www.tourisme.entredeuxmers.com

DOWN THE DORDOGNE

Just an hour east of Bordeaux is one of the prettiest stretches of water in Europe, the Dordogne river. Hugely popular as a recreational waterway, it's easily navigable, even by beginners. The section between Bergerac and Sarlat, around two hours from Bordeaux, flows at just the right speed to minimise paddling, and the scenery is diverse, including châteaux, medieval villages, prehistoric caves and a wide variety of birds and plants. Most hire canoes are for two people, but some hold up to four. The main canoe season is April to September, but with advance planning, you can usually arrange out-of-season canoeing, especially in the early spring and late autumn.

You should go with the flow of the river, east to west towards Bordeaux, so you'll need to take a train, bus or car from Bordeaux to start your adventure. Canoe companies offer self-guided trips from an hour to a week, and they can arrange hotels for you, ferrying your luggage from place to place so you can dawdle along the river without a care in the world. With the longer trips, you could keep going until you almost reach Libourne, an hour east of Bordeaux by train and just 10 or 15 minutes from St-Emilion. If you're coming back to the UK by Eurostar, trains from Libourne run direct to Paris.

Canoe trips depart from almost everywhere along this 490-kilometre-long river, but the most popular stretch is from Calviac, around two-and-a-half hours from Bordeaux near St-Julien-de-Lampon, to Tremolat. The scenery here takes in châteaux, cliffs and caves. You can cover it in a day, but two will allow for more stops along the way, and you'll want to take them. Périgord Loisirs is a reliable tour firm.

Making a start at Calviac, you quickly get in your stride, but even if you're completely hopeless, the river will carry you along slowly but surely. Before long, birds start swooping across your bow, and damsel and dragonflies act as guides. There's ample time to gawp at the castles and châteaux along the way, including the strange exterior of Château de Fénelon and the clifftop Montfort Castle. Thirsty? Pull over for a quick drink in Groléjac.

Back on the river, you pass an island bird sanctuary (keep your eyes peeled for black kites, herons and cormorants) and caves in the cliffs. If you're feeling peckish or just want to stretch your legs, stop off further along in La Roque-Gageac, a beautiful riverside village. On the river here, you'll suddenly be joined by some strange-looking craft – replica 19th-century gabare river boats. About five minutes from the village is a nice, open patch of grass, good for a picnic.

The last leg of your one- or two-day trip is possibly the most spectacular, thanks to the looming Castle of Castelnaud. If you want to take a side trip to the castle, pull over in Beynac and take a taxi or, if you're feeling really fit, walk up. To finish your day, you'll go past pretty Beynac village, where the canoe company will be waiting to take you and your canoe back to base or to your hotel for the night.

After all that hard work, you deserve dinner, so take a taxi to **Le Vieux Logis**, a Michelin-starred restaurant and hotel. Indulge in the six-course Périgord menu, for a taste of the region's finest fare, but beware that you'll be offered foie gras almost everywhere, so make sure to specify if you don't want it. Now you've refuelled, you're ready for another day on the Dordogne, making your way slowly towards Bergerac.

Perigord Loisirs have a base in Vitrac. Half-day canoe hire, €12 per person. Multi-day trips from €30 per person per day, staying at campsites, or €60 per person per day, half-board at two-star hotels, both including luggage transport.

Le Vieux Logis *Tremolat, 05 53 22 80 06, www.vieux-logis.com*

Perigord Loisirs *La Riviere, Vitrac, 05 53 28 23 43, www.canoeloisirs.com*

BORDEAUX

www.treesforcities.org

Trees for Cities
Charity registration number 1032154

We all care about reducing pollution.
We all care about tackling global warming.
We all care about our carbon footprint.

That's why Trees for Cities has planted
over 100,000 trees in cities at home and
abroad.

Leave your mark and join us today
to help create a greener future for
everyone.

To find out more about adult, joint, family
and child membership of Trees for Cities
visit:

www.treesforcities.org

Leave
Your
Mark

Create a green future for cities.

visit St Emilion and a few vineyards, Bordeaux tourist information does some good coach trips, but to really appreciate the area, you'll need a car or bicycle, but be warned it's very hilly.

Ideally, you'll have a car, allowing you plenty of time to wander through the vineyards and villages. A visit to **St-Emilion** is a must. Stroll through the cobbled streets, visit the monolithic church and join the excellent two-hour wine tasting course at the **Wine School of St-Emilion** for an introduction to the region's wines. The best scenery is south of St-Emilion, including plenty of fortified bastide villages, the Garonne and Dordogne rivers, and vineyards, sunflower fields, châteaux and castles galore. Stop off in Castillon-la-Bataille to watch the locals play pétanque by the river, lively La Reole for its Saturday morning market, Loubens and Bagas for their water mills and picture-perfect Castelmoron for its quaint houses with cascading flowers.

When it's time for food, stop at the Michelin-starred **Hostellerie de Plaisance** or stock up on provisions for picnics by the Garonne river (on picnic tables in Castillon-la-Bataille or on the ground near Barsac) or in the hills (try the Grotte Ferrand near St-Emilion).

For a real treat, book a classic convertible sports car with **Gourmet Touring**, which provides tailor-made tours of Entre-deux-Mers and the surrounding regions from £550 for four days. This is easily the most glamorous way to cruise around the countryside.

TRAVEL INFORMATION

Eurostar runs four times a day between Bordeaux and London, taking around seven hours in total, including a change in Paris between Gare du Nord and Montparnasse; fares from £99.

Ferries are another good option, with all the usual fast crossings from Dover to Calais, a six- or eight-hour journey from Plymouth to Roscoff, or the lengthier 20-hour overnight journey from Plymouth to Santander. In Calais, trains go to Bordeaux with a change in Lille, taking seven to nine hours. In Roscoff, trains take around nine hours, changing in Morlaix and Paris. Unless you're really keen to cut out the carbon, the Santander journey is best done with a car because getting a train or bus to Bordeaux is complicated and time-consuming. In a car, you can drive from Santander to Bordeaux in four-and-a-half hours.

Ferries between Dover and Calais take 90 minutes. **P&O Ferries** has up to 25 crossings a day, from £50 return with car and up to nine passengers; **SeaFrance** has up to 11 crossings a day from £52 return with car and up to five passengers.

Ferries from Plymouth to Roscoff take six or eight hours. **Brittany Ferries** has up to three crossings per day, costing around £100 return for foot passengers.

Ferries between Plymouth and Santander take around 20 hours. **Brittany Ferries** has two sailings a week, from £258 return, plus a two-berth cabin from £118 return or a reclining seat for £14 return. P&O Ferries has one crossing every three days, from £498 for a car and two people, including en suite cabin and all taxes, on board two nights from Plymouth to Santander and one night on the return trip.

Trains can be booked through **Rail Europe**.

WHEN TO GO

From Easter to All Saints.

Further reading
....

Robert Parker *Bordeaux* Know your wines. Alison Weir *Eleanor of Aquitaine: By the Wrath of God, Queen of England* A biography of the extraordinary woman who was wife to Louis VII of France and then Henry II of England, and mother of Richard the Lionheart and King John.

Websites
....

www.vins-bordeaux.fr
Santé!

www.bbc.co.uk/languages/french
Brush up before you go. Talking English slowly doesn't work.

www.canoe-france.com
River maps and further information to help with paddling.

St-Emilion
Office du Tourisme, pl des Créneaux
05 57 55 28 28
www.saint-emilion-tourisme.com

Wine School of St-Emilion
Ecole du Vin de St Emilion, 4 rue du Clocher, St-Émilion
www.vignobleschateaux.fr

Hostellerie de Plaisance
pl du Clocher, St-Emilion
05 57 55 07 55
www.hostellerie-plaisance.com

Gourmet Touring
06 32 80 04 74
www.gourmet-touring.com

Eurostar
08705 186186
www.eurostar.com
£5 booking fee if booked on the telephone

P&O Ferries
08716 645645
www.poferries.com

SeaFrance
0871 663 2546
www.seafranceholidays.com

Brittany Ferries
0870 907 6103
www.brittany-ferries.co.uk

Rail Europe
www.raileurope.co.uk

De Adriaan Windmill p149

Holland

ROUTE Harwich ▶ Hook of Holland ▶ The Hague ▶ Delft ▶ Haarlem ▶ Rotterdam

A smart passenger ferry to the Hook of Holland, gateway port to Holland's cities. From there. take the train to the handsome political capital, The Hague; the achingly pretty nearby Delft is a tram ride away. North, by train, is the medieval city of Haarlem. On the return to the Hook, stay in nearby Rotterdam where dockyards lean against stylish glass towers in a city renowned for its clubbing scene.

Written by **Claire Boobbyer**

Delft p147

Rotterdam p150

THE TRIP

Ferries chug across the 109 nautical miles of sea separating Harwich from the Hook of Holland both by day and by night. Of the two possibilities we recommend the later option: the journey passes in easy slumber in your own cabin and you wake, refreshed and ready to go, in Holland. On the day crossing, the initial excitement of putting to sea and seeing land drop away behind you is dissipated by the realisation that there's going to be nothing to see but sea for the next few hours, The time does seem to drag, even though there are two restaurants (one with waiter service, one a buffet), multiple cinema screenings, slot machines, children's play area and duty-free shop to keep passengers occupied during the six hours 15 minutes voyage.

The vast *Hollandica* ship carries 900 passengers with 398 cabins that are ultra-clean, spacious and comfortable, with abundant hot-water showers. The 44,327 tonne ship is so sturdy that for it to produce anything like a serious pitch would take serious storms and, while these are not unknown in the North Sea, most of the time you can hardly tell you're travelling on water.

 Harwich ▸ Den Haag Centraal
6 hours 55 minutes

 Art; history; nightlife

HOLLAND

THE DESTINATION

On the back of trading ships loaded with colourful and exotic spices sailing from the East Indies to Europe, the Netherlands became one of the richest countries in the world during the 17th century. At Delfshaven, now part of Rotterdam, Delft secured its outlet to the sea and started raking in the money from faraway lands. Such riches spawned great works of art – seen in all the cities' galleries and museums – and the finest buildings with a riot of decoration and a penchant for gabling. While all are historically important, today The Hague boasts a seaside resort and spa at Scheveningen; Delft factories still turn out the renowned delicate, and very expensive, pottery; visitors to tiny Haarlem are made dizzy by the number of culinary dens found in its warren of streets and Rotterdam, written off by many after its city centre was blitzed by the Nazis in 1940, has great museums and a fascinating architectural spread. The ongoing regeneration of vast swathes of old dockland and the nightlife – clubbing in a disused underground pass is the norm – give the city an edgy modernity that other Dutch cities, including Amsterdam, frankly lack.

The Hague, Delft and Rotterdam offer discount cards for museums, attractions and transport. These are available from tourist offices. Many museums are closed on Mondays.

It's an easy 25 minutes by train to The Hague, passing out of the suburbs of Rotterdam and quickly into those of The Hague. Head for the Central Station. If you arrive at Hollands Spoor station, which is a kilometre south of the centre, take a tram to the centre from outside the station entrance.

THE HAGUE AND DELFT

The Hague, the seat of government, has a self-important air evident in its streets of fine, tall, large-windowed buildings, its avenues of embassies and its political piles of bricks – the magnificent old parliament building and kooky PM's office, the audacious plastic-white modern town hall and the elegant Peace Palace with its superior interiors. It's a pleasure to wander around but for an overview hop on trams 1, 9 and 17.

Tram 1 takes you past the Richard Meier-built new Town Hall with its cavernous interior and elevated walkways, and up past the **parliament** and the towered **Vredespalais** or Peace Palace with its resident International Court of Justice. Telephone reservations at least a week in advance are required for the Peace Palace guided tours. It is worth the wait if only to see the gloriously tiled room, clad in turquoise blues and dominated by an enormous, ornate vase.

The tram, though, continues to Scheveningen, The Hague's North Sea resort, which has all the hallmarks of a British seaside town but with less clutter and rusty golden sands. In summer, the beach is packed with sun worshippers and kitesurfers; in winter, there's a regular stream of walkers and dogs, and should the wind prove too bracing there are plenty of cafés with cosy fires to retreat to. The crowning glory is the **Kurhaus** – a domed, five-star hotel whose dining room is topped by a breathtakingly frescoed ceiling anchored by a giant sparkling chandelier. With a nod to its bath-house origins, the **Vitalizee spa**, for naked thermal bathing and revitalising treatments, is next door. To fully appreciate what taking the waters did for Scheveningen visit the wondrous

Parliament
Binnenhof, Den Haag
070 364 61 44

Vredespalais
2 Carnegieplein, Den Haag
070 302 42 42/
tour reservations 070 302 41 37
www.vredespaleis.nl

Kurhaus
30 Gevers Deynootplein, Scheveningen
070 416 26 36
www.kurhaus.nl

Vitalizee
13F Strandweg, Scheveningen
070 416 65 00
www.vitalizee.nl

Kurhaus p146

Panorama Mesdag. This circular, 120-metre-wide painting reveals the seaside town in 1881, complete with horses, boats, sand dunes, bathers with sedan chairs, and mounted troops.

Tram 9 glides up Koninginnegracht, also to Scheveningen, passing dozens of flag-waving embassies. Tram 17 wriggles past the incongruous US embassy bunker, along Lange Vijverberg with its lovely buildings facing the central Hofvijver lake, the octagonal tower that is the PM's office and the parliamentary offices. It passes the **Prison Gate Museum** before heading into the Buitenhof square and looping around the prominent and wonderful **Grote Kerk**.

The star attraction is the **Mauritshuis** art gallery. Here, the wealth created by the 17th-century Golden Age took form in oils. Portraits of portly, rich men, clad in the most luxurious garments, gaze into the eyes of the commissioned painter. Here you will also find Johannes Vermeer's *Girl with a Pearl Earring* and his composite view of Delft. Rembrandt and Rubens also feature.

At the **Gemeentemuseum** you can see ceramics and wallpaper designs from the Rozenburg factory (1883-1917). The exquisite eggshell porcelain, decorated with lilacs and other floral patterns in art nouveau style, are stand-out items. (Rozenburg vases and other ceramics also enhance interiors of the Peace Palace). The museum is famous for its Piet Mondrian collection, although much of the work on show is not his later, more famous, abstract work, known as neo-plasticism.

After digesting the cultural offerings, it will be time for some more substantial consumption. Try the tiny streets south of the Paleis Noordeinde, with their cheek-by-jowl restaurants and bars, shops and churches. Or head to the Denneweg, past the luxurious ochre **Hotel des Indes** and the boutique shops, to the canal front where you can sup a beer or a hot chocolate, and eat at one of the many restaurants.

Tram 1 descends to Delft just 25 minutes south of The Hague. The small town, with its gabled buildings criss-crossed with cute canals and their diminutive bridges, might have been built to go on the cover of a chocolate box. Small artists' shops compete with Delftware outlets and there is a clutch of museums amid the cobbles. The **Museum Het Prinsenhof** gives a fascinating insight into the life and times of William of Orange, who led the rebellion

Panorama Mesdag
65 Zeestraat, Scheveningen
070 364 45 44
www.panorama-mesdag.nl

Prison Gate Museum
33 Buitenhof, Den Haag
070 346 08 61

Grote Kerk
Torenstraat, Den Haag
070 302 86 30
www.grotekerkdenhaag.nl

Mauritshuis
8 Korte Vijverberg, Den Haag
070 302 34 35
www.mauritshuis.nl

Gemeentemuseum
41 Stadhouderslaan, Den Haag
070 338 11 11
www.gemeentemuseum.nl

Hotel des Indes
54-56 Lange Voorhout, Den Haag
070 361 23 45
www.hoteldesindes.nl

Museum Het Prinsenhof
1 Sint Agathaplein, Delft
015 260 23 58
www.gemeentemusea-delft.nl

PASTA E BASTA

A fantastic night out!
Traditional Italian food
Live entertainment every night
Excellent wines
Student night every Monday

Nieuwe Spiegelstraat 8

020 422 22 22

www.pastaebasta.nl

against the entrenched Catholic Spanish in the 16th century; he was assassinated in 1584 and the bullet-ridden stone in front of which he met his end is now on show in the museum.

The highlight of the **Nieuwe Kerk** in the main square, facing the heavily decorated façade of the town hall, is the tomb of William of Orange. This elaborate marble grave, complete with loyal dog at the foot of his master, is a fine memorial. All Dutch royals are buried in a mausoleum beneath his columned resting place. A visit to the original **Royal Delftware factory** is a must for those interested in the blue-and-white pottery and its history. The **Vermeercentrum**, chronicling the life and times of the city's most famous artist, opened in early 2008.

To cater for the international clientele in The Hague, the city has a multinational cuisine. Tasty steaks are served up by friendly staff at **San Telmo**, a new Argentinian restaurant. The mainly black interior is the perfect backdrop for the tango shows. Nearby, on the Smidswater canal, is **Emile**, which is good for a light lunch. **Garoeda**, all wicker furniture, bonsai and objets from the Far East, is a very popular Indonesian with a variety of good-value set menus. **Zebedeus**, clinging to the wall of the Grote Kerk with its signature stained-glass wall hanging, does a good line in hearty home cooking and vegetarian dishes. For drinking, head to the Grote Markt and **De Zwarte Ruiter** for its bountiful beers and cosy interior, or to the popular **De Boterwaag**, the old butter weighing station, for its unusual and inviting spaces. In Delft, sit back for creamy hot chocolates, pancakes, coffees and sandwiches in the wonderfully inviting **Kleyweg's Stads Koffyhuis**.

Park Hotel Den Haag is a small, perfectly positioned hotel close to the Noordeinde Palace. Nights in a moored orange Brucker survival capsule will soon be available at the **Capsule Hotel**.

From Den Haag Central to Haarlem there are direct services or indirect trains via the university town of Leiden – the trains are double-deckers but no matter how high you get it's pretty flat.

HAARLEM

Haarlem is a small town with a big medieval heart. The outsized **St Bavo's** church dominates a huge, misshapen old cobbled market square, the Grote Markt, which also has a town hall, and converted meat and fish halls. The square is lined with cafés, snug bars, hotels and restaurants. But it's what has been done with the backstreets that is so intriguing. If possible, hire a guide – **Lard van der Pal** leads interesting tours – to take you through the streets and the history, and to see what Haarlem has done to blend new architecture with old. Visit *hofjes* (almshouses centred around a garden): the oldest *hofje* in the city, Hofjes Bakenes, is right next to the newest, Johan Enschedé-hof – a remarkable juxtaposition; see the glass façade of the Toneelschuur theatre blend into the older surroundings and walk under the old bell tower of the 19th-century money printing works that conceal the modern courthouse. It's all extremely clever. Further out is the **De Adriaan Windmill** that sits on the serpentine Spaarne, a watery ribbon on the city's east side.

The **Frans Hals Museum** is Haarlem's most important. The painter was famous for his enormous paintings of civil militias, the huge scale demonstrating the power and wealth of the men who sat on the boards of these forces, which were established to fight the Spanish during the 17th century.

Nieuwe Kerk
80 Markt, Delft
015 212 30 25
www.nieuwekerk-delft.nl

Royal Delftware factory
Koninklijke Porcelene Fles,
196 Rotterdamseweg, Delft
015 251 20 30
www.royaldelft.com

Vermeercentrum
21 Voldersgracht, Delft
015 213 85 88
www.vermeerdelft.nl

San Telmo
116A Kazernestraat, Den Haag
070 310 62 66

Emile
16 Maliestraat, Den Haag
070 345 11 00

Garoeda
18A Kneuterdijk, Den Haag
070 346 53 19

Zebedeus
8 Rond de Grote Kerk, Den Haag
070 346 83 93

De Zwarte Ruiter
27 Grote Markt, Den Haag
070 364 95 49
www.zwarteruiter.nl

De Boterwaag
8A Grote Markt, Den Haag
070 365 96 86
www.zwarteruiter.nl

Kleyweg's Stads Koffyhuis
133 Oude Delft, Delft
015 212 46 25
www.stads-koffyhuis.nl

Park Hotel Den Haag
53 Molenstraat, Den Haag
070 362 43 71
www.parkhoteldenhaag.nl

Capsule Hotel
287 Verheeskade, Den Haag
www.capsulehotel.info

St Bavo's
Grote Markt, Haarlem
023 553 20 40
www.bavo.nl

Lard van der Pal
Haarlem
023 527 01 77
lardvanderpal@hotmail.com
Or contact through the tourist office

De Adriaan Windmill
1A Papentorenvest, Haarlem
023 545 02 59
www.molenadriaan.nl

Frans Hals Museum
62 Groot Heiligland, Haarlem
023 511 57 75
www.franshalsmuseum.nl

HOLLAND

Hotel New York p151

Kijk-Kubus p151

Teylers Museum
16 Spaarne, Haarlem
023 516 09 60
www.teylersmuseum.nl

Azul
14 Lange Veerstraat, Haarlem
023 532 32 80

Stempels
9 Klokhuisplein, Haarlem
023 512 39 10
www.stempelsinhaarlem.nl

Golden Tulip Hotel Lion d'Or
34-36 Kruisweg, Haarlem
023 532 17 50
www.goldentulip.com

Spaarne 66
66 Spaarne, Haarlem
023 551 38 00

Café Fortuyn
21 Grote Markt, Haarlem

Laurenskerk
15 Grotekerkplein, Rotterdam
010 413 14 94
www.laurenskerkrotterdam.nl

Spido
www.spido.nl

Westelijk Handelsterrein
15 Van Vollenhovenstraat, Rotterdam

The **Teylers Museum** is full of curiosities. Its displays of fossils and bones in glass and wood cabinets, and early scientific instruments will delight children.

For such a small town there is a wealth of places to eat. The new Portuguese restaurant **Azul**, with its funky metal ceiling lights and multicoloured tiled walls, is strong on meat and delicious fish dishes. **Stempels** is a fairly new, smart hotel and dining room in the old printing works. Its lovely light rooms, some with ringside views of the church, are a snip. The quiet **Golden Tulip Hotel Lion d'Or** is conveniently situated close to the station. At **Spaarne 66**, with canalside views, the meaty dishes of hare hotpot, veal and pig are complemented by the lighter zucchini omelette with camembert and a pumpkin risotto for vegetarians. The brown bars are at their best around the main square and perfect for a tipple with the locals. Try Proeflokaal de Blauwe Druif and Den Uiver Proeflokaal. **Café Fortuyn** is a delightful, old-fashioned candlelit café with original 1930s decor that inspires dreamy coffee sessions.

Take the direct train from Haarlem back to Rotterdam (three trains per hour) or change at Leiden (two an hour).

ROTTERDAM

The largest seaport in Europe may be considered an ugly duckling by some, especially compared to its attractive neighbours. However, for those with a sense of rhythm and an architectural bent, this seafront city is well worth exploring.

The heart of Rotterdam was laid waste by Nazi bombs in 1940, when some 25,000 buildings were destroyed. The **Laurenskerk** shows a photograph of the handful of buildings that were left standing after the devastation. From the ashes, Rotterdam rebuilt in modern style and continues to do so, erecting challenging modern buildings in the centre and throughout its hinterland. For a waterside overview take a harbour cruise with **Spido**. If you need something more substantial when you land, try the 19th-century converted warehouses at **Westelijk Handelsterrein**, which have plenty of funky art galleries, restaurants and shops.

To appreciate the architecture, walk over the Williamsberg bridge to the Kop Van Zuid area passing the White House office building (one of the survivors of the bombing); the 38 slanting yellow 1984 cube houses or **Kijk-Kubus** will be behind you. Here you will see the raised oblong glass box of Unilever, and as you go further east, the new Luxor Theatre, the Renzo Piano telecoms building, the Las Palmas photo museum and finally on to the wonderful **Hotel New York**, the former head office of the Holland-America line with its Jugendstil façade, for a coffee or meal.

Crossing back over the iconic Erasmusbridge, there's more modern architecture to admire at the Museum Park, featuring the **Kunsthal** exhibition centre, designed by Rem Koolhaas, the angular **Netherlands Architecture Institute**, which branches out over water and is linked with the Sonneveld, a cool, 1933 perfectly preserved family house. The **Museum Boijmans Van Beuningen**, also in the Museum Park, is full of Old Masters. Pictures to look out for are Pieter Bruegel the Elder's extraordinary *Tower of Babel* (c1560), several hell-raising Hieronymus Bosch works (it can't have been much fun being in his head) and Rembrandt's *Titus at his Desk* (1655). For those interested in catching a glimpse of old Rotterdam see *De Grote Markt in Rotterdam* by Hendrik Maertensz Sorgh (1654). The *Tulpenkabinet* (c1635-50) by Herman Doomer honours the bulb trade with the tulips in mother of pearl.

Rising up a little out of the centre of Rotterdam, but worth making the trip, is the **Euromast**. Ascend the tower for its fabulous views and dine or take tea and cake at 100 metres in the Brasserie, with its funky white furniture, while gazing at the cranes stretching out to the industrial horizon. Continuing outwards, pretty little Delfshaven is a short walk from tram stop Schiemond on line 8. This quiet area belies a busy past when it was the port for the city of Delft during its Golden Age. Today, it is sleepy save for the only working **windmill** (a replica of the 1727 original) in Rotterdam, which churns out flour for the Ethiopian community, among others. The friendly miller will tell you everything you need to know. The windmill sits diagonally opposite the dilapidated Dutch East India Company headquarters across the water. On Voorhaven stands the **Pilgrim Fathers Church**. On 22 July 1620, the Pilgrims set off from this very point at the start of their epoch-making journey for America. However, they judged that their boat, the *Speedwell*, would not last the journey and so docked at Plymouth to board the *Mayflower*, the ship that would take them to the New World and into history.

Cheese, potato dishes, hot pots and kebabs can be found everywhere but in Rotterdam, as an entrepôt, there's more of an international flavour. Smart **De Loft**, which is in the subterranean converted warehouses, attracts stylish locals with its exposed brickwork, and good food and cocktails. **Dudok** is the place to hang out – all day if necessary. The spacious, old insurance company building has huge windows and reading tables. As well as good, wholesome food there's the unbeatable Dudok apple pie with cinnamon ice-cream. **Bazar**, with its hanging Moroccan lamps and old American signs, combines multiple Middle Eastern dishes in a menu that's popular with young locals.

Hotel Stroom is industrial cool; admire your chic in the hundreds of face mirrors tacked on to the large wall above the bar. Hostel **Room** has beds in an art deco building and **Stay Ok** is due to open a 230-bed hostel in one of the cube houses in August 2008. The **Golden Tulip Rotterdam-Centre** enjoys

Kijk-Kubus
70 Overblaak, Rotterdam
010 414 22 85
www.kubuswoning.nl

Hotel New York
1 Koninginnenhoofd, Kop Van Zuid,
Rotterdam
010 439 05 00

Kunsthal
Rotterdam
010 440 03 00
www.kunsthal.nl

Netherlands Architecture Institute
Rotterdam
010 440 12 00
www.nai.nl

Museum Boijmans Van Beuningen
Rotterdam
010 441 94 00
www.boijmans.nl

Euromast
20 Parkhaven, Scheepvaartkwartier,
Rotterdam
010 436 48 11
www.euromast.nl

Windmill
Distilleerketel, Delfshaven
010 477 91 81

Pilgrim Fathers Church
20 Aelbrechtskolk, Delfshaven
010 477 41 56
www.pilgrimfatherschurch.nl

De Loft
15/15 Van Vollenhovenstraat,
Scheepvaartkwartier, Rotterdam
010 241 75 06
www.deloft.nl

Dudok
88 Meent, Rotterdam
010 433 31 02
www.dudok.nl

Bazar
16 Witte de Withstraat, Rotterdam
010 206 51 51
www.bazarrotterdam.nl

Hotel Stroom
1 Lloydstraat, Rotterdam
010 221 40 60
www.stroomrotterdam.nl

Room
62 Van Vollenhovenstraat,
Scheepvaartkwartier, Rotterdam
010 282 72 77
www.roomrotterdam.nl

Stay Ok
www.stayokay.com

Golden Tulip Rotterdam-Centre
80 Leuvehaven, Rotterdam
010 413 41 39
www.goldentuliprotterdamcentre.com

HOLLAND

LOS PILONES
CANTINA MEXICO

enjoy the authentic mex-mex cuisine, atmosphere cocktails and a great tequila collection

Kerkstraat 63
1017 GC Amsterdam
Tel.: (020) – 320 4651
open from 16:00 – 24:00

1e Anjeliersdwarsstraat 6
1015 NR Amsterdam – Jordaa
(020) – 620 03 23
open from 16:00 – 24:00

www.LosPilones.com

fantastic views of the urban landscape, while the **Hilton Rotterdam** is extreme comfort in a central location – the best hotel for ease of hopping from one club to another.

Rotown, with live music, is for pre-clubbing drinks. Top venues include the typographically irritating **off_corso**, a converted cinema with different nightly sounds, and the five levels of enjoyment at the **Thalia Lounge**. Descend into the subway for **Club Catwalk** and weekend resident DJs. See www.mojo.nl for live artists dates and booking and www.rotterdaminfo.nl for festivals.

IN THE AREA

Amsterdam is not far from any of these cities. In fact, it's just a 16-minute train journey from Haarlem, with around seven connections an hour. Between Haarlem and The Hague – and on the railway line connecting them – is Leiden, seat of the country's oldest university and tantalisingly close to the tulip fields of the **Keukenhof**, the largest flower garden in the world, while Aalsmeer has the world's largest flower auction.

TRAVEL INFORMATION

Stena Line operates one day and one overnight sailing from Harwich to Hoek van Holland. Fares for one passenger start at £49 single. However, the 'Dutch flyer' deal means that fares including travel from any 'one' railway station to any station in Holland per passenger start from £29 single, making it cheaper to take train and ferry than the ship alone. For a car plus two passengers fares start at £59 single. Travel for a passenger with a bicycle starts at £29 single. **P&O** sails from Hull to Europoort, Rotterdam. Eurolines also travels from London Victoria to Holland and there are rail connections from Belgium.

Getting out of the Hook and into Holland is a cinch. The 30-minute train ride takes you from the port to Rotterdam. Change here for a 25-minute journey to The Hague. Delft, just south of The Hague, can be reached by train or tram. Haarlem is 40 minutes north of The Hague by direct train. To return to Rotterdam there are direct and indirect trains via Leiden, taking 52 and 55 minutes respectively.

The Netherlands' national rail network, **Nederlandse Spoorwegen**, links all these main places and many of the smaller ones with a regular and to-the-millisecond punctual service. If you buy tickets from the station offices, there is a €0.50 per ticket surcharge compared to buying tickets from the machines in station forecourts. Bicycles are charged at €6 for a day ticket. For getting round in The Hague, Delft and Rotterdam, the tram is useful but the city centres are compact and easily walked. Rotterdam also has watertaxis and a metro.

WHEN TO GO

No one goes to Holland for its weather. Of course, the sun might shine, the rain hold off and the wind die down, but then again… The advantage to this lack of certainty is that there is no time not to go. Low winter or high summer, there's plenty to see and do. The main thing to bear in mind is the tulip season, from mid March to mid May, when the fields are covered by a multi-coloured blanket of blooms.

Further reading

Anna Pavord *The Tulip*
Mike Dash *Tulipomania: the Story* There was a time in the 17th century when tulip bulbs were more valuable than gold. This is the story of fortunes made and lost.
Desiderius Erasmus *The Praise of Folly* One of the key works of Renaissance humanism.

Websites

www.htm.net
Dutch buses and trams.
www.watertaxirotterdam.nl.
What it says
www.denhaag.com
The tourist office of The Hague.
www.vvvzk.nl
Haarlem tourist information.
www.rotterdam.info
Rotterdam tourist office.

Hilton Rotterdam
10 Weena, Rotterdam
010 710 80 00
www.hiltonrotterdam.nl

Rotown
19 Nieuwe Binnenweg, Rotterdam
010 436 26 69
www.rotown.nl

off_corso
22 Kruiskade, Rotterdam
010 411 38 97
www.off-corso.nl

Thalia Lounge
31 Kruiskade, Rotterdam
010 214 25 47
www.thaliarotterdam.nl

Club Catwalk
33 Weena Zuid, Rotterdam
www.catwalkrotterdam.com

Keukenhof
www.keukenhof.nl

Stena Line
08705 70 70 70
www.stenaline.co.uk

P&O
www.poferries.com

Nederlandse Spoorwegen
www.ns.nl

Avoriaz

Portes du Soleil

ROUTE   London ▸ Paris ▸ Cluses ▸ Les Gets

Take a high-speed train ride across France to the largest ski area in the world, and go chalet-hopping between Avoriaz, Morzine and Les Gets, the latter a frontrunner in the fight to make skiing green and keep the mountains white.

Written by **Dominic Earle**

Avoriaz

Les Gets

THE TRIP

Unless you live in Inverness, it is probably easier to get to Les Gets than it is to get to Aviemore – and you may well find the latter bereft of snow. There are two flight-free options: one is to pack everything into the back of the car and gun the nine hours from Calais to the pistes, the other is to take the Eurostar to Paris Gare du Nord, then hop on the RER for two stops across Paris to Gare de Lyon and change on to the TGV direct to the valley town of Cluses (4hrs 30mins), just 22 kilometres from the slopes of Les Gets. Operators such as Ski Famille can organise either option, and the transfer from Cluses TGV station to your chalet. Alternatively, Altibus runs up to ten buses a day in each direction between the TGV station at Cluses and Les Gets bus station for €16 return – the journey time is approximately 40mins.

When you consider that budget airlines now charge anywhere in the region of £30-£40 to take a pair of skis or a snowboard to the Alps and back, plus an extra £7.98 (Easyjet) to £18 (Ryanair) for each bag in the hold, the argument for taking the train to the piste is growing stronger than ever.

 St Pancras International
Cluses (Haute Savoie)
7 hours 59 minutes

Active break; family holiday; landscape

Wanted.
Jumpers, coats and people with their knickers in a twist.

From the people who feel moved to bring us their old books and CDs, to the people fed up to the back teeth with our politicians' track record on climate change, Oxfam supporters have one thing in common. They're passionate. If you've got a little fire in your belly, we'd love to hear from you. Visit us at **oxfam.org.uk**

Be Humankind Ⓧ Oxfam

THE DESTINATION

The Portes du Soleil, sitting in the lee of mighty Mont Blanc, Europe's highest peak at 4,807 metres, offers a ski area of truly epic proportions, with 650 kilometres of piste and more than 200 lifts straddling the border between France and Switzerland. But size isn't everything and the real beauty of the area is in the fact that, unlike other mega-league resorts such as La Plagne, Les Arcs or Les Trois Vallées, it doesn't simply link up a string of soulless high-altitude carbuncles, but instead joins together a group of attractive, authentic mountain villages, which are decidedly more chocolate box than concrete box. The one major exception to this is the area's only truly high-altitude resort, Avoriaz. Car-free and perched above dramatic, sheer rock cliffs at 1,800 metres, it is a winding 14-kilometre-drive or cable-car ride up from the valley below. This chapter focuses on three of the most popular and easily accessible resorts from the UK – Les Gets, Morzine and Avoriaz.

LES GETS

Les Gets may be stuck on the fringes of the Portes du Soleil, with a bit of a trek to reach the vast area's highest skiing above Avoriaz, but thanks to an influx of British and Swiss families this cosy farming community has managed to transform itself into a kind of nappy valley sur neige. Children are everywhere, and the open-air ice rink and toy-town road train that travels between the lift stations add to the family atmosphere. Nowadays, there is a hint of a traffic problem, but all in all Les Gets is a charming spot, with chalets dotting the hillside and a traditional village centre. The introduction of a fast six-man chairlift from the outskirts of the village up to the main slopes means day-trippers can now park and ride, without having to clog up the narrow streets. Unfortunately, though, a complete ban on cars is unlikely as the village is on the through road to Morzine and Avoriaz, and narrow mountain valleys don't offer much scope for bypasses.

There's skiing on both sides of the village, but the main area starts at Chavannes, with a fast chairlift and slow gondola leading up to a wide, sunny plateau at a fairly respectable 1,400 metres. This is the main ski school meeting place – stumble up here at 11am and you'll be besieged by mini-racers – and also hosts a number of cafés and restaurants for a spot of piste-side bronzing. From here, a chairlift gives access to 'the bowl': Les Gets's best skiing with five chairlifts clustered together serving some rolling red cruisers, loopy blue variants and bumpy blacks. Alternatively, head in the other direction and you can meander all the way down through the trees to the neighbouring resort of Morzine. Talking of trees, one of the few advantages of Les Gets's frustrating lack of height is that most of the skiing takes place in the forest, with wide boulevards cutting through the trees – a real bonus when the weather sets in.

Les Gets' second ski area, Mont Chéry, is a five-minute trudge across the village from the main Chavannes lift base (the proposed 'white road' allowing skiers to cross the village with skis on is still more eco-dream than reality). The skiing here is much quieter, a single peak rising to a modest 1,820 metres

Les Gets

Les Gets

and accessed by a gondola and an aged chairlift. But it's worth the detour, especially the red Marmottes run down the back of the mountain, a lovely back-country cruiser to the limit of the area at L'Encrenaz. Mont Chéry is also home to the local **paragliding** operation, so if you fancy a spot of carbon-neutral flying then this is the place to get airborne.

Back down at ground level, Les Gets is remarkably active, with dog sledding expeditions, ice diving, ice skating and snowmobiling. But perhaps the finest way to escape the crowds is to slap a pair of tennis rackets to your feet and head off into the wild on a snowshoe trek. One of the best trips is to Jean-Claude Bonhomme's farm, where you can learn all the gooey details about the making of the famous chevrotin cheese and finish off with a warming shot of gnôle (local schnapps) before heading back to town. Book through the tourist office (04 50 75 80 80, www.lesgets.com).

After all that exercise, there are plenty of hearty, traditional Savoyarde options lining the attractive, semi-pedestrianised main street. Try the rustic **Vieux Chene** for Savoyarde specialities, **La R'mize** for meat and **Le Flambeau** for well-cooked French dishes. **Le Schuss** and Le Tyrol are tops for pizza. For something even cheesier, the **Fruitière des Perrières** is a supremely cosy auberge serving up cheese specialities from raclette to reblochonnade in the old cheese-maturing cellars.

Les Gets majors on family-run hotels and chalets. The best option is Ski Famille, which runs six spacious, well-equipped chalets in and around the resort, including a couple of upmarket options such as Le Chardon, which sleeps 22 and is set up on the hillside a five-minute walk from the village centre, with wonderful views across to the main ski slopes. With its fully inclusive childcare, Ski Famille is the ideal solution for families with toddlers – English nannies turn up at 8.30am five days a week and take your kids off to the in-house playroom, as well as making snowy sorties such as ice skating, a ride in the cable car, snowman-building and sledging. Meanwhile, you can burn around the mountains and even squeeze in a quick après-ski vin chaud before a minibus turns up to deliver you back to the chalet and the bosom of your family at 4.30pm. The children's supper is served up at 5pm, then it's time for bath and bed before heading back downstairs for a four-course blowout at 8pm, along with as much wine as you can drink (quite a lot after a day on the slopes). Dieters beware – prices also include a hearty buffet breakfast (eggs and pastries every which way) and afternoon tea (cake and biscuits every which way). All in all, a family skiing trip minus all of the stress and most of the guilt.

It is a sign of the times when a ski resort's brochure leads not with the number of snow cannons or cable cars, but instead with a double-page spread with the rather less sexy title of 'keeping up with current changes in mountain tourism'. Skiing has some way to go before it gets the environmental stamp of approval but lowly Les Gets stands out for schemes intended to keep the place looking less green and more white. These include free pocket ashtrays to stop butts littering the mountains when the snow melts, plus an eco-life day to pick up aforesaid butts, hands-free rechargeable lift passes, additive-free artificial snowmaking and piste-bashers that run on biodegradable oil.

On the hotel front, three-star is as good as it gets, notably at

Paragliding
04 50 79 87 06

Vieux Chene
04 50 79 71 93

La R'mize
04 50 79 75 57

Le Flambeau
04 50 79 80 66

Le Schuss
04 50 79 71 67

Le Tyrol
04 50 79 70 55

Fruitière des Perrières
04 50 79 70 04

the **Labrador**, with a swimming pool and in a peaceful location on the outskirts of the village, or the **Crychar**, which is convenient for the lifts and a green eco-warrior – it was the first hotel in the village to use geothermal energy to heat the bathwater. In the two-star category, the **Chamois** is central, while the **Alpen Sports** has good food. Or try **Les Gets Reservations**.

MORZINE

First the bad news. Morzine has two main problems – height and width. At just 1,000 metres village snow is in no way assured and it's also too big for its own good, with its two ski areas starting from opposite sides of the village and a trek or inefficient bus service in between. But these drawbacks don't seem to bother the hordes of faithful Brit families who set up camp here during the school holidays. The town itself holds the biggest appeal, a bustling, cheerful and authentically Savoyarde place with a sense of community. The development on both sides of the river is chalet style, with a pedestrianised zone, a range of shops and a market on Wednesday mornings. Other bonuses include excellent children's facilities and a wide network of blue runs, perfect for massaging your ego on the first day.

Although Morzine has free shuttle buses to ferry visitors between lift stations, a car is useful, especially in dodgy snow conditions. Many riders choose to head straight to nearby Avoriaz, either via the cable car from Les Prodains – a short drive or bus journey from the village – or a neighbouring chairlift accessing the network of slopes above it: from here the Combe du Mâchon chairlift opens up a web of challenging black runs on the Hauts Forts face. The Super Morzine gondola connects

Labrador
04 50 75 80 00
www.labrador-hotel.com

Crychar
04 50 75 80 50
www.crychar.com

Chamois
04 50 75 80 20
www.alpineelements.co.uk

Alpen Sports
04 50 75 80 55
www.alpensport-hotel.com

Les Gets Reservations
04 50 75 80 80
www.lesgets.com

PORTES DU SOLEIL

THE FAST TRACK TO THE PISTE

If you're really after doorstep skiing, then there's no slicker way to reach the mountains than aboard the Eurostar ski train. Running from December to April, there are two direct weekly services from London St Pancras to the Alpine valley towns of Moutiers (6hrs 30mins), Aime La Plagne (7hrs 2mins) and Bourg St-Maurice (7hrs 20mins). The overnight service departs on Friday evening and arrives early Saturday morning, giving skiers an extra two days on the slopes. Alternatively, the daytime service leaves London on Saturday morning and arrives in the mountains in the early evening. Resorts served include all the big-hitters, such as Méribel, Courchevel and Val Thorens (Moutiers), La Plagne (Aime La Plagne), and Val d'Isère and Tignes (Bourg St Maurice), but the smoothest passage of all is to Les Arcs. The Eurostar train stops at Bourg St-Maurice, from where a covered walkway leads directly to the seven-minute funicular up the mountain to Arc 1600, the lowest of Les Arcs's four purpose-built resorts. Having already bought your ski passes online via the website (www.lesarcs.com), you can check into your ski-in, ski-out apartment and check straight back out the back door and on to the slopes. On the return journey, you can either catch a train on Saturday morning, arriving home at St Pancras in time for tea, or alternatively enjoy another day on the slopes and a farewell fondue before heading down the mountain to catch the overnight service, arriving at St Pancras early Sunday morning. Minimum hassle, maximum vertical.

www.eurostar.com, 08705 186186. From £149.

Avoriaz

central Morzine to various blue runs leading ultimately to Avoriaz, but it's a long trek between the two resorts and crowds can quickly build up along the way. On the other side of the valley, most people are happiest capitalising on the excellent pistes around Le Pléney, reached via a gondola. From here a range of fast blue and red runs wind beginners and intermediates back to the town or to nearby Les Fys.

If diversification is the buzzword in skiing these days, then Morzine has it in spades with a huge number of activities open to non-skiers. Full- or half-day snowshoe expeditions led by **Hervé Le Sobre** take participants on trails through breathtaking surroundings. Morzine is also considered one of the European capitals of paragliding: this hair-raising sport can be attempted – in tandem with a professional, naturally – at the well-established **Ecole de Parapente**. Local hot-air balloon flights are run by **Cameleon Organisation** and cost from €245, while the **Indiana Parc** is an excellent adventure playground for children aged six and over, with gangways, bridges and Tyrolean traverses. There's also bungee jumping and ice diving under Lake Montriomond (again by Cameleon).

Morzine is bursting with good food, and so will you be after recharging the batteries at **La Chamade**, a gourmet place that is justifiably one of the village's most popular spots. If you favour Savoyarde specialities of the fondue variety, try **Le Grillon** near the tourist office.

The resort is dominated by chalet-style hotels, none of them above three stars and several unrated. Of the three-stars, **La Bergerie** is highly recommended, with an outdoor heated pool and sauna, while **Le Dahu** is noted for its food and its free shuttle to the lifts, which in Morzine is worth its weight in gold.

AVORIAZ

Avoriaz sits atop a cliff face, high above Morzine, and from a distance its landscape of looming buildings in bold red cedar with shingle roofs successfully blends into the mountains, no mean feat considering some of the concrete monstrosities that were put up in the Alps around the same time. Construction here began in 1966 under the direction of local boy and future sunglasses supremo Jean Vuarnet, who had returned from the 1960 Squaw Valley Winter Olympics a gold medallist and national hero. This is a relaxing place to hang out (unless you have the misfortune to be here in French school holidays when the place is rammed), with no cars allowed on the streets and a fleet of horse-drawn sleighs and electric snowcats to meet new arrivals. After that, it's walk or slide – Avoriaz is compact enough to walk through in ten minutes. Green rules here, with all manner of environmentally friendly schemes on the go, from free disposable pocket ashtrays to electric piste bashers.

If you want your kids to become Olympians, the Children's Village, run by top French downhill racer Annie Famose, which recently celebrated its 30th anniversary, will give them the best possible start. More experienced skiers will head straight for the adjoining valleys, although they shouldn't leave Avoriaz without sampling the steep and challenging Arête des Intrets and Coupe du Monde: the latter has staged many downhill World Cup competitions, and both are worthy black runs.

Hervé Le Sobre
06 19 42 95 57
www.alpirandovtt.com

Ecole de Parapente
04 50 75 76 39

Cameleon Organisation
04 50 75 94 00

Indiana Parc
04 50 74 01 88

La Chamade
04 50 79 13 91

Le Grillon
04 50 79 09 41

La Bergerie
04 50 79 13 69
www.hotel-bergerie.com

Le Dahu
04 50 75 92 92
www.dahu.com

The neighbouring Arare face, meanwhile, is home to a large number of interconnecting blue runs well suited to beginners (and an excellent snowpark for boarders). Red runs are fewer and farther between here: those that there are tend to be short and quickly run into less challenging terrain. Intermediates may be better off taking the Express du Tour from the centre of town and soaking up the tree-lined scenery of Les Lindarets, where two good (if not exactly epic) red runs are accessed by the Prolays and Lindarets chairs between them. From the bottom of these runs a series of chairs lead to the Abricotine blue run, more than seven kilometres of gently undulating piste that boarders should avoid like the plague.

Avoriaz's finest dining is in the restaurant in **Hôtel des Dromonts**, run by celebrity chef Christophe Leroy, who also runs eateries in St Tropez and Marrakech. **Les Trappeurs**, at the top of the gondola from Les Prodains, is the best of the informal eateries, with a choice between a quality brasserie and a café with a terrace. **Le Chalet d'Avoriaz**, the oldest restaurant in the resort, specialises in pierrades (meat slow-cooked on a hot rock), the perfect post-piste fare.

Avoriaz is dominated by apartments. If you don't fancy looking after yourself, then you can be pampered at the magnificent and fully restored **Hôtel des Dromonts**, Avoriaz's finest hotel. Other options include the three-star **Hôtel Neige-Roc**, which benefits from its situation at the Les Prodains end of the resort, meaning you can ski to the front door.

TRAVEL INFORMATION

Ski Famille offers seven-night chalet holidays in Les Gets, including accommodation on a half-board basis, childcare, afternoon tea and wine with dinner from £435 per adult and £395 per child. The price includes a Eurotunnel crossing and transfer from Geneva or the TGV station at Cluses (22 kilometres away). Eurostar/TGV fares (www.raileurope.co.uk) from London to Cluses start from £129 return.

Lugging luggage from Gare du Nord to Gare de Lyon isn't as backbreaking as it might sound. Walk off the end of the Eurostar platform, turn left, and follow the signs for RER line D. Take RER line D two stops direct to the Gare de Lyon. At both the Gare du Nord and Gare de Lyon there are escalators (and/or lifts) between the mainline station concourse, the RER concourse and the RER platforms, making it relatively easy even with luggage or a pushchair. To access the RER, there are also special wide ticket gates for passengers with luggage or pushchairs. Alternatively, a taxi between the two should cost about €15-€20.

Many of the listings featured above give telephone numbers only. No address is needed as agents and tour guides are likely to arrange to meet you not at a central office but at a convenient spot – usually where the activity is to take place.

WHEN TO GO

Late December-late April. Christmas/New Year is busy and snow can be unreliable. January is very quiet, with generally good snow but can be very cold. February usually has the best snow but most crowds (French half-term). March is ideal, with plenty of snow and sunshine, and longer days.

Further reading

We Learned to Ski Harold Evans Brian Jackman & Mark Ottoway The classic, old-school ski coaching manual.
The Chalet Girl Kate Lace Can Millie the maid move from bed-making to bedding a gorgeous ski instructor? Alpine romance to doze off to after the après-ski.
Inner Skiing W. Timothy Gallwey & Robert Krieger Forget the state of the snow; look at your state of mind. In case you though skiing was all about appearances...

Websites

www.snow-forecast.com
The best snow forecast site.
www.skiclub.co.uk/skiclub/resorts/ greenresorts
The Ski Club of Great Britain's green resort guide.
www.saveoursnow.com

Hotel des Dromonts
04 50 74 08 11
www.christophe-leroy.com

Les Trappeurs
04 50 74 17 33

Le Chalet d'Avoriaz
04 50 74 01 30

Hôtel Neige-Roc
04 50 79 03 21
www.neige-roc.com

Ski Famille
0845 644 3764
www.skifamille.co.uk

Nice port

Nice & the Riviera

ROUTE Folkestone ▸ Calais ▸ Nice ▸ Cap-Ferrat ▸ The Corniches ▸ Monaco ▸ Marseilles

Few things put more of a damper on a car holiday in the French Riviera than spending 12 hours stuck in jams on the *autoroute du soleil*. So skip the boring bits: catch the Eurotunnel train to Calais, drive straight on to another train, retire to your couchette and wake up next morning on the Côte d'Azur, rested and ready for the fleshpots of Cannes, the niceties of Nice and the money in Monaco. It's not the greenest holiday in this book – but it's definitely the most glamorous.

Written by **Edoardo Albert** and **Sam Le Quesne**

Le Negresco p164

Vieux Nice p165

THE TRIP

Simplicity itself. Drive to Folkestone and into the train. Drive off in France where you face a long and tiring journey of, oh, some 15 minutes to the Motorail terminal. Motorail staff load the cars on the train, allowing passengers time to stock up with food for the overnight journey (there's a bar on the train, but you have to bring your own food for the trip). Alternatively, pick up a hamper at Fortnum & Mason's before you leave – you might as well start off posh if you're heading for the South of France. Passengers for each car have their own couchette allocated, ideal for peace, privacy and an early start to holiday adventures. The night-train experience is unforgettable: either you'll sleep all night like a baby in a cradle on set auto-rock, suffer dreadful insomnia as you attempt to adapt to this new, unique rhythm, or – and this well may be the most stimulating of all possibilities – you'll wander down to the buffet car for a late brandy or an early coffee and make some friends. Do try to rise for the dawn passage into Provence – you can smell the sunshine through the window. Wake up slowly, then pick up the car in Nice and off you go. The Riviera awaits.

 Folkestone ▸ Nice Ville
8 hours 55 minutes

 Food & drink; beach; luxury

THE DESTINATION

Every cliché you've heard about the South of France is glaringly on show in the narrow, sun-drenched strip of land between the mountains and the sea that makes up the French Riviera. You'll find dramatic roads, hairpinning above abyssal drops into a turquoise sea (James Bond freaks love it), wallets the size of yachts and yachts the size of towns, an extraordinarily beautiful natural landscape (pockmarked with some of the most banal concrete bunkers), as well as multitudes of Eurotrash and a multitude of ways to trash your euros. But in among the consumption and conspicuous crassness are hints of a romantic past. The ghosts of Picasso, Renoir and Matisse linger on in the rows of painters hunched over canvases and in the sublime light and colour of the Côte d'Azur that they are trying to capture. The pastel shades of Vieux Nice, shutters drawn tight against the fierce light, bring reflections on a grander age of travel, when aristocrats escaped the chill, both seasonal and moral, of northern climes for the expansive air of the Mediterranean. And what nicer place than Nice to begin the journey along the Côte d'Azur – besides, that's where the train stops.

NICE

Prehistoric man set up camp some 400,000 years ago at the site known as Terra Amata at the foot of Mont Boron, not far from where Sir Elton John's pastel-pink hilltop mansion now sprawls. The Romans followed rather later (100 BC), with assorted barbarians, Saracens, Neapolitans and Savoyards coming in their wake. But amid much toing and froing over who was in charge, a small group of Britons in 1822 raised a subscription for the building of the seafront esplanade still called the promenade des Anglais. Queen Victoria came to visit, some 70 years later, and Nice was well on its way to becoming the fashionable resort for the wealthy and the well-born.

Today, France's fifth largest city often serves as a jumping-off point for the rest of the Côte d'Azur. But don't make that mistake yourself. Park yourself – and your sports car – at **Le Negresco**, Nice's most famous hotel and an inn that completely escapes, for both good and bad, the bland uniformity that blights almost every top-of-the-range hotel. It is, after all, a National Historic Building and the artistic creation of Madame Augier, its owner and the collector of the many paintings and sculptures that decorate the place. If your wheels are humbler, but you still want a central location (in fact, near Le Negresco), try **Hôtel de la Buffa**. Warm, welcoming staff, and clean, cosy rooms make up for the absence of any design flourishes.

Nice is walkable, so even if the car is expensive (and flash cars are as common as sunny days here) leave it at the kerb and take to the streets à pied. Before plunging into the labyrinth of streets that make up the old town, stroll along the promenade des Anglais. Here's where most of the action is: in-line skaters carve through the crowds, speedboats haul shrieking parascenders skywards, and swarthy boys flirt with bikini-clad girls at the ice-cream stands. The bay itself is one long stripe of bleached pebble and turquoise water, divided between the volleyball courts and crisp white sun loungers of the private beaches, and the colourful melee of the public ones.

Le Negresco
37 promenade des Anglais
04 93 16 64 00
www.hotel-negresco-nice.com

Hôtel de la Buffa
56 rue de la Buffa
04 93 88 77 35
www.hotel-buffa.com

Much of the Baie des Anges' pebbly shoreline is open to the public at all times of day, throughout the year. And it is on these public beaches that you can expect to encounter crowds in summer. If that doesn't faze you, then fine (just remember to leave any valuables at home – the normal seaside drill), but if you'd rather occupy a more exclusive patch of sunlight, you'll need to pay the entrance fee to one of the private beaches.

But assuming you're here for more than the heat, you'll scorn the fleshy delights of the beach and head for Vieux Nice. Walking among the tall, pastel-coloured buildings of rue Droite, the street feels cool as a forest floor, while high above you, washing lines are threaded from balcony to balcony, and the faded blue shutters are shut tight against the sun. The unassuming façades of the **Eglise de Gesù** or **Palais Lascaris**, both dating from the 17th century, are gateways into forgotten worlds, while the sudden surprise of the **Cathédrale de Ste-Réparate**, opening up among the tiny streets, is one of the most beautiful sights on the Riviera. But perhaps the greatest of Vieux Nice's treasures is the irrepressible cours Saleya, home to the flower market and many of the city's busiest bars and restaurants. Every morning (except for Mondays, when the thrift and antiques stalls move in), this wide pedestrianised street is colonised by an army of vendors perfuming the air with tubs of freshly cut flowers, and mounds of deliciously ripe fruit and veg. Traders travel in from the surrounding countryside, their vans groaning with the burden of everything from strings of pinkish garlic to lush bunches of herbs and sun-kissed peaches. The market is operational from dawn (when mustard-keen locals and kitchen boys are the only browsers) to lunchtime (when last-minute deals on perfectly ripe tomatoes are a picnicker's dream come true).

Most of Nice's other draws, in particular the museums devoted to Matisse and Chagall, are in Cimiez, the beautiful residential neighbourhood you can see quietly drowsing on its hillside a few miles above Vieux Nice.

Before heading there, have lunch in Vieux Nice. For the well-heeled, there's **Christian Plumail**, where the ever-changing menu is filled with exquisite seafood dishes, trout and duck creations, and desserts that will make short work of your bikini line. If further gastronomic adventures appeal, a journey into the weird and wonderful **Terres de Truffes**, where mycology becomes gastronomy, is recommended. Moving more towards the economy/compact end of the market, **Acchiardo**, which Mrs and Mrs Acchiardo run with their two children, is a wonderful local restaurant serving well-rendered versions of home-grown classics such as merda de can, or gnocchi stuffed with spinach, and a fairly priced wine list. **L'Escalinada** and **Lou Pistou** are further options for sampling typical niçois cooking – tripe is a speciality – at reasonable prices.

Suitably refreshed, it's time for art. You can walk up to Cimiez in about 30 minutes, which might be no bad idea after lunch, or take the bus (no.15 from place Masséna). If you decide to get the car, arm yourself with a map and plenty of patience. But really, Nice is a place for walking: unless you have to, leave the car until it's time to head to Monaco, and head up past the villas, considering how the other half lives.

Just off the lower reaches of boulevard de Cimiez is the **Musée National Message Biblique Marc Chagall**. Enclosed

Baie des Anges

Eglise de Gesù
pl du Gesù
04 92 00 41 90

Palais Lascaris
15 rue Droite
04 93 62 72 40

Cathédrale de Ste-Réparate
pl Rossetti
04 93 92 01 35

Christian Plumail
54 blvd Jean Jaurès
04 93 62 32 22
www.christian-plumail.com

Terres de Truffes
11 rue St-François de Paule
04 93 62 07 68

Acchiardo
38 rue Droite
04 93 85 51 16

L'Escalinada
22 rue Pairolière
04 93 62 11 71
www.escalinada.fr

Lou Pistou
4 rue Raoul Bosio
04 93 62 21 82

Musée National Message Biblique Marc Chagall
ave Docteur Ménard
04 93 53 87 20
www.musee-chagall.fr

www.treesforcities.org

Trees for Citie
Charity registration number 10321

We all care about reducing pollution.
We all care about tackling global warming.
We all care about our carbon footprint.

That's why Trees for Cities has planted
over 100,000 trees in cities at home and
abroad.

Leave your mark and join us today
to help create a greener future for
everyone.

To find out more about adult, joint, family
and child membership of Trees for Cities
visit:

www.treesforcities.org

Leave
Your
Mark

Create a green future for cities.

within the rigorous geometries of this bunker-like building (designed by Le Corbusier collaborator André Hermant) is the complete set of biblical paintings by Belarus-born painter and long-time Riviera resident Marc Chagall. The thematic thread that binds together these vivid canvases is the Old Testament, specifically the Song of Songs, Genesis and Exodus. Arresting and otherworldly, the imposing paintings are complemented by preparatory sketches made by the artist – the whole is meant to transmit, in Chagall's phrase, 'a certain peace, a certain sense of religion and a sense of life's meaning'.

Further up, sweeping round the corner of boulevard de Cimiez and avenue Régina, you can't miss the Excelsior Régina Palace. The hotel where Queen Victoria stayed each year from 1897 to 1899 and Matisse lived between 1938 and 1943 is now an apartment building. At the top of the hill the **Musée Matisse** stands among olive trees, behind the ruins of the Roman amphitheatre. The Genoese-style 17th-century villa houses a sizeable number of the artist's paintings, hundreds of his drawings and engravings, as well as an assortment of sculptures and illustrated books. Photographs and artefacts from Matisse's personal collection are also scattered around, giving space a lived-in feel in keeping with the breezy Mediterranean vibe of the villa's burnt-red façade and tall shuttered windows. From the vast cut-out *Fleurs et Fruits* in the museum's light-filled atrium to the pared-down delicacy of such paintings as *Tempête à Nice*, the breadth of Matisse's output is made abundantly clear in the progression of each display.

But in the end, all this is just some daubs on a piece of canvas. You want real art? Look up to the cobalt sky, and out to the azure sea. Test the sound of a V12 firing up in the quiet of a Mediterranean morning, Ferrari red blurred into a gasp of wonder against the teeming sunlight, an open road before you and a tank of petrol behind. Or turn the keys on the 2CV you've rented. We're out of here.

CAP-FERRAT

Take the D6098 boulevard Princess Grace de Monaco east out of Nice. Heading this way, the sea lies below the passenger door, tempting the inexperienced driver with flirtatious glimpses between stone pines. But don't fall for it: the pleasure is fleeting, the fall precipitous. There will be time for sightseeing later. Now's the time to drive.

A short journey along the coast is the highest concentration of carbon abusers and tax exiles on the planet – Monaco, with its racing drivers in their lavish pits, globetrotting tennis players by their pools, billionaires feasting on beluga. But first, turn right on to the D125, and the exclusive retreat of Cap-Ferrat. Money these days trumps pretty well everything else, meaning that most of the cape's previous illustrious residents – Charlie Chaplin, David Niven, W Somerset Maugham – wouldn't get a look in any more. For a glimpse of the sort of taste that used to accompany great wealth, stop at the **Villa Ephrussi-de-Rothschild**, an Italianate fantasy villa – again, the colour is Eltonian – built for Beatrice de Rothschild in the early 1900s. It houses her immense art collection, which focuses on the 18th century but also includes Impressionist paintings and those little priceless oriental knick-knacks without which no turn-of-the-19th-

Musée Matisse
164 ave des Arènes, Nice
04 93 81 08 08
www.musee-matisse-nice.org

Villa Ephrussi-de-Rothschild
1 ave Ephrussi-de-Rothschild, Cap-Ferrat
04 93 01 33 09
www.villa-ephrussi.com

La Canebière p169

Marseille p169

Casino
pl du Casino, Monte-Carlo
00 377-92 16 20 00
www.casino-monte-carlo.com

Musée Océanographique
ave St-Martin, Monte-Carlo
00 377-93 15 36 00
www.oceano.mc

century magnate's house was complete. Cap-Ferrat is ideal for walkers, so park up and set out on the beautiful, rocky, ten-kilometre path that winds around the Cap en route to the Plage des Fosses, a pebbly beach ideal for children.

THE CORNICHES

What better and more scenic roads could you find than the three Corniche roads that wind between Nice and Menton (the last town before the Côte d'Azur becomes the Italian Riviera)? The roads – low (Basse), middle (Moyenne) and high (Grande) – give you flashes of glittering surf, green manicured gardens and pretty villages. The Basse Corniche (D6098 – also known as the Corniche Inférieure) hugs the coast, passing through all the towns and resorts. It's ideal for letting people admire you in an open-top car, but not so good for actually getting anywhere. To take some of the strain, the wider Moyenne Corniche (D6007) was hacked through the mountains in the 1920s. The highest route – the Grande Corniche (D2564) – follows the ancient Roman Aurelian Way and is the most spectacular of the three.

These roads are tragically linked to our next destination, Monaco. On 13 September 1982, Princess Grace lost control of her car (a Rover 3500, sadly) on the N53, a treacherous descent full of hairpin bends that leads from the Grande Corniche to the Moyenne Corniche. It sailed off the road into a ravine; Princess Grace died from her injuries, although her daughter, Stéphanie, survived. There's no memorial at the spot, but a bunch or two of flowers can generally be seen by the roadside.

MONACO

Grace Kelly, star of *High Noon*, *Dial M for Murder* and *Rear Window*, swapped tinseltown for toy town when she married Prince Rainier of Monaco in 1956, ensuring with the birth of their first child the continued existence of the principality (a treaty with France had Monaco reverting to Paris if Rainier failed to produce an heir – nine months and four days after the wedding Princess Grace gave birth to a daughter, Caroline). The Grimaldis – then a bunch of Genoese pirates – seized the area in 1297 and had held on to it grimly ever since, overcoming the loss of nearby Menton and Roquebrune in 1848 by legalising gambling. Grace Kelly gave Monaco the glitter it needed to silver the financial shadows that accompanied Prince Rainier's transformation of the principality into an offshore tax haven (individuals pay no income tax, making it the home from home of many a magnate and a significant proportion of the world's Formula One drivers).

At dusk, unpack the tux and make like James Bond with a visit to the **Casino**. Or, at least, dress up a bit. For men, a sports jacket and tie are de rigueur. There's a €5 minimum bet at the roulette tables; the stakes are higher in the salons privés and the Club Anglais, which offer chemin de fer, trente-et-quarante, blackjack and craps.

Should luck not prove a lady, Monaco has an unexpected watery delight in the **Musée Océanographique**. Set in a beautiful fin-de-siècle building on a sheer cliff rising from the sea in Monaco-Ville, this wonderful aquarium was founded by oceanographer Prince Albert I in 1910. The old-style museum on the first floor is dedicated to his activities, with vast whale skeletons, original equipment and meticulously surveyed maps of Arctic islands. Downstairs is the aquarium, including the shark lagoon and reconstructed tropical reefs bright with colourful movement. Lantern-eye fish, long-horned cowfish, fish shaped like rocks, razor shrimps that can also be used as knives when bone dry, medusas and moray eels all give rise to shrieks of 'Rigolo!' from darkened corners of the eerie basement. There's a bar on the roof terrace and a restaurant.

Apart from that there's a lot of shopping. If you're staying, the **Hôtel de Paris** shares its history with Monte-Carlo itself. At the other end of the scale, **Villa Boeri**, within a short walk of the Casino, is the last of a line of budget lodgings a few doors over the Monégasque border in Beausoleil, and provides 30 clean, comfortable rooms, some with sea-facing balconies.

IN THE AREA

From Nice, there are ferry services to Corsica, as there are from Toulon, further west along the coast. To go further afield you'll need to drive to Marseilles, France's second city and oldest port. From here, ferries depart, in a babel of competing languages, for Corsica, Sardinia, Algeria and Tunisia.

Marseilles itself is France's second city, with a rugged, unpredictable charm. Here, the colours seem brighter and the cafés sexier than its neighbours. The graceful Vieux Port, home to France's most photogenic fish market, is the hub of local life. The quai de Rive Neuve contains the **Théâtre National de la Criée**, converted from old fish auction rooms; this area is also where you'll find the city's hippest nightspots. North is Le Panier, the oldest part of the city and one hard to resist for its narrow streets, steep stairways and pastel-coloured houses.

The North African district of Belsunce, around rue d'Aubagne, has a souk-like feel and a reputation for muggings. La Canebière is the city's main street and, although a little shabby, glamour can be found at the dynamic **Musée de la Mode**. Bohemian cours Julien sits on the site of the former central food market. These days, it is the city's most youthful area, home to fashion boutiques, bookshops, cafés and music venues.

TRAVEL INFORMATION

Book Eurotunnel tickets at www.eurotunnel.com. Motorail services from Calais to Nice run every Friday from mid-May to mid-September. There are Sunday services in July and August. The price (one way and per car, irrespective of the number of passengers) ranges from £470 to £660. The return journey, from Nice to Calais, runs on Saturdays (additional trains on Mondays in July and August), and costs £360 to £650. Book through **RailEurope**.

If you go car-less but want to hire a car on arrival, all the major car-hire companies have offices at the railway station. For something sexier than a hatchback, try **Elite Agencies**.

WHEN TO GO

Spring, summer, autumn. Summer can be blisteringly hot, though. Spare a thought for winter: cool but usually bright.

Further reading

Marcel Pagnol *Jean de Florette*
Marcel Pagnol *Manon des Sources*
  Pagnol's classic tales of land and love.
Carol Drinkwater *The Olive Farm: A Memoir of Life, Love and Olive Oil* From jobbing TV actress to olive grower.
JG Ballard *Super-Cannes* What lies beneath the slick surface.
F Scott Fitzgerald *Tender is the Night*
Peter Mayle *A Year in Provence* The book that started a publishing mini-industry.

Websites

www.nicetourism.com
  The official tourist website.
www.visitmonaco.com
  The principality's tourist website.
www.gracekellyonline.com
  A virtual shrine to the movie star and princess.

Hôtel de Paris
pl du Casino, Monte-Carlo
00 377-98 06 30 16
www.hoteldeparismontecarlo.com

Villa Boeri
29 bd du Général Leclerc, Monte-Carlo
04 93 78 38 10
www.hotelboeri.com

Théâtre National de la Criée
30 quai de Rive Neuve, Marseille
04 91 54 70 54
www.theatre-lacriee.com

Musée de la Mode
11 La Canebière, Marseille
04 96 17 06 00
www.espacemodemediterranee.com

RailEurope
0844 848 4070
www.raileurope.co.uk

Elite Agencies
6 ave de Suède
04 92 14 77 77
www.eliterent.com

Statue of Emanuele Filiberto p172

Turin

ROUTE London ▸ Paris ▸ Turin

Take Route One from Paris to Italy by TGV and the first big city you hit is Turin. But ease of access isn't its only virtue. The capital of Piedmont is stuffed with interest, from the palaces of the Savoy monarchs through the monuments of its car-manufacturing heritage to today's creative post-industrial metropolis. And did we mention the food? The chief beneficiary of the bounty of the Piedmont region, urban home of the Slow Food movement and inventor of chocolate as we know it, Turin knows how to please the palate.

Written by **Ruth Jarvis**

Via Po p175

Palazzo Madama p172

THE TRIP

Play your timetables right and you can have breakfast in the UK, lunch in France and dinner in Italy. There are two trains a day from Paris to Turin, leaving after an early lunch and a late lunch respectively. Catch the latter, and you can start the day with breakfast either at St Pancras's champagne bar or the Spanish-influenced Camino on the other side of King's Cross station, which does an excellent hot chocolate you can compare with the Torinese version you'll be sampling later. For a Paris lunch stop, you only have to cross the road from Gare du Nord to reach the very decent Terminus Nord brasserie.

The Turin trains leave Paris from Gare de Lyon, two fast RER stops from Gare du Nord. They are sleek double-deckers with good facilities throughout – but since first class carries only a small supplement you might as well go for the generous space it offers. The route takes you from Lyon through Chambéry and then the Alps.

If you'd prefer to spend most of the journey asleep, then catch one of the overnight Artesia sleeper trains to Milan and from there connect to Turin the next morning via a two-hour local train.

St Pancras International ▶
Turin **9hours 11 minutes**

Food & drink; shopping

TURIN

THE DESTINATION

Roman Turin was only a minor outpost of the Empire, and its one notable legacy was the grid-pattern street plan that gives the city a gracious topography and views clear through to the cradling Alps. Its dominant heritage comes courtesy of the Savoys, who adopted it as their capital in the mid-16th century and promptly summoned the greatest artists and architects of the age to extend and ornament it.

A wave of neo-classical building hit in the mid-19th century, when, as a prime mover in the Risorgimento, Turin briefly became the capital of a newly united Italy. Shortly after, the Industrial Revolution added its more utilitarian footprint. In 1899, Fabbrica Italiana Automobili Torino opened – more commonly known as Fiat – and dominated the city for nearly a century. The company's headquarters remain here.

Turin's city government has been pro-active in regenerating the industrial suburbs which, added to ongoing civic beautifications, makes this a good time to visit.

EAT, DRINK AND BE MERRY

Piedmont provides a rich larder for Torinese chefs to plunder. And rich is the word. Egg-heavy pastas, bathed in butter, provide the backdrop for heady white truffles brought from Alba. Frog's legs are a local delicacy, often served with risotto; generous applications of *maionese* improve the simplest salads; and meats marinate in robust wines. Cheeses are a course unto themselves. Even coffee is treated to an extra flourish when layered with melted chocolate and hot milk.

Piedmont is also famed for its chocolate, which has been produced – and perfected – here since the 17th century. This might account for its long and glorious tradition of café society; the locals are proud of their historic coffeehouses, some of them looking exactly as they did two centuries ago.

To drink, renowned local reds include Barolo and Barbaresco; Asti takes care of the whites, including spumante.

PIAZZA CASTELLO

Piazza Castello is the monumental heart of Turin: it's the core around which the city has developed, the hub of its street plan. It's a civic centre rather than a social one, surrounded by *palazzi* and fortifications, handsome but lacking architectural unity. It now forms part of an extensive pedestrian area linking many of the major sights. These include the **Duomo**, Turin's only major example of Renaissance architecture but best known as the erstwhile home of the Holy Shroud.

There are two major Savoy palaces here. **Palazzo Madama** has recently reopened as a museum of art, architecture and decorative arts. The Museo Civico d'Arte Antica is a light and open space, grand but not oppressive. Collections include medieval stonework; art from the Gothic to the Baroque; and decorative arts. At entry level, a glass floor gives views on to the Roman ruins below; the first-floor café is a decorative joy (particularly the cake stand). **Palazzo Reale** was the official Savoy residence. Its stern façade contrasts with interiors rich with stucco, gilt, frescoes and tapestries that make it one of the city's most impressive Baroque monuments (though note that it

Duomo
piazza San Giovanni
011 436 1540

Palazzo Madama & Museo
1 Civico d'Arte Antica
011 443 501
www.palazzomadamatorino.it

Palazzo Reale
1 piazzetta Reale
011 436 1455
www.ambienteto.arti.beniculturali.it

can be visited only on half-hour guided tours in Italian).

Just around the corner from the piazza is one of Turin's best restaurants, **AB+**. Sleek and discreet inside and out – it's hard even to spot the sign – this is Turin's contemporary restaurant du jour, critically rated and publicly fêted. Dishes are creative Italian/Mediterranean takes on locally sourced produce; for example, artichoke gnocchi with mullet and olives.

For more casual eating, we like the warm and inviting **Abrate**, a lovely café-bar, formerly a bakery dating from 1866. It has the original vaulted brick ceilings and flooring that's stripped back to reveal the 17th-century pavement of via Po. There's a dining area, a quick-serve counter for coffee, good sandwiches and pastries, and a kitchen producing light meals. Even more casual, but no less delicious, is **Grom**. The two friends who opened this shiny ice-cream parlour in 2006 rewrote the recipe for *gelaterie*. It's not just the surroundings – shiny and contemporary with few seats – but the product itself. The base is own-made using mineral water, and the flavours sourced in an obsessive quest for the best available. The dark Ecuadorean chocolate variety is the finest we've tasted in a month of sundaes.

A good bet for staying in the Piazza Castello area is the **NH Santo Stefano**, enjoyably characterful, despite being part of a big chain. From the outside, it resembles a watchtower, but it was built to delight rather than defend, rising above the smart foyer purely to create an unusual interior space. Rooms are also contemporary but more conventional; those on the fifth floor have sloping ceilings and excellent views.

AB+
13 via della Basilica
011 439 0618
www.abpiu.it

Abrate
10 piazza Castello Via Po
011 812 2206

Grom
4 via Accademia delle Scienze
011 557 9095
www.grom.it

NH Santo Stefano
19 via Porta Palatina
0115223311
www.nh-hotels.com

MANGIA ITALIA

Fast food is as addictive as heroin – and just as soul-destroying, according to scientists at Princeton University who, in 2003, found that the consumption of fast food transformed the process of eating into an act of despondency. It was a conclusion that had already been reached by Italy's Slow Food movement back in the 1980s, when McDonald's attempted to open a branch by Rome's Spanish Steps. A group of journalists, led by campaigner and writer Carlo Petrini, gathered at their neighbourhood osteria in the small Piedmont city of Bra to create a manifesto that celebrates conviviality, promotes local, seasonal ingredients and counters 'the degrading effects of fast food'. Taking a snail as its badge, the Slow Food movement was born. A dynamic non-profit group still based in Bra, it now has 83,000 members in 100 countries, and even a University of Gastronomic Sciences in Piedmont and Emilia-Romagna.

The Slow Food ethos is about the taste and enjoyment of food, but by necessity and design it is also about the ethics of provenance. Petrini is vehemently opposed to agri-businesses. He admits the food costs more, but he argues for its superior quality. Critics have hinted at elitism, but Petrini and his colleagues work hard to offer more than just *tagliarini* tossed with trendy values.

You might have thought that such small-producer ethics were incompatible with large-scale shopping. But in 2007 Slow Food took the game to the enemy by collaborating with commercial partners to open Eataly in Turin. Eataly is a food education centre and bookshop, but more visibly a large and lovely food shop (Eataly) and restaurant (Casa Vicina) complex packed with products given the Slow Food seal of approval. A mouthwatering experience all round.

Eataly *230/14 via Nizza, 011 1950 6801,*
www.eatalytorino.it.
Guido per Eataly – Casa Vicina, *224 via Nizza,*
011 1950 6840, www.casavicina.it.

Mole Antonelliana

IL QUADRILATERO ROMANO

North of the Duomo is Turin's least formal quarter, and its most bohemian. Round Porta Palazzo is a maze of magnificent churches and sprawling markets that is ballsy old Turin despite the inevitably encroaching gentrification. To the west of here, centring on piazza Emanuele Filiberto and via Sant'Agostino, is the now thoroughly trendy Il Quadrilatero Romano. But our favourite restaurant here is distinctly unreconstructed. The atmospheric, family-run **Trattoria Valenza** – like some of its clients – seems to be caught in a time warp. The dark interior is crowded with assorted memorabilia and the menu offers no-fuss, authentic local dishes including stuffed pig's trotters and excellent tripe with white beans. There is no wine list to speak of, but the house reds on tap are decent and cheap.

CENTRO

Piazza Castello might be the geographical heart of Turin, but the fulcrum of shopping, drinking, working and playing lies further south, along vias Roma and Po, with their arcades, and in the regular grid of streets between. Turin's two landmark museums are here, in contrasting style. **Museo Egizio** holds some 30,000 Egyptian artefacts. It's fascinating for fans of the subject, but loses the general audience with poor interpretation, an overwhelming number of objects and an awkward route through the rooms. **Museo Nazionale del Cinema**, on the other hand, is a delight. It's housed in the Mole Antonelliana, the distinctive spire/dome that dominates Turin's skyline. Fitted with two giant screens and a bank of red-upholstered recliners with built-in speakers, the dome's vast, light-haunted interior could have been made to evoke the spectacle of the medium, with extra drama provided by the periodic passage of the tiny lift that shoots up the centre on its way to the needle at the top. The interactive exhibits have similar chutzpah.

However short your stay, don't miss **Al Bicerin**. This tiny gem of a café was founded in 1763, and it's not difficult to picture gentlemen in powdered wigs and silk stockings among the marble tables and mirror-lined walls. Set on a delightful square opposite the church of La Consolata, the café also has outside tables at which to sip a *zabaione* (traditional hot egg-yolk drink) or a *bicerìn* (the rich and creamy local version of a mocha) in its purest form. If Al Bicerin is full, as it often is, **Caffè San Carlo** is just as august. A Turin institution, it impresses with its regal atmosphere and a sense that it has remained unchanged for centuries (it was the first café in Italy to install gas lighting, in 1832). Sitting at an outside table in the Baroque piazza of the same name is a real (though pricey) treat.

Fast-forward into the 21st century and you can find some of Italy's most fashionable pizzas at **Gramsci**, a suave dining room rumoured to be frequented by Torino football players. Or in more classic mode, you could try **Mare Nostrum**, probably the best fish restaurant in Turin.

Naturally, many of the city's hotels are clustered in the centre. Our pick at the top end is **Hotel Boston**, which positions itself as an 'art hotel' – a risky gambit, but one that pays off well, particularly in the public areas, which are remarkable.

It might occupy a rather nondescript 1950s building, but the family-run **Victoria** is everybody's favourite hotel in Turin. The

Trattoria Valenza
39 via Borgo Dora
011 521 3914
Closed Aug

Museo Egizio
6 via Accademia delle Scienze
011 561 7776
www.museoegizio.it

Museo Nazionale del Cinema
20 via Montebello
011 813 8560
www.museonazionaledelcinema.it

Al Bicerin
5 piazza della Consolata
011 436 9325
www.bicerin.it

Caffè San Carlo
156 piazza San Carlo
011 532 586

Gramsci
12 via Gramsci
011 540 635

Mare Nostrum
16 via Matteo Pescatore
011 839 4543

Hotel Boston
70 via Massena
011 500 359
www.hotelbostontorino.it

Hotel Victoria
4 via Nino Costa
011 561 1909
www.hotelvictoria-torino.com

style is country house, sometimes elegant (with antique furniture), sometimes cosy (with a real fire in the sitting room) and sometimes chintzy (although, since a recent revamp, less so than previously). The new spa is notably seductive.

L'Orsa Poeta is that rare and special thing: a city-centre B&B of genuine charm. Staying here gives you a glimpse into the residential life of Turin that takes place in the courtyards behind the grand frontages. You'll ride a caged lift and enjoy views over rooftops towards the Mole Antonelliana.

Built into the huge arches in the embankment along the west bank of the River Po from Ponte Umberto to Ponte Vittorio are the bars and clubs of I Murazzi, the heart of Turin's nightlife. Most are open year-round, but they come into their own in summer, when Torinese descend en masse to the waterfront from after work to after dawn.

LINGOTTO

A few kilometres south of the city centre, the Lingotto was the heart of Fiat's manufacturing empire. The factories are now silent, but urban blight is being fought off with a series of redevelopments, notably a park and venues originally built for the 2006 Winter Olympics and the conversion of the Lingotto complex, a former Fiat factory, into a US-style shopping mall. It contains a Renzo Piano-designed auditorium, cinemas and an art gallery, the **Pinacoteca Giovanni e Marella Agnelli**.

PURCHASING POWER

Turin has a good spread of shopping, from high-end designer boutiques to sprawling fleamarkets. Whatever you're looking for, piazza Castello is a good point of departure. South along glittering via Roma are bourgeois boutiques and celebrated confectioners; west up via Garibaldi is the cheap 'n' cheerful buzz of Europe's longest pedestrian precinct. Via Milano leads north from via Garibaldi towards piazza della Repubblica; on side streets such as via Bonelli and via delle Orfane are clusters of artsy emporia. Piazza della Repubblica is home to the **Mercato di Porta Palazzo**, Europe's largest open-air market, and entry point to the **Balon** fleamarket at weekends.

Parallel to via Garibaldi, via Barbaroux has antiques shops, home design, jewellers and candle shops. To the east of piazza Madama, via Po and piazza Vittorio have arcades to protect you from rain and sun as you browse through their mix of antiques, second-hand book stalls and fashion shops.

TRAVEL INFORMATION

Both day trains and sleepers are bookable through **Rail Europe**.

If you prefer to travel at night you can take the **Artesia** sleeper to Milan and connect to Turin on a two-hour local train.

WHEN TO GO

Turin is good year round. There is a trio of important cultural events in autumn dedicated to music (Settembre Musica), Slow Food (Salone del Gusto, alternate years) and film (Torino Film festival, second in Italy only to Venice). Details are available from the **Turismo Torino e Provincia**. Turin is designated **World Design Capital** for 2008 with a bristling roster of events.

Further reading
....
Carlo Fruttero & Franco Lucentini *The Sunday Woman* F&L began their successful series of il commissario Santamaria mysteries with this story.
Carlo Petrini *Slow Food: The Case for Taste* The manifesto of the Slow Food movement.

Websites
....
www.shroud.com
More information than you could possibly imagine about the Shroud of Turin.

TURIN

L'Orso Poeta
10 corso Vittorio Emanuele II
011 517 8996
www.orsopoeta-bed-and-breakfast.it

Pinacoteca Giovanni e Marella Agnelli
230 via Nizza
011 006 2713
www.pinacoteca-agnelli.it

Mercato di Porta Palazzo
piazza della Repubblica

Il (Gran) Balon
011 436 9741
www.balon.it

Rail Europe
0844 848 4070
www.raileurope.co.uk

Artesia
www.artesia.eu

Turismo Torino e Provincia
www.turismotorino.org

World Design Capital
www.torinoworlddesigncapital.it

Gamle Stavanger p179

Stavanger

ROUTE Newcastle ▸ Stavanger

Catch the overnight ferry to Stavanger, European Capital of Culture 2008, to explore its pristine old town, maritime heritage, arts scene and full-on nightlife. Then take a tour around the Rogaland coast for some lighthouse bagging and a trek through the spectacular scenery of Jæren, home to one of Europe's longest beaches.

Written by **Jonathan Lee**

Stavanger Harbour p179

THE TRIP

The prospect of spending nearly a day tossing around on the North Sea might be enough to put off most tourists, but the experience proves much more agreeable than the anticipation. With toddlers dancing to cheesy live bands and a sprinkling of grandfathers snoring stertorously in corners, the jaunt from Newcastle to Norway is more free-form floating wedding than ferry journey. Add in to the mixture piano sing-alongs and the buffet free-for-all – an endless belt of smoked salmon, pickled herring, sushi, salami and bubbling cauldrons of veal stew – and it's hard not to be won over by the general 'go on, have another one' bonhomie.

Beyond the possibilities for some serious bouts of blow-out indulgence, DFDS Seaways' *Queen of Scandinavia* offers plenty to fill the 19.5-hour trip to Stavanger, with two cinemas, 'pirate ship' children's play area, swimming pool and a nightclub for the weekend party crowd. And wherever you look, you'll find Norwegians with the glint of a manic pre-Christmas shopper in their eye — drawn to the comparatively cheaper fare of Newcastle's shopping malls.

 Newcastle ▸ Stavanger
19 hours 30 minutes

 Architecture; culture; landscape; active break

Swords in Rock p183

THE DESTINATION

Fire and ice, ocean and oil, boom and bust: Stavanger is a city of elemental extremes. Jutting out into the North Sea, it has a compact, picture-postcard centre built of whitewashed clapboard; fishermen still ply their catch straight from their boats and denizens are of the laid-back, have-another-herring-and-don't-worry-about-it variety. But the oil discoveries of the last four decades have put a commercial spring into the city's step: enter ugly business hotels, tower blocks and an endless stream of oil workers with expense accounts. Probe deeper again and you'll discover a scene of cutting-edge performance spaces and international art, funky late-night clubs and world-class cuisine.

Come in the summer and you'll find Norway's fourth largest city at its buzziest with the old port's pavement cafés heaving thanks to the balmy Gulf Stream and 20-odd hours of sunlight a day; a season that, at least according to locals, rivals the Costa del Sol in atmosphere. The winter months bring much shorter days, but crisp air and the possibility of skiing and a glimpse of frozen fjords if you are heading north.

This is also a city geared to inquisitive walkers – the maniacal driver is a rare species – and all key cultural attractions are easily reached on foot. If you plan to visit more than one museum, hang on to your first ticket and you'll get cut-price entry for subsequent stops. (See www.stavanger.museum.no for the list of participants.)

And if you find the likes of the British Museum a tad over-ambitious, you'll love the fact that it's local passions – the sea, sardines, petrol and putting out rampant blazes – that are given exhibition space.

Get your bearings atop the Valberg Tower, a 26-metre lookout built on a hillock in the town centre to spot outbreaks of fire – potentially catastrophic events for timber-built towns.

Watchmen warned the city by tolling bells and firing cannons, while today the octagonal 19th-century tower hosts a small exhibition complete with fire buckets and polished stirrup pumps. Sadly, the thing wasn't in place to save the city's **Cathedral**, a heavy 12th-century granite affair built in an Anglo-Norman style and given a Gothic makeover after being blasted by fire in 1272; don't miss Victor Sparre's stained glass, depicting New Testament scenes, on the eastern flank.

From the tower you should be able to spot at least a couple of Antony Gormley's life-size iron sculptures. His Broken Column project comprises 23 sandblasted figures standing at various points throughout the city, all gazing in exactly the same direction out to the swelling grey sea. Each has been planted at a specific height, running from just over 41 metres above sea level to right down to the water's edge to form a 'fractured' column.

From here it's a short stroll along spotless cobbled streets to the Østre Havn harbour, the home of the **Norsk Oljemuseum** (Petroleum Musuem), which hardly sounds like a $100 barrel of laughs but is a convincing paean to the black stuff featuring an excellent 3-D cinema, a life-size replica of a rig floor and some fearsome drill bits. If nothing else, it explains how the 'Christmas present' of 1969 – a bumper discovery of North Sea reserves – marked a return to the boom years after the demise of the fishing and shipbuilding industries.

Cathedral
Domkirkeplassen
51 84 04 00

Norsk Oljemuseum
Kjeringholmen
51 93 93 00
www.norskolje.museum.no

Other attractions lie to the south and south-west of the city's Breiavatnet lake. The **Stavanger Museum** is well worth a stop, housing a good natural history collection – including a huge fin whale skeleton – together with excellent life-size re-creations of local life including a cooper's workshop, a typical 19th-century street and a classroom. And against all the odds, the nearby **Museum of Archaeology** is the best place to take the kids. Beyond well-displayed Stone and Bronze Age flints is a 'time machine' taking children to a forest glade where they can don Viking capes and practise marauding across England.

The best art gallery is the **Rogaland Kunstmuseum**, a domed structure found on the western shore of Mosvatnet lake, south-west of the city centre. Take the path from the edge of town – it's a pleasant half-hour lakeside wend where your noisiest companions will be a gaggle of geese – to find a strong collection of 19th- and 20th-century paintings including excellent snowscapes by Enger Erling and symbolist works by Olaf Lange. The museum also majors on contemporary artists such as Pia Myrvold and Damien Hirst, while café staff are typically relaxed: you select your own sticky bun, pour yourself a coffee and put money in the pot.

GAMLE STAVANGER

No matter how brief your stay, Gamle Stavanger (Old Stavanger) on the west side of the Vågen harbour is a must-see. Your nose should draw you there: the nearby fish market's piles of prawns, crabs, sardines and smoked kippers give off a potent whiff. You'll soon hit a picturesque hotchpotch of wharf houses and narrow cobbled lanes; the best-preserved and biggest number of wooden buildings in northern Europe are pretty much unchanged since their construction at the turn of the 18th century. This time capsule is by far the town's most atmospheric corner: it's easy to imagine barnacle-encrusted fishermen hauling their catch along the cobbles, swapping yarns of terrifying swells.

Galleries and studios now pepper the Gamle Stavanger, but there's a decent doff of the cap to its seafaring origins at the **Maritime Museum**. Akin to exploring below decks in a creaking full-rigger, the museum is crammed with ships' wheels, diving suits, barrels, a sail-maker's attic and recreated merchants' offices and stores, all charting Stavanger's years as a herring town (1808-70), and as a shipbuilding and transport hub.

If you have the energy, wander further north towards the international ferry terminal and call in at the **Canning Museum**, a worthy but rather dusty collection focusing on the town's sardine processing industry through a recreated 1920s-era factory, complete with drying ovens and heavyweight machinery. It will really only appeal to the piscatorial equivalent of the trainspotter, but a good collection of retro tins and posters is a redeeming feature.

CAPITAL OF CULTURE

Alongside Liverpool, the Stavanger region was European Capital of Culture in 2008 (www.stavanger2008.no) – a year marked by vast banquets, Greek dramas, frenzied Nordic underground rock gigs and a great deal more besides.

One of the event's biggest legacies was Norwegian Wood, a project that saw international architects build sustainable,

NOTES

....
....
....
....
....
....
....
....
....
....
....
....
....
....
....
....
....
....
....
....
....
....
....
....
....
....
....
....

STAVANGER

Stavanger Museum
16 Muségate
51 84 27 00
www.stavanger.museum.no

Museum of Archaeology
10A Peder Klows Gate
51 84 60 00
www.ark.museum.no

Rogaland Kunstmuseum
55 Henrik Ibsensgate
51 53 09 00
www.rkm.no

Maritime Museum
17&19 Nedre Strandgate
51 84 27 00
www.stavanger.museum.no

Canning Museum
88 Øvre Strandgate
51 84 27 00
www.stavanger.museum.no

Time Out Travel Guides

Worldwide

All our guides are written by a team of local experts with a unique and stylish insider perspective. We offer essential tips, trusted advice and honest reviews for everything you need to know in the city.

Over 50 destinations available at all good bookshops and at timeout.com/shop

Time Out Guides

wooden buildings and bridges in and around the city. Check out the new wooden quarter in Siriskjær, a new boat house and a wharfside warehouse on Natvigs Minde, an island in Stavanger's harbour, and a new open-air theatre on the island of Hundvåg. Stavanger is also gaining a new concert hall in Sandvigå, which will be home to the city's symphony orchestra from 2011.

Meanwhile, 11 kilometres south lies a veritable frenzy of cultural openings. The **Sandnes Kulturhus** is home to a new national dance centre, while the town's new **Jærmuseet** encourages children and adults to explore technology and science through workshops and interactive exhibitions. Also, a new storytelling centre, **Odin's Eye**, is busy becoming a European centre for narrative art.

Lighthouse fanatics should check out the spectacular Rogaland coast, where artists and architects were invited to 'fill the gap between what a lighthouse used to be and what a lighthouse may yet become'. The lighthouses – some retaining works beyond 2008 – include Eigerøy (Eigersund), Kvassheim (Hå), Obrestad (Hå region), Feistein (Klepp), Tungenes (Randaberg) and Utsira (Utsira region).

EATING AND DRINKING

The city boasts a decent clutch of bars and restaurants, but oil-induced price hikes and the buoyant Norwegian economy, mean a night out can make a serious dent in your wallet. Dishes are hearty with herring, shrimps, venison and scallops appearing regularly. There's a concentration of bars around the Vågen harbour, a magnet for oilmen in the small hours.

To kick off, sink a few glasses of dark, sweet Bokkøl beer at the **N.B. Sørensens Dampskibsexpedition** on the Vågen harbour. Founded in 1897, it's a wooden-panelled hideaway chock-full of seafaring curios. Bar food includes solid stomach-fillers such as huge English breakfast-style fry-ups and glazed pork ribs served with lightning efficiency by cheerful waitresses, while there's a fine dining restaurant upstairs.

Another good session-starter is **Bøker & Børst** ('books and booze'), a chilled, low-lit bar attracting intellectual types perfecting the Peter Wessel Zapffe existentialist look. Try your hand at backgammon or chess, tuck into a decent slab of *bløtkake* (a creamy Norwegian gateaux) or kick back with a book.

The cheapest pub in town – with beer at half the price of other boozers at just 25 kroner a jar – is **München**, an underground den that owes more to the classic London-based TV series *Minder* than rustic Norwegian drinking holes. A long faux-mahogany bar serves grateful expats by the dozen, and the place is perpetually packed to the gills. If your pockets are a little deeper, head for **Gaffel and Karaffel**, a funky champagne bar and dining rooms set over several lavish floors. The menu sports reconstructed traditional British dishes including cod with mushy peas and roast pork ribs with red cabbage.

Meanwhile, the harbourside **Stim** ups the minimalist ante with frosted glass tables, an open kitchen, purple seating and extremely hip clientele. Choose from the likes of spicy fish soup, steamed black mussels, fallow deer and cloudberry parfait.

Those on the trail of haute Nordic cuisine should try **Setra**, which gives traditional ingredients such as reindeer, oysters and scallops the gourmet treatment in laid-back surroundings.

Casa Nostra p183

Sandnes Kulturhus
1 Mauritz Kartevolds Plass
51 60 20 10
www.sandnes-kulturhus.no

Jærmuseet
26 Storgate
51 97 25 40
www.jaermuseet.no

Odin's Eye
5 Olav Kyrresgate
www.fortellersenteret.no

N.B. Sørensens Dampskibsexpedition
26 Skagen
51 84 38 20

Bøker & Børst
32 Øvre Holmegate
51 86 04 76

München
Urgata, off Prostebak

Gaffel and Karaffel
20 Øvre Holmegate
51 86 41 58
www.tomat.no

Stim
In Skagen Brygge Hotel, 28 Skagenkaien
51 85 00 16
www.stim.as

Setra
8 Eiganesveien
51 52 86 26
www.restaurantsetra.no

NIGHTLIFE

Many bars stay open until 3am so late drinking sessions, combined with inebriated gyration, are popular pastimes. Die-hard partygoers flock to the Strandkaien quayside strip. If you only visit one venue, make it **Cementen** in Gamle Stavanger. It's nothing special to look at – rickety tables, tobacco-stained walls and a dash of ersatz in the form of posters of cheesy Spanish señoritas – but this tiny venue boasts a storming arthouse pedigree, hosting comedy, live music and club nights with rockabilly, Northern Soul, jazz and hard-core punk as regular fixtures. The kids behind the bar are bleeding-edge cool – size zero black jeans and stripy black and red jumpers are de rigueur – while many ex-staff are now professional actors, and scenes from the quirky comedy flick *Mongoland* were shot here.

While you're in the area, head a few paces up the hill to **Checkpoint Charlie**, a rock pub and nightclub attracting a slightly younger, angrier crowd. And if it all gets too much, repair to the white-walled minimalism of **Tango Bar & Kjøkken**, just paces away on the harbour, which serves decent cocktails and a strong cosmopolitan menu.

Locals also swear by **Café Sting**, a nightclub, art gallery and café found close to the Valberg Tower while the dye-in-the-wool avant garde set can be found on the other side of town at **Tou Scene** – an old brewery hosting good live gigs and experimental performance. Up the hill towards the business hotels is **Folken**, a grungy bar complete with glitterballs, ripped posters and sets by DJ Ivar! and the guitar legend that is Lars Lillo Stenberg.

Those who fancy sticking to one venue for the entire evening should try **Hall Toll**. This bar, concert venue, nightclub, lounge and restaurant, situated in the town's old custom house, attracts a hip, international crowd.

WHERE TO STAY

At first, tracking down characterful, well-priced accommodation in Stavanger seems as easy as unearthing a Viking longship: the city bristles with business-oriented hotels but it is possible to find some unpolished gems. Remember, too, that as the city is geared towards business trips, prices are high during the week but fall dramatically at the weekend.

Those on tight budgets should head straight for **Stavanger Bed and Breakfast**, which offers bargain stays on a quiet road around ten minutes' walk from the train and bus stations. Rooms offer hostel-style simplicity with en suite showers and TVs (although there are no en suite toilets), while breakfast will satiate even the most ravenous, comprising boiled eggs, salami and cheese, good coffee, all manner of gooey chocolate spreads and even smoked salmon. Owner Michael Peck is a walking tourist information kiosk too, with an encyclopaedic knowledge of local attractions and events.

Other budget possibilities include the **Youth Hostel**, situated three kilometres north-east of the centre, and the **Folken Bed and Breakfast**, a better-placed option in the centre of town.

One of the best options is the 28-bedroom **Skansen Hotel** – a mid-priced retreat right on the port. The staircases may be more at home in a multi-storey car park and the interiors are functional, but views across the water and an unbeatable central location make it a surefire punt.

Cementen
25 Nedre Strandgate
51 56 78 00
www.cementen.no

Checkpoint Charlie
5 Lars Hertervigsgate
51 53 22 45
www.checkpoint.no

Tango Bar & Kjøkken
25 Nedre Strandgate
51 50 12 30
www.tango-bk.no

Café Sting
3 Valberget
51 89 38 78
www.cafe-sting.no

Tou Scene
Lervigsveien, entrance from Kvitsøygt
51 53 05 95
www.touscene.com

Folken
16 Ny Olavskleiv
51 56 44 44
www.folken.no

Hall Toll
2 Skansengaten
51 51 72 32
www.hall-toll.no

Stavanger Bed and Breakfast
1A Vikedalsgaten
51 56 25 00
www.stavangerbedandbreakfast.no

Youth Hostel
19 Henrik Ibsensgate
51 54 36 36
www.hihostels.com

Folken Bed and Breakfast
16 Ny Olavskleiv
51 56 44 44
www.folken.no

Skansen Hotel
7 Skansegata
51 93 85 00
www.skansenhotel.no

STAVANGER

If it's self-catering you're after, try **Villa Blidensol** in the old town. It's a former stable, converted by a local boho artist into a neat little house complete with beams and a fireplace.

The adventurous should try **Casa Nostra**, a cooperman's cottage converted by Torunn Larsen, a woman with boundless energy and a cool design eye. It's situated around 15 minutes' walk east of the city centre in Stavanger's arty 'Manhattan' district. The only downside: there's only a single bed with an additional fold-out option.

Finally, if you're really stuck and don't mind travelling back to 1950s Britain, try the **Rogalandsheimen Inn** in a suburb 15 minutes' walk south of the port. The place resembles an old-style boarding house, but the owners are extremely friendly and there's 21st-century Wi-Fi internet access thrown in.

IN THE AREA

The most popular jaunt is the boat trip to Lyseford, home to both the vast Preikestolen (Pulpit Rock) – a 600-metre edifice towering above the fjord – and the famous Kjerag boulder, its 1,000-metre drop drawing base jumpers in droves.

Travelling to the fjord is straightforward – the **Rødne Fjord Cruise** runs day trips from Stavanger – while conquering Pulpit Rock is a little more complicated: take a ferry to Tau from Stavanger's Fiskepiren wharf, pick up the bus (June to August only) from Tau to Preikestolhytta lodge and then hike the two strenuous hours from there.

At Hafrsfjord, five kilometres outside Stavanger, is the Swerd i Fjell (Swords in Rock) memorial of the Battle of Hafrsfjord of 872AD, where Harald Hårfagre united Norway into one country. The monument was unveiled by King Olav in 1983. The three crowns represent the three districts that fought in the battle.

Hikers looking for a decent fix should head for Mosterøy, an island 25 kilometres north of Stavanger and home to the excellent **Utstein Kloster Hotell**, while the closest skiing can be found at **Sirdal**, two hours by bus to the east.

For a truly quirky trip, you could trek the coast staying at lighthouses or fishermen's huts en route with **Nordsjøløypa North Sea Trail**. Various historical excursions are also possible, including a tour of medieval and Viking sites. (Find out more at the **Museum of Archeology**.)

TRAVEL INFORMATION

National Express East Coast runs train services to Newcastle from London and other UK cities; advance purchase return fares between London King's Cross and Newcastle, booked online, start from £23 (standard class) and £75 (first class). **DFDS Seaways** runs two outward and two return sailings a week from Newcastle to Stavanger. Sailing time is 19.5 hours. Fares for two people plus a car start at £352 return, while foot passenger tickets go from £43 per person. Stavanger's excellent **tourist office** is based near the cathedral. To see the fjords pick up the **Hurtigruten ferry**, which pooters right into the Arctic Circle.

WHEN TO GO

May to September.

Further reading

Graham Clarke *Graham Clarke's Stavanger* Sketches in words and pictures of the town.
Hans Eyvind Næss *Will and Vision* (available from Stavanger Tourist Information) Fine coffee table book to the region.

Websites

www.stavanger-guide.com
www.guidecompagniet.no
www.fjordnorway.com
The complete guide to the crinkly bits.

Villa Blidensol
112 Øvre Strandgate
51 52 53 46

Casa Nostra
18 Badehusgata
92 85 02 98
www.casa-nostra.no

Rogalandsheimen Inn
18 Musegata
51 52 01 88
www.rogalandsheimen.no

Rødne Fjord Cruise
51 89 52 70
www.rodne.no

Ustein Kloster Hotell
4156 Mosterøy
51 72 01 00
www.utsteinklosterhotell.no

Sirdal
www.sirdalsferie.com

Nordsjøløypa North Sea Trail
www.northseatrail.org

Museum of Archaeology
www.ark.museum.no

National Express East Coast
08457 225 225
www.nationalexpresseastcoast.com

DFDS Seaways
0871 522 9955
www.dfds.co.uk

Tourist Office
3 Domkirkeplassen
www.regionstavanger.com

Hurtigruten ferry
www.hurtigruten.co.uk

STAVANGER

Buza p191

Croatian Coast

ROUTE London ▶ Paris ▶ Stuttgart ▶ Munich ▶ Ljubljana ▶ Rijeka ▶ Split ▶ Brac ▶ Hvar Town ▶ Vis ▶ Dubrovnik

A palm-fronded paradise is what many travellers seek these days. Brochure fantasies are forged in Thailand, the Maldives or the Caribbean – with long-haul flights and expense no object. But right here in Europe, in less than a day's flight-free travel from London, you can board a boat and head out to an unspoiled idyll of safe, crystal-clear waters, untamed wildlife and traditional Mediterranean cuisine. So kiss jumbo jets goodbye and embrace the wild, unspoiled coast of Croatia.

Written by **Peterjon Cresswell**

Dubrovnik p190

Split p188

THE TRIP

The best way to reach Croatia is in the comfort of one of Deutsche Bahn's City Night Line couchettes. That way you'll have plenty of time to think about how you're going to indulge in the 1,200 islands and 2,000 kilometres of Europe's most celebrated coastline.

Leaving Gare du Nord and the Eurostar behind it's a short walk to Gare de l'Est, from which one of the new Christian Lacroix-designed TGV Est trains speeds, cutting the journey time to Stuttgart to well under four hours. En route, the train passes through Champagne country as the sun thinks about setting, arriving at the southern German metropolis for an easy change of platforms to Munich. Another two hours or so and then it's time to board the night train for Rijeka, waking up in time to enjoy the mountain scenery and karst landscapes of Slovenia. If you decide to break your journey at the Slovene capital of Ljubljana, as the winter timetable demands, then you can enjoy a cool, cultured stopover. From Ljubljana, it's a quick hop of just over two hours to Rijeka in Croatia, including the almost forgotten thrill of a border crossing: you are leaving the EU behind.

 St Pancras International ▶
Rijeka **19 hours 46 minutes**

⭐ Beaches; history; landscapes;

....
....
....
....
....
....
....
....
....
....
....
....
....
....
....
....
....
....
....
....
....
....
....

CROATIAN COAST

Jadrolinija
16 Riva, Rijeka
+385 051 666 111
www.jadrolinija.hr

Trsat Castle
Petra Zrinskoga
no phone

Grand Hotel Bonavia
4 Dolac, Rijeka
051 357 100
www.bonavia.hr

Jadran
46 Setaliste XIII Divizije, Rijeka
051 216 600
www.jadran-hoteli.hr

Municipum
5 Trg Rijecke rezolucije, Rijeka
051 213 000

Zlatna Skoljka
12A Kruzna, Rijeka
051 213 782

Trsatika
33 Setaliste J
Rakovca 33, Trsat
051 217 455

Opium Buddha Bar
12A Riva, Rijeka
051 336 397

Capitano
3 Adamiceva, Rijeka
051 213 399

ARRIVAL: RIJEKA

The Croatian seaboard is one of rocky, natural beaches and Rijeka is the ideal hub for exploring it. As a result, few people spend more than a few hours here, but get past the industrial clutter lining the seafront and you'll find one of Croatia's more unusual destinations. On the promenade, or Riva, you'll find the main office of the Croatian state ferry company, **Jadrolinija**, where tickets are sold for the bulk of its destinations down the coast.

You may decide to stay in Rijeka for a day or so after the long journey down, but even if you are merely swapping modes of transport, you'll invariably have a few hours to kill before setting sail. To get a sense of what's in store, take a no.1 bus from the town centre to its terminus at Trsat, high above Rijeka. There, at **Trsat Castle**, is a panoramic terrace café and, beyond it, a jaw-dropping view of the Kvarner Bay. It's a much hyped vista and the reason for this will be immediately apparent to any visitor – as will the reason that land-locked Hungary greedily snaffled up this Adriatic outlet for itself in the mid 19th century.

ONE RIVER TO CROSS

Known as Fiume ('River') to both Magyars and Italians, Rijeka was founded by the Romans and was taken over by the Habsburgs in the 15th century. It fell under Hungary in the late 18th century. Just as Vienna had a sea outlet in Trieste, so Budapest created a harbour, Baroque buildings and sundry industry (including the world's first torpedo) here. Although the nearest Hungarian community was 350 kilometres away, the Magyars claimed Rijeka as theirs. When this legitimacy was challenged in 1868, the Hungarians switched papers on Emperor Franz Josef at the signing ceremony and a majority Slav population had to suffer another 50 years of Magyar rule.

Similar underhand practices in Slovakia and elsewhere caused the minorities under Austro-Hungarian rule to have a justifiable grievance, giving rise to World War I. Immediately afterwards, Mussolini's favourite poet, Gabriele D'Annunzio, went one better, invading with 200 soldiers to claim Fiume as Italian and his own state. The border between Italy and the newly created Yugoslavia was a little canal you'll see just off the main street, the Korzo. Il Duce, Hitler and Tito later came to rule, but Rijeka remains an anomaly even with the better harbour and transport links to Zagreb, Budapest and the rest of Europe that the World Bank's investment of €300 million provided.

For the time being, Rijeka can offer two excellent hotels – the **Grand Hotel Bonavia** and the seafront **Jadran** – and a handful of good restaurants. **Municipum** is top-notch and formal while **Zlatna Skoljka** provides quality seafood with less fuss. If you're up in Trsat, **Trsatika** offers juicy grilled dishes and a great terrace view. Nightlife takes place near the harbour. The **Opium Buddha Bar** and **Capitano** are trendy bars full of up-for-it locals, open late seven days a week. The last beer you'll drink in Rijeka is likely

to be at **Kavana Ri**, where you can rest on the first-floor terrace while gazing at the liner that will soon take you down the Adriatic.

Immediately ahead, Kvarner Bay, occasionally blasted by the vicious Bura wind, contains islands brimming with wildlife: Krk (connected to the mainland near Rijeka by a road bridge and containing Rijeka airport); Rab; Cres and Losinj, the latter two also linked to each other. Veli Losinj is the base for **Blue World**, a dolphin conservation project with workshops for school groups and volunteers. Boat tours recommended by the organisation include **Fran** and **Happy Boat**, both based at Veli Losinj harbour. On Cres, at the tiny hilltop village of Beli, the **Caput Insulae** monitors and cares for a population of rare griffon vultures. It also provides maps of hiking trails leading from there. Rab is most notable for its pretty beaches and tradition of naturism – this is where King Edward VIII and Wallis Simpson shocked the world by swimming naked. Key hotels on the island are run by the Imperial group (www.imperial.hr). The website www.kvarner.hr has details of hotels and the main restaurants in the region.

The coastal ferry to Dalmatia bypasses these islands, but in summer Jadrolinija boats and catamarans run regularly from Rijeka and, in the case of Krk, there's a bus too.

COASTING ALONG

The daily ferry service runs along the whole coastline from Rijeka to the very southern tip of the country, Dubrovnik, some 200 kilometres south of Split and right by the border with Montenegro.

Jadrolinija's fleet of 36 ferries, eight catamarans, one hydrobus and a handful of conventional ships serves some nine million passengers and two million vehicles every year. In summer, there are 400 departures a day. Facilities vary according to the boat, but if you're aboard the *Marko Polo* or the *Dubrovnik* then you can expect a decent restaurant, musicians, dancing and a playroom for children.

As for the cost, deck passes between Rijeka and Split, a journey of ten hours or more, are about €25. OK, you may only snatch a few hours' sleep in a chair but you would have spent more snacking in service stations if you were hitching it. A cabin

Kavana Ri
Brodokomerc Forum, Riva, Rijeka
051 311 019

Blue World
24 Kastel, Veli Losinj
051 604 666
www.blue-world.org

Fran
Veli Losinj harbour
098 627 012 mobile

Happy Boat
Veli Losinj harbour
091 792 1035 mobile

Caput Insulae
Beli, Cres
051 840 525
www.caput-insulae.com

Split

Bistro Black Cat
1 Segviceva, Split
021 490 284

Adriana
8 Riva, Split
021 340 000
www.hotel-adriana.hr

Slavija
2 Buvinina, Split
021 323 840
www.hotelslavija.com

Jupiter
1 Grabovceva sirina, Split
021 344 801
www.hotel-jupiter.info

Zbirac
Setaliste Bacvice bb, Bacvive
www.zbirac.hr

Tropic Club Equador
Kupaliste, Bacvice

Bota Sare
Bacvive
021 488 648

Academia Ghetto Club
10 Dosud, Split
021 346 879

Puls
1 Buvinina, Split
no phone

Villa Giardino
2 Novi put, Bol
021 635 286

Ribarska kucica
Ante Starcevica, Bol
021 635 033

berth is about €70, rising to €100 for the best bed on board. Add about €10 to these prices and you're valid for Dubrovnik. If you're driving across Europe, then an average car can be ferried from Rijeka to Split for about €60-€70.

Through the night the ferry chugs southwards until, come morning, it arrives at Split just as the harbourfront and recently revamped seaside promenade Riva are coming to life.

STORMING THE PALACE

Split is no picture postcard. Better to think of it as organic, or real. It consists of: a gutted Roman palace in the old centre, its alleyways housing a medley of bars and shops; the palm-lined Riva with attendant terrace cafés; the beach and nightspots a short walk away at Bacvice; and endless housing blocks sprawling to the back and beyond. Apart from ferry crews and the market traders by the palace, no one ever seems to be working. Splicani have a chip on their shoulder about where they come from and the fact that it's neither the capital nor as prestigious as nearby Dubrovnik, but their city can be a lot of fun.

Having stepped off the boat, breakfast can be enjoyed at the **Bistro Black Cat** near the Riva. Reasonably priced lodgings can be arranged at the **Adriana** pizzeria on the Riva, the **Slavija**, or at the cheaper, hostel-like **Jupiter**, the latter two just inside the palace complex. The day is best spent by the sea at Bacvice. To get there, walk away from the harbour, keeping the bus station to your left, over a slight incline and then over the train tracks. It's a city beach, with not the cleanest sea (which means pristine by Spanish standards) but there are showers and good bars. The clubby **Zbirac** is steps away while the late-opening **Tropic Club Equador** doubles as a disco – its huge balcony catches the sunset and dominates the three-level leisure centre in which you will also find the traditional Dalmatian restaurant **Bota Sare**.

Barhopping in the palace is de rigueur if you're staying over. The best place hands down is the **Academia Ghetto Club**, a tumble-down DJ bar and gallery accessed up a short flight of steps. The the popular disco-bar **Puls** is at the Hotel Slavija end. Choose a hotel room facing the back.

SPLIT SPLIT

Although more tourists are staying in Split for a night or two, in the end nearly all head on to the islands. And, because the boat service is designed to serve locals and their needs (many islanders work and/or send their children to secondary school on the mainland), prices are absurd. A passenger ticket from Split to any of the three holiday islands of Brac, Hvar or Vis, some two hours away, costs less than a short tube journey in London. There are catamarans too, more expensive but twice as quick, all boats are equipped with a bar and, for longer journeys, a restaurant.

The nearest island, Brac (www.brac.hr), is family-oriented and hell in high season. But it does have Croatia's most famous beach, Zlatni Rat, near Bol, a triangle of shifting sands and a haven for windsurfers. A Jadrolinija catamaran takes 50 minutes to reach Bol from Split; most ferries run to Supetar on the north side. Most hotels are of the package-holiday variety although the family-run **Villa Giardino** in Bol has character. The idyllic but pricey **Ribarska kucica** nearby will provide a memorable meal and there are plenty of bars around the harbour. In Supetar, the street Put

Vele Luke by the sea is also a bar hub; **Jastog** is the once in a holiday budget-buster of a restaurant, but worth it.

Hvar Town, Croatia's Monte-Carlo, is 50 minutes by catamaran from Split. The main settlement on the island of the same name attracts famous names and the yachting fraternity to its modest harbour and main square, although most partying takes place in private surroundings back on board. The one exception is **Carpe Diem**, a cocktail bar on the seafront, where Roman Abramovich orders the finest Russian vodka and Gérard Depardieu the cheapest local plonk. Cooler and more sympathetic is **Zimmer Frei**, a stark but friendly club-bar near the main-square church. Narrow Groda, officially known as Petra Hektorovica, is lined with restaurants, in particular **Luna** and its roof terrace, and trendy **Yaksa**. Hotels are run by **Suncani Hvar**, which has converted all three stars to four and higher, and upped rates to French Riviera norms. Alternatively, as everywhere in Croatia, families hire out rooms. More alternatively still, a 15-minute boat ride organised by the hosts will bring you to the **Villa Irming**, a detached villa with a barbecue grill and plenty of outdoor activities.

Remote Vis, meanwhile, is another matter. An army base under Tito so not developed for either industry or tourism – in fact, closed to Westerners for decades – Vis is surrounded by wonderfully clear waters ideal for divers. The **Issa Diving Center**, based at the one big resort hotel, the **Bisevo** in the main town of Komiza, can offer 22 guided itineraries for divers of varying abilities. From Komiza harbour, boats leave around 9am for the Blue Cave, a natural phenomenon on the nearby tiny island of Bisevo. Just before noon, as the sun shines through a side entrance, the cave is bathed in an eerie blue light. Most boat tours also include a lunch or picnic nearby. Komiza is where you'll find restaurants such as the **Konoba Jastozera**, where dining tables are placed over a turquoise sea, attracting A-list celebs in high season. Less showy, set in Vis town where the boat arrives from Split, is the **Kantun**, an ideal bar-restaurant to try the local Vugava wines. The yachting crowd prefers the **Vila Kaliopa**, a Dalmatian restaurant in the verdant grounds of a 16th-century mansion. The **Hotel Paula** is a lovely, family-run stone-house hotel in Vis town.

Jastog
7 Bana Josipa Jelacica, Bol
021 631 486

Carpe Diem
Hvar Town, Hvar
www.carpe-diem-hvar.com

Zimmer Frei
Groda, Hvar Town, Hvar
098 559 6182 mobile

Luna
Groda, Hvar Town, Hvar
021 741 400

Yaksa
Groda, Hvar Town, Hvar
091 277 0770 mobile

Suncani Hvar
www.suncanihvar.com

Villa Irming
Sveta Nedelja, Hvar
021 745 768
www.irming.hr

Issa Diving Center
96 Ribarska, Komiza, Vis
021 713 144
www.scubadiving.hr

Bisevo
96 Ribarska, Komiza, Vis
021 713 144

Konoba Jastozera
6 Gunduliceva, Komiza, Vis
021 713 859
www.jastozera.com

Kantun
17 Biskupa Mihe Psica, Vis Town, Vis
021 711 306

Vila Kaliopa
32 Vladimira Nazora, Vis
021 711 755

Hotel Paula
2 Petra Hektorovica, Vis Town, Vis
021 711 362
www.paula-hotel.htnet.hr

Dubrovnik

The coastal ferry via Split from Rijeka goes on to Stari Grad on the north side of Hvar, with far fewer amenities but a reasonable selection of sleeping and eating options. It then calls into Korcula, alleged birthplace of Marco Polo, built by the Venetians with an old-town vibe that appeals to an older generation of tourist. The hotel stock, mainly provided by the **HTP group**, is disappointing, but the **Massimo Cocktail Bar** and **Morski Konjic** restaurant should satisfy visitors of most ages.

DOWN TO DUBROVNIK

After steaming for some 20 hours down the coast the ferry from Rijeka finally pulls into Dubrovnik. It's worth the wait. The city is the heart of what was once called Ragusa, an independent trading and maritime power (think Venice) that once challenged La Serenissima. These days it may be an overpriced tourist centre, but the impressive outline of this stone citadel cannot fail to wow the first-time visitor.

What you see today is what Napoleon's generals would have seen 200 years ago when their entrance ended centuries of self-rule. Seeing this, it's hard to believe that 15 years ago much of this Adriatic jewel was destroyed by Serbian bombs, an action of no strategic value in the context of the war that divided Yugoslavia and gave Croatia its independence from Belgrade. The city rebuilt itself and embarked on the self-promotion that has seen its fortunes rise. Dubrovnik, haughty, cultural and intellectual, has always been a separate entity, in attitude at least, and attracted A-list celebrities since the 1960s.

High-end hotels, especially prestigious ones run by the Adriatic Luxury Hotels group (www.gsresortshotels.com), cater to such stars although off-season you might find them surprisingly affordable. For a home-from-home right in the Old Town, look no further than Marc van Bloemen's **Karmen Apartments**. Nearby, as London-born Marc will explain, are the cheap seafood options of the **Kamenice**, overlooking the main market, and the pricier but

HTP group
www.htp-korcula.hr

Massimo Cocktail Bar
Kula Zakerjan, Korcula
020 715 073

Morski Konjic
Setaliste Petra Kanavelica, Korcula
020 711 878

Karmen Apartments
1 Bandureva, Dubrovnik
020 323 433
www.karmendu.com

Kamenice
8 Gunduliceva poljana, Dubrovnik
020 323 685

quality alternative of the **Dubrovacki kantun**, where local produce is put to superb use. Mention must also be made of the wonderful **Wanda**, whose care and international experience in the kitchen put the tourist traps in the same street to shame. Right on the Old Harbour, the **Lokanda Peskarija** offers great local cuisine at outstandingly low prices – hence the queues around the block every summer evening. From here, little boats make the 15-minute journey to Lokrum, an island nature reserve of nudist beaches and strange tradition. No one can spend the night there, apart from the guards who ensure that everyone is on the last boat back to Dubrovnik.

There are also day trips to recently independent Montenegro and its coastline of virgin beauty interspersed with brash resorts.

The main street in town, Stradun, and offshoots, are full of bars and cafés. By now everyone knows about the **Buza** bar, signposted ('Cold Drinks') by the Jesuit church, but it still does not detract from a slightly pricier beer looking out on to the open sea from its cliff-face location. The **Buza I** bar is a less fussy option, with the bonus of being able to dive into a moonlit Adriatic.

Daytime activities are not limited to sunbathing. Sea kayaking is popular, with beginners made to feel welcome by **Adriatic Kayak Tours**, a local outdoor adventure company run by an enthusiastic American who fell in love with Croatia. A half-day's paddle on a calm sea involves a few minutes of instruction, a ride to Lokrum island, lunch there and then back again by kayak.

The main harbour where the ferry docks is at Gruz, a fair trek with luggage or a 70-kuna taxi ride from the Old Town. From here, regular boats also leave for the Elafiti Islands, real get-away-from-it-all isles, where locals live from growing melons and running restaurants the quality of **Kod Marka** on Sipan. Aficionados are known to plan entire holidays around his hospitable and unbeatable cuisine.

TRAVEL INFORMATION: GOING HOME

Ferries between Croatia and Italy are run by **Jadrolinija**, **SEM Marina** and **Adriatica**. Some of the Croatian coastal ferries go on from Dubrovnik to Bari in southern Italy, from where a train every two hours takes eight to reach Milan. Or you could head back to Split from Dubrovnik, a four-and-a-half-hour coach ride – Dubrovnik has no train station. From Split, there is at least one nightly service to Ancona, halfway up the east coast of Italy. A deck pass is about €40, a standard cabin berth about €100.

Between June and September there is also the option of a **SNAV** fast boat, which takes four-and-a-half hours from Split to Ancona, although arriving at a somewhat inconvenient 9.30pm. The standard ticket is €81, with rates available at €63 and €36 out of high season and with advance booking.

By train it is about four hours from Ancona to Milan, from where a direct train to Paris takes seven, finally pulling into Paris-Lyon. A simple journey on RER line D of seven minutes takes you to the Gare du Nord, and the Eurostar to London St Pancras International.

WHEN TO GO

September is the best time to visit Croatia. Hotels drop their rates, the sea is warm and so is the sun.

Further reading

Marcus Tanner *Croatia, a Nation Forged in War* Focused account of the background to the the 1991-5 war.
Jane Cody & John Nash *Croatia Cruising Companion* The sailor's handbook.
Rebecca West *Black Lamb and Grey Falcon* One of the classics of travel writing.
Robert D Kaplan *Balkan Ghosts* Written just before Yugoslavia tore itself apart, Kaplan gives the wider context.

Websites

www.croatia.hr
www.visit-croatia.co.uk
www.dalmatia-cen.com
Dalmatian tourist board site.
www.titoville.com
Does the impossible: makes Tito funny.

Dubrovacki kantun
5 Boskoviceva, Dubrovnik
020 331 911

Wanda
8 Prijeko, Dubrovnik
098 944 9317 mobile

Lokanda Peskarija
Na Ponti, Dubrovnik
020 324 750

Buza
9 Crijeviceva, Dubrovnik
no phone

Buza I
Ilije Sarake, Dubrovnik

Adriatic Kayak Tours
www.adriatickayaktours.com

Kod Marka
Sipanska luka, Sipan
020 758 007

Jadrolinija
www.jadrolinija.hr

SEM Marina
www.sem-marina.hr

Adriatica
www.adriatica.it

SNAV
www.snav.it

Cares Gorge p196

España Verde

| **ROUTE** | Plymouth ▸ Santander ▸ Santillana del Mar ▸ Cabezón de la Sal ▸ Arriondas ▸ Cain ▸ Cares Gorge ▸ Poncebos ▸ Potes ▸ Panes ▸ Alevia |

Take a comfortable car ferry to Santander, one of Spain's most underrated cities, followed by a beach break in the perfectly preserved town of Santillana del Mar. Then it's time to fuel up on hotpot and go deep into the heart of 'Green Spain', exploring the steep slopes, lush valleys and unspoiled villages of the Picos de Europa.

Written by **Chris Moss**

Potes p196

Faro de Santander

THE TRIP

At 20.5 hours, the long haul from Plymouth to Santander on Spain's Cantabrian coast could be slotted into the 'Journeys' section of this book. In fact, t's a painless and even pleasant half-a-day and one night crossing on a smart ship, the *Pont-Aven*, run by French irm Brittany Ferries. There's a pool and leisure area, a wrap-around promenade, cinemas, a disco and games oom to keep the young 'uns occupied, all spread over ive spacious decks. The ship carries 2,400 passengers ut, somehow, it never feels packed, and the cabins are lean and cosy. Whether you go for the self-service buffet r the waiter-served restaurant, there's cheap, decent vine and a plate of frites and steak for the evening neal; the staff are efficient and keen to help. The Bay f Biscay has a reputation for gales and grim sailings.)ccasionally, crossings can be rough, but more common s a nice, sleep-inducing heave-ho during the night. Spain's national rail network, Renfe, only links the nain cities of España Verde to Madrid. For getting round, he FEVE train goes to Arriondas and along the coast to alicia; but to explore the Picos properly you'll need a ar, a bicycle or extremely good legs (and lots of time).

 Plymouth ▸ Santander
20 hours 30 minutes

 Active break; family holiday; food; landscape; walking; wildlife

THE DESTINATION

The rain in Spain certainly doesn't stay on the plain. It lashes it down right here, turning the steep, sensually shaped mountains of the north-west coast into a lush, verdant barrier that keeps Castile far away and gives the natives of Cantabria, Asturias and Galicia a sense of separateness and regional pride. This chapter focuses on Cantabria and Asturias – the two provinces most easily accessible from Santander.

SANTANDER

Elegant, wealthy Santander is a favourite holiday resort for inner-city Spaniards who flock here to enjoy the mild weather and long beaches. The main thoroughfares are the Avenida Reina Victoria and the Paseo de Pereda, lined by 18th- and 19th-century French-style architecture, manicured public gardens and pretty balconies overlooking the Cantabrian Sea. Most other streets are modern – unlike the rest of Cantabria, which is Romanesque – as Santander was almost completely rebuilt after the ancient hub of the city was destroyed by fire in 1941.

The city's most illustrious man of letters was Marcelino Menéndez y Pelayo (1856-1912). He is buried in the fort-like 13th-century **Catedral**, which was restored after being seriously damaged in the afore-mentioned 1941 fire, and his 50,000-volume library forms the basis of the **Biblioteca Menéndez y Pelayo**. Guided tours are available. Opposite is the Casa Museo, which displays the writer's modest study.

History runs deep in this part of Spain, and Roman ruins were discovered beneath the north aisle of the cathedral in 1983. If you want to delve deeper into the region's distant past, the **Museo Regional de Prehistoria y Arqueología de Cantabria** has valuable Roman and prehistoric artefacts discovered in the province – some of them dating from 15,000 years ago.

Santander has always aspired to rival San Sebastián for discreet urbaneness but it has never quite matched the Basque city. Nor have Cantabria's chefs caught up with those of the Pais Vasco or even Galicia yet – but **Sebal** is a coolly contemporary, Michelin-starred centre of excellence. The grilled anglerfish is a must-taste, and ox steak comes with fresh rosemary and port. The namesake chef at **Zacarias** is the local authority on Cantabrian recipes and his *alubias rojas* (red beans with sausage) and other local stews are possibly the tastiest in Spain.

When it becomes time to sleep, the best beds in town are at the ultra-luxurious **Hotel Real**, built in 1917, and the modern, stylish **NH Ciudad de Santander**.

With more than five kilometres of clean coastline, Santander offers a plethora of beachlife from tiny coves to wide golden sands; families enjoy those with calm waters (Los Peligros, La Magdalena and Bikinis), while the surfers tend to go for the wind and wilder waves of El Camello, La Concha, El Sardinero, Molinucos and Matalefías.

Just 40 kilometres west of Santander is Santillana del Mar (or Santillana-by-Sea), an immaculate-looking town paved throughout with huge cobblestones – the kind of perfectly preserved provincial town Spain seems to specialise in and one where motor cars look utterly out of place. At the heart of the historic centre is the 12th-century **La Colegiata** church, an

Catedral
Plaza José Equino Trecu
94 222 60 24

Biblioteca Menéndez y Pelayo
6 C/Rubio
94 223 45 34

Museo Regional de Prehistoria y Arqueología de Cantabria
4 C/Casimiro Sáinz
94 220 71 09

Sebal
7 Andrés del Río
94 222 2515

Zacarias
41 General Mola
94 221 23 33

Hotel Real
28 Paseo Pérez Galdós
94 227 25-50
www.hotelreal.es

NH Ciudad de Santander
13-15 Menéndez Pelayo
94 222 7965
www.nh-hotels.com

La Colegiata
Plaza Abad Francisco Navarro
63 983 0520

mpressive hulk of Romanesque grandiosity where the bones of the local patron, Saint Juliana, are kept.

Santillana's streets are lined with *casonas*, the typical residences of Spain's rural nobility, often adorned with a heraldic shield bearing a coat of arms. The architecture looks harmonious – pale grey, austere, impenetrable – but the town evolved between the Middle Ages and the 18th century and features buildings from all periods. There are dozens of stores selling local foodstuffs – try the picón de tresviso blue cheese, the salted venison, the anchovies, and the *bizcocho* or sponge cake. It all looks touristy enough, but this is a living, breathing town and people decorate their balconies with flowers out of pride, not for visitors' photos. Santillana's **Museo de al Inquisicion** is a lively collection of iron maidens, chastity belts and things for sticking into people, covering the history of torture throughout the ages.

There are Paleolithic caves all over northern Spain and it really is a case of seen one.... But just two kilometres outside Santillana is the Altamira Cave, discovered in 1879 and now a UNESCO World Heritage Site. The 300 metres of walls are decorated with 150 engraved figures and polychromatic paintings of bisons and boars.

Santillana is very close to its Mar. It's a pleasant drive to and along the coast and you can take a back road (the CA-125) down to Cabezón de la Sal, a tranquil town surrounded by farms. A few kilometres south of Cabezón, off the main road, is **El Jardin de Carrejo**, a beautiful stone house built in 1881, set in gardens.

Potes p196

GOING GREEN

Where Cantabria meets Asturias and León is the 647 square kilometre **Parque Nacional Picos de Europa**, a kind of Wales on steroids for those who hate the crowds and clichés of southern Spain. There are three major massifs in the park – the Central, Eastern and Western – with several peaks rising in excess of 2,000 metres (the highest, Torre de Cerredo, has an altitude of 2,648 metres). The rock is chiefly limestone and glacial action has created a dramatic region of alpine karst, with challenging jagged summits that draw the world's best climbers. Some of Europe's deepest caves are in the Picos park, including Torca del Cerro and Sima de la Cornisa, which both go more than 1,500 metres below sea level.

The Picos support an ever-diminishing group of shepherds who, in the summer, migrate from the valleys with their sheep, goats, cows and pigs. Asturias is famous for its dairy farming and is nicknamed 'land of cheeses' by some: the *queso cabrales* is everywhere, and is still made mainly by local artisans – many of whom continue to mature their cheeses in caves.

To warm up for the Picos, it's wise to do a lowland village walk. The **Posada del Valle**, a delightful stone house in the tiny hamlet of Collia, is an ideal base for walking. British host Nigel Burch lavishes plates of home-grown roots and shoots on his guests, as well as the tender meat of the rare Xaldas sheep – of Celtic origin – that he raises. The *posada* has its own farm trail where guests can see what Nigel and his wife, Joann, are doing in the way of conservation work, with wildflower meadows integrated with low-intensity farming and vegetable patches.

The views from the rooms are stupendous, with ridges of serrated hills separated by cradles of verdant pastureland.

Museo de al Inquisicion
1 Jesús Otero
942 840 273

El Jardin de Carrejo
Carrejo
942 701 516
www.eljardindecarrejo.com

Parque Nacional Picos de Europa
www.picoseuropa.net

Posada del Valle
985 84 11 57
www.posadadelvalle.com

Catedral de Santander p194

Orujos for sale in Potes

The cottages on the saddles between the hills are painted in bright pastels, their flower gardens bursting with luminous colour even when storms turn the sky an ominous grey.

The Asturias Village Walk – Nigel provides maps and guides – takes you right into this landscape. It begins with an easy downhill walk into the town of Arriondas, where you can grab a *café con leche*, and buy some picnic food, before boarding the little FEVE train and travelling four stops to Sevares. From here, you begin the trek back to the *posada*. The route takes you down back roads that connect tiny pueblos and many thriving little farms. The rolling hills make for easy strolling, and little chapels and copses of dense woodland provide shade or, as is more likely, shelter from the rain and an opportunity to pause and take a drink. The most noteworthy building in these Asturian villages is the *oriel* or raised granary, which provides cover during the frequent showers to livestock while using the animals' body heat to dry the stores.

It's just as well that the walking is not too strenuous since, arriving back at the *posada*, there's a tough final climb back to Nigel's vegetable patches, where tea and cake are always waiting

INTO THE HIGH PICOS

The Cares Gorge – a 1.5-kilometre-deep rift that divides the Central and Western massifs – is one of the most popular walks in the Picos de Europa park. It runs between Cain and Poncebos – you can start at either end. From the Cain end, at first you have to bow your head to pass beneath the jutting shelves that hang from the cliffs, but then the canyon retreats slightly, allowing you views of rocky peaks in the distance and of the vegetation clinging to the vertical walls.

You are only a few hundred metres west of the mighty Naranjo de Bulnes, which, at 2,519 metres above sea level, is one of the highest mountains in the Picos range. It's called the Naranjo (or Orange) because at sunrise and sunset the grey limestone horn at the summit glows bright orange. The slopes are clad in holm and cork oaks, chestnuts and hazels, which are the basis of the ecosystem that supports wildcats, chamois, foxes and a handful of Cantabrian brown bears.

The Gorge itself is a straightforward walk. The 12 kilometres take from two to four hours to cover, depending on how often you stop for photo opportunities and rests. If you park at one end, either arrange for a taxi to collect you four hours later at the other end – or walk back.

POTES AND PANES

Potes, in Cantabria, is a pretty little market town full of winding lanes and well worth a few hours – the town hall is in a handsome 13th-century tower – and also an ideal base for exploring the Picos. Here, there are several quaint hotels and some lovely restaurants serving traditional regional cuisine. The **Casa Cayo** is a wood-framed mountain-style property, built in the 1930s, with big bedrooms and a decent restaurant; for food and drink, the **Asador El Balcón** has an extensive menu of local dishes and stocks wines and *orujos* (liquers) from across Spain.

The perfect post- or pre-climbing energy supplement is *pote asturiano* – served everywhere (even in Cantabria) and in all seasons. The 'pot' is a hot cauldron of pork shoulder, cured pork, *fabes* (white beans), potatoes, *chorizos* (sausages), *morcillas*

Casa Cayo
6 Cantabra
942 730 150
www.casacayo.com

Asador El Balcón
Epifanio Sánchez Mateo
942 730 464

Transcántabrico p198

(blood pudding), ham off the bone, cabbage and seasoning. Like all great stews, you feel as if you're eating the landscape around you, not to mention the local fauna. The sauce should be thick but not so much that it has absorbed all the ingredients with their separate flavours. There are countless variations on the *pote*, as well as rival broths: the *cocido lebaniego* is a similar concoction, though with chickpeas. If in doubt, just say 'guiso' or 'stew'.

The only challenge is: when to eat these hearty meals? At night it is something of a dream inducer, but can you pack one away for breakfast before a hike?

Panes, Asturias, is another crossroads town and a useful gateway for the Picos. Just above it is Alevia, a charming hamlet full of traditional houses – some grand mansions with several storeys, others workers' cottages made from rough stone.

Stay at the **Casona D'Alevia**, a beautifully renovated 15th-century farmhouse crammed with dark-wood furniture and antiques. It's run by Gregorio and his wife, Lupe, who was born here – her father was a skilled artisan and his primitive iron tools are displayed proudly on one of the walls.

While some of the lowland farming villages are still very much alive, Alevia's peasant families have moved on and most of the grander houses are now used as summer residences by wealthy *madrileños* – they place a premium on high places for their second homes. Out of season it can be a bit of a ghost pueblo.

Still, it's pretty enough and there are great views over the valley below. As for eating, you can't do better than to dine at the Casona – Lupe's pote is awesome. But beforehand, pop out for a drink at Alevia's sole entertainment arena – La Bolera – a grocer's as well as a snack bar and drinking den.

Speaking of drink, the only tipple worth having around here is cider. Around Potes – and across Asturias – are dozens of apple orchards, as well as a number of *lagareros* or cider breweries. Cider, or *sidra*, is considered to be the region's 'wine' and is produced under a Denomination of Origin just like the best vintages. The Asturian tradition goes back at least to Roman times, and some 30 varieties of apple are grown, which are then carefully blended to produce the balance of sweetness and acidity the local palate favours.

It is traditionally poured by an expert server (or *escanciador*) – and even backwater canteens seem to have one. The bottle is raised high above his or her head to oxygenate the brew as it falls

Transcántabrico dining car

Casona D'Alevia
Alevia, Peñamellera Baja
985 414 176
www.casonadalevia.com/

Further reading

Tim Moore *Spanish Steps* The subtitle is One Man and his Ass on the Pilgrim Way to Santiago. A ruder Bill Bryson.

Websites

http://english.turismodecantabria.com
A comprehensive website for visitors.
www.visitasturias.co.uk
What it says.
www.idealspain.com/pages/Places/greenspain.asp
All about the top edge of the country.
www.spain.info/
The official tourist website.

FEVE
www.feve.es

Transcántabrico
www.transcantabrico.feve.es

Brittany Ferries
08705 360360
www.brittanyferries.co.uk

into the glass below. Small amounts are poured and these are supposed to be drunk immediately before the drink loses its bubbles – a custom that invariably leads to instantaneous tipsiness. Any dregs are poured on to a woodchip-strewn floor or a trough along the bottom of the bar.

Alevia is well off the tourist circuit so the old dear at the bar will give you a label-less bottle, a bucket and a little glass. Expect much spillage and lots of scrumpyesque sensations.

The mountains of north-western Spain may not be Europe's highest range, but the Picos de Europa probably get their name from the fact that they were the first thing sailors returning to the Bay of Biscay could see – so they are certainly high enough. Having done a lowland stroll and the gorge, you may want to take on a long hike across the peaks. Guides in Potes, Panes and all the other main centres can arrange the logistics and camping for small groups.

But even if you go to España Verde to feast and drive along the wonderful roads, the whole region reveals a fresh side of a country we sometimes think we've thoroughly done. The deep clefts in the coast and the folds in the mountains have a strange effect on travel round Cantabria and Asturias, and as-the-crow-flies distances mean very little – this is a land of corners, coves and crannies, many of them unexplored.

IN THE AREA

España Verde stretches west into Galicia and east into the Basque Country and Catalunya. Go in either direction for wonderful regional cooking, plenty of climbing opportunities and, in Catalunya, arguably the best adventure tourism infrastructure in Spain – Val d'Aran in the Pyrenees is the place to go quad-biking, horse-riding, climbing and white-water rafting. If heading in this direction, consider P&O's Bilbao–Portsmouth ferry service. At more than 33 hours, it's slow, but it means you won't have to retrace your steps.

The Camino de Santiago is Europe's most popular pilgrimage route – if you really want to get to know Green Spain, then take on the 780-kilometre trudge from St-Jean-Pied-de-Port in France to Santiago de Compostela. If you walk at least 100 kilometres, or cycle 200 kilometres, you will get a *compostela* – a certificate of accomplishment – on arrival.

If the little **FEVE** train doesn't quite hit the spot, check out the **Transcántabrico**, a luxury service operated by the same firm that runs through Santiago de Compostela, Oviedo, Ribadesella, Llanes, Santillana del Mar, Santander and Bilbao. There are departures from spring through autumn.

TRAVEL INFORMATION

Brittany Ferries has two sailings a week to Santander departing from Plymouth every Sunday and Wednesday. Crossing time is just under 20 hours. Fares for a car plus two passengers start at £258 return; plus a two-berth cabin from £118 return or a reclining seat for £14 per person return.

WHEN TO GO

Spring, summer and autumn, but always be prepared for rain.

Journeys

Journeys

Orient Express

Orient Express

ROUTE London ▸ Paris ▸ Vienna ▸ Budapest ▸ Belgrade ▸ Sofia ▸ Istanbul

Roll through history as you ride on Europe's most famous railway line – well, lines, now it's been cut up. You can arrange your own journey to Istanbul, taking the traditional route and using public trains– or revive the grand style and take the luxury sleeper from Venice to Paris.

Written by **Peterjon Cresswell**; 'Orient Excess' by **Cathy Phillips**

Zagreb railway station p205

Grand Bazaar p210

Westend Café, Vienna p206

THE JOURNEY

 Culture; luxury

'Touch nothing!' Poirot's words as he enters the train carriage crime scene in Sidney Lumet's 1974 star-studded film version of *Murder on the Orient Express* might still ring true for today's traveller following along in his hallowed tracks. Those intrepid enough to take the classic original train route between Paris and Istanbul – a journey of almost exactly 48 hours – can expect an authentic experience a world away from the luxury of expensive faux vintage voyages or the easy leisure of 21st-century frontier-free continental rail travel. Once you cross to the other side of Vienna – truly the gates of Europe, now as then – everything gets a little exotic and unfamiliar, a bit edgy and weirdly trapped in time. This is something out of the comfort zone of normal tourist travel. 'Balkan' is the word that best describes it. Only when you reach your goal of Istanbul Sirkeci, and find stills from Lumet's Oscar-winning film decking the walls of the station's tourist-friendly Orient Express restaurant, does the sense of accomplishment come, together with the odd feeling that you have played your own bit part in the long-running lore of the world's most legendary train.

ORIENT EXPRESS

TRACK HISTORY

You will be heading to the very edge of Europe, through the battlefields of Balkan conflicts from the 1800s to the 1990s. A short walk from Sirkeci to the transport hub of Eminonu is a regular ferry across the Bosphorus to the tiled, frescoed station of Haydarpasa and the Monday morning Taurus Express to Damascus. The train once divided at Aleppo (where Poirot first boarded), one part heading in the direction of Mecca, the other to Baghdad. The line was German-built (as were Sirkeci and Haydarpasa), a move in the grand colonial game as the Ottoman Empire crumbled in the run-up to World War I – but that's another story.

On today's trains you will be safe – but watch your belongings as you would do anywhere else. You won't be ambushed by bandits as the original Orient Express occasionally was, nor will you cross the Black Sea by rowing boat as the first passengers did in 1883, nor will you be bartering with peasants for chickens while stuck in a nine-foot, ten-day snowdrift, the impasse of 1929 that gave Agatha Christie the inspiration for her novel published five years later.

Around the same time, Graham Greene set out to write a crowd-pleaser that was turned into a little-known film in 1934. His alarmingly anti-Semitic *Stamboul Train*, another tale of murder and Balkan intrigue, reflects the heyday of the great railway era, when spies, diplomats and counts hobnobbed in ornate dining cars between major stops on the grand tour. Greene's book was published in the US as *Orient Express*, though trainspotters will point out that the train of the title was, in fact, a completely separate Ostend–Istanbul service. A literary and celluloid genre ensued. Great rail hotels were constructed, such as the Esplanade in Zagreb, since impressively rebuilt.

That apart, the post-war era has not been kind to the Orient Express. Just as World War I moved Europe's borders and forced the renamed Simplon Orient Express to re-route via the newly opened Simplon Tunnel, Venice and Trieste (thus avoiding Germany and Austria), so the aftermath of World War II imposed an Iron Curtain in its path. Visas and strict border controls came into force. While society's upper crust slowly died out in the West, in the East it was airbrushed from history. Opportunists, itinerant workers and hustlers took advantage of this historical anomaly on wheels. Socialist countries asserted their identity, adding carriages bearing the colours and symbols of their national rail carrier.

The original Wagons-Lits company, formed by pioneering Belgian Georges Nackelmackers, founder of the Orient Express, sold or leased all parts of the train. Passengers could choose whether to journey via Hungary, Romania or Yugoslavia. By the time Paul Theroux rode the Direct Orient Express in the mid 1970s, the first stage of his *The Great Railway Bazaar* from London to Yokohama via Singapore, he was moved to write, 'the Orient Express, once unique for its service, is now unique among trains for its lack of it', and compared it unfavourably to trains crossing some of the poorest regions of Asia.

It last ran in 1977. While direct services from Paris to Istanbul still rolled on, the success of Lumet's film inspired American businessman James B Sherwood to relaunch a luxury service from London to Venice, using coaches revamped for the movie, echoing the style and tradition of the day. The Venice-Simplon Orient Express has been a success and created a vogue for posh chartered trains. Another upmarket sleeper, the Danube Express (www.danube-express.com), from Budapest to Prague, Poland, Croatia and points east was inaugurated in May 2008.

In Paris, the Gare de l'Est is the gleaming new terminus for the LGV Est TGV extension, which will halve the journey time to Strasbourg and has already brought Frankfurt more than two hours closer. An immediate consequence of its inauguration in June 2007 was the removal of the 'Orient Express' from international rail timetables – there was no longer a direct service from Paris to Vienna and on to Istanbul. Indeed, ask the short-memoried staff for 'Istanbul' at the booking office at the gaudy gare ('52 shops!') today and they will look at you incredulously. Their French rail SNCF computer network agrees, throwing up obscure French village destinations beginning with 'Ist-'. 'Istanbul? Isn't that in Turkey? That's a two-day journey! Surely you should fly?'

ALL ABOARD!

Rail romantics need not despair. Reaching Vienna requires easy, scheduled and punctual platform changes at Frankfurt or Stuttgart and Munich, then at Wien West itself, after which the train heads for Budapest and rolls on for two nights to Istanbul, via Serbia or Romania. The Gare de l'Est staff at platform 6, where the daily service east sets off at breakfast time, can print you out a confusing schedule of possibilities – simply punch 'Paris-Istanbul' into German rail's www.db.de for an easy breakdown of the two daily options between the traditional bookends of European train travel, the timings varying slightly according to season. One more tip: Gare de l'Est staff will quote an alarming ticket price for the Paris–Vienna leg alone. Again, do not despair, for investment in an InterRail Global Pass (www.raileurope.co.uk) allows over-26s ten days' worth of flexible all-Europe travel within a 22-day period for a current price of £281. Considering that journeys taken after 7pm count as the following day, you can do a handful of overnighters, pay sleeper supplements and cut down on hotel bills, and stretch the trip out to a fortnight. If you come back via Zagreb on the original Simplon route, you pass the places where the action takes place in Agatha Christie's thriller: Slavonski Brod and Vinkovci, railway towns now just inside the border of Croatia. Greene set his denouement in Subotica, just over the Hungarian border in modern-day Serbia.

As the train leaves Paris early in the morning, it makes sense to stay at a cheapish station hotel the night before. Eurostar travellers from London arrive at the Gare du Nord, surrounded by establishments whose names relate to accessible Belgian destinations: **Hôtel Brasserie des Belges**; **Hôtel de Bruxelles et du Nord**; **Restaurant Paris-Liège**. (The Orient Express, halfway between Nord and Est stations, is a kebab joint.) Est, ten minutes' walk via a grand staircase on rue d'Alsace, carries more historical baggage in its place names. Convenient connections between Paris and Germany have not always been a boon. The taxi-filled square outside, place du 11 Novembre, and adjacent main road rue du 8 Mai 1945, mark victory days

Blue Mosque p210

ORIENT EXPRESS

Hôtel Brasserie des Belges
35bis rue St-Quentin
01 48 78 25 30

Hôtel de Bruxelles et du Nord
28 rue Dunkerque
01 48 78 25 15

Restaurant Paris-Liège
36 rue St-Quentin
01 42 81 59 93

Hofburg, Vienna

La Strasbourgeoise
5 rue du 8 Mai 1945, Paris
01 42 05 20 02

Best Western Paris Est
4 rue du 8 Mai 1945, Paris
01 44 89 27 00
www.bestwestern.com

Dorint Biedermeier
28 Landstrasse Hauptstrasse, Vienna
01 716 710
www.dorint.com/wien

Palmenhaus
Burggarten, Vienna
01 533 1033

Zum Schwarzen Kameel
5 Bognergasse, Vienna
01 533 8125

Westend
128 Mariahilfer Strasse
01 523 3183

Demel
14 Kohlmarkt, Vienna
01 535 1717

Griesensteidl
2 Michaelerplatz, Vienna
01 535 2693

Stephansdom
Stephansplatz, Vienna
01 5155 2376

in both world wars. Within the bland commerce of the revamped station stands a stern monument to the railway workers who died at the hands of the Nazis, while a plaque commemorates the 70,000 Jews deported to death camps from here. One place mentioned, Compiègne, was the site of the Armistice signature between France and Germany in 1918, in an Orient Express train carriage; Hitler chose the exact same setting for the truce after France fell in 1940, swapping the seats round.

Alsace, the border region served from Gare de l'Est that has changed hands over the centuries, provides the inspiration for the culinary offerings of pork and sauerkraut around the station. **La Strasbourgeoise** is a wonderfully ornate restaurant of carved wood and glazed windows, a pretty mural depicting a nameless Rhine village in peaceful times. Breakfast (€6.20) is served from 7am, refreshing, white Alsatian wines all day. Best Western has two hotels alongside, including the **Paris Est**.

Whichever route you take through Germany, the half-day journey from the City of Lights to Vienna should be a pleasurable, passport-free breeze, changing platforms according to numbers already indicated on the Deutsche Bahn timetable.

OH, VIENNA

Arrival into Wien Westbahnhof, Vienna West, allows a gentle introduction to the intrigue awaiting over the next 36 hours. No, you won't be greeted by passport-checking military as Joseph Cotton was as he strode on to the platform in Carol Reed's *The Third Man*, but Vienna's role as a revolving door between East and West soon becomes apparent. The sleeping carriage of your train to Istanbul could be a sleek, Austrian Schlafwagen or a dowdy, Romanian vagon de dormit, the latter patrolled outside by an ill-dressed employee in tell-tale cheap footwear.

If you buy your sleeper ticket through official means in Vienna or three hours later in Hungary, you may also be allocated a comfort-free Bulgarian spalen vagon sleeper tacked to the end of the train in Budapest. Balkan characters and blonde-from-a-bottle dames smoke while awaiting a train to or from points east, shunning the pricey local Schnitzel or Tafelspitz dishes offered at the station's sleek è Express restaurant (the è Café upstairs has cheaper snacks and a nice view of the platform).

Downstairs at this modest two-tiered international hub (a central station for Vienna is now being built) stands a statue of the Habsburg Empress Consort Elizabeth. Popularly known as Sissi, reluctant wife of Franz Joseph, she was stabbed through the heart by an assassin on the shores of Lake Geneva. The statue was erected when the station was built in the mid 1800s, when both she and the Habsburg Empire oversaw an eastern dominion soon to foment revolution.

Moderate hotels in the Ibis and Mercure chains surround the station, although a simple hop by rail or U-Bahn line 3 to Wien-Mitte brings you to the period-style **Dorint Biedermeier**. Staying with tradition, baroque restaurants such as the **Palmenhaus** and **Zum Schwarzen Kameel**, and coffeehouses such as **Westend**, **Demel** and **Griesensteidl** are all within easy reach in the Innere Stadt. The latter stands in the shadow of the vast Imperial Palace, the Hofburg, a complex of stately buildings and gardens. The other must-see is **Stephansdom**, Vienna's cathedral with a lift to the top of the north tower.

ORIENT EXCESS

As the gleaming blue-and-gold carriages of the Venice Simplon-Orient-Express (VSOE) pull out of Venice's Santa Lucia station, at the start of the 36-hour journey to London, the sleeping car steward comes round to each compartment to check if everything is to your satisfaction and which sitting you'd like for lunch. It's a far cry from the hurly-burly of most modern-day travel – and the reason why thousands of passengers a year fork out nearly £1,500 for the one-way trip. Speed is not the point, nor cost: it's the chance to experience the kind of old-fashioned luxury travel typical of the 1920s and '30s, an era when the accents matched the cut-glass tableware and everyone dressed for dinner.

Despite the name and the company blurb, this isn't really the original Orient Express, but it's as close as dammit. The carriages are authentic 1920s beauties, built for the Compagnie Internationale des Wagons-Lits et des Grands Express Europeens railway company, which ran the Orient Express in its heyday. All polished wood and delicate art deco marquetry, with Lalique tulip-shaped lights and shiny brass fittings, each sleeping car is subtly different in design; there are also three sumptuously decorated dining cars and one bar car, complete with pianist. The travel of yesteryear has its drawbacks: the sleeping compartments (singles, doubles or – the most roomy – interconnecting doubles) are masterpieces of space-saving design, with beds that transform into couches during the day and limited washing facilities tucked away in a cabinet. Coal-fired boilers are still used to heat the water, there are no showers, and the toilets are at either end of each carriage. But, boy, is it romantic.

The man behind the rebirth of the Orient Express was American businessman James Sherwood, who scoured Europe to find historic carriages and then restored them. The first VSOE left Victoria station in 1982, and romance returned to rail travel. The Venice–Paris–London route (or vice versa) is by far the most popular – and most frequent, with twice-weekly departures from March to November – but there are also services via Vienna, Budapest, Prague or (new for 2008) Krakow, as well as a ten-day trip from Paris to Istanbul with overnight stops in Budapest and Bucharest.

Current passengers may not live up to the Agatha Christie stereotype (there's a disappointing lack of retired colonels, maiden aunts and petulant starlets and certainly no murders), but they're a varied lot, with plenty of French, German, American and Japanese travellers to alleviate the train-loving Brits who dominate. For some, the VSOE is the highlight of a wider European adventure; for many it's a special trip to celebrate a silver wedding, birthday or other anniversary. To keep with the pre-war vibe, jeans, shorts and trainers are a no-no, mobile phones are discouraged and dressing for dinner is encouraged. The atmosphere is less stuffy and formal than you might expect, aided by the bonhomie of the 40-strong cosmopolitan staff, many of whom have been working on the train for years. In fact, an infectious air of celebration predominates – especially in the bar car before dinner, when the whole train seems to have squeezed in for pre-prandial drinks and a natter. This is the kind of rail journey where people want to talk to strangers.

The longest-serving member of staff is French chef Christian Bodiguel; after 23 years with VSOE, he's mastered the art of turning out high-class dishes in a tiny galley kitchen. The three-course lunch and four-course dinner are definite high points. Monogrammed crockery, starched linen and waiters in gold-trimmed white jackets add to the air of elegant nostalgia. Lunch and dinner are included in the fare, as are afternoon tea and breakfast (both taken in your compartment), but drinks are extra.

In between mealtimes, there's plenty of time to admire the passing scenery as the train trundles at a sedate average 72kmph through the Italian Dolomites to Innsbruck (for a brief halt), then via the Swiss Alps and across France to Paris. By the time you return to your compartment after dinner, the steward has made up the bed and before you know it you've arrived at Gare de l'Est.

The final leg of the journey is a bit of a letdown. At the Channel you wave a fond farewell to the lovely Wagons-Lits carriages, clamber on a coach to cross through the tunnel, then take a brown and cream British Pullman train from Folkestone to Victoria station. And then it's back to noisy, bustling, unromantic modern London with a bump.

Orient Express 0845 077 2222, www.orient-express.com

ORIENT EXPRESS

Keleti station

BALKANISED

Even today Vienna and its then twin ruling capital of Budapest head the rail network within the old empire – mainline services to Zagreb, Belgrade and Sarajevo depart or terminate at either hub and usually call at both. Such was the force by which the Hungarians assumed their role in the Dual Monarchy, that Magyar became the language of official communication between train staff and passengers – even when passing through the future Yugoslavia.

Blue city buses serve the streets of suburban Budapest as you approach the Danube. The train makes a brief stop at Kelenföld station – 'getting off at Kelenföld' is local slang for withdrawal before ejaculation – then crosses the river. With the Citadella monument high above and 'bridges looped across like sparkling necklaces' (Patrick Leigh Fermor), the Danube here is broad and dramatic. The track runs past the newly gentrifying waterside Ninth district, past the national Ferenc Puskás football stadium, built in the great player's day, before pulling into the once mighty nexus of Keleti railway station.

Now a shabby ruin boarded up here and there, Keleti ('East') at least still has a proud exterior fronted by statues of James Watt and George Stephenson and the rather splendid **Baross Terasz** café-restaurant in one corner, although a pianist no longer serenades passengers from a grand centrepiecing the interior. On the expansive concourse Gypsy families gather around sagging bags, taxi drivers and flat-owners hustle for business while a catchy jingle ('Do-la-sol-LA-mi-fa-MI') introducing each train announcement over the tannoy earns its composer, Emil Petrovics, another couple of forints. If you fancy staying over, the four-star **Best Western Hungária** opposite the station has a sauna, gym and Habsburg-style restaurant. Its typical Magyar mains are meaty and quite spicy – *pörkölt* is the stew you would think of as goulash. If you have a real appetite, then bean soup (*bableves*) is another speciality. Gere Attila is the best domestic wine producer these days. Bear in mind that the famous Tokaj is a very sweet dessert wine – and very expensive. For a local meal to remember, the **Múzeum** by the National Museum is Hungarian with all the trimmings. There is an all-night cake shop and bar next door if you're staying up. Taxis parked at main train stations are somewhat pricey – hail one from the street or take the easy-to-use metro.

Before boarding the solitary maroon-and-rust Bulgarian sleeping coach you should stock up on supplies (including toilet paper) as the native conductor can only provide a plastic beaker misshapen by hot, undrinkable coffee in exchange for a euro coin. Euros in small denominations are useful, although Serbian dinars, Bulgarian lev and Turkish lira are the host currencies en route. He also takes your ticket and reservation. (He will keep your reservation – if you need it back, ask him to photocopy it at Dimitrovgrad or Sofia.) Cyrillic signs warn against using the toilet at stations – they should warn against using it at all. Compartment notices in Bulgarian, French, German and Italian (why does Italian always get a look-in?) suggest you not lean out of the window – you would have to unlock it first. Pictographs above your quarter-moon of tabletop indicate light and heating. Out of the summer season you should have a dowdy cabin (probably all the dowdy cabins)

Baross Terasz
Keleti pályaudvar, Budapest
www.meko.hu

Best Western Hungária
90 Rákóczi út, Budapest
01 889 4400
www.bestwestern.com

Múzeum
12 VIII. Múzeum korut, Budapest
01 267 0375

to yourself. This might allow scope for conversation with your conductor, a situation for miscommunication famously described by Dezsö Kosztolányi, Hungary's greatest writer of short stories, born when his home border town of Subotica was the Hungarian Szabadka. Kosztolányi's journey involved hours of meaningless head-nodding or shaking depending on his interlocutor's tone – yours may be similar. Serbian customs guards noisily rouse you from sleep, their firm and officious handling of your passport beckoning you to the Balkans beyond the notable civility of Hungary.

As dawn breaks, the train crawls through Belgrade's suburbs en route to its peeling main station, where shabby men fill empty bottles from dodgy-looking water fountains. Dingy railway hotels such as the **Astorija** outside offer cheap rooms, while the Kafe Pekara Express and Zeltourist Express by the platforms provide local Jelen beer and strong coffee. For more class, the revamped four-star **Balkan Hotel** in town has comfortable rooms and the stylish Orient Express café-restaurant, with a bizarre map-mural of the Simplon route bookended by a busby-bearing British grenadier and a Turk in a fez.

Venture outside and you'll find the pedestrianised main street, Kneza Mihaila, lined with terrace cafés. At the far end stands Kalemegdan, a park complex and 17th-century fortress, the city's most prominent landmark, containing sundry museums (the most interesting being the Military Museum) and Belgrade's best-known nightclub, **Anderground**. For eats, head to downtown street Skardarska and **Tri Sesira**, **Sesir Moj** and **Ima Dana**.

Out of Belgrade, past Nis, the ruin of the Serbian economy becomes apparent, abandoned buildings and disused quarries left to their fate. Scenes of almost medieval servitude are played out amid unpaved paths and errant chickens. Horses dutifully clip-clop loads between villages, while Gypsy menfolk commandeer a bare car chassis as another viable means of transport. The frontier stops of Dimitrovgrad and its Bulgarian counterpart of Dragoman hardly project an image of fortress-like security between a non-EU nation (ie Serbia) and a new member. All is shabby and rusting, the road alongside lined with Turkish trucks backed up for miles at the border post.

The Bulgarian capital of Sofia lies 90 minutes ahead, like Belgrade, best appreciated in daylight on the journey back. The evening train pulls in to a confusing array of platforms. You should just have enough time to pick up more supplies before changing for your sleeper to Istanbul. Pay the conductor for your couchette with a handful of euros and remember that Bulgarians shake their heads for 'yes' and nod for 'no'.

If you decide to break your journey to visit one of Europe's least visited cities, an easy trip on a rusty tram into the centre brings you to Vitosha, Sofia's main street, capped by the mountain of the same name in the distance. Halfway down is Sveta Nedelya church, impressive enough, but nothing when compared to the immense Aleksandar Nevsky Cathedral nearby. **Otvyad Aleyata, Za Skafa** is a reliable restaurant choice for local cuisine – Bulgaria is known for its fresh produce, peppers, tomatoes and cucumbers. Bohemian Bilkova Apteka is one of the best bars in the Balkans, let alone Bulgaria, while nearby **Chervilo** is a see-and-be-seen nightclub. For boutique digs, try the **Maria Luisa** or the 1930s' conversion **Residence Oborishte**.

Venice-Simplon Orient Express p205

Astorija
1A Milovana Milovanovica 1A
011 2645 422
ww.astorija.co.yu

Balkan Hotel
2 Prizrenska, Belgrade
011 2687 466
www.balkanhotel.net

Anderground
1A Pariska, Belgrade
011 328 2526

Tri Sesira
29 Skardarska, Belgrade
011 324 7501

Sesir Moj
27 Skardarska, Belgrade
011 322 8750

Ima Dana
38 Skardarska, Belgrade
011 323 4422

Otvyad Aleyata, Za Skafa
31 Budapeshta ulitsa, Sofia
02 983 5545
www.beyondthealley.com

Bohemian Bilkova Apteka
22 Tsar Shishman, Sofia

Chervilo
9 Tsar Osvoboditel bulevard, Sofia
02 981 6633

Maria Luisa
29 Maria Luisa, Sofia
02 980 5577
www.marialuisa.bol.bg

Residence Oborishte
63 Oborishte ulitsa, Sofia
02 814 4888
www.residence-oborishte.com

Regent Esplanade p211

Orient Express restaurant
Sirkeci Terminal, Istanbul
0212 522 2280

Museum
Sirkeci Terminal, Istanbul
0212 520 6575
Closed Sun, Mon

Events Hall
Sirkeci Terminal, Istanbul
0212 458 8834

Orient Express
34 Hüdavendigar cad., Istanbul
0212 520 7161
www.orientexpresshotel.com

Haghia Sophia
Sultanahmet, Istanbul
0212 522 1750

Topkapi Palace
Bab-i Humayun Cad., Gulhane, Istanbul
0212 512 0480

Blue Mosque
17 Meydani Sok., Istanbul
0212 458 0776

ISTANBUL HO!

The train takes six hours to get from Sofia to Svilengrad, one of Europe's most bizarre border posts. True, the station on the Turkish side, Kapikule, has been done up with bright neon, shrubbery and the striking red-and-blue, star-and-crescent motifs of Turkish State Railways, TCDD. Each office of the two-storey block features a stern, staring portrait of Ataturk. It is at this point that Turkish train conductors thrust €7 in exact change into your hand and demand, smilingly, that you buy them 20 red-and-blue packs of Muratti cigarettes from the fat, unshaven character sat flicking through an equally fat pile of notes behind the chicken wire of the solitary duty-free hut. Next to it is the hatch where a woman dressed like a cleaning lady dispenses tourist visas, British citizens £10 in the exact sterling denomination only. You then take your passport to be stamped in a bare stone room not unlike a cattle market. Then 90 minutes after Svilengrad you chug into Turkey.

Within four hours the train is hugging the Sea of Marmara and negotiating the endless outskirts of Istanbul. Slowly, dilapidated wooden houses give way to glimpses of the Bosphorus through fortifications protecting the Haghia Sophia and other famed sights of Istanbul. Rounding the Sultanahmet, with little drama and much creaking, the train pulls up: Sirkeci, the last outpost of the European rail network.

The station has been done up almost as if to resemble how it was on the set of Lumet's film, without the peddlers, merchants or Lauren Bacall. The **Orient Express restaurant** serves Turkish standards amid suitable decor; souvenirs from the original train also line the walls of a nearby modest **train museum** and Sufi musicians and dancers entertain thrice a week at the **events hall** next door. A railed-off bust of Ataturk is mounted on a marble plinth with the national slogan 'Ne mutlu Türküm Diyene!' – 'Happy is he who can say, "I am a Turk"'.

Cheap hotels surround Sirkeci, including the **Orient Express** with a loosely themed bar-restaurant and boxy rooms. In the other direction, the Galata Bridge, lined with fishermen, leads to the nightlife hub of Beyoglu and the Pera Palas hotel (www.perapalas.com), built by Wagon-Lits for Orient Express passengers in 1892 and under reconstruction until late 2008.

A short walk away, Sultanahmet contains most famous sights, namely the **Haghia Sophia**, the mother church of the Byzantine Empire and then, after the fall of Constantinople, the chief mosque of the Ottoman Empire; it's now a museum. The imperial enclave of the **Topkapi Palace** is nearby as is the **Blue Mosque**. Both a sight and shopping hub is the Grand Bazaar, a maze of street traders, most notably of jewellery and fabrics.

GOING HOME: FROM EAST TO WEST

The train back leaves Istanbul somewhat dramatically at 10pm sharp according to the grand Nacar clock hanging over platform 1. Two grim Bulgarian carriages are attached to a cosy Turkish one, a Hungarian one in MÁV blue and a Romanian CFR one bound for Bucharest. A horn blast and a travel legend is relived.

The warm, padded Turkish cabin, equipped with a sink, a reading light and fold-down armrests, will be yours, maybe even the entire carriage. The Turkish conductor offers chat in basic German and nibbles of carob ('for virility!'), but little else –

again, take supplies. Lean back and after the border shenanigans and welcome sunrise, watch the whole of bucolic Bulgaria pass by your window. At Sofia, you pull into the brutalist Socialist Tsentralna Gara in its mid-morning glory, shabby pensioners sleeping on its wooden benches by a mounted locomotive in use from 1918 to 2000. Beyond the bingo halls and casinos, dusty, dilapidated, slow-paced Sofia allows for a swift Astika beer in the hour-long layover.

Heading up to Belgrade and beyond, train pass travellers can choose the southern Simplon route for variety. At Belgrade, no mention is made on the posted timetable of Zagreb, although the last carriage, no.275, of the lunchtime train runs to the Croatian capital. Cornfields, ruined buildings and the occasional stark, white Orthodox church form the landscape until the border post at Sid, a surprisingly unstressed crossing considering these were the killing fields in 1991. Past the Croatian checkerboard flag at Tovarnik, a landscape of cornfields, ruined buildings and the occasional stark, white Catholic church runs until the main stops of Vinkovci and Slavonski Brod, settings for the original *Murder on the Orient Express*. The German-made carriages are comfortable, with the considerable addition of an equally comfortable buffet car. Although offering only sausages and Ozujsko beer, and stern advice on the menu not to sing or play music, the civilising influence of sitting à table is palpable. You are back in the West. Later on, the Austrian buffet menu will forbid 'any parlour or card games'. Order and decorum rule.

At Zagreb, beside the landmark Glavni Kolodvor station, the opulent **Regent Esplanade** was built in 1925 for Orient Express passengers and was completely renovated with the glitzy Emerald Ballroom and all kinds of spa treatments after the 1990s war. Here, perhaps in the Esplanade 1925 Lounge & Cocktail Bar, you might contemplate your route back (Ljubljana? Trieste? Venice?) across a Europe now free of borders.

TRAVEL INFORMATION

To do this trip, it is best to buy an InterRail Global Pass; this gives you any five days travel out of 10 and costs £185 (or £119 for under-25s). There will be small supplements for sleeper trains. UK ticket agents don't sell through tickets to Istanbul.

Keep a modest supply of the currency of each country you will be passing – the euro zone stops at Slovenia. Always take toilet paper and water. Keep your passport safe but easy to pull out. Avoid talk of politics in the Balkans – you'll be out of your depth.

Note that at the time of press, the rail service to northern Kosovo was suspended. Services to other parts of Kosovo were unaffected. The line and border were open but following violence in North Mitrovica, the FCO advised against all travel to North Mitrovica, and all but essential travel to Northern Kosovo.

WHEN TO GO

High summer is when trains are busiest – the rest of the year you'll have entire carriages to yourself. The Balkans can be harsh in winter – as evidenced by the snowdrift that inspired the original *Murder on the Orient Express*. In deep winter, check the weather forecasts before you travel – and for news of any train strikes. Hungarian workers have recently been playing hard ball.

Further reading

Agatha Christie *Murder on the Orient Express* One of Christie's best Poirot mysteries.
Graham Greene *Stamboul Train* A gripping spy thriller by the great writer and traveller.
Paul Theroux *The Great Railway Bazaar* From London to Tokyo and back again by train.
Andrew Eames *The 8.55 to Baghdad: From London to Iraq on the Trail of Agatha Christie* After her first marriage broke up Christie took the Orient Express to Iraq. Some 60 years later, Eames followed in her footsteps.
John Lukacs *Budapest 1900: A Historical Portrait of a City and its Culture*

Websites

www.gotohungary.co.uk
www.pestiside.hu
  The Hungarian 'Onion'.
www.sofiaecho.com
  English-language news of Bulgaria.

Regent Esplanade
1 Mihanoviceva, Zagreb
01 456 6666
www.regenthotels.com

Mount Titlis cable car p215

Swiss Rail Orgy

ROUTE London ▸ Paris ▸ Basle ▸ Lucerne

Switzerland, with its scenic lakes and soaring mountains, panoramic
trains, paddle steamers and revolving cable cars, is on your doorstep.
Make your hub Lucerne, and you're an hour or so from Basle or Berne,
less than three from Geneva and 50 minutes from Zürich. Boats, rack-rail
trains and panoramic cable cars, they all start their journey from Lucerne.

Written by **Peterjon Cresswell**

Golden Pass p216

Unterwalden steamboat on Lake Lucerne p215

Swiss postal bus

THE JOURNEY

If God had invented a transport network, it would have been a scruffier version of Switzerland's. It's not just the landscape porn you see at almost every turn, or the way a sun-dappled, whimperingly twee vale often sits beneath an ominous storm-capped mountain. It's also the ease and comfort of gliding from A to B and the scale and topographical extravagance of the railway network. Perhaps it was the constant encounter with the sublime that made Swiss engineers so daring, but orgiastic train trips abound. Indulge in the panoramic luxury of the Voralpen Express, board a century-old paddle steamer across Lake Lucerne, eat an apple on the William Tell Express or take the dinky Zentralbahn Alpine train to the world's first rotating cable car to finish at the glacier park atop 3,000-metre-high Mount Titlis – all is smoothly interlinked and carefully co-ordinated. Usually, your train, boat or yellow postal bus (some road routes are post buses integrated into the schedule) are waiting for you a platform hop away, their departure timed to allow you to whizz over from the major towns. Forget the blinging watches; you are sitting on a precision timekeeper.

Landscape; trainspotting

Bermina Express p219

Swiss Rail Pass
www.swisstravelsystem.ch

SBB
www.sbb.ch

Rio
12 Barfüsserplatz, Basle
061 261 3472

Café des Arts
6 Barfüsserplatz, Basle
061 273 5737

Kunstmuseum
16 St Alban-Graben, Basle
061 206 6262
www.kunstmuseumbasel.ch

Kunsthalle Restaurant
7 Steinenburg, Basle
061 272 4233

Mérian am Rhein
2 Rheingasse, Basle
061 685 1111
www.hotel-merian.ch

Hecht am Rhein
8 Rheingasse, Basle
061 262 220

THE HEART OF THE MATTER

Switzerland's compactness helps to make travel a pleasure, nothing being more than a few hours away at most. But the Swiss travel system and its **rail pass** makes the most of the feats of engineering that created the Alpine tunnels and mountain passes at the turn of the 19th century. And it is constantly being improved. Slicing through the Alps, the tunnels of Lötschberg, opened in December 2007, and Gotthard, set for 2012, allow international trains to operate at high speeds, cutting the journey times from Basle or Zürich to Milan by an hour, and moving freight by rail rather than road. By 2009, Geneva will be a three-hour train ride from Paris.

These measures were voted for by referendum. Most of the train network is still state-run by **SBB**. No wonder that, per head, more Swiss use trains than any other European nation.

Within cities, the tram and S-Bahn system rivals Germany's. Between them, inter-city trains are set at the same times past each hour. Miss one and you know when the next one is. Timetables, massive departure boards, clear signposting and multi-lingual announcements are ubiquitous. Luggage lockers abound – you can even have your bags sent on ahead. (And if you were to fly in, Switzerland's Fly Rail Baggage service allows you to check in to any airport in the world and have your bags sent to your final destination via Zürich, Geneva or Basle.) Cycles can be hired from one of a hundred stations and left at another. The catering is first class, whether it's the seasonally changing menu by Helvetia or communal servings of pasta in fresh sauces by Tavolago in the Italian-speaking areas.

In the heart of Europe, Switzerland has any number of access points. With the Eurostar out of London, from Paris you can head to Switzerland via Basle, a city on the Rhine adjoining three countries. Its airport is in France; some platforms of one train station (SBB) are in France, the platforms of another ('Basel Bad') station are in Germany. Border towns are always interesting – make a stop here by all means. The city is divided by the Rhine into residential Kleinbasel and Grossbasel, where all the action is. The focal square of Barfüsserplatz is lined with cafés: authentically retro **Rio** is where generations of locals congregate; the **Café des Arts** opposite is a cultured spot for coffee or lunch. Behind the square, separated by a tangle of narrow lanes, is the Münster cathedral, built in the 12th and 13th centuries. Just across Steinenberg is the **Kunstmuseum**, filled with Klees, Chagalls and Gauguins. The nearby **Kunsthalle Restaurant** offers more substantial cuisine in an arty setting. Just across the river, Rheingasse is lined with bars and hotels – the **Mérian am Rhein**, with balconied rooms overlooking the river, offers quiet comfort at around €170. The nearby **Hecht am Rhein** is much plainer and less than half that price. The other side of the tram lines is Basle's red-light district but this stretch offers revelry with no strings attached.

An hour or so away is Lucerne, in Switzerland's historic heart. This is the region of William Tell, where cantons united to overthrow the ruling Habsburgs. Thanks to its picturesque lakeside location, tourism has been the bedrock of Lucerne's economy for 150 years, hence the plethora of decent if high-priced hotels and range of day trips. There is even a Transport Museum (Verkehrshaus, Lidostrasse 5, www.verkehrshaus.org)

filled with hands-on models of Alpine trains and tunnels, with a planetarium, IMAX cinema and tethered hot-air balloon alongside. The main historic sight is the Chapel Bridge, decorated with panels depicting local history, including one of William Tell. Restaurants cater to the tourist trade – the riverside **Schiff** has character and rooms for rent too. The **Wilden Mann** and the **Hofgarten** are also lovely choices for accommodation. The rooms at the **Pickwick pub**, the other side of Chapel Bridge from the station, are very good value in winter. Nightlife around the focal Old Town involves unsophisticated drinking – quality partying and live music are provided by **Schüür** at the back of the train station.

EASY HOPS

Setting off from Lucerne, the hourly **Voralpen Express** shuttles between two lakes, from Romanshorn on Lake Constance and Lake Lucerne, skirting three others, including Lake Zürich. Boat trips, hiking and cycle tours are easily arranged from many stops. The shore resort of Romanshorn is easily and cheaply accessible across the water from Friedrichshafen over the German border if you're coming via Stuttgart or Munich. The Voralpen passes through picturesque villages and rolling countryside, past St Gallen and Mount Rigi. The whole journey lasts three hours.

Many of Switzerland's forms of transport are almost as attractive as the mountains themselves: rack rail, cogwheel and narrow-gauge trains, funiculars and cable cars. Of these, the most stunning is the **Titlis Rotair**, the world's first revolving cable car that does a full 360-degree panoramic spin round as it reaches the Titlis Glacier Station at the summit. All year round, the glacier station of restaurants, shops, a sun terrace and Europe's highest karaoke bar also offers the Ice Flyer Chairlift over the crevasses to the Titlis Glacier Park. Here, just below the peak, you can slide down a snow run on a gigantic tyre, the Snow Tube, and other wacky devices. More conventional abseiling, hiking and glacier walking are other attractions.

The hub of all this outdoor activity, Engelberg, is the pretty terminus of the dinky Zentralbahn line direct from Lucerne an hour away. A Swiss Pass is valid for Engelberg and also gives a 50 per cent discount for many attractions atop Mount Titlis. The bright red, hourly **Zentralbahn** train starts out round Lake Lucerne before taking a vertiginous route illustrated at each window-seat table. The train takes a steep climb past the power station at Obermatt station, lurching through large, hillside spruces as it ascends to reach Engelberg. Behind the quaint, Dutch-run **Hotel Alpina**, visible from the platform, is a path leading to the cable-car station less than ten minutes' walk away. There, as you gaze at the live shots on Mount Titlis from a fixed camera beamed on to a screen in the main ticket office, you can choose from all kinds of multi-day and ski passes up the slopes – the standard day ticket to Titlis is SFr53-59 for adults, SFr21-24 for under-15s. Other accommodation options include the winter-only **Berghotel Trübsee** at 1,800 metres and the classic, fin-de-siècle **Bellevue** outside Engelberg station. The journey on the Rotair cable car lasts five minutes, from the winter-only ski hut, sun terrace and café at Stand, 2,428 metres high, itself reached by a gondola across a beautiful lake from

NOTES

Schiff
8 Unter der Egg, Lucerne
041 418 5252

Wilden Mann
30 Bahnhofstrasse, Lucerne
041 210 1666
www.wilden-mann.ch

Hofgarten
14 Stadthofstrasse, Lucerne
041 410 8888

Pickwick pub
6 Rathausquai, Lucerne
041 410 5927
www.hotelpickwick.ch

Schüür
Tribschenstrasse 1, Lucerne
www.schuur.ch

Voralpen Express
www.voralpen-express.ch

Titlis Rotair
www.titlis.ch

Zentralbahn
www.zentralbahn.ch

Hotel Alpina
34 Erlenweg, Engelberg
041 637 1340

Berghotel Trübsee
www.truebseehof.ch

Bellevue
Bahnhofplatz, Engelberg
041 637 1213
www.bellevue-engelberg.ch

the well-equipped station at Trübsee, 1,800 metres high. From here you can also take a cable car to Jochpass, and descend by hiring a pedal-free Devil Bike, hefty with fat tyres for trundling over the stones in summer. At Geschnalp on the lower slopes you can also hire a Trotti Bike, tall-framed contraptions ideal for the more gentle run down to the main station at Engelberg.

EPIC TRIPS

Lucerne is the setting-off point for the flagship of the Swiss train fleet, the seven-hour **Golden Pass**. This engine of shimmering gold glides past Lake Lucerne, over the Brünig Pass, on to Interlaken, past Gstaad and down to Montreux on the shores of Lake Geneva. The premier trains on this service contain vintage carriages and swivel armchairs in the panoramic coaches. From here a thrice-daily boat to Geneva takes five hours, the regular and equally picturesque train just over an hour.

From Interlaken, you can also change on to **Jungfraubahn**, up to the highest railway station in Europe at Jungfraujoch. From Interlaken Ost (a kilometre east of town – Interlaken West is nearer the centre), trains of the Bernese Oberland Railway (or BOB) run as far as Lauterbrunnen. From there, Jungfrau trains either head south to Mürren, or east through Wengen, both free for Swiss Pass holders. To continue on to the 3,454-metre peak of Jungfraujoch, holders receive a 25 per cent discount on the equally steep ticket price – the first train of the day is the cheapest. A tunnel runs through the Eiger to a platform just below the summit. Try to time your journey for a clear day – a view from the summit is broadcast on www.jungfrau.ch. Lifts serve the various attractions there: a restaurant, exhibitions and sledge rides. Footpaths lead off from many of the stops, accessible in summer. If you break your journey up at Wengen, the **Regina Hotel** offers quality rooms and fare, and stunning views. Book ahead, especially around the time of the annual World Cup Skiing event at Wengen. More atmospheric is the **Jungfrau at Wengernalp**, a hotel and restaurant facing the Eiger, Mönch and Jungfrau mountains. Wengenalp stands at some 1,900 metres, about three kilometres south of Wengen on the Jungfrau line. Byron stayed there to compose poetry, Richard Wagner to write music.

Another celebrated, spectacular route is the **Glacier Express**. The most convenient station from Lucerne to pick up this panoramic service is Visp, two hours away via Berne – this is once-in-a-lifetime stuff.

The name is a misnomer. The Glacier Express from Zermatt via Visp to Davos or St Moritz crawls along at an average 40kmph, across some 300 bridges, through some 90 tunnels and over the 2,000-metre-high Oberalp Pass. The journey here is definitely the thing. Inaugurated in 1931, the route changed in 1982 with the opening of the Furka Base Tunnel, the train no longer having to skirt the Rhône Glacier on the way up to the Furka summit. The Glacier Express was further improved in 2006 with air-cushioned, air-conditioned interiors whose hush underscores the jaw-dropping scenery around you. Eight trains run daily in summer, two in winter. On Premium trains, dinner can be served at your seat. (Tables are often busy in the vintage dining car.) Originating from Zermatt, the car-free ski village nestled up by the Matterhorn, the bright train in

Golden Pass
www.goldenpass.ch

Jungfraubahn
www.jungfraubahn.ch

Regina Hotel
Wengen
033 856 5858
www.wengen.com

Jungfrau at Wengernalp
033 855 1622
www.wengernalp.ch
Christmas-Easter only

Glacier Express
www.glacierexpress.ch

TAKING THE BOAT TRAIN

In this age of high-speed European rail travel, it's reassuring to know that a pre-war paddle steamer forms part of a timetabled journey through the heart of Switzerland. It links with a train to form the William Tell Express (www.wilhelmtellexpress.ch), named after the fabled character whose legend is marked at various sights along the way. Tell's famed defiance of Habsburg rule, proving his marksmanship by shooting an apple from his son's head, killing the Austrian bailiff with the same crossbow and escaping across Lake Lucerne, ties in with the foundation of the Swiss confederation. Rütli meadow, close to another landing site, was where a three-canton oath was taken in 1291. Works celebrating the Tell legend, most notably a Friedrich Schiller play and a Rossini opera, led to a boom in tourism here in the 19th century.

Today's route links Lucerne with Ticino, the Italian-speaking Swiss region Mediterranean in character and cuisine. 2008 sees the 20th anniversary of the route and 80th of the paddle steamer that serves it, the *Stadt Luzern*, the youngest of the vintage vessels taking tourists around the lake. Special events are planned for spring and summer.

The journey begins at Lucerne station, a short rail hop from all major Swiss towns. The quay is immediately outside, past a vintage carousel and the grand columns of the original 19th-century station that burned down in 1971. Alongside runs the River Reuss. Just beyond nearby Spreuer Bridge is the Needle Dam that controls the flow and level of water in the lake. Ahead awaits a vintage, two-deck paddle steamer, built in 1928, of carved wood and shiny brass, its pistons centrepiecing the lower deck. After two long hoots of the horn to signal departure, passengers gravitate to a side restaurant, a crossbow over the entrance, the Oberdeck restaurant or deck seating in the outdoor sun. Canoeists glide by, locals wave with both hands from the balconies of their picture-postcard cottages. No wonder Wagner spent so many idyllic summers at Tribschen; the first main settlement you pass is the composer's house now a museum (www.kulturluzern.ch/wagner-museum). In a further musical footnote, Beethoven's Piano Sonata No.14 was named the 'Moonlight Sonata' after the waves on Lake Lucerne.

Your ticket reservation entitles you to a plat du jour in the upstairs restaurant, many ingredients (deer salsiz, Alpine cheese, smoked trout) produced by lakeside farmers. The bar also serves local wines (Weisser Schwyzer, Féchy La Colombe), beers (Eichhof Braugold, Ramseier Burehöfler) and grappas (Willisauer Chrüter, Pflümli) as a commentary in sing-song Swiss German rings out the landing stages as the boat skips from bank to bank in its three-and-a-half hour journey.

Most bear a 'Grüezi' ('Welcome') sign, with a restaurant and hotel alongside, and with it the experience of two centuries of tourism. The Tellsplatte (www.seerest-tellsplatte.ch) restaurant near Sisikon is close to the spot where Tell is meant to have jumped free; the picturesque Hobby Hotel Terrasse at Vitznau (www.hobbyhotel.ch) allows access to the Rigi cogwheel rail (www.rigi.ch), the mountain of the same name and its spectacular views.

After old-style dancing to accordion tunes and yodelling from the Oergeli-Stärne in-house band, passengers disembark at Flüelen, fluttering flags of the Swiss confederation lining the quay. A mere 20 steps away, a first-class train carriage, apparently entirely made of panoramic window, awaits. It speeds through the deep ravines of the Reuss Valley before climbing up to the Gotthard Tunnel, seemingly high in the clouds. After a full ten minutes of blackness from Göschenen to Airolo, a seven-year feat of 1880s' engineering that cost nearly 300 lives, train announcements switch from German to Italian: Ticino. After the cantonal capital of Bellinzona, two hours from Flüelen, the train runs on for 20 minutes to the lakeside resorts of either Lugano or Locarno, the latter ideally located for the scenic Centovalli line (www.centovalli.ch).

Zürich p214

Swiss-flag colours heads north for an hour up to Visp, the route lined with avalanche shelters, the Alps towering over the tinted roof-glass. If extremes are what you're after, you might go the whole hog and begin your voyage at Zermatt, where you can also take the Gornergratbahn. This rack railway opened in the late 1890s and climbs to 1,800 metres to a vantage point and the three-star **Kulmhotel Gornergrat**. The highest hotel in the Swiss Alps, the Kulm is surrounded by 29 4,000-metre peaks and its towers are used by scientists to observe the heavens with radio telescopes. It also offers a sun terrace, two restaurants, snowboarding and mountain biking.

Back on the main train, from Zermatt or Visp you head along the Rhône Valley to Brig, an international train hub whose importance has increased with the recent opening of the Lötschberg Tunnel to accommodate a fast-speed service between Geneva and Milan.

The section from Zermatt to Brig can be undertaken using your basic Swiss Pass – the Glacier Express otherwise carries a surcharge and mandatory seat reservation. From Brig, it climbs to the entrance of the Furka Base Tunnel at Oberwald, emerging some 15 kilometres later near the resort of Andermatt in the Urseren Valley and the entrance of the Gotthard Tunnel. Here you will find another, shorter rack rail service, which goes to Göschenen.

From Andermatt, the train climbs over the Oberalp Pass, past the source of the Rhine, before steeply descending to Disentis, known as Mustér in the Romansh of these parts. Switzerland's fourth language is spoken in villages here, where you might hear a hearty 'bun di!' for 'good morning'. Disentis is also known for its eighth-century Benedictine monastery. The line then passes through pretty Ilanz (Glion) before heading to the capital of the Romansh region, Chur, pronounced 'koorr'. This is the Graubünden of south-east Switzerland, whose regional rail, **Rhätische Bahn**, has mountain routes and post buses galore. It also contains the holy trinity of upmarket ski resorts: St Moritz, Davos and Klosters.

From Chur you can head east to Davos or, far more spectacularly, reverse south for St Moritz. Doing this allows you to cross the Landwasser Viaduct, the train passing over its famous arches before being swallowed into the sheer rock face, and the Albula Pass, a maze of tunnels and viaducts. Once through the Albula Tunnel, there is a gentle descent past Celerina (site of the famous bobsleigh Cresta Run) and, eight hours after Zermatt, St Moritz.

This year-round spa and ski resort is one of the most expensive destinations in Europe. However, out of ski and high-summer season, you can find some real accommodation bargains. The lovely **Waldhaus am See**, for example, sauna, steam room, lakeside location and all, offers doubles for less than €100 in April, May, October, November and the first three weeks of December – it's ten times that, even 15, at peak tourist time. The modest **Bellaval** is a year-round cheapie at around €100. It's also right next to the train station.

St Moritz is also a major stop on the **Bernina Express**, another panoramic route, with compulsory seat reservations, this time with onboard commentary in German, Italian and English. Pack your passport – the route terminates in Italy.

Kulmhotel Gornergrat
www.matterhorn-group.ch

Rhätische Bahn
www.rhb.ch

Waldhaus am See
6 Vic Dim Lej, St Moritz
081 60 00
www.waldhaus-am-see.ch

Bellaval
55 via Grevas, St Moritz
081 833 3245
www.bellaval-stmoritz.ch

Bernina Express
www.rhb.ch

Also subtitled as a journey from glaciers to palm trees, in two-and-a-half hours, the Bernina originates in Chur and calls at St Moritz before scaling the Bernina Pass. Just south of St Moritz the train skirts Diavolezza and its 125-person cable car to the ski slopes at Diavolezza and Lagalb. Staying on the train, you descend at a steep angle via the still waters of Lake Bianco, through forested slopes towards Poschiavo. A favourite stop off point is panoramic Alp Grüm, only accessible by train or after a hearty climb on foot. Nearby the summer-only **Hotel Belvedere** offers simple, affordable rooms and a fabulous view from the restaurant terrace. In pretty Poschiavo, you'll find the imaginatively converted **Hotel Albrici** amid the other historic buildings.

The Bernina continues to speed downhill towards the Italo-Swiss border, past the border stop of Campocologno to Tirano, where there are Swiss and Italian train stations alongside each other, separated by a customs post. The recommended **Bernina** restaurant stands outside, with rooms for rent upstairs. Trains head to Milan every couple of hours. In summer, a bus links with the Bernina and makes the three-hour journey to Lugano, in Switzerland, also the terminus of the Palm Express, a daily summer and weekend off-season panoramic post bus from St Moritz via Lake Como. At Lugano, a funicular built into the station takes you to the grand city centre, fringed by the lake of the same name. The aptly named **Splendide Royal** offers panoramic views from the rooms on the top floor.

The other key resort in Ticino, the Italian part of Switzerland, is Locarno. On the shores of Lago Maggiore, the sunniest spot in Switzerland is the terminus of the famously picturesque Centovalli line from Berne. The route has been recently facilitated by the opening of the Lötschberg Base Tunnel, and the **Lötschberg-Centovalli** now takes under four hours from Berne via Lake Thun to the Valais and the Hundred Valleys. The route passes briefly through Italy, so don't forget your passport. The final stretch glides past chestnut forests and waterfalls to Locarno, where the **Alexandra Hotel** stands between the station and the lake, with views from the higher floors. You can also take advantage of the summer-only **boats** and hydrofoils serving the lake.

TRAVEL INFORMATION

Take the Eurostar from St Pancras International to Gare du Nord and then a TGV from Gare de L'Est to Basle SBB; it's a further 70-80 minutes to Lucerne. The journey should take 8-10 hours. London-Lucerne returns start from £132. A one-country pass allowing six days' travel in Switzerland in any one month costs £148 from RailEurope (www.raileurope.co.uk). A Swiss Flexi Pass for six days in a month costs €246, slightly more but it covers the boats and post buses included in the Swiss Travel System; it also gives 50 percent discounts on mountain-top trains and cable cars (www.swisstravelsystem.ch) and doubles as a museum pass to 400 attractions across Switzerland.

WHEN TO GO

Year-round. No 'leaves on the line' dramas in Switzerland and even avalanches are unlikely to cause lengthy delays.

Further reading

Jim Ring *How the English Made the Alps* Or how the English invented the Sublime and were occasionally Ridiculous.
Adam LeBor *Hitler's Secret Bankers*
Patricia Highsmith *Small G: a Summer Idyll* The author's last novel, about Zürich's underbelly.
Anita Brookner *Hotel du Lac*
Max Frisch *Man in the Holocene* Alpine existentialism.

Websites

www.swisstravelsystem.com
www.rail.ch
www.myswitzerland.com
www.alptransit.ch
www.meteoswiss.ch
www.swisshelpdesk.org
www.swissinfo.org

Hotel Belvedere
081 844 0314
www.belvedere-engadin.ch
Summer only

Hotel Albrici
piazza da Cumun, Poschiavo
081 844 0173
www.hotelalbrici.ch

Bernina
piazza Stazione, Tirano
0342 701 302
If calling from Switzerland, use +39

Splendide Royal
7 riva Caccia, Lugano
091 985 7711
www.splendide.ch

Lötschberg-Centovalli
www.centovalli.ch

Alexandra Hotel
43 via San Gottardo, Locarno
091 743 2523
www.hotel-alexandra.ch

Boats
www.navlaghi.it

SWISS RAIL ORGY

Bergen p222

Polar Circle

An overnight ferry trip from Newcastle will bring you to the UNESCO World
Heritage city of Bergen for a circular trip around the heartlands of Norway
and Sweden – with options for hops across to Finland and Denmark –
taking in soaring fjords, island treks and the Northern Lights. After that
there's time for a quick stop in Stockholm, Scandinavia's buzziest city,
before heading back via the summer resort of Kristiansand.

Written by **Jonathan Lee**

The Hurtigruten p223

THE JOURNEY

A t 27.5 hours, the trip from Newcastle to Bergen gives you time to knit a 20-foot scarf with matching mittens. Fortunately, DFDS's *Queen of Scandinavia* provides ample distraction in the form of live bands, sauna sessions, treasure hunts and, if you're really at a loose end, bingo.

With space for 1,638 passengers, punters range from Norwegian party girls – drinks on the boat, drinks in Newcastle, drinks on the boat – to sinewy British army cadets itching to crawl about on icy tundra. Despite the steady flow of booze, the mood is mellow enough for young families and middle-aged cruiseaholics.

But it's after landfall that the epic nature of this trip really becomes apparent. Not to beat around the bush, Scandinavia is big and empty. But, of course, being Scandinavia, there's also an efficient railway system that will get you to most places you might want to visit and, failing that, boats for the less accessible destinations. After that, half an hour of brisk walking will take you to places seemingly untouched since the morning of the world. Breathe deep. You've arrived.

⭐ Landscape; wildlife

Lofoten p225

THE DESTINATION

Distances across Norway, Sweden, Denmark and Finland are vast but getting around is a breeze. Trains are efficient, sleek barrels of shimmering steel with reclining seats and smart sleepers for overnight trips. With ScanRail passes hitting the buffers in 2007, an **InterRail** Global Pass is the best option, giving you unlimited travel across all four countries, while hopping on a ferry is the most enjoyable way to explore the spectacular fjords of the Norwegian coastline or skip across to Finland or Denmark.

Your biggest challenge will be cost. Oslo and Copenhagen are among the world's priciest cities and simple pleasures such as sinking a few beers can empty your wallet with Scandinavian efficiency. Eke out funds by taking sleeper trains – you'll cover more ground and pay just a small supplement on top of your pass fee. Also, go for 'universal access' tickets to cultural attractions in the bigger cities.

Timing is critical. In deepest winter there's a good chance you'll witness the Northern Lights around the North Cape beyond Tromsø, but sightseeing is limited: once you're inside the Arctic Circle you're plunged into near permanent darkness and boat trips into the fjords are few and far between due to harsh weather conditions and lack of demand.

In summer, when temperatures hit a balmy 22°C, you can go into sightseeing overdrive with up to 24 hours of daylight a day and there's a chance to experience the 'midnight sun' (mid May to end of July). Little snow, though, unless you head far north.

Autumn ushers in a palette of russets and golds, but probably the optimum time to travel is in the spring: you should still see the ice sheets of the Finmark plateau, while the landscape is blossoming into life.

BERGEN

Mention Bergen to Max, one of the barmen on the *Queen of Scandinavia*, and he'll go all misty-eyed and start gushing about snow-capped mountains and opulent mansions…then he'tell you that it hammered down on 80 consecutive days recently, almost breaking the all-time record. That's Bergen for you – drop-dead beautiful and wetter than a trout's armpit in a monsoon.

Rain or shine, though, this UNESCO city is definitely worth a couple of days' stop-over. Set against a magnificent backdrop of seven mountains, the town boasts a bustling quayside and the impressive 18th- and 19th-century quarter of Bryggan – perched on a hillside overlooking the central harbour and criss-crossed with cobbled lanes and ice-cream-hued timber houses. It's also the starting point for Hurtigruten trips into the Arctic Circle.

As a former European City of Culture, Bergen musters a sophisticated tourist scene, with trips to the fjords (contact the helpful **tourist office**) being the most enthusiastically pushed. Other attractions include Edvard Grieg's home of **Troldhaugen**, situated just outside town and featuring an atmospheric concert hall, and the **Fløibanen funicular railway**, which runs up to Mount Fløyen and affords great views.

The place to stay is the **Det Hanseatiske Hotel**, found on the east side of Vågen harbour on the edge of Bryggan. This boutique hotel comprises 16 timber-clad rooms linked by

InterRail
www.interrailnet.com

Tourist Office
Vågsallmenning Square, Bergen
55 55 20 00
www.visitbergen.com

Troldhaugen
65 Troldhaugsveien, Bergen
55 92 29 92
www.kunstmuseeneibergen.no

Fløibanen funicular railway
Vetrlidsallmenning 21
55 33 68 00
www.floibanen.com

Det Hanseatiske Hotel
2A Finnegården, Bergen
55 30 48 00
www.dethanseatiskehotell.no

creaking wooden gantries; imagine Sir Walter Raleigh's galleon with a rococo revamp – all heavy beams, roll-top baths and lush velvet. Beyond the creaking olde worlde charm lie mod cons such as wireless internet access and cable TV, with house manager Kristine Sirevåg on hand if you get your wires in a twist.

If you have the time, don't miss a trip on the **Flåmsbana**, found 166 kilometres east of Bergen and accessed by bus, boat or train from the city. As one of the most beautiful, and certainly one of the steepest, railways in the world, the line winds some 20 buttock-clenching kilometres from Myrdal to Flåm through hairpin bends, mountains, steep ravines and waterfalls. As a bonus, it drops you at Aurlandfjord, a tributary of Sognefjord, the longest fjord in the world.

THE HURTIGRUTEN

Some 15 Hurtigruten passenger ships ply the coast between Bergen and the northern town of Kirkenes, deep in the Arctic Circle just ten kilometres from the Russian border. Boats stop at 34 ports along a 2,000-kilometre stretch, running from verdant fjords in the south to the icy plateaux of Lapland. The ships also provide a vital lifeline to these remote communities.

Coastal express boats are by far the most relaxed way to take in central and northern Norway. You can kick back on the viewing deck and watch fjords, snowy peaks and glaciers chug by, while wake-up calls ensure you don't miss out on the light show of the Aurora Borealis (Northern Lights). The docking schedule also gives you a few hours in the most interesting ports such as Ålesund, Trondheim and Tromsø.

The boats offer reasonable restaurants, 24-hour cafés, bars and souvenir shops, together with play areas and clubby lounges offering stocks of board games and books. Don't expect cutting-edge design, though: the 482-berth MS *Nordlys* sports headache-inducing swirly carpets and tired cabins so, if you can, try to book the latest addition to the fleet, the MS *Fram*. Built in 2007, it offers a gym, sauna and jacuzzis.

Whichever boat you choose, you won't starve: the buffet breakfast offers boot-filling mountains of herring, salami, boiled eggs, pastries and fresh fruit, while evenings bring an approximation of fine dining with the likes of salmon and cauliflower doused in heavy sauces. You can pay for meals ad hoc or go for a blowout full-board ticket.

Ships depart daily from Bergen, and the committed can go for the full-on 12-day trip to Kirkenes and back. Hurtigruten also runs guided walking tours around some of the towns, and onward coach and boat trips to take in glaciers, islands, mountains and wildlife including puffins and whales. If time is limited, try at least to visit the UNESCO World Heritage Site of Geirangerfjord – arguably Norway's most striking fjord and home to gigantic waterfalls.

NORTH TO ÅLESUND

It's a breezy overnighter on the Hurtigruten from Bergen to this small art nouveau town, one of the most rewarding stops along the Norwegian coast. It's also a more relaxed jumping off point into fjords, in contrast to tourist-oriented Bergen.

Ålesund's fairytale spires, gables and brightly painted, carved frontages belie an altogether more sombre tale: in 1904, a fire

POLAR CIRCLE

Flåmsbana
57 63 21 00
www.flaamsbana.no

swept through the timber town, destroying 850 houses and leaving 10,000 people homeless. Remarkably, only one person died, and by 1907 the town had been completely rebuilt, with Norway's finest young architects melding the dominant design style of the times with a spirited Romanticism.

The result is one of the world's most charming art nouveau towns: a glorious flight of fancy featuring quiet cobbled streets, good galleries and museums and some excellent restaurants. The undisputed highlight is the **Art Nouveau Centre**: a beautifully restored pharmacy building featuring gleaming teak counters, a grand carved staircase and an excellent 'time machine' recounting the fateful inferno. If the place is closed, curator Aud Farstad might even open up for you, typical of the Norwegians' high-trust, flexible attitude.

The place to stay is the 45-room **Hotel Brosundet**, a funky guesthouse situated right on the water's edge with great views across to the mountains. The front desk's Merethe Aarseth will happily point you in the direction of **Sjøbua Fiskerestauran**, one of Norway's best fish restaurants found just five minutes away.

If you have time, don't miss a meander down the waterside lane of Moloveien, where you can see viscous glass bubbles being blown at **Ingrid's Glassverksted** and rummage through two floors of bric-a-brac at Edel Rakvåg's **Trankokeriet Antikk** – an emporium and coffee shop stuffed full of chandeliers, old sea chests, lobster pots and wooden sledges.

On Ålesund's doorstep is the Sunnmøre coast, dotted with fishing villages and tiny islands, and great for trekking, birdwatching and fishing. Find out more at the **tourist office**.

TRONDHEIM

Zipping northwards on the Hurtigruten brings you to **Trondheim**, regarded by many as the last bastion of civilisation before the wastes of the Arctic Circle. In truth, the city is dominated by shopping centres, and its cultural highlights, which include a decent classical music scene can be bagged in half a day.

The prime draw is the vast Gothic cathedral – the finest medieval specimen in Scandinavia. **Nidaros Domkirke** was built on the tomb of St Olav, a marauding Viking chieftain (born 995) who conquered Norway in 1015, crowned himself king and promptly introduced Christianity to the country.

Fire and the Reformation soon reduced the cathedral to rubble, but rebuilding has created a green-tinged monolith, defended by mythical beasts growling at the base of its towers. A highlight is the western flank's huge rose window and gallery of carved figures – including Apostles, Adam and Eve and the prophets – while inside offers little more than all-enveloping gloom, redeemed by Joachim Wagner's restored Baroque organ. Situated next to the cathedral is the 12th-century **Archbishop's Palace** – well worth a look and housing an army museum and the glittering Norwegian crown jewels.

The town also has an excellent museum of decorative arts, **Nordenfjeldske Kunstindustriumuseum**, home to a collection of chairs by Mario Botta, Gerrit Rietveld and Marcel Breuer.

As for a bite to eat, try the Bakklandet district over the river from the cathedral. Hidden in this studenty quarter is **Bakklandet Skydsstation**, an 18th-century Wyatt Earp-style coaching house with wood-burning stove and beaten-up piano.

Art Nouveau Centre
16 Apotekergata, Ålesund
70 10 49 70
www.jugendstilsenteret.no

Hotel Brosundet
5 Apotekergata, Ålesund
70 11 45 00
www.brosundet.no

Sjøbua Fiskerestaurant Brunholmgt
1 Brunholmgt, Ålesund
70 12 71 00
www.sjoebua.no

Ingrid's Glassverksted
Molovegen 15, Ålesund
474 16 371
www.ingridsglassverksted.no

Trankokeriet Antikk
16b Moloveien, Ålesund
70 12 01 00
www.trankokeriet.no

Tourist Office
Skateflukaia, Ålesund
70 15 76 00
www.visitalesund.com

Trondheim
www.trondheim.com

Nidaros Domkirke
11 Bispegaten, Trondheim
www.nidarosdomen.no

Archbishop's Palace
Erkebispegården
www.nidarosdomen.no

Nordenfjeldske Kunstindustriumuseum
3-7 Munkegaten
73 80 89 50
www.nkim.museum.no

Bakklandet Skydsstation
33 Øvre Bakklandet
73 92 10 44
www.skydsstation.no

ONWARDS INTO THE ARCTIC CIRCLE

The Hurtigruten ploughs bravely on into the Arctic Circle – crossed around 80 kilometres north of Mo – via Tromsø, with its smattering of good bars and restaurants, and finally docking at Kirkenes, close to Russia.

Away from the coast, it's really only an area for those with bags of time and a desire to plunge into the wilderness. But hopping across to the Lofoten islands – spotting seabirds, whales, dolphins and seals en route – makes a good summer pursuit, while the **Ice Hotel**, found over the Swedish border in Jukkasjärvi, is a perennial winter favourite with its -5°C suites and ice bar, and dog-sled and Sámi safaris.

THE TRAIN SOUTH INTO SWEDEN

It's 800 kilometres from Trondheim to Stockholm, a route best tackled courtesy of Norway's state-owned **NSB** railway. Bar the mirthless ticket inspectors, it's an experience that puts UK efforts to shame: standard class feels like first with leather seats, adjustable headrests and flip-out tables, and the buffet car has a limitless supply of Ringnes lager (light but inoffensive), meatballs and chocolate muffins.

You'll whizz past pine forests and carve up snow-bound plains with ease, and after half an hour pull into Hell station, an appropriately desolate place that merits at least one daft photo. In summer the town hosts the **Hell Music Festival**, where rockers get to headbang to the likes of Deep Purple and the home-grown Blind Archery Club and Dimmu Borgir.

Crossing the border into Sweden at Tevedalen slices into prime skiing territory: the hillsides dotted with wooden chalets, pine forests and placid lakes. Then it's all change at Östersund to pick up the sleeper train to Stockholm. Sweden's **SJ** network offers similarly high standards, albeit on a dinky scale. Three narrow bunks are stacked into larder-size sleeper compartments with corner sinks and hooks to hang your clothes. Crisp sheets and pillows make it all very civilised, that is until your slumber is broken by a passenger getting on at 3am and stepping on your face en route to an upper bunk. The best approach: splash out and book all three bunks or request the upper one. There's respite at Stockholm, however: if you arrive at some ungodly hour you can sleep on for an hour or two before being asked to leave the train.

STOCKHOLM

This city's sophisticated streak is evident from the off: you'll arrive at the train hub of T-Centralen (Central Station, Vasagaten), packed with trendy cafés and bars, while the Tunnelbana (underground system) combines efficient transport with radical art: each station on the blue line has been given a conceptual makeover, with Radhuset's volcanic fractures and Vreten's Magritte-style blocky clouds proving two highlights.

Stockholm offers a bewildering array of cultural attractions. The cheapest way round is to buy the Stockholm Card (around £27 for 24 hours, available from the **tourist offices** at T-Centralen and on Kungsträdgården), which provides access to 75 museums and attractions, free public transport, maps and throws in a couple of sightseeing boat trips too.

Stockholm

POLAR CIRCLE

Ice Hotel
www.icehotel.com

NSB
www.nsb.no

Hell Music Festival
www.hellmusicfestival.com

SJ
www.sj.se

Tourist Office
T-Centralen, Vasagaten, Stockholm
Kungsträdgården, Stockholm
08 50 82 85 08
www.stockholmtown.com

Flåmsbana p223

The time-pressed should try to bag the **Moderna Museet** (Modern Art Museum) and the **Arkitekturmuseet** (Architecture Museum), found side-by-side on the east of the island of Skeppsholmen, some 30 minutes walk from T-Centralen.

The building alone is a marvel: a voluminous, airy hangar of gleaming marble and floor-to-ceiling glass affording great views across the harbour, while the collection features quirky sculpture by Truls Melin and good A-list pieces by Pollock, Judd, Picasso and Scandinavia's very own Edvard Munch. The architecture museum is less engaging, but includes a fun mini-estate for the kids to clamber around and a timeline running from tenth-century wooden longhouses to 21st-century hotels and libraries.

Another key attraction is the cobbled quarter of Gamla Stan – packed with tourists and home to the hulking Baroque **Kungliga Slottet** (Royal Palace) and the **Nobelmuseet** (Nobel Prize Museum) – a brave but rather lacklustre attempt to bring the legacy of the dynamite magnet-turned-philanthropist to life.

For a quirky and inexpensive stay, try the **AF Chapman**, a 19th-century rigger moored on Skeppsholmen and well placed for the modern art and architecture museums. Part of the youth hostel network, the boat was completely renovated in 2008, creating authentic cabins below deck. If it's full, there are more rooms in the hostel on land, together with a handy café bar, laundry room and shop. Staff offer good tips on decent late-night clubs and bars too.

EAST TO FINLAND

Stockholm is a good departure point for Finland, a country often dismissed as the poorer Scandinavian cousin, largely due to its refreshingly underdeveloped tourist scene. In reality, you'll find boundless hospitality and some of the world's most unsullied and beautiful mountains, forests and lakes here.

The 17-hour journey from Stockholm to Helsinki is touted as one of Scandinavia's most beautiful; the boat wends through the Åland Islands – a 6,500-strong archipelago offering invigorating fresh air and acres of secluded beaches, plus great sunset shots. Ferries are run by **Tallink Silja Line** and **Viking Line**, and offer the usual shops, saunas, casinos and nightclubs.

Finland also hosts excellent summer music festivals – one of the highlights being the **Savonlinna Opera Festival**, held in a castle north of the capital – while it's also a haven for hiking, sailing and cross-country skiing.

BACK TO OSLO

It's just six hours by train – bang on time as always – from Stockholm to the Norwegian capital. Founded in the 11th century, the coastal city manages to be both a busy commercial hub and a cultural enclave celebrating more than 1,000 years of Nordic heritage.

Anybody who fancies themselves in a horned helmet should check out the **Vikingskipshuset** (Viking Ship Museum), situated over the bay in Bygdøy, a short ride from the city centre by bus (no.30) or summer ferry (no.91 from City Hall Pier). The Oseberg longboat is the most extraordinary exhibit; built around AD 815, it features an ornately carved prow and stern – lit to throw curling shadows across the ceiling – while there's a good collection of Viking ephemera including boots and furniture.

Moderna Museet
08 51 95 52 00
www.modernamuseet.se

Arkitekturmuseet
08 58 72 70 00
www.arkitekturmuseet.se

Kungliga Slottet
1 Slottsbacken
08 60 01 000
www.kungahuset.se

Nobelmuseet
Börshuset
08 53 48 18 18
www.nobelmuseum.se

AF Chapman
8 Flaggmansvägen
08 463 22 66
www.stfchapman.com

Tallink Silja Line
www.tallinksilja.com

Viking Line
www.vikingline.fi

Savonlinna Opera Festival
www.operafestival.fi

Vikingskipshuset
35 Huk Aveny
22 13 52 80
www.khm.uio.no

A couple of hundred yards up the road is the **Norsk Folkemuseum**, which allows you to indulge in a few Han Christian Andersen-themed fantasies. The museum's park is home to 155 log buildings dating from the 13th century onwards, including a Stave church, stores and houses, complete with moss-covered roofs and icicles in winter. You can fast-forward to the 19th century by wandering along a period street, complete with grocery stores.

Oslo makes a good stepping off point for those keen to take in Denmark on this tour. **DFDS Seaways** ferries to Copenhagen take around 16 hours, putting vast tracts of green space, sandy beaches and the UNESCO castle at Helsingør – the setting for Shakespeare's *Hamlet* – within easy reach.

THE FINAL LEG TO BERGEN VIA STAVANGER

The eight-hour railway trip from Oslo to Stavanger is hardly Scandinavia's most picturesque, but it does take in open skies and lakes so vast they could be seas. It's here that you get a true sense of how sparsely populated the country is: a land mass a third bigger than the UK for just 4.7 million people, with many living in remote farmhouses perched amid sweeping valleys if this leg is anything to go by.

This journey can be broken at Kristiansand, the closest thing the Norwegians have to the French Riviera. The place has a certain small-town charm, while the seafront's numerous bars are where the Norwegians let their hair down. And if you're regretting skipping Denmark, **Color Line** ferries will take to you to North Jutland's Hirtshals in just two to 4.5 hours. Otherwise, it's a quick trip past the Jaeren coast into Stavanger.

Bus and car are options for the final scamper north, but the **Hurtigbåt** express boat is by far the best way to zip around the craggy outcrops that separate Stavanger from Bergen.

Departing from Stavanger's Østre Havn harbour, you'll glide past a jagged Hebridean landscape of rocky inlets and islets sprayed with spume and punctuated by stubby, winking lighthouses. And the further north you go, the barren escarpments rear ever more dramatically skywards, climaxing with those rain-inducing mountains of Bergen.

TRAVEL INFORMATION

National Express East Coast runs train services to Newcastle from London and other UK cities; advance purchase return fares between London King's Cross to Newcastle, booked online, start from £23 (standard class) and £75 (first class). **DFDS Seaways** runs two outward and two return sailings a week to Bergen. Sailing time is around 27.5 hours. Fares for two people plus a car start at £352 return, while foot passenger tickets go from £43. **Hurtigruten** ferry trips along the Norwegian coast start at £695 for seven nights, running south to north (Bergen to Kirkenes) or north to south (Kirkenes to Bergen). An **InterRail Global Pass** gives you unlimited travel across all four countries, with supplements for sleepers. Prices start at £117 (for under-26s, £182 if you're over) for five days' travel in a ten-day period.

WHEN TO GO

May-September. It's cold and dark the rest of the year.

Further reading

Knut Hamsun *Hunger* Hard to believe it was written in 1890.
Lars Saabye Christensen *The Half Brother* Life through four generations of an Oslo family.
Erlend Loe *Naïve. Super* How to find some meaning in life when you're a 25-year-old Norwegian. Better than it sounds.
Sigrid Undset *Kristin Lavransdatter* Nobel Prize winning author's masterwork, following the eponymous heroine through her life in 14th-century Norway.

Websites

www.visitnorway.com
www.visitsweden.com
www.visitfinland.com
www.visitdenmark.com
Spot a common theme among the national tourist sites?

Norsk Folkemuseum
10 Museumsveien
22 12 37 00
www.norskfolke.museum.no

DFDS Seaways
www.dfds.co.uk

Color Line
www.colorline.com

Hurtigbåt
http://eng.tide.no

National Express East Coast
08457 225225
www.nationalexpresseastcoast.com

DFDS Seaways
0871 522 9955
www.dfds.co.uk

Hurtigruten
020 8846 2666
www.hurtigruten.co.uk

InterRail Global Pass
www.raileurope.co.uk

Sifnos p233

Greek Odyssey

| **ROUTE** | London ▶ Paris ▶ Venice ▶ Patras ▶ Zakynthos ▶ Ithaka ▶ Kefalonia ▶ |
| | Athens ▶ Piraeus ▶ Aegina ▶ Spetses ▶ Mykonos ▶ Santorini ▶ Naxos |

Odysseus was so desperate to return to Ithaka that he sailed for ten years to get back to its warm seas and starry skies. You can get there rather quicker than that, although leaving may be more difficult. The seas around Greece are Europe's ultimate water-themed amusement park, the easy pleasures balanced by the ancient history and mythology. You'd need aeons to explore every cove and quay, but the ferry is a practical, modern means of seeing a lot, slowly.

Written by **Monica Guy**

Santorini p233

THE JOURNEY

In an age when trains look like planes and go faster than Ferraris, slow boats have an obvious charm. Cast a glance at a map of Europe, and Greece, with its ragged coastline and chaos of islets, cries out to be given more than the retsina-and-plate-smashing treatment package tourists endure on Kos, Corfu and Crete. The logistics are as easy as π: hop over to Paris on the Eurostar, sleep through the night to Venice and board the ferry to Patras in Greece. En route you get the view of Venice as you leave the port and the chance to land at Greece's third biggest city on the northerly ear of the Peloponnese.

As a major port and commercial centre, Patras is heaving with bars, restaurants and shops. But best of all, it allows you to connect to the ferry routes serving the myriad Greek islands – their exact number is almost as mythical as their history. However many times you return, you'll never have 'done' them all. Nonetheless the intricate web of ferries, sea taxis and private boats allows you to make a start on your odyssey – and will certainly give you an angle on the coasts and coves that air travel doesn't allow.

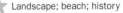 Landscape; beach; history

FIRST PORT OF CALL

Before it became the urban hub of the Peloponnese, Patras was the playground of the Spartans and an ancient treasure trove. The one sight you can't miss is Olympia. Birthplace of the Olympic Games in 776 BC, it is now a modern museum and huge partially reconstructed area of ruins, with stories of naked athletes and bare-breasted women, power, prowess, riches and sporting glory. The whole area nearly burned to the ground in the terrible fires of August 2007; the charred mountainsides and spindly black whiskers of burnt-out trees are a desolate sight but the ruins – saved by a mysterious sudden wind change at the last minute – are still magnificent. Take the train and change at Pyrgos; total journey time is around two hours.

IONIAN ISLANDS: BACK TO NATURE

The best bit about landing at Patras is the chance to visit the nearby Ionian islands. If you're a turtle-lover or scuba-diver – or simply get off on seeing cobalt seas and sandy beaches surrounded by olive groves and plum trees – head straight to the Ionian island of Zakynthos. **Ionian Ferries** run boats direct from Kyllini port, an easy 1.5-hour bus ride from Patras.

Laganás Bay, near Kéri village on Zakynthos, is a major breeding ground of the endangered loggerhead sea turtle. Strict laws are in place to protect the turtles, but Timos, the friendly, experienced owner of **Diving Center Turtle Beach**, offers scuba diving trips and courses between early May and October. Beginner courses (PADI open water and CMAS*) take five days. Ask Timos for advice on where to stay – there's only one hotel but plenty of apartments and locals' rooms to rent in season.

If your ambitions are on a smaller scale and all you want to do is chill out in a quiet, sleepy port town dotted with harbour-side cafés and populated by slow-moving Greeks, take the **Strintzis** ferry from Kyllini to Ithaka instead. The idea that this was Odysseus' home island is a fiction designed to attract tourists, but it's an excellent place to relax and eat your first fresher-than-fresh fish; one of the best restaurants is **Liberty**.

The one hop you can't miss in the Ionian is to Kefalonia, only recently but rightly made famous by Louis de Bernières's middlebrow classic *Captain Corelli's Mandolin*. Avoid the capital Argostoli and head straight for Fiskardo, the only town in Kefalonia saved by the gods in the 1953 earthquake and now a sparky sailing and fishing port lined with Venetian-style houses.

There's little in the way of serious history or culture in Fiskardo, but as a destination for sailors and travellers in the know, the town manages to remain both lively and understated. If you've found romance and want to revel in it, stare up at the skies from one of the six pools in the new luxury **Emelisse Hotel**, a 15-minute walk from Fiskardo town and rather cheesily overlooking the beautiful bay of Emblissi. You can get free diving lessons as well as rent bikes or sea kayaks, and one of the restaurants has an infinity pool and jacuzzi in the centre.

GETTING AN ISLAND MENTALITY

Greece is not in any sense a single, uniform country and never has been. Thousands of years ago, its men were fighting tooth and nail. Small empires came and went, democracy and

Ionian Ferries
210 324 9997
www.ionianferries.gr

Diving Center Turtle Beach
Zakynthos
26950 49424
www.diving-center-turtle-beach.com

Strintzis Ferries
www.strintzisferries.gr/strintzis

Liberty
Coastal Road Mylos, Ithaka
2674 032 561

Emelisse Hotel
Emblissi Bay, Kefalonia
267 404 1200
www.arthotel.gr/emelisse

dictatorship swapped and swapped again, whole islands sided with the Persian enemy to get back at fellow Greek neighbours. Petty territorial squabbles cost millions of lives. The fact that the Olympic Games could take place at all is remarkable and they're the exception that proves the rule; Greek states signed a special treaty guaranteeing the postponement of hostilities to allow athletes and visitors to travel freely to the Games. Greece was a cradle of civilisation, perhaps, but civilised it was not.

Modern ferries have replaced the triremes but the islands' huge variety isn't much changed today. However many times you return, you'll never have 'done' the Greek islands. But an intricate web of ferries, sea taxis and private boats allows you to make a start – and will certainly give you an angle on the coasts and coves that air travel doesn't allow.

That's not all. In one sense, sea travel is boringly practical, simply the easiest, cheapest, most popular way to get about. But in another, there's also a real buzz about the ports and the boats. Piraeus, just nine kilometres from Athens (regular trains run direct from Patras to both central Athens and the Piraeus), is the hub for the ferry network. Watching the ships queue up to enter the packed quaysides, hearing the shouts of deckhands and passengers, and taking deep draughts of the fishy aroma is a heady way to start a trip. Chaos is a Greek word, so expect it. If you're a planner, plan ahead or your head will spin. If you're an impulse traveller, embrace chance and let the Fates rule.

Wherever you go, take care to choose your vessel – and budget. The ugly Flying Dolphin hydrofoils and catamarans are quicker but double the price and mostly filled with businessmen. You'll meet other island-hoppers on the decks of ordinary slow ferries. Fun doesn't come on a plate in any sense of the phrase. Ferry food has a reputation for caterpillar-crawling sandwiches and deck seating for leg-numbing hard white benches. Take picnics, cameras, books and games and join in with your neighbours; each time you disembark it will be with a whole new group of friends.

What's also special about the slower ferries, though, is that you're never far from nature, from the water, wind and salty spray. The sunlight will make you sneeze, the blue sky will pierce your eyes, but the gentle rock of the boat is restful and you'll have time to take in each new landscape as you approach your destination. It's not something you can easily experience elsewhere in the world or on another form of transport.

EPICUREANS EAT HERE

You can warm up your hopping legs in the Argo-Saronic cluster of islands around Piraeus. The islands' proximity to the mainland make them a favourite with both Athenian yacht-owners and with the international jet set and they're revelling in a growing reputation for gourmet food and thumping nightlife. Regular fast ferries run by **Hellenic Seaways** connect Piraeus to all the islands. Interconnections depend on the time of year so you may have to pop back to Athens, but most journey times are under an hour. **Aegean Flying Dolphins** and **Nova Ferries** also run shuttles between Piraeus and Aegina.

Fish is the staple almost everywhere and in most ports you can watch the fishermen hauling in their catch then eat it later that evening in a harbour restaurant. Squid and swordfish are

Hellenic Seaways
21041 99100
www.hsw.gr

Aegean Flying Dolphins
21041 21656

Nova Ferries
21041 26181

Naxos p233

omnipresent, and depending on the season and on fishermen's luck you might get lobster or something more unrecognisably exotic. In almost every single case, simply grilled with a slice of lemon and a drizzle of olive oil is the tastiest way to enjoy it.

Sweet teeth are a genetic feature of most Greeks, and on every island you'll be urged to try and buy the local sticky speciality. One of the simplest and best desserts is rich Greek yoghurt drizzled with local honey – with its sharp sting you'll feel as though you're eating the bees mixed in with it.

If simplicity is the rule of thumb in food, this rolls over to restaurants in general. In Greece, gourmet doesn't go with luxury and expense. Starched white tablecloths and fancy websites are often a bad sign; upmarket restaurants and hotels cater for large wallets rather than trained tastes and hungry appetites. The best beds are often in the homes of locals or in a nearby campsite (see www.panhellenic-camping-union.gr) and the best eats are usually in the nameless restaurants tucked away at the back of markets or on the darker side of town – they've got no tables spare for a reason. Go-where-the-locals-go has never held so true.

Some seventeen miles, or 40 minutes by fast ferry, from the Piraeus is Aegina, the mythological home of Achilles. In ancient times a huge naval power, the island is now rather more tamely known for its pistachios and has a magical harbour lined with bars and fish restaurants shielding a network of cobbled shopping streets. You'll eat the finest fish ever in one of the tiny lunchtime restaurants at the back of the daily fish market, where waiters stand puffing cigarettes at the kitchen counter while their mother chats and steams and grills inside. Pop your head round the corner of the kitchen and point out what you want, or even buy it fresh in the market and take it along.

If simple's best, that doesn't mean there's nowhere to splash out if you're in the mood for a blowout. The distinctive smell of Spetses, a two-hour trip from Athens, will hit you as you roll into port – citrus trees and pines cover the whole island. There are only a handful of cars due to strict regulations, and most people get about the place by horse and carriage.

Run by three brothers, the 22-room **Orloff Resort** is as hip and quirky and off-the-conventional-tourist-path as the island of Spetses itself. You can hire anything from studios to a luxury five-bedroom house, all based around simple geometrical shapes, bright splashes of colour and furniture fabricated from local wood by the island's artisans. The **Orloff restaurant**, run by the same owners, is one of the finest around, serving up the same mix of traditional and contemporary that the hotel offers. Both places are slightly out of the main town of Dapia, so if you want to mix with the jet set stroll into the centre for a cocktail at **Throumpi** coffee bar or, even better, whichever place looks like it's flavour-of-the-month with the best-looking people.

PACKAGE TOURS AND MINOTAURS

The Aegean's Cyclades live up to any of the myths about the Greek islands and also harbour some of the modern excesses. Mountainous interiors, deep caves and golden beaches, brassy booze-fuelled nightlife, calm, harbourside quiet and clear, starry nights – the Cyclades have them all. A thick network of regular ferries between Piraeus and the Cyclades and around the

Orloff Resort
Old Harbour, Spetses
22980 75444
www.orloffresort.com

Orloff restaurant
Old Harbour, Spetses
22980 75255

Throumpi
Spetses
22980 74640

islands themselves are operated by **Blue Star Ferries, NEL-Lesvos Maritime** and **Skopelitis Lines**. Rule of thumb: if the temperature's over 15 degrees, there'll be a ferry running from wherever you are to pretty much wherever you want to go. Spontaneity is the best way to plan around here.

If you can't resist looking at a guidebook, you'll read all about Mykonos and Santorini, the former for its bright, white shining buildings, flash yachts and bling, the latter for its huge volcanic crater, black sand beaches, spectacular views and donkey rides. From Mykonos, a tour by **Windmills Travel** to the hot, dry, protected island of Delos is obligatory for Oxbridge academics and pop-Classicists alike.

The inevitable crowds and high prices of a popular tourist destination interrupt good fantasies, but as usual in Greece, there are places to which you can escape. On Santorini, hire a car from any of the numerous operators in Fira town and drive a few kilometres north to Oia, devastated by a huge earthquake in 1956 and only just recovering. It's a lot quieter than Fira but a far better spot for buying authentic handmade jewellery and original art from the craftsmen who have clustered in the area.

The **Perivolas** – a collection of small houses carved out of caves, with a café-bar in a converted wine cellar and an infinity pool that's possibly the eighth wonder of the world – is the finest getaway spa hotel on the island. To really leave the crowds behind, put your hiking boots on for a steep walk down 300 steps to the town's small port of Ammoudi. You'll find a few sea taxis bobbing around and their drivers haggling for a price to take you to the beach on the tiny nearby island of Thirassia. Take a picnic and arrange a time for pick-up later in the day.

If it's simply soft, smooth landscape you want, with gentle mountains, thick blankets of warm, blue sea spotted with colourful fishing boats, then you don't have to go as far as Santorini or pay the high prices of Mykonos. Stick instead to the central islands of Paros, Tinos, Naxos and Amorgos, or the less touristy western islands of Sifnos and Serifos.

Naxos is the big brother of the Cyclades, a 430-square-kilometre playground of alternately packed and deserted beaches, mountains, rocks, trees and flowing springs. The main port and town is Hora on the west coast, sometimes called Naxos Town and the best place to stay in terms of hot nightlife, facilities and sandy beaches. Try and get a ferry that docks around sunset and the Portara – a huge stone gate built in 522 BC as part of a temple to Apollo near the harbour – will give you a superbly romantic welcome to the island. Soundtrack: Richard Strauss's *Ariadne auf Naxos*, an opera based on Hesiod's tale of how Ariadne, after helping Theseus defeat the Cretan minotaur, was abandoned by him on Naxos and later married the god of wine Dionysios. Modern-day lovers take note.

Best beds in Naxos Town are at the family-run **Hotel Grotta**, an unpretentious modern boutique-style hotel with a beautiful sea view. For something cheap and charming right on the beach, take a 30-minute drive to the Oasis Studios at Mikri Vigla; the owner Manolis will arrange transfers and trips as well as kite-surfing and other beach activities. You'll be slathering for a break from Greek food by now so seek out the **Old Inn** in Naxos Town, a German-run restaurant set in a former monastery based around a courtyard. It must be the only place

Piraeus p231

Blue Star Ferries
21089 19820
www.bluestarferries.com

NEL-Lesvos Maritime
22510 26299
www.nel.gr

Skopelitis Lines
22850 71256

Windmills Travel
22890 26555
www.windmillstravel.com

Perivolas
Oia, Santorini
228 607 1308

Hotel Grotta
Naxos
22850 22101
www.hotelgrotta.gr

Old Inn
Naxos
22850 26093

GREEK ODYSSEY

in the whole of Greece where you can eat smoked pork and blood sausage and where you can choose between some excellent German wines in the cellar inside a small chapel.

When you've slept it off and fuelled up again, get out exploring. The most popular beaches are near Naxos Town along the west coast, so if you leave these behind you'll find yourself in blissful solitude. Cars are cheap and easy to hire, but if you want the breeze in your hair as you whizz round the deserted, dusty roads grab a scooter. Careful, careful, as island roads aren't the safest; insist on insurance and a helmet and check out the bike thoroughly before leaving. **Mike's Bikes** is one of the most reliable operators.

As you leave the main town heading south along the coast (few roads have names) you'll pass golden beach after white-sand beach. Head inland from Kastraki past the village of Sagri to wind higher up increasingly difficult paths, finally bursting out on to the hilltops. Rocky tracks with wooden, handmade signposts trail off from the single main road – one trail near Sagri leads to an almost perfectly reconstructed museum and

Mike's Bikes
Agios Georgios, Naxos
22850 24975

GREEK ODYSSEY

CLASSICS MADE EASY

If the Greek islands are the ultimate water wonderland, they also come with theme-park downsides: queues, crowds, confusing tickets and higher prices for the faster rides. So take it slowly on an easyCruise, an economy-price, snapshot tour through some of the best sites Greece has to offer. There's a direct connection to Odysseus' home island of Ithaka on the Classical Greece tour, as well as to Patras, Corinth, Itea (near Delphi) and Aegina island. Other itineraries offer other treats.

In essence, an easyCruise is a basic, clean, floating hotel with a hot tub and spa, restaurant, bar and an ever-changing seafront location. All transport is included – mostly short hops while you sleep – and you'll have long days and evenings in port. Dress code? Wear something. Guided tours? Good value, in English, and only if you fancy it. You can eat and drink on the ship if you want – canteen food, cheap and cheerful enough – but you're not obliged to. You can be extravagant if you like, but you don't have to fund anyone else's extravagance.

Some of the best features of an easyCruise are those not advertised: early morning crossings through the narrow Corinth Canal or under the

spectacular 2,880-metre cable bridge joining Rio and Antirrio; the free nightly entertainment – wine-tasting, belly-dancing and cocktails; and the ease of meeting other travellers. And on the Classical Greece itinerary, a travelling classics expert who'll give the trip an extra depth you can't get from guidebooks. It's worth considering an easyCruise as a cheap and cheerful introduction to island-hopping.

The seven-day Classical Greece tour is only available spring and autumn, but the ship's itinerary mid May to mid September around the Ionian sea (including stops in Albania and Corfu) has a similar format. Summer prices for a seven-day trip start at £132 for two people sharing a standard (very basic) cabin or £660 for two people sharing a more civilised suite with balcony. Short four-day breaks to Aegina and the Cycladic islands of Mykonos, Paros and Sifnos are available May to October.

Between mid April and mid October, the new, larger *easyCruise Life* will be sailing around the Aegean islands of Syros, Kalymnos, Kos, Samos, Mykonos and Paros, with stops and pick-ups at both Athens and the Turkish port of Bodrum.

For more details, see www.easycruise.com.

emple to Demeter, empty except for a few staff. With a rudimentary map you can seek out the crumbling mountain village of Apiranthos or the kouroi statue at Apollonas on the northern tip of the island, lying where it fell in the sixth century BC. There's a quiet nudist area at the end of Plaka beach and countless little coves along the west and south coasts, so make up a picnic and seek out a hilltop or deserted beach.

Short ferry rides from Naxos – ask at the port for times – will take you to its eastern baby sisters. The best beaches are in Donoussa and clearest waters in Koufonissia, or try Heraklia for its caves and coves and Schinoussa for its tiny picturesque port. Facilities are basic or non-existent, which is part of the attraction if you're after an escape. Take supplies and rent a room from locals for the night. There are usually several locals waiting around as the ferries dock offering rooms to visitors, or you can ask in a bar or café. Don't be browbeaten into accepting before you've seen the room and agreed a price, but there's a lot to be said for private rooms – local tips, understanding the community and excellent breakfasts of freshly made bread served with home-made jams, local soft white cheese and honey.

N THE AREA

From the north-east Aegean it's easy to hop over to Turkey. **Miniotis Ferries** operates a twice-daily ferry service in summer from Chios to the lively if tourist-scarred port of Çeflme.

From Santorini in the Cyclades, hop to Crete with **Lane Lines** for the controversially reconstructed ancient site of Knossos and for some beautiful mountain scenery. You can head straight back to Athens from Crete with **Minoan Lines**.

On the way back from Patras to Venice, the same ferry route you took to get to Greece will let you stop off at Corfu. Its noisy, hedonistic nightlife makes for a shattering finale and you'll have a shorter trip for the hangover home.

RAVEL INFORMATION

Standard one-way fares for the overnight Stendhal train from Paris to Venice start at around €55 (www.sncf.com or www.artesia.eu). Ferries from Venice to Patras via Corfu and Igoumenitsa are run by **Minoan Lines** and **Anek Lines**, and take around 31 hours. Fares start at around €85 return for basic deck accommodation.

For ferry timetables and online booking around Greece check www.gtp.gr, www.ferries.gr or the websites of the major companies, but be aware that delays and cancellations in bad weather are common. Call the Port Authority (1440) to confirm the day's sailings.

WHEN TO GO

July and August are not only hot but Greece's time for high winds and rocky seas, which can mean uncomfortable sailings on some of the Flying Dolphins and catamarans. It's also peak tourist season, so accommodation, ferry berths and beach space are at a premium. The best time for island-hopping is around April-June and September-October, when the winds are calm and the sun gentle rather than searing.

Further reading

Simon Goldhill, *Love, Sex & Tragedy: How the Ancient World Shapes Our Lives* A defence of what was once taken as the basis of any decent education.
Herodotus *The Histories* The father of history wrote the history of the Greco-Persian wars.
Homer *The Odyssey* Try the translation by Robert Fagles.

Websites

http://odysseus.culture.gr
The Greek Ministry of Culture.
www.islandstrolling.com
Personal island-hopping website.
www.godchecker.com
Know your Hephaestus from your Vulcan.

Miniotis Ferries
www.miniotis.gr

Lane Lines
28410 25249
www.lanesealines.gr

Minoan Lines
020 8206 3420
www.minoan.gr

Anek Lines
020 7431 4560
www.anek.gr

Boarding the bus p239

Polish Plains

ROUTE   London ▸ Krakow ▸ Warsaw ▸ Gdansk

Follow in the footsteps of over half a million Polish emigrants with a sociable coach journey to Poland's cultural capital, Krakow. From the cobblestones and cellar bars of the country's old capital, travel along the nation's backbone, stopping off in the gritty present-day capital, Warsaw, before unwinding along the Polish seaside belt in the historic port city of Gdansk.

Written by **Rory Boland**; 'Booze Cruises & Baltic Boating' by **Edoardo Albert**

Krakow p239

Warsaw p242

Poznan p243

THE JOURNEY

Since Poland joined the EU an estimated 600,000 Poles have packed their bags and made the journey to the UK, many of them rolling across the Continent by coach. Now, as business picks up at home, Poles are again clambering aboard, but this time to travel in the other direction, on one of Europe's grand coach trips.

As epic as the journey might be, it's certainly no pleasure cruise. There are 25 hours of road separating London and Krakow, at the end of which you and your arse are unlikely to be on speaking terms. As for through-the-window entertainment, the trip takes in no must-see cities and no great mountains high or valleys deep; in fact, for much of the drive you'll be zipping along the flat-as-a-pancake autobahn. So why go? Because climbing aboard will give you more insight into Poles and Eastern Europe than any church, museum or plane ride, and because it's a cultural feast of vodka, sausage and history.

The camaraderie on board is key to everyone's survival and you'll find the varied crowd of old ladies, labourers and students eager to share stories and fill you in on Poland's rollercoaster history. Impressions of Poland and Poles are almost solely based on the country's forced stint under communism. As a result, Poles have a wholly undeserved reputation for being dour, dull, drunk and about as much fun as athlete's foot; one spin on the London–Krakow express is a surefire solution to these clumsy stereotypes. Long the rivals of the Italians and the French in regard to culture and the arts, the Poles remain

Beach; budget; history; trainspotting

Wanted.
Jumpers, coats and people with their knickers in a twist.

From the people who feel moved to bring us their old books and CDs to the people fed up to the back teeth with our politicians' track recor on climate change, Oxfam supporters have one thing in common. They're passionate. If you've got a little fire in your belly, we'd love to hear from you. Visit us at **oxfam.org.uk**

Be Humankind ☮ Oxfam

Registered charity No. 202918

a highly educated and well informed people, deeply interested and engaged in world affairs, while centuries of do-or-die battles with their neighbours and rolling military occupations have also left Poles with a streak of deep and dark black humour. Their history has landed them with a reputation for a fondness for the bottle and, while exaggerated, there is no doubting that Poles like a pint; and the on-board history lesson is unfailingly lubricated by beers and vodka.

Buses are clean and modern; all feature air-conditioning, nightlights, toilets and often videos, albeit in Polish. Stops usually come every four hours, allowing ample opportunities to fill up on German Bratwurst. Buses generally come armed with an English-speaking guide who will make announcements in both Polish and English, although most, if not all passengers will be able to speak English too.

A myriad of companies run buses to just about every major city in Poland, with all departing from either the main London Victoria coach station or the nearby Victoria Green Line station. Two of the most reliable are **Eurolines** and Polish company **Sindbad**. Departures roll with demand, but a coach to Krakow leaves at least once a day, and more frequently during the peak summer season. Prices are as cheap, if not cheaper than, the budget airlines plying the same route, with one-way tickets hovering around £60 and returns at £90. As with the airlines, an early booking saves money.

THE DESTINATION

Despite the end of the Cold War, Poland has mysteriously remained locked out in the cold when it comes to European tourism. Long misrepresented and maligned as a land of colourless communist architecture and cabbage, this Grand Tour of the country's royal cities reveals some of Europe's most stirring and seductive cities. Characterised by their captivating old towns, whose cobblestone streets and clandestine courtyards house a sharply dressed selection of bars, restaurants and clubs, Krakow, Warsaw and Gdansk offer a seamless combination of beauty, brains and beaches.

CRACKING KRAKOW

Krakow is, quite rightly, Poland's biggest tourist draw and as soon as you set eyes on this ancient capital you'll wonder why the Poles ever leave. As the only major Polish centre to escape the Nazi's dynamite, Krakow's Old Town is a fairytale collection of regal palaces, grand churches and opulent townhouses, sown together by irresistible cobblestone streets and a beautiful market square. The capital of Poland for over 500 years, and now the favoured home of artists, students and dropouts, the city is the backdrop for a cultured mix of galleries, clubs and riotous cellar bars.

Krakow's standout attraction is its Old Town (Stare Miasto), listed as a UNESCO World Heritage Site. The area's majesty is most apparent in the monumental market square (Rynek Glowny), an architectural gem that will stagger visitors expecting the grim hammer-and-sickle blocks of communist architecture. Yet the Old Town, unlike many in the region, isn't a museum piece, and most of the townhouses have been

NOTES

Eurolines
08717 818181
www.nationalexpress.com

Sindbad
0870 850 2054
www.sindbad.com.pl

Gdansk p244

converted into bars and restaurants. In summer, many establishments spill on to the pavements, turning the streets into a circus of al fresco wining and dining.

At the heart of the market square is the splendid Cloth Hall (Sukiennice). Built in the 16th century, this vast building was long home to the city's wheelers and dealers, a tradition kept alive by the daily craft market that cuts underneath the hall.

In the north-east corner lies **St Mary's Church**. This imposing red-brick cathedral is one of the oldest in the country, with the first building on the site dating from 1222. The original church was destroyed by Mongols, an event commemorated today by a lone trumpeter who takes to the church tower to play each hour. The trumpeter's performance is cut short, however, the end marking the point when the original watchman was skewered by an arrow in the neck as he tried to sound the alarm.

South on ul. Grodzka, one of the finest streets in the city, lies **Wawel Castle**, home to Poland's kings and queens for over 500 years before the capital was shifted to Warsaw. The castle grounds are extensive, with highlights including the state and assembly rooms and a world-class collection of artworks.

For a taste of Krakow's Jewish heritage head for the excellent **Dawno temu na Kazimierzu**, which is set in the city's Jewish quarter of Kazimierz, inside a row of recreated, turn-of-the-19th-century Jewish traders' shops. Try the earthy *czulent*, a stew of beans, mince and potatoes. Back on the market square sit down at **Wierzynek** for expertly executed Polish classics, such as salmon in white wine and dill sauce. The restaurant has a guest list stretching back over 500 years that would shame anything in the Michelin guide, including Steven Spielberg, François Mitterand, George Bush Sr and, more recently, the young ladies from Miss World.

As for places to stay, if you have the money it's possible to indulge all your childhood prince and princess fantasies in the **Wentzl**. Arguably Krakow's finest hotel, it has wonderful views over the market square. For a more wallet-friendly stay try the boisterous **Goodbye Lenin Hostel**.

There is a healthy selection of day trips outside the city walls, but for something different, dip into the history books with an enthralling trip to Krakow's outskirts and the district of Nowa Huta, one of only two 'ideal' Soviet towns ever realised. Stalin himself is said to have green-lighted the project, which aimed to create the perfect workers' suburb. The murderous old man clearly had no eye for architecture, and the area is a mongrel cross of severe Stalinist style, with a splash of Renaissance thrown in. The area's daunting Soviet-style buildings are a fascinating insight into the Soviet Empire's gloomy plans for the world. The best way to see Nowa Huta is with **Crazy Guides**, which offers a tour of the area inside communist-era German Trabants or the recommended Polish Fiat 126p, a car with all the grace of a washing machine.

An essential but painful excursion is to the former Nazi concentration camp at **Auschwitz**. While the main site has been converted into a comprehensive museum of the Nazi atrocities, the attached, and much bigger, Birkenhau has remained as it was when the Germans retreated and makes for a tough but moving visit. Buses frequently make the 90-minute journey; at the main PKS bus station look for buses marked Oswiecim.

St Mary's Church (Kosciol Mariacki)
rynek Glowny, Krakow
www.bazylika-mariacka.krakow.pl

Wawel Castle
Podzamcze, Krakow
012 422 51 55 ext 219
www.wawel.krakow.pl

Dawno temu na Kazimierzu
1 ul. Szeroka, Krakow
012 421 21 17

Wierzynek
15 rynek Glowny, Krakow
012 424 96 00
www.wierzynek.com.pl

Wentzl
19 rynek Glowny, Krakow
012 430 26 64
www.wentzl.pl

Goodbye Lenin Hostel
23 ul. Joselewicza, Krakow
012 421 20 30
www.goodbyelenin.pl

Crazy Guides
05000 91 200
www.crazyguides.com

Auschwitz
www.auschwitz.org.pl

BRANCH LINE: LVIV THE DREAM

Long Poland's second city, Lviv, or Lwow as it's known in Polish, was sliced off by the Soviet Union at the end of World War II and now falls just inside the Ukrainian border. With EU citizens no longer needing visas to visit Europe's biggest country, there has never been a better time to visit. Lacking the tourists of Prague and Krakow, but with all of their appeal, Lviv's august boulevards and elegant squares are classically Central European and the city has an undeniable run-down charm. A direct train runs from Krakow once daily, with a journey time of five to six hours; or take a train to the Polish city of Przemysl and catch one of the hourly trains to Lviv.

WARS WITH WORDS

Cheap, frequent and unfailingly on time, Polish trains are great value. The bad news is that they tend to jog rather than sprint to their destination, but luckily the Krakow–Warsaw route is one of the quickest in the country and you can expect to cover the 260 kilometres in just under three hours.

Polish trains, run by **PKP**, come in all shapes and sizes, with some seemingly stopping at every field and farmhouse along the way. Plying the Krakow–Warsaw route, and onwards to Gdansk, are Intercity (IC) and Express (Ex) trains, which only stop in major centres. First-class IC boasts power connections for laptop addicts, while both services in both classes offer an in-seat buffet service. For a more involved dining experience head for the restaurant car, known forebodingly as Wars. This offers full meals and, in the near future, beer and wine. Dated white tablecloths and wilting net curtains can make Wars look like a step back to socialism; however, the car attracts the train's most gregarious travellers, and is a great place to hook up with the locals.

The train compartments themselves are similarly convivial, with passengers slotted in shoulder to shoulder in rows of four (second class) or three (first class) facing the row opposite, making conversation a foregone conclusion.

The communal aspect of the journey means there are a few ground rules to be observed; men should unfailingly help women to lift heavy bags on to the overhead luggage racks, or face the wrath of fellow passengers, while a short hello or goodbye when entering and exiting is also appreciated. Keep in mind if you're cold or hot that the opening of windows requires a parliamentary debate and vote, with discussion usually continuing until you've reached your destination anyway.

The trip from Krakow to Warsaw offers views over slender pine forests, which – should you take this line in winter – are the only defence against the onslaught of Poland's plunging winter temperatures. Rolling through Warsaw's sprawling suburbs, trains arrive at the city's monolithic Centralna station, which proves as intimidating on the inside as it is on the outside. Built in the early 1970s, the building was designed as a statement of communist achievement, to convince people the country wasn't falling apart. The leadership actually bussed people in from around the country to see this feat of socialist engineering. Today the station *is* falling apart, but it remains a fascinating insight into the country's communist past.

Krakow p239

POLISH PLAINS

PKP
www.pkp.pl

Warsaw

Holy Cross Church (Kosciol sw. Krzyza)
3 ul. Krakowskie Przedmiescie, Warsaw
www.swkrzyz.pl

University of Warsaw
022 552 00 00
www.uw.edu.pl

Palac Radziwillow
48 ul. Krakowskie Przedmiescie, Warsaw

Royal Castle (Zamek Krolewski)
4 pl. Zamkowy, Warsaw
022 35 55 305
www.zamek-krolewski.com.pl

Warsaw Uprising Museum (Muzeum Powstania Warszawskiego)
79 ul. Grzybowska, Warsaw
022 539 79 05
www.1944.pl

Centre for Contemporary Art (Centrum Sztuki Wspolczesnej)
Zamek Ujazdowski, 6 al.Ujazdowskie, Warsaw
022 628 76 83
www.csw.art.pl

Wilanow Poster Museum (Wilanow Muzeum Plakatu)
10/16 ul. St Kostki Potockiego, Warsaw
022 842 48 48
www.postermuseum.pl

Hotel Rialto
73 ul. Wilcza, Warsaw
022 584 8700
www.hotelrialto.com.pl

DON'T MENTION THE WARSAW

If Krakow is Cinderella, then Warsaw is the ugly sister. For 200 years Poland's capital found itself the boxing ring for Europe's title fights. Bombed, invaded and occupied, the city was finally destroyed, brick by brick, by maniacal Nazis, and at the end of World War II 85 per cent of Warsaw lay in a heap of rubble.

However, just like the country, the capital picked itself up, dusted itself off and rebuilt. In just over ten years Warsaw was back on its feet. The results are what's on show today, a mish-mash of socialist-realist planning, restored Baroque palaces and, more recently, towering skyscrapers. Warsaw's tumultuous history makes it one of the most compelling cities in Europe, and the streets are charged with tales of revolt, revolution and heroics. Warsaw proudly wears the scars of its battles, from statues and memorials, to bullet-riddled buildings.

The best route to get a feel for the former glories of Warsaw is along the main street of ul. Nowy Swiat through Krakowskie Przedmiescie and into the reconstructed Old Town (Stare Miasto). Once the route Poland's kings and queens travelled on their coronation day, the streets contain some of the city's finest buildings, including **Holy Cross Church** where, rather morbidly, Chopin's heart is sequestered inside an urn; the refined halls of the **University of Warsaw**, whose buildings line the street; and **Palac Radziwillow**, host of the Warsaw Pact signing and now the crashpad for Poland's presidents. Guarding the end of the route is the **Royal Castle**, which once housed the Polish royal family. The building was dynamited by the Nazis in the closing months of the war and only rebuilt in the 1970s. Luckily, much of the furniture and interior decorations were spirited away before the Germans rolled into town and today you can throw a critical eye over the stylish royal interiors.

More of the city's sufferings are on display at the award-winning **Warsaw Uprising Museum**. Chronicling the city's 63-day uprising against Nazi occupation, the museum has a comprehensive collection of authentic exhibits, eyewitness accounts and video footage, which combine to paint a blow-by-blow picture of the city's heroic, yet doomed resistance.

Today, Warsaw is shaking off its grey communist overcoat and quickly earning a reputation as the motor that powers Eastern Europe. Increasing affluence has given the city a cosmopolitan confidence, which has triggered a slew of top-class bar and restaurant openings, and streets such as ul. Chmielna and plac. Trzech Krzyzy have established the city's hedonistic credentials.

Poland is also rediscovering its artistic roots. Before the communists deployed their censors, the country enjoyed an enviable reputation in Europe for producing provocative and edgy art, long before the term 'modern art' had been coined. The country is again establishing itself as a major player on the international art scene, particularly in photography and sculpture. One of the best and most successful galleries has been the **Centre for Contemporary Art**. Elsewhere, Polish poster art, long considered among the best in the world, is also enjoying a renaissance. This quirky art form is best seen at the **Wilanow Poster Museum**, which is set in the impressive surrounds of Wilanow Palace.

Confirming its appearance on the tourist trail, Warsaw's first boutique hotel, the **Hotel Rialto**, opened in 2006. Decked out in 1920s art deco, each of the luxurious rooms has been individually designed, and everything from toiletries to furniture hand picked. Further down the price scale, but no less creative, is the **Oki Doki** hostel, with themed rooms decorated by local artists, such as the House of Vincent inspired by Van Gogh.

Legend has it that **Under the Red Hog** was once the official state restaurant for communist party hobnobs. This was where the likes of Fidel Castro and Mao Zedong pow-wowed with Polish leaders over hot button topics such as dialectical materialism, collective farming and the ubiquity of cabbage. Nowadays, the restaurant serves up superlative Polish classics with a modern twist, amid a collection of Soviet memorabilia. Across the road is **Chlodna 25**, where Warsaw's counter-culture sips cocktails and debates revolution.

BRANCH LINE: WOLSZTYN

Most of Europe's steam trains have been reduced to museum exhibits, only allowed to wheeze along a few kilometres of track. The exception is here, in Poznan. Claiming to be Europe's last steam-powered mainline service still in commercial operation, the Wolsztyn–Poznan route is served by a steam engine several times a day. Powering through the pine forests that pepper the area, the train can reach a respectable top speed of 80kmph as it ferries commuters to work and back. Tickets can be bought at Poznan Glowny train station, with the journey taking around two hours. Wolsztyn has a small but attractive centre to distract visitors for a few hours before returning on the service in the afternoon. The best route to Poznan itself is via Warsaw, where trains leave hourly for the three-hour journey.

More enthusiastic steam fans can contact British steam train buff Howard Jones, who helps fund and maintain the service, and offers the chance for rail enthusiasts to get behind the regulator and drive the train in the **Wolsztyn experience**.

POTATO FARMING

It's back to the crumbling concrete of Warszawa Centralna for the onward journey to Gdansk. Like the Krakow–Warsaw route, almost all trains are either IC or Ex, with roughly one train every two hours. Catch the Friday evening 'party train', from 6pm or later, and join Warsaw's dedicated drinkers as they make their way to the infamous clubs and bars of Sopot.

At over five hours, the journey reputedly takes longer now than before World War II, although track works are set to bring the journey time down to three hours before the Euro 2012 championships.

Much of the journey cuts through Poland's rural heartlands, with isolated family farms fenced in by potato fields. While modernisation and modern equipment is seeing many small farming communities pack up their potatoes and leave, Poland retains strong farming traditions and the sight of a donkey and cart, while rare, isn't unknown.

The undoubted highlight of the trip up is the hulking red-brick walls of **Malbork Castle**. Built in the 13th century as the headquarters for the Teutonic Knights, the castle is by far the biggest of its kind in Europe. Much of it is visible through the train windows, just outside the town of Malbork. However, the castle is well worth a half-day stop on the way to Gdansk.

Wolsztyn experience

POLISH PLAINS

Oki Doki
3 pl. Dabrowskiego, Warsaw
022 826 51 12
www.okidoki.pl

Under the Red Hog (Oberza Pod Czerwonym Wieprzem)
68 ul. Zelazna, Warsaw
022 850 3144
www.czerwonywieprz.pl

Chlodna 25
25 ul. Chlodna, Warsaw
http://chlodna25.blog.pl

Wolsztyn experience
www.wolsztyn.co.uk

Malbork Castle
1 ul. Staroscinska, Malbork
055 647 0800
www.zamek.malbork.pl

G'DAY GDANSK

Few cities on earth can claim to have played such a pivotal role in world events as Gdansk. Master of opening ceremonies for World War II, with the war's first shots fired at the city, Gdansk would find itself in the spotlight again 50 years later. But more on that below.

Despite emerging from World War II completely flattened, after being steamrollered by both the British air force and the Soviet

BOOZE CRUISES & BALTIC BOATING

Gdansk and Gdynia once hosted a flotilla of ferry connections to Scandinavian and Baltic cities. Unfortunately much of the ferry business has sunk, and now the only regularly scheduled departures are from Gdynia to Karlskrona, Sweden, with **Stenaline** (www.stenaline.co.uk), and Gdansk to Nynashamn (for Stockholm), with **Polferries** (www.polferries.pl).

But if you just want to get on a boat, try a Polish booze cruise with **Zegluga** (www.zegluga.pl), and make the trip to the Russian enclave of Kaliningrad, formerly Konigsberg. Leaving once daily from both Gdynia and Gdansk, the ferry simply docks at the port of Baltijsk in Kaliningrad and turns around. For Poles the journey is strictly business, as they fill up on a bar full of cut-price, duty-free spirits. Although you can't get off you will have an opportunity to see plenty of stony-faced Russian soldiers and a scrapyard of Russian military might on the dockside. In classic Russian bureaucratic style, the enclave occasionally enforces passport registration and/ or visas for foreigners, even though you can't actually disembark. Check ahead of time.

Elsewhere in the Baltic there are a number of lavish sea voyages. After the fall of the Soviet Union, cruise ship companies were quick to take advantage of the natural advantages of having what amounts to a huge lake surrounded by historic cities and some of the most unspoiled landscapes to be found on the Continent.

Although connected, via the Danish Straits, to the North Sea the Baltic is the drainage basin for about

1.6 million square kilometres of generally very green surrounding land. All the rain that falls there has to go somewhere, and it runs into the Baltic, adding some 660 cubic kilometres of fresh water to the sea every year. As a result, the water in the Baltic is notably fresher than in the oceans and, in those parts of the sea furthest from the world's oceans, the sea water actually becomes fresh. Should your cruise take you into the upper reaches of the Gulf of Bothnia, separating Sweden and Finland, have a taste. The water is sweet, and the marine life reflects that fact, with many fresh water fish and plants living in the open sea.

From mid November the sea begins to freeze and, in an average year, some 45 per cent of the Baltic will be covered, making cruising a summer-only activity. But the advantage to that is the long nights, with the sun hardly setting at all in the far north, giving plenty of time to explore the historic port cities of the area. Vague memories, from school history lessons, of the Hanseatic League are brought to life by the sight of the wealth that the trade guild's monopoly brought to cities such as Gdansk (or Danzig as it was often known), Stockholm, Riga and Tallinn. Add to that the raised-from-the-marsh new Russian city of St Petersburg, Helsinki and Copenhagen, and the question becomes more what to leave out.

Experienced cruisers know, however, that the holiday depends at least as much on their vessel and its crew as it does on its route. Ships cruising the Baltic include **Celebrity Cruises**'s (www.celebritycruises.com) *Century* (1,814 berths) and *Constellation* (2,043 berths); and **P&O**'s (www.P&O.com) *Aurora* (1,870 berths) and the brand-new super liner *Ventura*, due to be launched in spring 2008. For those who prefer their boats to be more intimate, **Silversea**'s (www.silversea.com) fleet of four ships takes either 382 or 296 passengers.

But even in the Scandinavian countries, sailing across the Baltic needn't cost a fortune. **Viking Line** (www.vikingline.fi) operates a budget service between Helsinki and Stockholm and Helsinki and Talinn, and **Silja Line** (www.tallinksilja.com) operates ferries between Riga and Stockholm, and also between Rostok in Germany and Helsinki.

Red Army, Gdansk has been painstakingly rebuilt to its pre-war splendour and the city's streets are filled with the treasures of its trading past. Architecturally influenced by fellow 15th-century Hanseatic League members, the city's slim and lavishly decorated burgher houses, set along wide streets, are more reminiscent of Amsterdam than Warsaw or Krakow.

An independent city state until it was grabbed by the Prussians in the 19th century, Gdansk's rich trading past is shamelessly paraded along the ul. Dluga main street. **Dwor Artusa** is perhaps the finest of the street's ostentatious mansions and it's easy to see how its lavish interiors set the pace of 16th-century interior design in the city.

Running parallel to ul. Dluga is Gdansk's most seductive street, ul. Mariacka. Paved in cobblestones and banked by the hand-crafted houses of the city's bold and beautiful, the street is now host to market stalls peddling Gdansk's most famous product, expertly crafted amber. Dominating the skyline is the imposing red-brick **Kosciol Mariacki**, said to be the biggest brick church in the world; its tower gives excellent views over the city.

Never far from the headlines, Gdansk was the site of possibly the most important event of recent history. In 1981, a portly electrician at the city's Lenin shipyards led the workers in forming an independent trades union, Solidarity. The movement shook the foundations of communism in Central and Eastern Europe, and would ultimately bring down the Berlin Wall. The shipyards (Stocznia Gdanska) are now home to a number of monuments to the strike, while the **Roads to Freedom** museum, currently housed in Solidarity's headquarters, contains a wealth of photos, film and documents chronicling the struggle.

Stretching north of Gdansk is the Polish seaside belt, and while the chilly Baltic doesn't exactly invite a dip, the broad, white sandy beaches that hug the coastline can rival anything served up on the Med. Beach headquarters are in Sopot, a short 20-minute metro ride north of Gdansk. Formerly the playground for Kaisers and Tsars, Sopot has earned itself a reputation as Poland's party capital and the town hosts some of Poland's best clubs. Enjoy the warm welcome at the **Language Pub** to kick off the night, while **Atelier** sees revellers dance the night away, before emptying on to the beach to watch the sunrise and, finally, fall over.

Further north, via Gdynia – a decent stop in its own right for its selection of ethnic restaurants – is Hel. Or at least, its peninsula. The headland slices into the Baltic, lined by beaches and dunes on either side. It's a two-hour train ride to the tip of the point and Hel town itself, with impressive views on either side as you go. You might have gone to Hel, but the town is heaven for fresh seafood. Trains leave Gdynia main station roughly every two hours, more often during the summer.

TRAVEL INFORMATION

The bus from London to Krakow with Eurolines costs from £55 (one way) and £83 (return). For anywhere else in Britain add £15 to cover connection(s) to London, single or return.

WHEN TO GO

Winter is not ideal.

Further reading

George Weigel *Witness to Hope*
The definitive biography of one of the 20th century's most influential Poles, Pope John Paul II.
Henryk Sienkiewicz *With Fire and Sword; The Deluge; Fire in the Steppe* A trilogy of historical novels, set in the time of the Polish-Lithuanian Commonwealth.
Richard Lukas *Forgotten Holocaust: The Poles Under German Occupation, 1939-1944* Further proof that Poland was not a good place to be mid century.

Websites

www.polandtour.org
The website of the national tourist office.

www.solidarnosc.org.pl
Solidarity still exists.

Dwor Artusa
19 ul. Dluga, Gdansk
058 301 7061

Kosciol Mariacki
5 ul. Podkramarska, Gdansk
058 301 39 82
www.bazylikamariacka.pl

Roads to Freedom
24 ul. Waly Piastowskie, Gdansk
058 769 29 20
www.fcs.org.pl

Language Pub
8/1 ul. Pulaskiego, Sopot

Atelier
2 al. Mamuszki, Sopot
058 555 89 06
www.klubatelier.pl

Eurolines
08717 818181
www.nationalexpress.com

Mustapha Blaoui p253

2:04 to Morocco

ROUTE   London ▶ Paris ▶ Madrid ▶ Ronda ▶ Gaucín ▶ Algeciras ▶ Ceuta ▶
Chefchaouen ▶ Fès/Meknès ▶ Marrakech ▶ Essaouira ▶ Tangiers ▶
Algeciras ▶ Madrid ▶ Paris ▶ London

Yes, you can escape to the winter sun without flying. Epic journeys are
all about the subtle thrill of anticipation and learning to look through the
window. Travel 2,000 kilometres across the continent, through changing
cultures and landscapes from London to Morocco, and you'll really feel
you deserve a lie down and a cup of mint tea.

Written by **Tanya Sassoon and Laura Middleton**

Tarifa p250

Gaucin p249

Sherry stop in Ceuta p250

THE JOURNEY

History; landscape; shopping

Long gone are the days when air travel was an exciting adventure; now it is merely the necessary drudgery that must be endured before your real holiday begins. But when you go by train – and more so when countries are crossed and boats are boarded – the adventure and the holiday start immediately. If you're in a hurry to get to Morocco, go Easyjet. Otherwise, take it slowly, enjoy the journey for its own sake and plan in some overnight stops as an integral part of your holiday plans. It's better to think of a two-week trip to Morocco as one week travelling through Europe, and a week in Morocco.

Taking the Eurostar allows for a pause in Paris, but save a stay there for the return journey. Now, with travel lust tingling, is no time to stop. Push on to Madrid and your first tentative steps into the heat and light of southern climes. Spain, of course, is the western bridge between Christendom and the Dar al-Islam. A stop in Andalucía, with its strong Moorish influences, is a must before crossing the Straits of Gibraltar to Africa. And acclimatise yourself to atmospheric, small-town Morocco before heading for the honeypot of Marrakech.

THERE AND BACK AGAIN

Start as you mean to go on – take a break before you leave. A good way to mark the beginning of your adventure is with a toast at St Pancras International's 315-foot-long champagne bar while watching the trains depart (hopefully not yours).

A 2pm Eurostar gets you to Paris's Gare du Nord with enough time to get to Gare d'Austerlitz for the evening Trenhotel to Madrid. However, if you are planning to have a picnic aboard the Trenhotel, it's worth stocking up at the better-equipped Gare du Nord. Then catch the orange line 5 on the metro to Austerlitz. The Trenhotel allows boarding 45 minutes before departure, which gives you time to settle in. If you have a Club Class or Grand Class ticket, you can go to the Sala Club near platform 14 for a complimentary tea, coffee, beer or juice.

NIGHT TRAIN

The **Trenhotel**, run by Elipsos, is a joint venture between France's SNCF and Spain's Renfe railway companies. The Francisco de Goya service from Paris to Madrid departs Gare d'Austerlitz every night, except Saturday. While the overnight train journey is painless, saves the cost of a night in a hotel and goes from city centre to city centre, Elipsos's promise that you will benefit from 'all the comforts of a hotel' rather depends on what class of ticket you can afford. The basic option, complete with super-reclining seat and free earplugs, is probably best suited to the impecunious young with robust backs. At the other end of the scale, the Grand Class offers a double 'roomette', fully equipped en suite shower room, and a three-course dinner and breakfast, all experienced while the scenery rushes past your window. The intermediate classes are comfortable, with two- (Club Class) and four-berth (Tourist Class) rooms, the latter being the best option for families.

Whichever class you find yourself in, a bit of luxury can be had by all. The onboard restaurant car is a delight. Although those in Grand Class (whose ticket includes the à la carte Gourmet Menu: starter, main, dessert, wine, spirits and liqueurs) have preference, the friendly guards will ask those in other classes if they wish to dine too.

A chef cooks the food fresh in the small on-board kitchen. Starters might include white asparagus; there are mains of monkfish, veal entrecote or cuttlefish; and desserts of crème caramel, cheese and, if you're lucky, a gorgeous chocolate cake with raspberry coulis. The food is complemented by a good range of Spanish, Italian and French wines. There is also a children's menu, and, with 72 hours notice, vegetarian and special-diet meals. For non Grand-Class diners, dinner, including a starter, main course, dessert and wine, costs from €30 (credit cards accepted). And once dinner is over, the bar is a good place to watch France roll by on summer evenings while nursing a coffee or drink. Both the bar and restaurant are open until 2am.

A tip: if you have breakfast in the restaurant (€9, included with Grand and Club Class tickets), on the Paris–Madrid trip try to sit on the left (as you face the direction of travel) – the view is spectacular, and if you're lucky you'll be dazzled by a wonderful sunrise before arrival.

Trenhotel
www.elipsos.com

MADRID

The Trenhotel gets into Madrid at 9.13am. From here, you could take a train direct to the port of Algeciras, or break your journey at Ronda and Gaucín. Either way, the next train doesn't leave until around 3pm. Of course, you could simply stay on for a day or two in Madrid, but assuming the muezzin's call is luring you irresistibly southwards, the first priority is dumping the luggage.

Chamartín station, where you arrive, is some way north of the centre, so take the metro, transferring from line 10 to line 1 at Plaza de Castilla station after one stop, to the new Atocha Renfe station, from where your onward train departs. After lodging your bags it's worth taking a look at the old Atocha station building, with its covered tropical garden and colony of terrapins. But you've come a long way and, unless you're writing a thesis on the architecture of transport, it's time to hit the museums.

To set yourself up for a busy few hours of sightseeing, grab a Madrileño-style breakfast of *chocolate con churros* (deep-fried doughnut strips that you dip into thick, strong hot chocolate) at **El Brilliante** in the square just in front of the station. With the sugar kicking in, head across the square to the **Reina Sofía**, which houses a huge collection of modern art including Picasso's *Guernica*. Continuing with the art binge, if you have time, a few hundred metres up the road is the **Museo del Prado**, with its collection of Spanish paintings by artists such as Goya, Velázquez and El Greco, as well as hundreds of works by foreign artists. Make sure to take a look at its striking new extension.

The downside of all this art is that it's yet more time inside. After 13.5 hours on a train, you might well want a space less confined and that wish can be granted at the pretty **Real Jardín Botánico**, just south of the Prado.

Useful free city maps (which include a plan of the metro) are available from most hotels and metro stations.

RONDA & GAUCÍN

It's a five-hour train-ride from Madrid to Algeciras, so to break your journey and get an early taste of Islamic architecture, it's worth stopping in Andalucía. You couldn't do better than a night or two in Ronda or the nearby tiny hillside town of Gaucín. The classic postcard view of **Ronda** is looking up at the clifftop buildings ranged on either side of the gorge of the Guadalevín. The gorge is spanned by the late 18th-century Puente Nuevo (New Bridge), which links the old Moorish citadel in the south to the newer town. However, the most emblematic of the town's fine buildings is the **Palacio de Mondragón** in the old town. Home to a succession of Moorish governors it is now a museum, but by far its most charming feature is its formal garden, which runs right to the edge of the cliff.

Bullfighting's Spanish stronghold is Andalucía and Ronda's **Plaza de Toros** is one of the oldest bullrings in Spain. It was here that local torero Pedro Romero (1754-1839) established the blueprint for modern bullfighting techniques.

Ronda has long captured the imagination of travellers, and it sometimes struggles to cope with the influx of tourists who are disgorged by the coachload from mid-morning onwards, so try and save your own sightseeing for early or late in the day.

For dinner, book a table at **La Gota de Vino**. An excellent young chef prepares creative cuisine – the garlicky grilled mushrooms

Moorish cuppa: mint tea

El Brilliante
8 plaza Del Emperador Carlos V, Madrid
91 528 6966

Reina Sofía
52 C/Santa Isabel, Madrid
91 774 10 00
www.museoreinasofia.es
Closed Tue

Museo del Prado
paseo del Prado s/n, Madrid
91 330 28 00
www.museodelprado.es
Closed Mon

Real Jardín Botánico
2 plaza de Murillo, Madrid
www.rjb.csic.es

Ronda
www.turismoderonda.es

Palacio de Mondragón
plaza de Mondragón s/n, Ronda
952 87 84 50/08 18

Plaza de Toros
15 C/Virgen de la Paz, Ronda
952 87 41 32

La Gota de Vino
13 C/Sevilla, Ronda
952 87 57 16

are particularly delicious. There is a huge range of accommodation in and around Ronda, but be sure to book in advance. A reasonably priced, central option is **Hotel Morales**.

South-west of Ronda is Gaucín, one of the area's best-known *pueblos blancos* (white villages). Gaucín is just an hour away from Ronda by train, with around four services a day, but, confusingly, 'Gaucín' train station is actually in El Colmenar – a 14-kilometre drive from Gaucín. Taxis are scarce, so ask your hotel to book a car to collect you. Alternatively, a bus from Ronda serves Gaucín intermittently. The village itself is perched more than 600 metres up in the Serranía de Ronda, and has amazing views – on a clear day you can see the mountains of Morocco and, at night, the twinkling lights of Tangier. Wander through the winding, cobbled streets, then take a walk around the ruined Moorish castle that overlooks the town.

Once an appetite is earned, it can be paid off with good tapas at Bar Paco Pepe in the main square – any local can direct you. The few hotels in Gaucín include **Hotel Caballo Andaluz** at the entrance to the village and **La Fructuosa** in the centre.

For true fans of 'slow travel' the **Djebel Musa House & Studio** offers week-long stays and is a beautiful place to wind down before you hit Morocco. Situated on the edge of the mountain, it has the village restaurants, shops and bars on its front doorstep, and the views, seclusion and infinity pool at the back door. The main house is for rent during the summer months.

Beautiful though Spain is, you can't stay forever: there's a boat to catch. Buses do go from Gaucín to Algeciras, but check for times, as they don't always run on the weekend. Alternatively, the train runs a few times a day and takes an hour. Set off early unless you intend to spend the night in Ceuta.

INTO AFRICA

If you arrive by train in the busy port town of Algeciras, the ferry terminals are just a five-minute walk away. There are about 12 departures a day to Ceuta, but do allow yourself at least an hour for check-in, security, passport control and the long walk to the ferries. There are many different ferry companies and the journey takes 1.5 hours, or just 30 minutes on the faster boats. The crossing allows you time to prepare for Africa as it comes into focus in front of you and the mix of Arabic, French and Spanish spoken on the ferry is a taste of what's to come.

Weather permitting, stand on deck and absorb the scenery: the striking Moroccan mountains loom ever closer as you cross the Straits of Gibraltar. Look behind you too, at The Rock and the sun-blessed, wind-blasted beach resort of Tarifa. Some six million years ago Europe and Africa were joined at this point; 13 kilometres may not seem like far to move in all that time, but we are talking continents here.

A EUROPEAN PAUSE

Ceuta is a curious town. Occupied by the Portuguese in 1415, it became part of Spain in 1580 and has remained so ever since, although the Moroccan government claims sovereignty. It's a good place to stock up on Spanish supplies – sherry, beer, ham – before moving on. To get into Morocco you'll need to catch a taxi to Fnidek, across the border. Aim to get one of the *petits*

Hotel Morales
51 C/Sevilla, Ronda
952 87 15 38
www.hotelmorales.es

Hotel Caballo Andaluz
Ctra. A-405, Km 0, Gaucín
952 15 11 47
www.hotelcaballoandaluz.es

La Fructuosa
67 C/Convento, Gaucín
617 69 27 84
www.lafructuosa.com

Djebel Musa House & Studio
C/Arrabalete, Gaucín
952 15 12 48

taxis, which are smaller and cheaper than *grands taxis*, for the four-kilometre journey. Remember Ceuta is in the same time zone as Spain, whereas Morocco is on GMT/UTC year-round.

Being one of the main crossing points between Europe and Africa, the border itself is heavily protected by the Spanish Guarda Civil, who aren't shy about shouting at unruly Moroccans. The crossing should be short and painless (if you're not Moroccan) and there appear to be separate queues for foreigners. Ignore touts trying to sell you a customs form, which are free from the passport counter.

Once across the border, you may need to negotiate your way through eager taxi drivers vying for your custom, but think of it as preparation for the rest of your trip. At the most it should cost Dh25 to Fnidek and this might be your first – but no means last – opportunity to hone your haggling skills. Once in Morocco, the shift from Spanish Catholicism to Islam is evident. Both men and women wear the traditional *djellaba* (a long hooded cloak), providing warmth in the winter, cool shade in the summer. A common complaint from those flying straight into Marrakech is the shock to the system of its traffic, noise and the crowded narrow shopping streets of the medina. For less of a crash landing, start your Moroccan adventure in Chefchaouen and ease yourself into the culture.

CHEFCHAOUEN

Moroccan state buses (CTM) are comfortable: some even have reclining seats. Buying tickets should be easy, but if you're finding it hard to work out which counter to go to, someone will always point you in the right direction. Forget polite queuing and get straight on once the bus doors open and keep your ticket, as the conductor may want to check it a few times. Buses from Fnidek to Tetouan take 1.5 hours. There are hourly buses until 6pm from Tetouan to Chefchaouen, with the same journey time.

Carved quite literally into the side of the Rif mountains, the blue-washed walls of Chefchaouen's medina offer delightful and mystical meanders. Looking out over the roof terraces and down on to the medieval streets of this pretty town, you could have been transported back in time – apart from the odd satellite dish.

The medina is full of shops, restaurants and cafés, and its focal point is Plaza Uta El Hamman, with plenty of opportunities for drinking mint tea and watching the world go by. Behind the Kasbah and Uta El Hamman is an artisans' market, selling a variety of leather, textiles and ceramic handicrafts. Note that being so near to Spain, the second language here is Spanish, although most locals working in the tourist industry will speak some French too.

But don't limit yourself to the town centre. It's worth walking a couple of kilometres along the Ras el-Maa river to the edge of town and the ruined mosque, where you'll see women gathering to do their washing. The views from the mosque of Chefchaouen are simply breathtaking.

For more adventurous walks in the beautiful Rif mountains, or a swim in one of the nearby rivers, ask your hotel to help you organise a day trip. You could visit the Talassemtane national park. **Chaouen Rural** offers tailored trips within the region.

Ronda p250

Chaouen Rural
www.chaouenrural.org

As well as having North Africa's most varied scenery, Morocco also offers some of its bet food, and Chefchaouen has plenty of places to try it out. The enchanting **Restaurant Tissemlal**, inside the Casa Hassan hotel, serves a great traditional tagine and on chilly evenings a welcoming open fire will beckon you. The upmarket hotel has a magical feel to it, and the elegant terrace tops it off.

The **Al-Kasbah Restaurant** has good food and does a mean hot chocolate. Sit in one of the external booths decked out with cushions and curtains and watch the world go by, or dine on one of the roof terraces for spectacular views of the mountains or the medina. **La Lampe Magique**, though a bit pricey, has good food and a great view of the main square.

Chefchaouen has an abundance of hotels and guesthouses; you should have no trouble finding one if you arrive in the morning. However, during the peak seasons (Christmas and New Year, mid June to mid September) rooms do get booked up. Reasonable hotels include: **Hotel Barcelona**, which has a great roof terrace, the magical hideaway of **Dar Terrae** and **Casa Hassan**. It can get cold at night – very cold in the winter – and you will have to pay extra for heating, or just ask for more blankets.

The area around Chefchaouen is Morocco's main cannabis-growing region. You will see people wreathed in the pungent smoke and, inevitably since you're a decadent Westerner, be offered some 'kif' to buy. A polite 'No, thank you' should suffice, although touts can be persistent.

HEADING SOUTH

You will need to get a bus to either Fès (four hours, four buses daily), or Meknès (five hours, three daily) in order to catch the train south to Marrakech, so either of these imperial cities is an obvious next stop on your trip. And you really should make time for them – both the old town of Meknès and the medina of Fès are UNESCO World Heritage Sites.

Fès's maze-like medina is an assault on the senses with its intense colours and smells. The bargaining with shopkeepers, and dealing with touts and unofficial guides will get you trained up for Marrakech. Meknès is smaller and much more laid-back, but is just as worthy of its status. The legacy that remains from its days as the capital under Sultan Moulay Ismail (1672-1727) has led to it being called the Versailles of Morocco.

The train from Fès to Marrakech takes just over seven hours (seven trains daily, the last leaving at 2.50pm), and also stops at Meknès (6.5 hours to Marrakech, seven daily).

The Moroccan railway company (**ONCF**) compares well with its European equivalent. The trains are reliable, as is the price and timetable information on its website (in French but reasonably easy to navigate even for the non-Francophone). There are second-class 1970s-style compartments and, as seats are unreserved, if you hunt you'll be able to find empty berths or even whole compartments free to stretch out in, though they fill up quickly. Finding a seat in the main carriages is not usually a problem. However, if you want to make an overnight trip, you will need to book in advance and pay a supplement.

So far as journey provisions are concerned, on longer journeys a man with a food trolley passes through the train once or twice

Restaurant Tissemlal
22 rue Targui, Chefchaouen
039 986 153
www.casahassan.com

Al-Kasbah Restaurant
rue Targui, off Uta El Hamman,
Chefchaouen

La Lampe Magique
rue Targui, Chefchaouen
065 406 464

Hotel Barcelona
12 rue Targui, Chefchaouen
039 988 506

Dar Terrae
ave Hassan I, Chefchaouen
039 987 598

Casa Hassan
22 rue Targui, Chefchaouen
039 986 153
www.casahassan.com

ONCF
www.oncf.ma

selling treats, water and a limited choice of sandwiches. Better to stock up beforehand on the roasted nuts that are sold everywhere in Morocco. It's a real treat to pick and choose from cashew nuts, peanuts, almonds, pistachios – at less than £1 for a big bag.

Ah, but what about the toilets? To be honest, they're pretty rank. The seats are filthy and the locks often broken. This proves quite a conundrum for women – attempting to squat on a moving train while hoping no one opens the door can provide more than enough excitement for one journey.

The concept of personal space is not the same as in the UK, so you will find yourself up close and personal with a whole cross-section of Moroccan life. People are friendly, often offering you a taste of their food, and helping you get off at the right stop (many stops aren't well signposted, making this a little tricky).

And, as if to prove that teenagers really are the same the world over, playing music out loud on your phone is just as popular in Morocco – albeit with Arabic music, and the occasional unashamed sing-along. Whereas in the UK it seems to be done to assert some sort of territorial right, in Morocco it's as if the protagonists genuinely think everyone else must surely want to listen too, for hours on end…

MARRAKECH

A great introduction to the Red City (so called because of the colour of its clay walls) is a dusk visit to the city's main open space, Jemaa El Fna – another UNESCO World Heritage Site. The sprawling square, also known as 'La Place', borders the souks and really comes alive as the sun goes down.

Rows of makeshift kitchens are set up with tables and benches, many specialising in one particular dish and these tend to be grouped together. They serve everything from kebabs and delicious lentils to mashed potato sandwiches, boiled sheep's head, and snails cooked in broth. Carts selling freshly squeezed orange juice, and many more selling dates line the edges of the square.

The rest of Jemaa El Fna takes on the air of a circus. Locals, who outnumber tourists in the evening, crowd around the assorted performers, who include storytellers, musicians and snake charmers. Towering above it all is the 77-metre high toweer of the Koutoubia Mosque (Mosque of Booksellers), the symolic heart of the city.

While La Place is one of the world's great open spaces, a visit to the souk is instant immersion in a *Thousand and One Nights* world of alleys and mysterious cubby-hole shops, where it's hard not to believe that that carpet really might whisk you up into the sky. Getting lost is inevitable and part of the experience. Seek out some downtime at the peaceful **Jardin Majorelle & Museum of Islamic Art**, which is now owned by Yves Saint Laurent, or treat yourself to a massage at **Hammam Menara**. The souk looks like a chaotic labyrinth but is in fact a patchwork of individual markets, most specialising in goods such as antiques, spices, carpets and leather. If you want a one-stop shop, go into **Mustapha Blaoui**'s emporium.

For budget hotels, rue Bab Agnaou is the place to go, but the popular **Hotel Gallia** comes top of the class. For a *riad* (a house in the traditional style with enclosed garden) with a spa attached

Koutoubia Mosque

Jardin Majorelle & Museum of Islamic Art
ave Yacoub El-Mansour, Guéliz, Marrakech
024 30 18 52
www.jardinmajorelle.com

Hammam Menara
Quartier Essaada, Marrakech
No phone
Tue, Thur, Sat men only; Mon, Wed, Fri, Sun women only

Mustapha Blaoui
142-144 Bab Doukkala, Marrakech
024 385 240

Hotel Gallia
30 rue de la Recette, off rue Bab Agnaou, Marrakech
024 445 913
www.ilove-marrakesh.com/hotelgallia

Further reading

Paul Bowles *The Sheltering Sky*
Paul Bowles *A Hundred Camels in the Courtyard*
William Burroughs *Naked Lunch*
Arturo Pérez-Reverte *The Seville Communion*
Washington Irving *Tales of the Alhambra*

Websites

www3.telus.net/OscarNieto/ Directory.html
World Flamenco Directory
www.magicmorocco.com
Food, culture, history

Jnane Mogador
116 riad Zitoun El Kedim, Marrakech
024 426 324
www.jnanemogador.com

Hotel Farouk
66 ave Hassan II, Guéliz, Marrakech
024 431 989
www.hotelfarouk.com

Le Mechouar
ave Oqba Ben Nafia, Essaouira
024 475 828
www.lemechouar-essaouira.com

Hostal Fez
7 C/Rio, Algeciras
095 60 99 088
www.hostalfez.com

SOUP-ER KITCHENS

It's like going to the caff, only not for a fry-up. If you're late to bed or early to rise, you might be lucky enough to stumble on a street stall selling soup. Although rarely discovered by holiday-makers, soup stalls can be found in medinas all over Morocco. At around 3am, housewives looking to make a few extra dirhams will provide hot, hearty harira soup and bread to workers and fishermen. Harira is traditionally eaten to break the fast of Ramadan. Made from chickpeas, lentils, tomatoes, celery, parsley, sometimes rice, and Morocco's favourite spice, cumin, the harira at these stalls is usually meat-free to keep prices low.

try the **Jnane Mogador**. If you'd prefer somewhere away from the hustle and bustle of the medina, **Hotel Farouk** is a basic but clean choice, with great views of the sunset from the top rooms.

ESSAOUIRA

Morocco has some of the finest beaches in the world. To sample them head east to Essaouira, a coastal town three hours by bus from Marrakech. As well as being Morocco's best-known windsurfing centre, it is also a fishing town. Walk along the wave-lashed ramparts that starred in Orson Welles's *Othello*; wander through the walled medina (another UNESCO World Heritage Site); check out the ruins of Borj El-Berod, an old fort that supposedly inspired Jimi Hendrix's 'Castles Made of Sand'; go quad biking or camel trekking on the dunes at the far end of the beach; sunbathe or try kitesurfing nearer to town; watch the fishermen land their catch – and then eat it in one of the nearby fish stalls. A good place to stay – and eat, drink and dance to live music and DJs – is **Le Mechouar**. There is currently talk of adding belly-dancing lessons to its repertoire.

HOMEWARD BOUND

On arrival we dipped our toes only gradually into Moroccan waters, arriving via Ceuta; as old hands we leave, with confidence, from the port of Tangiers. You can book the whole trip from Essaouira to Tangiers in Essaouira – the 6am bus connects with the 9am train out of Marrkech, which should arrive in Tangiers in time to get one of the last ferries to Algeciras. You can't connect to Madrid until the following morning; for your overnight in Algeciras the *riad*-style **Hostal Fez** has friendly staff and is very accommodating.

Next morning get the 8.30am train to Madrid, arriving at 2pm. The Trenhotel departs at around 7pm, and comes in to Paris at 8.30am the day after.

TRAVEL INFORMATION

Before you book on the Trenhotel find out about **Elipsos**' deals and discounts on its website – not all travel agents are aware of these. A one-way Grand Class ticket could cost as much as €291 per person – or as little as €149 for the same ticket when booked as part of a Mini Couple Offer. The Francisco de Goya service also offers discounts to ISIC cardholders, under-26s, over-60s, couples (any two people) and families (any three to four people). Rail pass holders can get seats for as little as €45 one-way. Children under four go free, and special arrangements can be made for travel with bicycles. Search for discounts or you might end up paying more for a reclining seat (top price of €131) than for a Club Class bed (€105 as part of the Mini Couple Offer) – not something you'd want to find out as you struggle to get comfortable in your seat and wrestle with your earplugs. See www.elipsos.com or call RailEurope on 08448 484 064.

WHEN TO GO

Winter. Mainly to make the point that you can escape it using flight-free transport. But a packed compartment in August in Andalucia or Morocco is another good reason for avoiding the southern summer sun.

Barcelona's Rambla p257

Iberia

ROUTE Plymouth ▸ Bilbao ▸ San Sebastián ▸ Barcelona ▸ Madrid ▸ Lisbon ▸ Porto ▸ Douro Valley ▸ Galicia

As you sail into Bilbao, the Iberian peninsula opens before you like a book. There are many, many beautiful routes, but a trip through the capitals of the Basque Country, Catalonia, Spain and Portugal is still one of Europe's grand tours. Enjoy galleries and the gourmet food, sample the new wines of the Douro Valley and collect shellfish in Galicia's Rias Baixas.

Written by **Chris Moss**

Gaudy Gaudí p258

Slow boat to Bilbao

Hotel de las Letras p259

★ Architecture; art; culture; food & drink; landscapes

THE JOURNEY

The cities, towns and villages of Spain and Portugal are ideal for short breaks and beach holidays, which is why millions of Britons, Germans, Scandinavians and other sun-poor northern Europeans fly down there every year. But to get a deeper sense of Iberia there's nothing better than travelling overland, savouring the changing flavours, diverse landscapes and temperature shifts, not to mention the distinct languages and people. Spain is a patchwork of nations – Catalonia, the Basque Country, Andalucia, Galicia, Asturias – and even the regions of Portugal, despite its diminutive size, have differing identities and lifestyles.

P&O's Portsmouth–Bilbao ferry service is no *Bluebird*, taking 29-35 hours (depending on weather and tides) to get round the jutting capes of Normandy and Brittany and across the Bay of Biscay. But the vessel, the *Pride of Bilbao*, has a Langan's Brasserie, a swimming pool and even a wildlife officer to help passengers spot whales and dolphins. There are colouring competitions and face-painting classes for children, and a cabaret, casino and cinema for the older kids.

BILBAO, BRIEFLY

It was as long ago as 1997 that Frank Gehry's glittering titanium Guggenheim Museum pushed Bilbao into the limelight, but this wealthy, industrial city has not been resting on its architectural laurels since. Recent showstoppers include Norman Foster's metro system, Santiago Calatrava's bird-like airport terminal and his glass-decked Zubizuri footbridge. As part of the tenth anniversary celebrations for the museum, the huge La Salve Bridge that pierces one end of the 'Goog' was redesigned by French artist Daniel Buren.

The **Guggenheim Bilbao** is not the only notable building on the River Nervión; other landmarks include the high-spec **Palacio Euskalduna** concert hall and **Museo de Bellas Artes**.

East of the river is the Old Town, where the Siete Calles ('Seven Streets') district is thick with bars, restaurants and monuments such as the Gothic **Catedral de Santiago**, the Mercado de la Ribera market and the church of San Antón. Along and beyond the river's west bank, the city's new architecture is a perfect counterpoint to the classic Spanish forms of the Old City. For a bird's-eye view, take the funicular (every 15 minutes) from the plaza of the same name up to Artxanda, which overlooks the city.

Bilbao is not a great place to stay long, so far better to have a busy day here and then catch the night train towards the Mediterranean coast. If you do decide to overnight, the **Hotel Miró**, designed by Antoni Miró, and Ricardo Legorreta's **Sheraton Bilbao** offer cool comfort near the Guggenheim.

TERRA DE PAS

There are daily trains between Bilbao and Barcelona, and occasional luxury night services with sleeper cars. The direct Talgo services pass through Zaragoza, Lleida, Reus and Tarragona, using the old track via Monzón-Río Cinca and leaving the new AVE line free for faster trains to/from Madrid. The journey time is between nine and 11 hours and you arrive in Barcelona's Sants station, joining the millions of other visitors descending on the Catalan capital each year.

The mile-long Rambla buzzes with street performers, flower sellers, shoe shiners and pickpockets. Towards the top end is the unmissable Boqueria, one of the biggest food markets in Europe, and at its best first thing in the morning. The area to the east of here, with the Gothic **Catedral** at its heart, is a maze of evocative alleys opening on to quiet squares – Plaça del Pi, Plaça Sant Josep Oriol and Plaça del Rei.

The area to the other side of La Rambla is the Raval, the last (and crumbling) bastion of ungentrified old Barcelona. It boasts a couple of great museums: **MACBA** (Museu d'Art Contemporani de Barcelona), a gleaming white edifice housing modern art; and **CCCB** (Centre de Cultura Contemporània de Barcelona), a showcase of fascinating exhibitions and festivals.

To the other side of the Old City is the fashionable Born area, where boutiques and bars multiply by the week. For more serious pursuits, there is the **Museu Picasso** and the magnificent 14th-century basilica, **Santa Maria del Mar**. At the top of this area, just off the Via Laietana, is the **Palau de la Música Catalana**, a breathtaking example of Modernisme (Catalan art nouveau).

Guggenheim Bilbao
2 avda Abandoibarra, Bilbao
944 359 080
www.guggenheim-bilbao.es
Closed Mon

Palacio Euskalduna
4 avda Abandoibarra, Bilbao
944 035 000
www.euskalduna.net

Museo de Bellas Artes
2 MuseoPlaza, Bilbao
944 396 060
www.museobilbao.com

Catedral de Santiago
1 plaza Santiago, Bilbao
944 153 627

Hotel Miró
77 Alameda de Mazarredo, Bilbao
946 611 880
www.mirohotelbilbao.com

Sheraton Bilbao
29 Lehendakari Leizaola, Bilbao
944 280 000
www.sheraton.com

Catedral
pla de la Seu, Barcelona
93 342 82 60
www.catedralbcn.org

MACBA (Museu d'Art Contemporani de Barcelona)
1 plaça dels Àngels, Barcelona
93 412 08 10
www.macba.es
Closed Tue

CCCB (Centre de Cultura Contemporània de Barcelona)
5 C/Montalegre, Barcelona
93 306 41 00
www.cccb.org
Closed Mon

Museu Picasso
15-23 C/Montcada, Barcelona
93 256 30 00
www.museupicasso.bcn.es
Closed Mon

Santa Maria del Mar
plaça de Santa Maria, Barcelona
93 310 23 90

Palau de la Música Catalana
2 C/Sant Francesc de Paula, Barcelona
93 295 72 00
www.palaumusica.org

IBERIA

Leading uphill from the Plaça Catalunya, the Passeig de Gràcia takes you through the centre of the Eixample district. This wide boulevard is home to some of the finest examples of Modernisme. Gaudí's curving apartment block, **La Pedrera**, is about halfway up, and across the road is **La Manzana de la Discordia**, where buildings by the three greatest figures of Modernisme – Gaudí, Domènech and Puig i Cadafalch – stand together in wildly clashing styles. To the north of here is Gaudí's unfinished masterpiece, the **Sagrada Família**, Barcelona's most emblematic building. Two great hotels are in the Eixample: if you want to sleep in a converted Modernista mansion, check into **Casa Fuster**; the sleek **Hotel Omm** is close by and close in quality.

Much smaller and quirkier, but still stylish, is the **5rooms**. Down in the Raval is **Hotel Peninsular**, a characterful plant-filled former convent with suitably spartan facilities.

Gourmet Catalan cooking is available at **Comerç 24** in the Born and **Cinc Sentits**. For a taste of more traditional Catalan cuisine there's the rambling and tourist-friendly **Can Culleretes** in the Barri Gòtic. For seafood and paella, it's difficult to go wrong in the Barceloneta fishing district. **Ginger**, behind the City Hall, and **Quimet i Quimet** over in Poble Sec are good places for tapas, but for straightforward drinking head to the many bars on and around the Passeig del Born.

To get from Barcelona to Madrid, hop on the AVE high-speed line, which was completed in February 2008 and passes through Lleida, Zaragoza and Guadalajara on its way to the capital. There are 17 trains every day between 6am and 9pm and the non-stop service covers the 550 kilometres in as little as 2 hours 38 minutes, making it one of the world's fastest long-distance trains.

MADRID'S MUSEOS

Barcelona has had the hype but the Spanish capital is one of the world's most irresistible cities. It has the rich, proudly Spanish traditions – bullfighting, flamenco, *horchata* in Retiro park. It has the food – brown sticky stews, wood-roasted suckling pig, fish (Madrid, as capital, gets the best seafood). It has a decadent nightlife scene and world-class museums. That this is something of a secret is the best part of all.

To get oriented, Madrid has three reference points: the Puerta del Sol, the city's absolute centre; the Plaza Mayor, the Golden Age core; and the Plaza de Cibeles, with its extravagant architecture. The Habsburg dynasty figured large in the history of Madrid until 1700, and the area bounded by Sol, the Plaza Mayor, the Palacio Real and San Francisco el Grande, the oldest part of the city, is commonly known as 'Los Austrias' after them. An elegant arcaded square with some lurid murals added in the 1990s, the Plaza Mayor was where the greatest festivals and ceremonies of imperial Madrid were held, as well as bullfights and carnivals. These days it hosts coin and stamp collectors' markets on Sundays and lively dance bands during fiestas.

Sol is Madrid's most photographed square, home to the emblematic bear and strawberry tree statue, as well as the famous Tío Pepe sign. The area north and east of Sol is dominated by the two great avenues of Calle Alcalá and Gran Vía. Alcalá has a wonderful variety of 19th- to early 20th-century

La Pedrera
92 passeig de Gràcia, Barcelona
902 40 09 73
www.lapedreraeducacio.org

La Manzana de la Discordia
35-45 passeig de Gràcia, Barcelona

Sagrada Família
401 C/Mallorca, Barcelona
93 207 30 31
www.sagradafamilia.org

Casa Fuster
132 passeig de Gràcia, Barcelona
93 255 30 00
www.hotelcasafuster.com

Hotel Omm
265 C/Rosselló, Barcelona
93 44540 00
www.hotelomm.es

5rooms
72 C/Pau Claris, Barcelona
93 342 78 80
www.thefiverooms.com

Hotel Peninsular
34 C/Sant Pau, Barcelona
93 302 31 38
www.hpeninsular.com

Comerç 24
24 C/Comerç, Barcelona
933 19 21 02
www.comerc24.com

Cinc Sentits
58 C/Aribau, Barcelona
93 323 94 90
www.cincsentits.com

Can Culleretes
5 C/Quintana, Barcelona
93 317 30 22
www.culleretes.com

Ginger
1 C/Palma de Sant Just, Barcelona
93 310 53 09

Quimet i Quimet
25 C/Poeta Cabanyes, Barcelona
93 442 31 42

buildings, including the striking **Círculo de Bellas Artes**, with its fine café. Look out too for the handsome **Real Academia de Bellas Artes de San Fernando**, with 13 works by Goya.

Most people, though, are here for the trio of world-famous art museums: the **Thyssen-Bornemisza**; the giant, neo-classical **Prado**; and the **Museo Nacional Centro de Arte Reina Sofía**, Spain's national gallery.

The avenues and the art, and a bit of strolling round Retiro park, will soon work up an appetite. Traditional gutsy stews are the order of the day in Madrid's restaurants. The classic stop for suckling pig and roast lamb is **El Sobrino de Botín**, much loved, needless to say, by Ernest Hemingway. Soaring temperatures in summer, however, can make this kind of food hard to stomach. Three cheers, then, for tapas. The streets around plazas Santa Ana and Mayor all but bristle with old-school bars where you can pick at plates of squid, tortilla, olives and *patatas bravas*.

For something a bit more nouvelle, head up to the newly – and still only partially – gentrified Chueca neighbourhood, and be sure to stop at **Café Oliver**. If it's sublime seafood you're after, look no further than the bustling **Ribeira Do Miño**.

Everything you've heard about traffic jams in the small hours and office workers heading straight to work from the clubs is true: the *madrileños*' reputation as party fiends is more than justified, despite municipal meddling and earlier closing times than previously. Perennial drinking favourites are **Viva Madrid** and the dusty old *tabernas* around Los Austrias, with aproned barmen and vermouth pulled from silver taps. For a younger, funkier atmosphere, Malasaña has it all, from cineaste's delight **Pepe Botella** to the Iberian *Friends* set that is **La Ida**.

Of the unusually funky wave of Madrid hotels to open in recent years, the very latest in designer chic is the **Hotel Puerta América**. It has a starry cast of designers and architects behind it, among them Zaha Hadid, Jean Nouvel, Ron Arad and Norman Foster. Other recent openings include the boutique hotels **Hotel Urban** and **Hotel de las Letras**. Other mid-range options include the classy **Hotel Palacio San Martín**. Budget chic is the latest vogue in Madrid: two forerunners are the **Room-Mate Mario**, on a graceful side street near the opera house, and the high-tech **Petit Palace Ducal**, just off Gran Vía.

EAST THROUGH EXTREMADURA

Spain may dangle off the Continent like a *bota de vino* hanging from a *hidalgo*'s saddle, but Madrid is one of the great European rail hubs. From Chamartin, trains go north. From Atocha, trains go south to Andalucía and east to Murcia and Valencia. It's all very tempting, but we're heading west.

With baguette, some slices of *jamon ibérico* and a bottle of water – and one of wine – in hand, climb aboard the Lusitania, the overnight train from Madrid to Lisbon, invariably filled with groups of note-swapping InterRailers and boisterous Spaniards on weekend breaks. The route takes you through Talavera de la Reina and Cáceres, one of the grandest and most beautiful towns in Extremadura. Although Portugal's border with Spain hardly seems to exist any more, with passports rarely checked, you'll still notice a difference as you head west. The language softens and slows – as do the people – and if you get off to buy a sandwich at the station, you'll find the prices have dropped.

Círculo de Bellas Artes
42 C/Alcalá, Madrid
91 360 54 00
www.circulobellasartes.com

Real Academia de Bellas Artes de San Fernando
13 C/Alcalá, Madrid
91 524 08 64
http://rabasf.insde.es

Thyssen-Bornemisza
8 paseo del Prado, Madrid
91 369 01 51
www.museothyssen.org

Prado
paseo del Prado s/n, Madrid
91 330 28 00
www.museoprado.es

Museo Nacional Centro de Arte Reina Sofía
52 C/Santa Isabel, Madrid
91 774 10 00
www.museoreinasofia.es

El Sobrino de Botín
17 C/Cuchilleros, Madrid
91 366 42 17
www.botin.es

Café Oliver
12 C/Almirante, Madrid
91 521 73 79
www.cafeoliver.com

Ribeira Do Miño
1 C/Santa Brígida, Madrid
91 521 98 54

Viva Madrid
7 C/Manuel Fernández y González, Madrid
91 429 36 40

Pepe Botella
12 C/San Andrés, Madrid
91 522 43 09

La Ida
11 C/Colón, Madrid
91 522 91 07

Hotel Puerta América
41 avda América, Madrid
91 744 54 00
www.hotelpuertamerica.com

Hotel Urban
34 carrera de San Jerónimo, Madrid
91 787 77 70
www.derbyhotels.es

Hotel de las Letras
11 Gran Vía, Madrid
91 523 79 80
www.hoteldelasletras.com

Hotel Palacio San Martín
5 plaza de San Martín, Madrid
91 701 50 00
www.intur.com

Room-Mate Mario
4 C/Campomanes, Madrid
91 548 85 48
www.hhcampomanes.com

Petit Palace Ducal
3 C/Hortaleza, Madrid
91 521 10 43
www.hthoteles.com

IBERIA

LOFTY LISBON

All of a sudden, it's hilly streets, washing lines, salted cod and custard tarts. For centuries, ships set out from Europe's westernmost capital to explore the world. Today, Lisbon is more of a destination: a picturesquely hilly city on a beautiful estuary with friendly locals, good food and wine at affordable prices.

Lisbon's historical roots lie elsewhere. According to legend, it was founded by Ulysses – its name is supposedly a corruption of his – but the earliest remains, including a theatre dedicated to Nero, are Roman. When the Moors invaded from North Africa in the eighth century, they built a castle on the site of a hilltop Roman fort. After Christian forces threw them out in 1147, the **Castelo de São Jorge** was rebuilt and restored, and it is worth the climb for the panoramic views. The same is true of many of the city's other *miradouros* – lookout points. Downhill is the bairro of Alfama, whose name (Al-Hama – fountain) and maze of streets recall its Moorish origins.

Opposite the Romanesque **Sé** or cathedral is the Baroque church of **Santo António** and, next to the church, the quirky **Museu Antoniano**. Santo António is Lisbon's favourite native son (officially he's called St Anthony of Padua but *lisboetas* claim him as their own and hold an all-night party in his honour every 12 June).

Parque das Nações – the site of Expo 98 – offers child-friendly attractions such as the **Oceanário** aquarium.

Lisbon's grid-like downtown, the Baixa, is a sharp contrast to Alfama. It was laid out after the massive 1755 earthquake that, together with the resulting fires and tidal wave, killed thousands. The new Baixa – between Rossio and the riverside Praça do Comércio, with its arcades and triumphal arch – was an attempt to impose order.

On the hillside west of Baixa is the elegant Chiado, with shops and cafés such as the famous **A Brasileira** – all wood panelling and modernist paintings. Further up is the funky Bairro Alto, where clothes stores open mid-afternoon and bars get going around midnight.

Portugal's Golden Age was during the 15th- and 16th-century era of 'Discoveries', when explorers set sail from Belém, west of the city. Here, the **Jerónimos** monastery and the Tower of Belém are prime examples of Manueline architecture, a late Gothic style incorporating maritime and tropical motifs. This museum district harbours among others the **Coach Museum** and an arts centre, the **Centro Cultural de Belém**.

Outside Lisbon, leafy Sintra is a former royal resort dubbed by Byron 'glorious Eden'; the Baroque **Palácio de Queluz** is a less bombastic Versailles; and **Mafra**'s palace-convent is as bombastic as they come. The region's many beaches range from the promenades and strands of the Estoril coast through wild Guincho – great for windsurfing – to pretty coves north of Cabo da Roca (the continent's western tip). The Atlantic waters are cold but the surfing is good. South of the river are more beaches on the Caparica coast.

Newish design hotels include the **Heritage Avenida Liberdade** and **Bairro Alto Hotel**. **Pensão Londres** is up the road.

Lisbon offers global cuisine as well as the *bacalhau* (salt cod) and fresh seafood for which Portugal is renowned. In Bairro Alto, **Sinal Vermelho** is a mid-priced option, **Pap'Açorda**

Castelo de São Jorge
Castelo, Lisbon
21 880 0620/0626

Sé
Largo da Sé, Lisbon
21 887 6628

Igreja de Santo António
Largo de Santo António da Sé, Lisbon
21 886 9145

Museu Antoniano
24 Largo de Santo António da Sé, Lisbon
21 886 0447

Oceanário
Esplanada Dom Carlos I, Parque das Nações, Lisbon
21 891 7002
www.oceanario.pt

A Brasileira
120 rua Garrett, Lisbon
21 346 9541

Jerónimos
praça do Império, Lisbon
21 362 0034
Closed Mon

Coach Museum
praça Afonso de Albuquerque, Lisbon
21 361 0850
Closed Mon

Centro Cultural de Belém
praça do Império, Lisbon
21 361 2400

Palácio de Queluz
Queluz
21434 3860

Palácio Nacional de Mafra
Terreiro Dom João V, Mafra
261 817 550

Heritage Avenida Liberdade
28 avenida da Liberdade, Lisbon
21 340 4040
www.heritage.pt

Bairro Alto Hotel
2 praça Luís de Camões, Lisbon
21 340 8222
www.bairroaltohotel.com

Pensão Londres
53 rua Dom Pedro V, Lisbon
21 346 2203
www.pensaolondres.com.pt

Sinal Vermelho
89 rua das Gáveas, Lisbon
21 343 1281

Pap'Açorda
57 rua da Atalaia, Lisbon
21 346 4811

a swish alternative. Gourmets dine at **Eleven**.

Thanks to a mild climate, the Bairro Alto's streets often fill with barhoppers clutching Caipirinhas and beer. Visit the hip **Clube da Esquina** or the boho **B'Artis**. **Pavilhão Chinês** is worth a look for its ultra-kitsch decor.

VINTAGE PORTO

But to get to know the Portuguese, you'll really have to go up the coast. Most InterRailers will be heading straight up on the fast, clean inter-city route to Porto, Portugal's second city in the north. Porto straddles the Douro river with its spectacular double-decker coat-hanger bridge of Dom Luis. The overland metro runs right over the top level, flying past pedestrians with no barrier in sight. From the top of the bridge, along the riverside Ribeira or from outside the port cellars of Gaia is where most people see the Douro.

Porto is one of Europe's great trading cities, its dockside alive with ships coming and going. Its most famous import was Bobby Robson, who won the cup once and the league twice as manager of the local team, FC Porto. Even more famous is its chief export – port.

Portugal is England's oldest ally, and it's in Porto that the British left their most visible mark, in the form of the fortified wine that is Portugal's biggest export. The port cellars are still there, in Vila Nova de Gaia, and offer guided tours.

Nestling in a deep gorge, the Old Town, a UNESCO World Heritage Site, is implausibly picturesque. Climb the 240 steps of the Torre dos Clérigos, an 18th-century tower designed by Italian architect Nicolau Nasoni and view the panorama that sweeps across to the Atlantic. The neo-classical **Palácio da Bolsa** has a neo-Moorish ballroom that took 18 years to build and is gilded with 18 kilos of gold.

The fortress-like Romanesque cathedral, **Sé do Porto**, founded in the early 12th century, offers fine views from the chapterhouse and courtyard. The narrow, steep streets known as *ilhas* (islands) cascade down to the waterfront Ribeira district, where the Gothic exterior of the Igreja de São Francisco belies an 18th-century interior dripping with gilt. The houses of the poor but pretty Miragaia neighbourhood are built on arches because of regular flooding.

The locals' nickname, *tripeiros* (tripe-eaters), dates back to 1415, when Porto's patriots donated all their best meat to a Portuguese fleet off to conquer Ceuta in North Africa. Tripe is still a speciality, but the snack of choice is now the *francesinha*, a meat and cheese sandwich drenched in spicy sauce.

Seafood can be pricey. Along the waterfront Cais da Ribeira, at no.39, the **Filha da Mãe Preta** (closed Sun) is cosy. Locals prefer swanky **Dom Tonho**, upstairs at no.13, owned by local bluesman Rui Veloso. The refined Portuguese cuisine at **Bull & Bear** (closed Sun) has won it a reputation as Porto's top restaurant. If you want to take a look inside the port lodges and do a spot of tasting, call into the **tourist office** on the waterfront in Vila Nova de Gaia, and staff will give you a map and list of companies that open their doors to visitors.

The coolest place to sleep in town is also the crustiest. The **Albergaria Miradouro** has original 1960s teak and brown wallpaper interiors, and bedside lamps Shaft would die for.

IBERIA

Eleven
rua Marquês de Fronteira, Lisbon
21 386 2211
www.restauranteleven.com

Clube da Esquina
30 rua da Barroca, Lisbon
93 866 1134

B'Artis
95 rua do Diário de Notícias, Lisbon
21 342 4795

Pavilhão Chinês
89 rua Dom Pedro V, Lisbon
21 342 4729

Palácio da Bolsa
rua Ferreira Borges, Porto
223 399 000
www.palaciodabolsa.com

Sé do Porto
Terreiro da Sé, Porto

Filha da Mãe Preta
39 rua Cais da Ribeira, Porto
222 055 515

Dom Tonho
13-15 rua Cais da Ribeira, Porto
222 004 307

Bull & Bear
3431 avenida da Boavista, Porto
226 107 669

Tourist Office
avenida Diogo Leite, Porto
223 703 735
www.portoturismo.pt

Albergaria Miradouro
598 rua da Alegria, Porto
225 370 717

Douro Valley vineyard

Porto-Pocinho train

GOLDEN VALLEY

At the end of the 17th century, England and France went to war again. Unable to source their wine from Bordeaux, English wine merchants travelled to Porto in search of new supplies. The local wine didn't travel well so they added brandy and fortified it. The new drink, port, was a massive success. In the mid 18th century, the Douro was divided up by the British port exporters, and 335 stone markers were erected to show the demarcated zone where port could officially be produced.

You can travel up the valley on a railway that hugs the north bank of the meandering river. The Porto–Régua–Pocinho service runs between 7am and midnight daily (the earliest train leaves from Porto's Campanhã station), with departures every two hours; for some trains you have to change at Régua and/or at Marco de Canvaseses.

It's a pleasure just to ride up and down the line, but a stopover at Pinhão is strongly recommended. As you chug along the valley, look out for the names of port wineries: Sandeman, Taylor's, Cockburn's. Boats ply up and down the river. Goats cling to the places where even the intrepid winemakers can't reach. As you go further east, deeper into the Douro, you'll see just how steep the land is.

Pinhão may not be the prettiest of Portuguese towns, but it has a very smart hotel, the **Vintage House**, and it is close to a Douro Boys estate, the **Quinta do Vale Dona Maria**, which can be visited if you ring in advance.

On the south bank of the river, a short taxi ride from Pinhão – or from Régua – is **D.O.C.**, a chic new restaurant. It's a perfect place for an early evening meal: try a bottle of local wine with some creamy local cheeses, cured meats and conserves, and then sit back and watch the setting sun turn the valley gold (*douro* means 'golden').

If Douro is port of entry to wine heaven, just north of here Galicia is the antechamber to food heaven. Trains depart Porto's Campanha station for the border at Redondela de Galicia where you swap to a Spanish train – they are quite slow, but you should be in Pontevedra in less than four hours. From here, catch a bus or taxi for the 25-kilometre ride to Cambados.

TO THE SOURCE

A small port town in the Rias Baixas (low rivers), Cambados is a lovely place to slow down after the long haul across Iberia, and a 17th-century parador will ease the unwinding. **Parador de Cambados** is ideally located for beachcombing, strolls along the prom – walk north to see the busy port – and general idling. Cambados still has a few old fishermen's houses, some of them with scallop shells for decoration on their outside walls. There are plenty of nice bars and small restaurants in town, but for lunch and/or dinner catch a taxi to **O Tio Benito**. Here the *pulpo* is served with cheap red Barrantes wine that comes served in bowls. The bold flavours of the octopus go well with strong reds and the peasant-style drinking somehow feels right. More refined meals – or palates – are best accompanied by the local *albariño* wines, many of which are produced nearby.

But the best reason for spending the night here is to start the next day with a walk on the shore. There are daily 'clam tours' along the coast and the parador will arrange one for you – insist

Vintage House
Lugar da Ponte, Pinhão
254 730 230
www.relaischateaux.com/vintage

Quinta do Vale Dona Maria
Quinta do Vale Dona Maria
22 374 4320
www.quintavaledonamaria.com

D.O.C.
222 Estrada Nacional, Folgosa
254 858 123
www.restaurantedoc.com

Parador de Cambados
Pº Calzada s/n, Cambados
986 542250
www.paradores-spain.com

O Tio Benito
4 avenida de Bouza Martín, Ribadumia,
near Cambados
986 710 287

on English if your Spanish is poor. The guide will give you a few key words of the *galego* tongue to get by, including *empanada* (the Galician pasty), *marisquera* (female shellfish collector) and, above all, *ria,* which is a drowned river valley defined by its tidal seawater rather than any inland source.

The bays are full of *marisqueras*, bent over collecting pink clams. They use long rakes to drag through the sand and expose the blackish earth below. Once the shells are brought up, they are quickly assessed for size and anything at or above four centimetres goes into a collecting bucket. The smaller shellfish are reprieved and thrown back on to the sand to bury themselves and get older and bigger.

END OF THE WORLD

It's an hour along the northbound line from Pontevedra to Santiago de Compostela. After a wander through the town's austerely beautiful streets, and a visit to the crypt of the **Catedral de Santiago**, where St James's bones are stored, take a seat at **Casa Camilo**, off the city's main food and drink gauntlet, Raíña. Ask for a cold beer and, with a knowing nod, a plate of *percebes* – or goose barnacles. In order to harvest the *percebes*, a fisherman must row up to a rockface, often during rough seas. He ties a rope to his ankle and places a knife in his teeth before leaping into the water and swimming like mad to get to the rock, where he hacks the barnacles off and stuffs them in a net bag around his waist, finally swimming back to the bobbing boat. All this before the next wave breaks, which might just dash his brains out on the jagged rocks. Galicians tell visitors their region *huele a mar*, 'smells of the sea'. *Percebes* taste of it, compressed, intensified, purified.

Other Galician standards are grilled hake with fresh herbs, *chipirones* (baby squid) and *pulpo a la gallega* (octopus). You can try them all at the lovely on-site restaurant of the **AC Palacio del Carmen** hotel, a gorgeous convent conversion.

Santiago, as the climax of many a pilgrimage, is a natural place to end an Iberian itinerary – though, of course, you'll have to go home, and can choose between heading back to Madrid or taking a train along the northern coastline back to Bilbao. If you want to experience a different sort of end, hire a car and explore the Costa da Mort (Coast of Death), named for the huge number of shipwrecks that have occurred here, before heading to Fisterra, the 'end of the earth', and the end of Spain.

TRAVEL INFORMATION

P&O's the *Pride of Bilbao* makes the southbound crossing in 35 hours and returns in 29 hours: this means two nights on the voyage out and one night on the way back. You leave Portsmouth about 9pm, have one night on board, a full day and then another night on board, then you arrive about 8am the following morning. Spanish rail timetables are available at http://horarios.renfe.es/hir/ingles.html. You can print off a timetable for the Douro Valley trains as well as inter-city services in Portugal at www.cp.pt.

WHEN TO GO

Spring and autumn are best.

Further reading

George Orwell *Homage to Catalonia* Orwell's classic account of his experiences during the Spanish Civil War.
CHJ Sansom *Winter in Madrid* Spy novel set in World War II Madrid.
Graham Greene *Monsignor Quixote* A peregrination through modern Spain.
José Saramago *The Year of the Death of Ricardo Reis* Dense novel by 1998 Nobel Laureate for Literature.

Websites

www.douroboys.com
Winelands.
www.wonderfulland.com
All about Portugal.
www.galiciaguide.com
What to do and see in Galicia.

Catedral de Santiago
praza de Praterías, Santiago de Compostela
981 581 155
www.catedraldesantiago.es

Casa Camilo
24 rua de Raíña, Santiago de Compostela
981 584 593

AC Palacio del Carmen
C/Oblatas, Santiago de Compostela
981 552 444
www.ac-hotels.com/main.asp

P&O
08716 64 64 64
www.poferries.com

Deutsche Bahn p268

InterRail

ROUTE   London ▶ Europe

'Where are you going on holiday this year?' 'Europe.' That's about as precise an answer as you'll get out of an InterRailer. Think of it as a club dedicated to freedom, serendipity, ever-changing vistas. If you fancy joining, it's easy now there are no age restrictions. Get a pass that gives you five travelling days in ten or go for a month's continuous travel, do the Prado, the Vatican, the Northern Lights, and then go to Hel and back.

Written by **Monica Guy**, **Edoardo Albert**, **Peterjon Cresswell** and **Chris Moss**

Eat a paella

Sunbathe

Sightsee

Go sailing

Check the time

Keep moving

THE JOURNEY

It's a city worker's mid-commute fantasy. On arrival at St Pancras, Waterloo or Victoria, everyone debouches and slumps to work. He or she leaves the fray and saunters, gilt-edged ticket in hand, on to the concourse, scans the departures, and walks confidently towards a train bound for the Continent. A Eurostar or perhaps a boat-train, the better to ease gently into the experience. This is just the beginning of a month-long, joyously pointless, unhurried and uncharted train trip through as many countries as come around before the magic ticket expires.

Sound a bit much for a train ticket? Try it. Set off for a month with a rucksack, a couple of novels, some music. Open-ended rail travel is about casting off routines and learning to slow down and enjoy the details: taking in the architecture of the grand terminus; watching the departing trains with a knowing eye; noting how the pigeons panic as an engine sounds its farewell whistle. You can almost smell the excitement in railway stations. Long the preserve of the under-26s, the InterRail is now open to everyone and for more manageable periods. But it still feels young and even a little bit dangerous.

... whatever you make of it

Flight-free Lisbon

THE EXPERIENCE

To some, InterRail might sound a bit naff, a bit 1980s, the kind of thing gap-yearers did before the USSR imploded and long-haul became the norm. But no. Europe still surprises all who explore it, and a rail trip is likely to reveal more secrets than any other holiday. There's a real buzz in travelling along the tracks of history – and you'll also be tracing your own route, marking out your own path.

You'll probably spend just a few days in each place, but the trip will never feel like a short city break. Whereas weekend escapists have to prioritise and plan, InterRailers can gleefully overdose on everything or, equally, ignore everything. You might see Van Eyck's altarpiece in Bruges just after dawn, some Gaudi in the evening, Picasso's *Guernica* in Madrid the following day. Then 24 hours later you're eating Polish dumplings for dinner or indulging in ironic wassail in a Munich beer hall. Or you might just lie back in a crumbling hostel and soak up the country – what was it's name again – through osmosis. You'll never feel guilty as the pass in your pocket murmurs, gently: oh, you can come back and see it all later...

InterRailing is often intimate: couchettes, six to a tiny cabin, six tiny cabins to a carriage, one toilet for the lot. You are squeezed in, knocking knees with your neighbours, all going to bed together – travel with a group of friends, or be prepared to make them. One guy's got a guitar, another offers round the wine, a group of Slovenian girls squeeze in seven to a six-berth cabin and giggle at the train guard, the quiet one with the red hair and glasses turns out to be a stand-up comic. English is normally a common second language, but you'll learn to sign and translate. Cabin-swapping, excitement bouncing off the walls, and if the fine crockery from the restaurant car were here, it would be flying everywhere.

InterRail gives you the run of Europe's growing spider's web of routes and destinations. In the west, trains are fast, safe, comfortable and reliable. In the east, they are 'characterful'. The EU is opening out. Borders are still there, but crossing them is easier. And InterRail has grown up. There are no age restrictions now, no zone divisions either. So put a pinch of salt on rite-of-passage reminiscences and nostalgic talk of the grand old days of trains with their shiny brass knobs, stiff-capped guards and puffing steam – the belle époque of rail travel is now.

WHERE SHALL I GO?

On the face of it, the answer to this question is easy: to see the sights of Europe? The best-known InterRail pass – called a global pass – covers most of Europe and is primarily a fast-track inter-city affair, and while you do see landscapes through the window, and can easily stop over in a few villages out in the countryside, if you really wanted to see a region or a single country properly you'd buy an InterRail country pass.

But InterRailing is often more about socialising. The places serve largely as a backdrop to the hothouse intrigues and passions that flourish among a small group of travellers, intimately locked together for days and weeks on end. For InterRailers in this category, the freedom and flexibility of the rail pass offers the huge advantage of the quick getaway. Things getting too intense? Can't bear the sight of him/want to whisk her away? Just hop on a train to somewhere, anywhere, new.

On the other hand, if you're shy or misanthropic, or a few years older than your classic InterRailer (18-25) and have decided that you've got all the friends you've time for, then where you go really does matter. Perhaps you want to see some of the things that were missed last time round? Here, perhaps, a little more planning might be in order – see box The Over-26 Club p271.

CLOCKING UP MILES

So you're young, you've got time, you've got energy in excess, but what you haven't got is money. There's cash for the ticket and maybe £20 a day, but that's it. This is not going to buy accommodation in Europe's top-flight hotels; in fact, it's not even going to procure a regular night's sleep in crash-and-burn hostels. What to do? Easy: sleep on the train. After all, you're going to be using the railway to get to places, the ticket's paid for and sleeping on the train means you get where you're going without having to waste any money on accommodation. So, if we factor in at least seven nights on trains, that sees the daily budget go up to £25, maybe £30 a day. Suddenly, it's beginning to look quite possible. And you might even be able to afford to eat.

Make sure you pick up a copy of the most current *Thomas Cook European Rail Timetable*. Over the next month this will serve as bible, almanac, oracle, confidant and pillow, plus being a handy place to jot down travel tips from other travellers. Hide behind it when weirdos enter your compartment. It will become strangely addictive. Even if Thomas the Tank Engine never blew your whistle and the only thing you remember from *The Railway Children* is Jenny Agutter's red bloomers, you will find yourself developing an obsessive interest in trains, timetables, wagon formations and good connections.

Aboard, there are only two other topics that vie with the timetable as foci of interest: what to tote and what to walk. Backpacks – their contents, reliability, suitability as pillows, security and stealability – are a topic of endless interest, only rivalled by what to wear on your feet. Flip flops or sandals, trainers or boots? Will it get too hot for boots in Italy, but then what to do if you want to go trekking down the Amalfi coast…? Questions, questions. Half the fun lies in thinking over the possibilities and outcomes, playing a half-excited, half-fearful game of what if? as the day of departure rolls nearer.

TRAVEL ALONE OR TRAVEL TOGETHER?

Even if you set off alone, you won't stay that way for long. As Douglas Coupland noted in his novel *Shampoo Planet*, you'll make plenty of 'mutually disposable friends' as you go, relationships nearly as intense and as brief as those in the trenches of the Somme. InterRailing could have been designed to ensure that the young people of Europe come into brief but intimate contact with each other: individuals and groups in random motion but funnelled through major hubs, both transport and tourist, ensuring regular mixing; overnight journeys crowded into six-person couchettes, a mini-youth hostel on wheels; and the shared experience of being the only

INTERRAIL

Catch the AVE to Zaragoza

people for whom the next few weeks offer a canvas blank and waiting to be written upon.

This brings us to one of the great misconceptions of InterRailing and, indeed, travelling in general. You set off with grand ideas of gaining insights into different cultures and people, but what you actually end up doing is meeting lots of people who are pretty well the same as you. It's perfectly possible to go the whole trip and, apart from waiters, barmen and hostel receptionists, only speak to other InterRailers. A moment's post hoc thought reveals the reason: wherever you go, the only other people who have the time and inclination to sit nursing a beer on a beach for a whole evening in prospect of the anticipated glory of the sunset, or to go skinny-dipping into a sea of luminescent plankton, are people like you. On holiday, with time, and no ties. In fact, a useful rule of thumb to bear in mind when dealing with the locals: if they want to spend an extended period of time in your company, it's because they either want your body or your money and, in some cases, both.

Still, this limited range of contact is, in fact, one of the reasons for the success of InterRail. After all, which would you really prefer: long talks with a niçois granny about life in the inter-war years, or skittering eye contact and halting conversation with lissom Scandinavians and dark-eyed Italians? For the young, travel is about relationships, and relationships are about sex. More than a few passionate affairs have begun in whispered conversations on overnight trains. The days of *Brief Encounter* may be long gone, but you may have trouble encountering your briefs the day after the night after a wine-soaked ride along the Riviera.

ROUTES AND REGIONS

Now if you are an aspiring situationist, dice man or self-styled 'experimental traveller', you may be averse to planning your InterRail in any shape or form. In which case, just hop on and off trains willy-nilly and see where they take you – though be warned, there are supplements on special trains for InterRail pass holders.

Of course, the whole of this book amounts, in InterRailing terms, to a set of suggestions that can easily be combined in a vast travel collage. Perhaps you want to link the 'Polish Plains' chapter to the 'Swiss Rail Orgy', thus comparing steam to electricity and clock-accurate timetabling to whimsy and wishful thinking. Or combine 'Iberia' with 'España Verde' and do a full circle of Spain and Portugal, before zooming off to see the cities featured in '2:04 to Morocco'. Check out the four 'Hubs' chapters too, as they list some of the long-distance services departing from Paris, Brussels, Cologne and Lille.

Still can't make your mind up? Below is a further set of wholly unauthoritative suggestions for planning your perfect pan-European holiday...

DON'T FORGET GERMANY!

The **German rail** network – Deutsche Bahn – serves as a punctual, swift and comfortable conduit between London, Paris and Brussels and the eastern hubs of Warsaw, Prague, Budapest and beyond to Russia. But the huge network also invites scenic relaxation along some of Europe's most beautiful

German rail
www.db.de

stretches – down the Rhine, around the Alps or through the Harz Mountains. From Cologne, the train for Frankfurt follows the picturesque bends in the Rhine, where the hills are topped with castles and carpeted with vineyards; from Munich, the service terminating at the ski capital of Garmisch-Partenkirchen links with the narrow-gauge station alongside. From there, a little train chugs up the side of the Zugspitz, Germany's highest mountain, the summit accessed by cable car from the transit point of Eibsee. Below, to the south, is Austria.

The 110-kilometre-long Harz Mountains, in former East Germany, are criss-crossed by narrow-gauge tracks used by the local Harzer Schmalspurbahnen (HSB) network, partly served by steam locomotives. These are not heritage railways run by enthusiasts but rather a hangover from the old system. The most spectacular line, named after the Brocken mountain, runs between Drei Annen Hohne and Bad Harzburg, almost reaching the summit in between. Getting off at the highest point allows for wonderful views of hilly forests and the chance for a meal at the panoramic restaurant. Bocken is equidistant from Dresden and Berlin, major stops on the line that runs south to Prague, Bratislava and Budapest.

SOUTH TO THE SUN

As well as the new super-fast Barcelona–Madrid AVE service, covered elsewhere in this book, there are fast services from Madrid-Atocha to Córdoba (2hrs) and Seville (2.5hrs). In 2008, a new line from Madrid to Malaga was opened, covering the 550 kilometres in just 2.5 hours. Note that InterRail holders have to pay a supplement of around €10 to use the AVE. Equally impressive are the Alaris service from Madrid to Valencia and the Euromed from Barcelona to Valencia. The passholder fares for both routes start at around €7 one way – this supplement must be paid in the ticket office in the departure station, and is subject to availability.

Italy is the other obvious sunseekers' route. There is a lovely line connecting Trieste and Udine – with seafront for half the journey – and Rome–Naples has long been a classic. Look out for the trolley guy with Neapolitan blue eyes, as he engages you in conversation then tries to rip you off. The train is transferred to a boat to get you to Sicily.

Virtu Ferries' 600-passenger MV *Maria Dolores* sails from Catania to Valletta in Malta (3hrs) every day, increasing to two to three crossings daily during the high season.There is also a shorter crossing to Pozzallo (90mins).

Greece is mainly about boats as the **Hellenic Railways Organisation** runs extremely slow, undependable local trains. There is, however, a fair service connecting Athens with Salonika, with some trains continuing to Alexandrupoi near the Turkish border. The Athens–Kalamata line crosses the Corinth Canal and covers the 250 kilometres in a stupendous seven hours. When this book went to press the railways on the Peloponnese were being 'restructured' so there is a good chance there is no train at all on this line.

Croatia is desperately bad for trains but the national operator **Hrvatske Îeljeznice** improved the Zagreb–Knin–Split line in 2007 and introduced a reasonably fast inter-city service (under 5hrs). It's a few euros more expensive than the bus so locals

InterRailers' porn

INTERRAIL

Virtu Ferries
www.virtuferries.com

Hellenic Railways Organisation
www.ose.gr

Hrvatske Îeljeznice
www.hznet.hr

Madrid by boat

stay away, meaning you may get the whole train – all two carriages of it – to yourself. Get a seat with a table and write up your holiday notes. A man comes round with free coffee, and a free if less than tasty sandwich for you.

STEAMING ALONG ON STATE-RUN RAILWAYS

Eastern Europe is far more than the beach, of course. Crossing from the sometimes-too-civilised West, you'll find many national networks have managed to 'preserve' their Soviet-style trains with cracked, PVC seats and separate compartments, officious-verging-on-Kafkaesque border guards and magical, bare scenery. These countries are changing at a frightening pace. Right now is the time to go.

Budapest–Kiev takes forever. Consider starting the journey not in the Hungarian capital but Miskolc, an ex-industrial hellhole near the Slovak border where drink and decay rule over daily life. Once you reach the Ukrainian border, you have to jump off as the gauge is different – Stalin was afraid of invasion by rail – and this is where you buy your ticket for Kiev for small change. Gaze out of the window at irradiated farmland and peasants with 18th-century equipment. On this route by bus, gangs of robbers used to give passengers notes to tell the next gang down the line that they had already been robbed. In Kiev in the early 1990s the authorities banned photocopiers as everyone was copying the local currency. This is not a pretty rail holiday, but next time someone tells you Europe is all the same and all very rich these days, you can tell them where to go – literally.

THE BIG ONES

For some travellers it's all about length. If Kiev simply isn't far enough, there is still a direct service from Berlin Hbf to Astana in Kazakhstan, via Warsaw, Brest and Minsk and 55 other towns (taking 98 hours, 48 minutes, or thereabouts, and crossing six borders).

The longest rail journey in the world is a hotly disputed matter – as hot as train banter gets, anyway – but it's sometimes said that Porto–Saigon is about as extensive as they come for a west-to-east epic. You'll have to change trains at Coimbra, Hendaye, Paris, Cologne, Moscow and Beijing and will need at least 12 days, 24 pot noodles, three novels, some wet wipes and perhaps a canny combination of sleeping, Imodium and laxative pills. Portugal to Vietnam, without crossing water or taking off. You could go on and on, of course, and extend your trip by taking the new line to Lhasa – but you're sort of heading west – that is, back home – then, so it doesn't count.

AND THE LITTLE ONES

One way to get an oblique experience of Europe is to think of all the places you may never go to and use your pass to see them. How about a holiday in these: Gibraltar, Lichtenstein, Luxembourg, San Marino, Kalinngrad, Vatican City?

COMING HOME

Wherever the train has taken you, however long the journey, there comes a time when the adventure stops. It's time to go home. The young will, most likely, stumble off the train, hollow eyed with exhaustion, on the border line of malnutrition as a result of a diet of baguettes, pizza and cheese, and with an urgent need of a shower. They will have had a ball. Their elders will be more fragrant, have better photos and will have gained, rather than lost, weight. They will have had an enjoyable trip. But there really is nothing like the first time.

TRAVEL INFORMATION

It's all change at InterRail – forget the old zoning system and age restrictions. Youths aged 12-25 get a discounted rate and tickets for children aged 4-11 are half-price. Under-4s travel free. First-class passes are also on offer.

InterRail is valid in 30 countries, covering most of Europe; Northern Ireland, Albania, Kosovo, Russia, Belarus and Ukraine are not covered by the pass. An InterRail pass is not valid for free travel in your own country of residence. Eurostar is a private company and not included in the InterRail scheme – passholders are entitled to travel in standard class for £50 single or £100 return. If they feel like treating themselves to champagne and a three course meal on board, 'leisure select' single tickets are £90 and returns are £180.

InterRail Global Passes start at £182 for an adult over 26 and give you free rein of regular trains in all European countries included in the scheme. Chose between unlimited travel for 22 days or one month, or a flexi-option of five days' travel within

THE OVER-26 CLUB

InterRail isn't just for impoverished students. You can get a pass at any age, for luxury travel as well as budget. Take the first-class option, settle back and relax.

The Luxury Night Train The CityNightLine sleepers running between many main cities in Germany, Austria and Switzerland are the shining white knights of overland train travel. Deluxe Class is the ultimate luxury option, with proper, comfortable beds, a tiny bathroom, card-locked cabins and privacy. You'll see the restaurant as you walk down the platform towards your cabin. White tablecloths and deep red wine in fine glasses, the smells of fresh bread and stewing duck from the slits in the windows. The food is excellent and you can choose à la carte if the full, rich menu will make you dream.

Depending on the type of sleeper cabin they choose, InterRail passholders can use these trains for a supplement that starts at around €20. See www.citynightline.ch.

The Pleasure Romp The Paris chapter of this book gives details of the fast train to Reims for a champagne tour. How about following this up with a trip from Paris to Toulouse on the new luxury iDTGV route? Choose between obligatory silence and sleeping kits or DVDs, video games, magazines and chattering over coffee. See www.sncf.com.

The Winter Ride Scandinavia isn't the first choice for young student InterRailers but it's a dreamland for anyone with a bit more padding in their pocket. Cross from Oslo to Bergen on the slow Bergen Line over the so-called 'roof of Norway', passing frozen lakes, snowy pines and smoking *hyttes*. Look out for Hardangerjøkulen, Norway's second largest glacier, when the train stops at Finse, 1,222 metres above sea level. Then stop just afterwards at Myrdal and take a helter-skelter ride on the Flåmbana: 20 kilometres of dizzying mountains, brake-screeching valleys and torrential waterfalls down to Flåm station near the Aurlandfjord, a narrow branch of the world's longest fjord, Sognefjord. Hire a bike and brake your way down the winding rocky paths on that, coming back up on the train. It's cold and fresh and blows your mind. See www.flaamsbana.no; 30 per cent discount for InterRail passholders.

RailEurope
0844 848 4070
www.raileurope.co.uk

ten days, or ten days' travel within 22 days. Buy a One-Country Pass if you want to explore just one country. There are four bands or 'levels', priced according to regions – so if you want a month on Germany's expensive, extensive network you'll pay a lot more than you would to spend the same period travelling round the handful of lines in a smaller, poorer country. In fact, it's so cheap to hop around the Level 4 countries (Bulgaria, Czech Republic, Republic of Macedonia, Serbia, Slovakia, Slovenia and Turkey) that you might as well just buy tickets when you need them.

Express and overnight trains always require reservations and a supplement – watch out for these, as you could get stung. Some ferries are included in the pass and some private rail lines and rack railways give discounts – check the Traveller's Guide on www.interrailnet.com and always ask before boarding.

Trains in your country of residence are not included, but UK resident passholders under 26 can get a discount for travel to the border and back. Eurostar offers set price tickets to passholders at around £50 single from London to Paris.

The InterRail pass is only available to European residents. See www.raileurope.co.uk or call 0844 848 4070. If you live outside Europe, see www.eurail.com instead.The offical agent for the InterRail in the UK is **RailEurope**. They can give advice on services and supplements and can pre-book seats – vital for many of the fastest trains, especialy in busy periods such as summer. Seat reservation supplements are payable for many services and they can be paid in sterling through RailEurope. There are also supplements for cross-border luxury trains such as Elipsos (Paris to Madrid or Barcelona), Artesia (Paris to Rome or Venice) and Paris to Berlin.

For those carrying single-country passes, there are discounts on cross-border journeys to neighbouring countries.

If in doubt, call the InterRail help desk on 08448 484 046.

WHEN TO GO

Go any time of the year, but if you want a sun-and-sand trip, aim for summer's shoulder months. Peak holiday time – July, August and September – means hot sweaty carriages full of schoolkids and backpack-laden Antipodeans.

TRAVEL LIGHT

Advertisers' Index

Directory

Trains, stations, buses, ports, ferries, cars, tickets, tourist information, phone numbers and all the other stuff you need to plan your escape.

Written by **Edoardo Albert** and **Chris Moss**

GETTING AWAY

TRAIN

St Pancras International
Pancras Road, London, NW1 2QP
020 7843 4250, www.stpancras.com
Eurostar
Eurostar House, Waterloo Station, London, SE1 8SE
Customer relations 01777 777879, www.eurostar.com
National Rail Enquiries
08457 48 49 50, www.nationalrail.co.uk
Eurotunnel
Train carrying cars between Folkestone and Calais in just 35 mins.
08705 35 35 35, www.eurotunnel.com

BUYING TICKETS

Eurostar.com is linked with the ticketing systems of the seven train operators that use St Pancras, Kings Cross and Euston – Virgin Trains, First Capital Connect, National Express East Coast, East Midlands Trains, Chiltern Railways, Hull Trains and London Midland – so you can buy through-tickets from places like Leeds, Manchester and York to all the destinations served by Eurostar. This service is due to be extended to more cities in mid-to-late 2008.

If travellers miss a train due to a late-running connecting service, they will be able to travel on the next available Eurostar or domestic train at no extra cost.

Still, because of time zones, and because timetables and connections are liable to change, booking train tickets that involve anything more than catching the Eurostar to Paris can be confusing. One way around this is to book via a reputable ticket agency, and another is to investigate some of the independent sources of advice and information on rail travel. Below we list some useful websites, and most of them also have real, live people available at the other end of a telephone line if it all gets too complicated.

www.bahn.de The site for German railways: generally acknowledged as the best for working out routes and timetables.
www.raileurope.co.uk Comprehensive booking service for European rail travel, InterRail and offical UK agent for SNCF, the French railway operator; charges same rates as SNCF and other European agencies, subject to currency exchange rates.
www.eurostar.com Fast booking and offers for Paris and other French destinations, Brussels and Belgium, and The Netherlands.
www.rail.ch The Swiss railways site.

www.thalys.com The site for the high-speed train service linking France, Belgium, The Netherlands and Germany.

www.voyages-sncf.com France-based trains and travel.

www.seat61.com The man to go to for independent advice on rail travel.

www.europeanrail.com An independent rail company, good for advice on tours and unusual routes. Charges £5 for a quote which is refunded if you purchase a ticket.

www.festtravel.co.uk Another independent operator, worth trying for rail tours and tickets.

www.internationalrail.com A rail specialist. Contact for tours and tickets.

www.interrailnet.com Official pan-European site for InterRail passes.

http://horarios.renfe.es/hir/ingles.html Spanish railways site – English-language version.

CAR TRAINS

The summertime Motorail service, which allows you to load your car onto a TGV train and travel down to the south of France in a 4- or 6-bed couchette, runs from Calais to Toulose, Brive and Narbonne, or Calais to Avignon, Fréjus/St Raphael and Nice. Details from www.raileurope.co.uk, 0844 848 3339.

Motorail services from Calais to the south of France run every Friday from 16 May to 12 September 2008, with a similar timetable likely in future. There are extra Sunday services between 20 July and 24 August. The return journey, from the south of France to Calais, runs on Saturdays from 17 May to 13 September 2008 (additional trains on Mondays between 21 July and 25 August).

There is a separate, year-round Autotrain service from Paris to Avignon, Bordeaux, Brive, Fréjus/St Raphaël, Lyon, Marseille, Narbonne, Nice, Toulon and Toulouse. The cars are carried overnight on train carriers to the destination; you follow in a separate train. For further information call RailEurope on 08448 484 050, or Rail Savers (www.railsavers.com, 01253 595555).

A motorail service runs from 's-Hertogenbosch in the Netherlands to Livorno and Bologna in Italy, and Avignon in France. The weekly service runs between June and September, with outbound trains on Friday nights and returns on Saturday nights. The website (www.autoslaaptrein.nl) of the company that runs the service, AutoSlaap Trein, is only in Dutch but tickets can be booked through Rail Savers (www.railsavers.com, 01253 595555).

For ferries to the Hook of Holland and Rotterdam, both of which are within an easy drive of 's-Hertogenbosch, see below.

Another possibility is the excellent motorail service of Deutsche Bahn from Düsseldorf. There are services to, in Germany, Munich; in Austria, Innsbruck, Salzburg and Villach; in Italy, Bolzano, Verona and Alessandria; and in France, Narbonne. See www.dbautozug.de for further details. Düsseldorf is about a three hour drive from the Hook of Holland and Rotterdam; for details on ferry crossings see below.

BOAT TRAINS

Believe it or not, these throwbacks to ye smoky days of steam still exist. Few trains now hook up specifically with a ferry schedule, and the chances of a boat waiting for you because of a delay are slim. Allow at least an hour between your planned arrival time and the ferry departure as there is normally a minimum 45-minute check-in. Rail timetables at www.nationalrail.co.uk.

● **Via Dover** Southeastern operates ervices from London Charing Cross and London Victoria to Dover Priory every 30 minutes. www.southeasternrailway.co.uk

• **Via the south coast** South West Trains run services between London Waterloo and Portsmouth Harbour, Southampton, Poole and Weymouth. www.southwesttrains.co.uk

• **Via Plymouth** First Great Western operates the service betweem London Paddington and Plymouth, as well as the Night Riviera Sleeper, ideal if you have a morning sailing (calling at Reading, Taunton, Exeter, Newton Abbot). www.firstgreatwestern.co.uk; CrossCountry runs services from the Midlands and north. www.crosscountrytrains.co.uk

• **Via south Wales** First Great Western connects London Paddington, Reading, Bristol and Cardiff with Swansea, Fishguad and Pembroke. www.firstgreatwestern.co.uk

• **Via north Wales** Virgin Trains operates the service between London Euston and Holyhead, via Crewe. www.virgintrains.co.uk

• **Via Newcastle** National Express East Coast operates the service between London and Newcastle. www.nationalexpresseastcoast.com

• **Dutchflyer** City-to-city travel for passengers wishing to travel from Britain to Holland, especially useful if you are close to Norwich, Colchester, Ipswich or London Liverpool Street. From just £25 single. www.stenaline.co.uk/ferry/rail-and-sail/holland/

• **Ireland** Two ferry operators and five rail firms have created an alliance to offer central booking for all the UK-Eire services. www.sailrail.co.uk

INTERNATIONAL ROUTES

At the end of the four 'Hubs' chapters, we give a list of easy connections from the respective cities. There are several other key interchange cities in Europe, and many long-distance, border-hopping services. The following is a list of some recommended long journeys that involve no change of train:

Basel-Innsbruck–Salzburg–Linz–Vienna
Bucharest-Athens
Budapest–Bucharest
Frankfurt (Main)–Nürnberg–Linz–Vienna
Frankfurt (Main)–Nürnberg–Prague
Moscow–Irkutsk–Ulan Bator/Beijing/Vladivostok
Munich–Salzburg–Linz–Vienna
Oslo–Copenhagen
Riga-Vilnius-Lviv
Stockholm–Copenhagen
Stuttgart–Munich–Salzburg–Klagenfurt
Warsaw–Minsk–Moscow
Zurich–Barcelona

FERRY

As well as the services featured in this guide there are scheduled ferry services between the following ports.

Aberdeen–Lerwick (Shetlands)/Kirkwall & Stromness (Orkneys)
The phone number for Abderdeen port is 01224 597000.
Northlink Ferries (www.northlinkferries.co.uk) operates from Aberdeen: booking 0845 600 0449, administration 01856 885500.

Cairnryan (Scotland)–Larne (Northern Ireland)
For port information ring 0870 2424777.
P&O (www.poferries.com) sail from Cairnryan; 08716 645645.

Dover–Calais/Boulogne/Dunkerque
The phone number for Dover port is 01304 240400.
P&O (www.poferries.com) sail from Dover; 08716 645645.

SeaFrance (www.seafrance.com) sail from Dover; 08705 711711.
Norfolk Line (www.norfolkline.com) sail from Dover; 0870 870 10 20.

Fishguard–Rosslare (Eire)
The phone number for the Fishguard harbour master is 01348 404425.
StenaLine (www.stenaline.co.uk) sail from Fishguard; 08705 707070.

Fleetwood–Larne (Northern Ireland)
The phone number for the port master is 01253 872 323.
Stena Lines (www.stenaline.co.uk) sails from Fishguard; 08705 707070.

Harwich–Esbjerg (Denmark)/Hook of Holland (The Netherlands)
The phone number for the port is 01255 242000.
Stena Lines (www.stenalines.co.uk) and DFDS Seaways (www.dfds.co.uk) sail from Harwich.
Stena Lines general reservations 08705 707070; lost luggage (Harwich route only) 01255 243333; ferry information 08705 755755.
DFDS Seaways 08702 520524; sailing information 08705 444333.

Heysham–Douglas (Isle of Man)
The Isle of Man Steam Packet Company (www.steam-packet.com) sails from Heysham; 0871 222 1333.

Holyhead–Dublin (Eire)/Dun Laoghaire (Eire)
The phone number for the port of Holyhead is 01407 606666.
Stena Lines (www.stenalines.co.uk) and Irish Ferries (www.irishferries.com) sail from Holyhead, with Stena Lines sailing both routes and Irish Ferries going to Dublin.
Stena Lines general reservations 08705 707070; ferry information 08705 755755.
Irish Ferries 08705 171717.

Hull–Zeebrugge (Belgium)/Rotterdam (The Netherlands)
The phone number for the port is 01482 327171.
P&O (www.poferries.com) sail from Hull; 08716 645645.

Kirkwall–Lerwick–Torshavn (Faroe Islands)–Sejdisfjorur (Iceland)
The phone number for Kirkwall harbour master is 01856 872292.

Liverpool–Douglas (Isle of Man)/Dublin (Eire)
The phone number for the port is 0151 949 6000.
The Isle of Man Steam Packet Company (www.steam-packet.com) sails from Liverpool to Douglas; 0871 222 1333.
P&O (www.poferries.com) sails to Dublin; 08716 645645.

Liverpool (Birkenhead)–Belfast (Northern Ireland)
The phone number for the port is 0151 949 6000.
Norfolk Line (www.norfolkline.com) sails from Birkenhead: 0844 499 0007.

Newcastle–Amsterdam (The Netherlands)/Stavanger (Norway)/Haugesund (Norway)/Bergen (Norway)
The phone number for the passenger terminal is 0191 257 1373.
DFDS Seaways (www.dfds.co.uk) sails to Amsterdam; Bergen (via Stavanger and Haugesund); Haugesund (via Stavanger); Stavanger; 0871 522 9955.

Newhaven–Dieppe (France)/Le Havre (France)
The phone number for the port is 01273 612900.
Transmanche Ferries (www.transmanche.co.uk) sail to Dieppe; 0800 917 1201.
LD Lines (www.ldlines.co.uk) sail to Le Havre and Dieppe; 0844 576 8836.

Pembroke–Rosslare (Eire)
The phone number for the port manager is 01646 623420.
Irish Ferries (www.irishferries.com) sail from Pembroke; 08705 171717.

NOTES

TOUR OPERATORS

The following firms offer package and tailor-made flight-free trips.

Andalucian Adventures
Painting and photography holidays.
01453 834137
www.andalucian-adventures.co.uk.

Andante Travels
Archaeological tours.
01722 713800
www.andantetravels.co.uk.

Arblaster & Clarke
Wine-tour specialists.
01730 263111
www.winetours.co.uk.

Baltic Holidays
Tailor-made tours and city-hopping coach trips.
0845 070 5711
www.balticholidays.com.

Cruise People
It involves boats.
020 7723 2450
http://members.aol.com/CruiseAZ/home.htm.

Danube Express
A luxury hotel train.
www.danube-express.com.

Dragoman
Overland adventures in a truck.
01728 861133
www.dragoman.com.

Equine Adventures
Get on your horse and ride.
0845 130 6981
www.equineadventures.co.uk.

European Bike Express
The coach takes you and your bike to where you want to ride.
01430 422111
www.bike-express.co.uk.

European Rail
Rail tours of the Continent.
020 7619 1080
www.erail.co.uk.

Explore
Adventure holidays worldwide.
0844 499 0901
www.explore.co.uk.

Gascony Secret
Self-catering in south-west France.
0844 800 1637
www.gascony-secret.com.

Inntravel
Walking, cycling and riding holidays.
01653 617949
www.inntravel.co.uk.

Kirker Holidays
Short break specialist.
020 7593 2288
www.kirkerholidays.com.

Plymouth–Roscoff (France)/Santander (Spain)
The phone number for the port is 08709 000429.
Brittany Ferries (www.brittany-ferries.co.uk) sail from Plymouth; 08709 076103.

Poole–Guernsey (Channel Islands)/Jersey (Channel Islands)/St Malo (France)/Cherbourg (France)
The phone number for the passenger terminal is 01202 207215.
For inquiries about the Brittany Ferries Poole–Cherbourg sailings, ring 08709 000 359.
Condor Ferries (www.condorferries.co.uk) sail to the Channel Islands and St Malo; 01202 207216.
Brittany Ferries (www.brittany-ferries.co.uk) go to Cherbourg; 08709 076103.

Portsmouth–Fishbourne (Isle of Wight)/Ryde (Isle of Wight)/Guernsey (Channel Islands)/ St Malo (France)/Cherbourg (France)/Le Havre (France)/Caen (France)/Bilbao (Spain)
The phone number for the port is 023 9229 7391.
Brittany Ferries (www.brittany-ferries.co.uk) sails to Caen, Cherbourg and St Malo; 08709 000 389.
Condor Ferries (www.condorferries.co.uk) sails to Guernsey and Cherbourg; 01202 207216.
LD Lines (www.ldlines.co.uk) sails to Le Havre; 0844 576 8836.
Wight Link (www.wightlink.co.uk) sails to Fishbourne and Ryde; 0871 376 4342.
P&O (www.poferries.com) sails to Bilbao; 08716 645645.

Ramsgate–Ostend (Belgium)
For queries about sailings, phone 01843 595522.
Transeuropa Ferries (www.transeuropaferries.co.uk) sails to Ostend – note this service does not take foot passengers; 01843 595522.

Rosyth–Zeebrugge (Belgium)
Superfast Ferries (www.superfast.com); 0870 234 0870.

Scrabster–Stromness (Orkneys)
For inquiries about NorthLink sailings phone 0845 600 0449.
Northlink Ferries (www.northlinkferries.co.uk) operates from Scrabster: booking 0845 600 0449, administration 01856 885500.

Stranraer–Belfast (Northern Ireland)
The phone number of the port is 01776 706266.
Stena Lines general reservations 08705 707070; ferry information 08705 755755.

Troon–Larne (Northern Ireland)
The phone number for the port is 01292 281687.
P&O (www.poferries.com) sails to Larne from Troon; 08716 645645.

Weymouth–Guernsey (Channel Islands)/Jersey (Channel Islands)/ St Malo (France)
Condor Ferries (www.condorferries.co.uk) sails to the Channel Islands and St Malo; 01202 207216.

BUS

Buses and coaches may be slow, prone to getting held up in traffic jams and about as sexy as, well, air travel these days, but they are both cheap and green. To take cheapness first, Eurolines (www.eurolines.com), one of the biggest coach operators in Britain and the Continent, offers the following fares:

London–Paris £40 return £21 single
London–Warsaw–£72 return £48 single
London–Amsterdam £40 return £21 single
London–Prague £65 return or £44 single

For any other starting point in Britain, add £15 to the fare to cover the cost of connecting buses to London (note that the £15 is added only once, even in the case of a return journey). Thus Liverpool, Plymouth, Cardiff, Edinburgh or Aberdeen–Paris costs £55 return (ie £40 London–Paris + £15 add-on fare return Liverpool–London); £36 single (ie £21 London-Paris + £15 add-on fare for connection to London from Liverpool).

London, Liverpool, Manchester, Leeds, Birmigham, Newcastle–Dublin £39 return or £22 single (several direct services operate to Dublin so there is no add-on fare).

Eurolines Passes allow travel between over 40 cities for either 15 or 30 days. Prices from £119 for 15-days or £159 for 30 days.

As far as being green is concerned, coach travel produces significantly lower carbon dioxide emissions per person per mile of travel than going by either plane or car, with a typical journey from London to Paris producing 10.6 kilograms of carbon dioxide per passenger on a coach journey, as compared to 52 kilograms on a normal plane flight and 49.3 kilograms in a car of average fuel efficiency and carrying the average load of passengers (which is only 1.6 people, if you're interested). For destinations further afield the differences become even more marked: London to Vienna by coach produces 22.6 kilograms of carbon dioxide by coach, 171.8 kilograms by car and 190.9 kilograms by plane.

CAR

When driving to or on the Continent, you should take the following documents with you:

Driving licence (full and valid)

International Driving Permit
If required by the country you're visiting (which include Bosnia, Bulgaria, Czech Republic, Hungary, Iceland, Italy, Montenegro, Portugal, Romania, Russia, San Marino, Serbia, Slovakia, Slovenia, Spain – including Balearic and Canary islands, Turkey, Ukraine, but check before going). Photographic British driving licences will be accepted by EU countries, but if you have an older type of licence it's best to get an International Driving Permit.

Vehicle registration document

Motor insurance certificate

You must display a GB sticker if your number plate does not state your country of origin. The new EU number plates obviates this but outside the EU the GB sticker remains necessary.

A warning triangle (to display in case of breakdown) is compulsory in many countries. Take one with you.

Reflective jackets are also compulsory if you break down in many European countries.

A first aid kit, fire extinguisher and spare bulbs are all good pieces of kit to take with you.

Before leaving, adjust your headlights so that when driving on the right oncoming drivers are not dazzled.

It's also wise to take out breakdown cover. The AA (www.the aa.com), RAC (www.rac.co.uk) and other motoring organisations provide cover through most of Europe.

TOUR OPERATORS

Motor Home Holiday Swap
You own a mobile home (RV); someone in Germany does too. Why not swap?
www.motorhomeholidayswap.com.

Nonstop Sail
Specialist family-run firm running adventure sailing trips.
01803 833399
www.nonstopsail.com.

PTG Tours
Rail-based culture tours.
01235 768855
www.ptg.co.uk.

Rail Select
Personalised railway tours.
01904 521921
www.railselect.com.

Railbookers
Train specialists.
0844 482 1010
www.railbookers.com.

Real Holidays
Central & Southern Italy rural accommodation specialist.
020 7359 3938
www.realholidays.co.uk.

VFB Holidays
Introduced the concept of gîte holidays to the UK 38 years ago.
01452 716840
www.vfbholidays.co.uk.

Traveller
Small group tour operator specialising in cultural holidays.
020 7436 9343
www.the-traveller.co.uk.

Voyages of Discovery
Cruises on the MV *Discovery*.
01444 462150
www.voyagesofdiscovery.com.

TOURIST BOARDS

Many official tourist board websites – and indeed, local offices – are quite hopeless, but the following all offer information in English and are genuinely useful.

www.koelntourismus.de
www.visitflanders.co.uk
www.holland.com
www.uk.pas-de-calais.com
www.bordeaux-tourisme.com
www.visitnorway.com
www.nicetourism.com

DIRECTORY

TELEPHONE CODES

The telephone numbers given in the marginal listings give local codes only. If dialling from the UK, use 00 followed by these codes:

Austria	43
Belarus	375
Belgium	32
Bosnia and Herzegovina	387
Bulgaria	359
Croatia	385
Czech	420
Denmark	45
Estonia	372
Finland	358
France	33
Germany	49
Gibraltar (UK)	350
Greece	30
Hungary	36
Ireland	353
Italy	39
Kosovo	381
Latvia	371
Liechtenstein	423
Lithuania	370
Luxembourg	352
Macedonia (FYROM)	389
Monaco	377
Netherlands	31
Norway	47
Poland	48
Portugal	351
Rumania	40
Russian Federation	7
San Marino	378
Serbia and Montenegro	381
Slovakia	421
Slovenia	386
ain	34
n	46
d	41
	90
	380
	44

ope 279

c-free Europe

HIRE CARS

All the major car-hire companies are represented in Europe.

Avis
www.avis.co.uk

Budget
0844 581 9998, www.budget.co.uk

Easycar
08710 500 444, www.easycar.com

Europcar
0870 607 5000, www.europcar.co.uk

Hertz
www.hertz.co.uk

Thrifty
0808 234 7642, www.thrifty.co.uk

BICYCLE

Getting to Europe with your bike isn't too difficult, particularly if travelling by ferry. Depending on the route and operator, the bike might be carried for free or incur a small charge, but at least it won't need to be dismantled and put into a bike bag.

If travelling by Eurostar, bicycles can be taken as carry-on luggage so long as they are dismantled and put in a bike bag. If you don't fancy wielding the spanners, bicycles can be transported on Eurostar as registered baggage for about £20 each way, although Eurostar only guarantee collection within 24 hours of checking the bike in. The best bet would be to check the bicycle in the day before you travel yourself, but that's obviously only possible for people living relatively near St Pancras International.

Once in Europe, bikes can normally be carried in bike bags but always check ahead. Local trains often have luggage vans where bicycles can be carried without need for disassembly, but the fast international trains don't generally have this facility. For further details see the train operators of whichever country you're travelling to.

EUROVELO

Of course, just about the greenest possible holiday would be one where you cycled to your destination, and the EuroVelo scheme of long-distance cycle routes across Europe just might make that possible. The routes are planned by the European Cyclists' Federation (www.ecf.com) and, when complete, will consist of 12 trails of some 66,000 kilometres, stretching from the furthest tips of Europe and criss crossing its heart. About 45,000 kilometres is already in place, with notable journeys including the Atlantic Coast (Route 1), the Mediterranean (Route 8) and the Atlantic–Black Sea (Route 6). This last route is also known as the European Rivers Cycle Route and a series of hotels 'Accueil Vélo' are signed up and linked to the scheme, offering comfortable beds, high-energy breakfasts, secure bicycle parks and breakdown assistance.

WALKING

The hard-core rambler, or someone with the itch for a life-changing challenge masked as a holiday, should think about taking on one of the 11 long distance walking routes across Europe, stretching from an all but Arctic north through to the balmier shores of the south. And, of course, there can be no greener form of transport than Shanks's pony. For more information on European long distance paths see the European Ramblers' Association site (www.era-ewv-ferp.com).